REFORMATION AND RESISTANCE
IN TUDOR LANCASHIRE

REFORMATION AND RESISTANCE IN TUDOR LANCASHIRE

CHRISTOPHER HAIGH

Lecturer in Modern History
University of Manchester

CAMBRIDGE UNIVERSITY PRESS

Published by the Syndics of the Cambridge University Press
Bentley House, 200 Euston Road, London NW1 2DB
American Branch: 32 East 57th Street, New York, N.Y.10022

© Cambridge University Press 1975

Library of Congress Catalogue Card Number: 73-88308

ISBN 0 521 20367 8

First published 1975

Printed in Great Britain
at the the University Printing House, Cambridge
(Euan Phillips, University Printer)

Contents

For Clare and Lucy

Preface

This book is an attempt to test some of the suggested explanations of the origins and course of the English Reformation by a consideration of one county outside the orbit of the capital and the universities, and to relate religious change to social, economic and political influences. It has long been realised that Lancashire, of all counties, stood out against change, but there has been no serious attempt to explain this, though J. S. Leatherbarrow has described some of the symptoms of county conservatism in his *Lancashire Elizabethan Recusants*. I have tried to indicate why the palatinate was different, though I should admit that I sometimes suspect that the contrast is between Lancashire and what the conventional wisdom tells us happened elsewhere, rather than between Lancashire and what actually took place in the rest of England.

The debts I have accumulated during the seven years devoted to the book are immense. I must be numbered among the many whose major intellectual debt is to Geoffrey Elton, who forged my interest in the Reformation while I was an undergraduate, contributed by his advice to my Ph.D. dissertation, and watched over the progress of the present work with his usual kindness. His erudition and encouragement have been invaluable. Although I have often disagreed with him, the pioneering studies of Professor A. G. Dickens have been a frequent source of stimulation since I began my researches.

The first two parts of the book are, to some extent, a shortened version of my thesis, which was prepared under the benevolent guidance of Gordon Rupp, Basil Hall, John Roskell and Benjamin Drewery, but I have added some new material and modified my arguments here and there. The whole work has been read in draft by Professor Elton, Margaret Bowker and my wife, and Part Three by John Bossy, John Martin and several of my 1972–3 special subject students; without their vigilance, the book would contain many more errors. Dr Bossy generously allowed me to read the typescript of his *English Catholic Community*, and the considerable help I received from this is acknowledged in the appropriate footnotes.

Many others have contributed, including Patricia Turner, Janet Jarecki, Anne Scarth, John Addy, John Fox and Peter Jones; my gratitude to those I have omitted to mention is no less great. The map is based on one published by the Institute of Heraldic and Genealogical Studies, and I am grateful for permission to use it. I share the historian's perennial debt to the staffs of all the archives I have used, but in particular I would like to thank those of the Borthwick Institute, the Lichfield Joint Record Office, the Public Record Office and, above all, the County Record Office at Chester, where Brian Redwood and his colleagues have been kinder than one had any right to hope. More recently, I did not know how helpful publishers could be until I encountered the staff of Cambridge University Press. I must thank my colleagues at Manchester for ensuring that I had enough teaching and administrative duties to prevent me rushing into print without proper time for reflection, and my students for their patience in hearing rather more of Lancashire than of any other English county. Their forbearance is exceeded only by that of my wife.

I have thought it worthwhile to explore the relationship between official policy and local religious practice over the whole of the sixteenth century, so that for reasons of space and expertise some problems are treated more cursorily than would be true in a work specialising on a section of the period. There are, perforce, fewer comparisons than I would have liked, and in the footnotes I have normally restricted myself to the citation of the primary materials upon which my own conclusions are based. These, however, seemed acceptable weaknesses, in the cause of establishing, as far as the evidence allows, the chronology of the Reformation at the popular level, and of attempting to show that in the north-west at least religious change was a slow and far from unimpeded process.

I have modernised the spelling and punctuation of quotations, and all dates are given in the New Style.

August 1973   CH

Abbreviations

APC	*Acts of the Privy Council*
BIY	Borthwick Institute, York
BM	British Museum
Bailey, 'Churchwardens' accounts of Prescot', I and II	F. A. Bailey, 'Churchwardens' accounts of Prescot, 1523–1607', *Transactions of the Historic Society of Lancashire and Cheshire*', XCII and XCV
CCR	*Court Rolls of the Honour of Clitheroe*
CPR	*Calendar of Patent Rolls*
CRO	Cheshire County Record Office, Chester
CRS	*Catholic Record Society Publications*
CS	Chetham Society
CSPD	*Calendar of State Papers, Domestic*
CSPF	*Calendar of State Papers, Foreign*
CSPS	*Calendar of State Papers, Spanish*
CU	Cambridge University
Church Goods, I-III	*Inventories of Church Goods in the Churches and Chapels of Lancashire, 1552*
Clergy List	'List of the clergy in eleven deaneries of the diocese of Chester, 1541–2', ed. W. F. Irvine, *Miscellanies relating to Lancashire and Cheshire*, Record Society of Lancashire and Cheshire, XXXIII
DNB	*Dictionary of National Biography*
Derby Correspondence	*Correspondence of Edward, third earl of Derby*
Douai Diaries	*First and Second Douai Diaries*
Duchy Pleadings	*Pleadings and Depositions in the Duchy Court of Lancaster*
EHR	*English Historical Review*
FOR	*Register of the Archbishop of Canterbury's Faculty Office*
Haigh, *Lancs. Monasteries*	C. Haigh, *The Last Days of the Lancashire Monasteries and the Pilgrimage of Grace*
J Eccl. Hist.	*Journal of Ecclesiastical History*
LCL	Leeds City Library, Manuscripts Department
LRO	Lancashire County Record Office, Preston
L & C Wills, I–V	*Lancashire and Cheshire Wills and Inventories*, Chetham Society, Old series, XXXIII, LI, LIV; New series, III, XXVIII
L & C Wills, VI	*Lancashire and Cheshire Wills*, Record Society of Lancashire and Cheshire, XXX
L & P	*Letters and Papers, Foreign and Domestic, of the Reign of Henry VIII*

Abbreviations

Lancs. Chantries	*History of the Chantries within the County Palatine of Lancaster* (Reports of the Suppression Commissions)
Lich. RO	Lichfield Joint Record Office
NS	New series
OS	Old series
Ordination Reg.	'Ordination register of the diocese of Chester, 1542–1558', ed. W. F. Irvine, *Miscellanies relating to Lancashire and Cheshire,* Record Society of Lancashire and Cheshire, XLIII, 1902
PRO	Public Record Office
Prescot Accounts	*Churchwardens' Accounts of Prescot, Lancashire, 1523–1607*
Reg.	Register
'Richmond Registers', I–III	'Registers of the archdeacons of Richmond, 1361–1477', ed. A. H. Thompson, *Yorkshire Archaeological Journal,* XXV, XXX, XXXII
State Civil and Ecclesiastical	'State civil and ecclesiastical of the county of Lancaster', ed. F. R. Raines, *Chetham Miscellanies,* Old series, V, Chetham Society, Old series, XCVI
THSLC	*Transactions of the Historic Society of Lancashire and Cheshire*
TLCAS	*Transactions of the Lancashire and Cheshire Antiquarian Society*
TRHS	*Transactions of the Royal Historical Society*
VCH	*Victoria History of the County of Lancashire*
Valor	*Valor Ecclesiasticus*
Whalley Act Book	*Act Book of the Ecclesiastical Court of Whalley*
YAJ	*Yorkshire Archaeological Journal*

References to the state papers are normally to folios, but where the foliation is confused I have used document numbers.

Where article references are to the reprinting of an original document, rather than to a piece of research, the article title is given at first reference only, and journal references thereafter.

Key to map opposite: The ecclesiastical structure of Lancashire, c. 1600

Deanery of Furness
1 Kirkby Ireleth
2 Ulverston
3 Hawkshead (1578)
4 Cartmel
5 Pennington
6 Dalton
7 Urswick
8 Aldingham

Deanery of Kendal
9 Warton
10 Bolton-le-Sands
11 Halton
12 Heysham

Deanery of Lonsdale
13 Whittington
14 Tunstall
15 Melling
16 Claughton
17 Tatham

Deanery of Amounderness
18 Lancaster
19 Cockerham
20 Garstang
21 St Michael's-on-Wyre
22 Poulton-le-Fylde
23 Lytham
24 Kirkham
25 Preston
26 Ribchester
27 Chipping
28 Part of Mitton, Yorks.

Deanery of Blackburn
29 Blackburn
30 Whalley

Deanery of Leyland
42 Penwortham
43 Croston
44 Leyland
45 Brindle
46 Eccleston
47 Standish

Deanery of Manchester
31 Rochdale
32 Bury
33 Bolton-le-Moors
34 Dean (1541)
35 Prestwich
36 Radcliffe
37 Middleton
38 Manchester
39 Ashton-under-Lyne
40 Eccles
41 Flixton

Deanery of Warrington
48 Wigan
49 Ormskirk
50 North Meols
51 Halsall
52 Aughton
53 Sefton
54 Walton
55 Childwall
56 Huyton
57 Prescot
58 Warrington
59 Winwick
60 Leigh

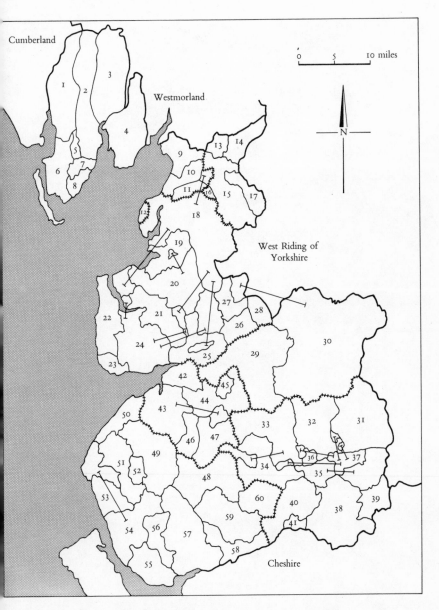

The ecclesiastical structure of Lancashire, *c.* 1600

PART ONE

1

The government of the Church

Lancashire lay at the periphery of the structure of the early Tudor Church, easily overlooked and probably neglected. Throughout the sixteenth century the county was to pose major problems for the officers of Church and state, but the ecclesiastical machinery which existed to cope with these difficulties was cumbersome and inefficient. Proper administration was made impossible by the notoriously poor communications of Lancashire. In 1533 a herald complained that his duties in the area had forced upon him 'as evil a journey as ever I had', and as late as 1617 it was thought that a royal progress through the north-west might have to be curtailed as the king's coach would be unable to negotiate Lancashire roads.[1] Other counties had poor roads, but in the case of Lancashire a further difficulty disrupted ecclesiastical government. The county was sixth in England in size, but until 1541 its northern and southern divisions were each merely small parts of two of the country's largest dioceses, and each section lay far from its cathedral city.

Lancashire south of the Ribble formed the northern part of the archdeaconry of Chester, in the diocese of Coventry and Lichfield. The archdeaconry's distance from Lichfield had forced the bishop to grant the archdeacon a measure of independence, and from at least the middle of the fourteenth century there were conflicts over the extent of the respective jurisdictions.[2] In 1447 and 1453 two bishops of Lichfield tried to prevent further trouble and recognised administrative necessities by granting the archdeacon almost episcopal powers within Chester, in return for an annual composition.[3] The

[1] *Visitation of Lancashire, 1533*, ed. W. Langton, 43; *CSPD* 1611–18, 471.
[2] W. Mather, 'Some aspects of parochial administration in the archdeaconry of Chester in the latter half of the fourteenth century', University of Manchester M.A. thesis, 1932, 175–8, 201–13.
[3] Lich. RO, Reg. Booth, B/A/1/10, fos. 37v–38; Reg. Boulers, B/A/1/11, fos. 37–37v.

1

fee due to the bishop was still being paid in the sixteenth century, and it is probable that the arrangement survived until 1541.[1] The early Lichfield court books show that only a small number of cases went beyond the archdeacon's court at Chester to the Lichfield consistory, and these were mainly disciplinary proceedings against the clergy and appeals against local decisions.[2] Although there are a number of office cases in the earliest surviving probate act books at Lichfield, for the years 1532 to 1540, none originated in the archdeaconry of Chester, and it is clear that wills from the area were proved locally rather than before the bishop's officers.[3] But Chester did remain subject to episcopal visitations, and there is evidence that the parishes or the religious houses were visited in 1502, 1504, 1517, 1521, 1525 and 1530. There was thus some attempt to combine a necessary decentralisation of authority with an overall supervision by the bishop.

As the archdeaconry enjoyed a degree of autonomy, it was important that the calibre of its officials should be high. Chester was regarded as the senior archdeaconry in the diocese and it yielded a substantial income,[4] so it became a lucrative prize for royal servants and rising churchmen. Between 1499 and 1541, Chester was held by three future bishops, John Veysey, Cuthbert Tunstall and William Knight, administrators, diplomats and benefice-collectors on a grand scale, and they can have had little more than a financial connection with the archdeaconry.[5] But it was far from unusual for archdeacons to be non-resident, and day-to-day administration was normally entrusted to deputies. The early records of the archdeacon's court at Chester tell us little of the work of the first two of the sixteenth-century officials of Chester, but by the early 1520s the archdeaconry seems to have been in a poor state and Archdeacon Knight found it necesssy to bring in Adam Beconsall, who was something of an ecclesiastical trouble-shooter. Beconsall, a Cambridge-trained canon lawyer, specialised in difficult and delicate tasks; he went to Chester for a short time to sort out its administrative problems, he was later employed by Thomas Cromwell to tie up the estate of a deceased bishop to the advantage of the king, he acted as a monastic visitor and he became the government's expert on the

---

[1] P. Heath, 'The medieval archdeaconry and the Tudor bishopric of Chester', *J Eccl. Hist.* XX, 246.

[2] Lich. RO, B/C/2/1–3, *passim*. Only 13 Lancashire cases went to Lichfield in the years 1524–35.

[3] CRO, EDA 2/1, *passim*; *Calendar of Wills in the Consistory of Lichfield*, Index Library, VII, *passim*.

[4] In 1535 the net pre-tax income was said to be £65 10s, but a more realistic assessment in 1541 gave £111 13s 4d (*Valor*, V, 201; CRO, EDA 3/1, fo. 35v).

[5] C. Haigh, 'The Reformation in Lancashire to 1558', University of Manchester Ph.D. thesis, 1969, 6–8.

Church in Wales.[1] In November 1522 Beconsall was given a commission as official of Chester, with power to deal with almost all cases in the archdeacon's court, and to conduct visitations of clergy and laity.[2]

The administration of Chester was improved under Beconsall, for he set about his duties with vigour and was responsible for some perceptive initiatives. He seems to have realised that several of the archdeaconry's problems resulted from its unusual size, for officers could not maintain contact with affairs at the parish level and litigants might have to travel long distances to the court. To reduce inconvenience Beconsall began to hold sessions of his court at three centres in south Lancashire, as well as at Chester, but this was only a partial solution. In 1523 or 1524 Beconsall took a more dramatic step and established a second court at Bury, under a commissary, to deal with cases from the north of the archdeaconry. This proved, however, to be an abortive experiment, for the official himself was often absent so that the commissary had to suspend his court at Bury and sit as judge in Chester.[3] The new system collapsed completely when Beconsall resigned his office and was succeeded by the commissary; the Bury court was abandoned and the archdeaconry was once more ruled from Chester alone. But the exercise illustrates some of the problems faced in Chester; largely because of the size of the archdeaconry the bishop had to delegate power to the archdeacon, the archdeacon had to employ an official, and the official needed the assistance of a commissary.

As the chain of command lengthened and effective jurisdiction passed further down the hierarchy, so episcopal control was weakened, and Bishop Rowland Lee of Lichfield claimed in 1535 that he had no authority in the archdeaconry.[4] In this situation, lesser officers were allowed too much independence and administration suffered. Beconsall's successor as official was Richard Smith, rector of Bury and commissary of the short-lived court there, but he was a quarrelsome character, unpopular with his parishioners, and willing to profit from his position by receiving bribes.[5] By 1535 the affairs of the archdeaconry had declined to such a serious state that Adam Beconsall found it necessary to send Thomas Cromwell a series of reports on the work of his former colleague. Beconsall thought that sexual laxity was widespread among the clergy and gentry of the

[1] *CU Grace Book* Γ, 168, 247; *L & P,* IX, 32, 34, 35, X, 522, XI, 244, 607, 806.
[2] CRO, EDA 2/1, fos. 44–45.
[3] CRO, EDC 1/3, fos. 2, 18, 19, 28; *Duchy Pleadings,* III, 61, 63.
[4] *L & P,* IX, 712.
[5] CRO, EDC 1/8, fos. 64/1, 77v, 78, 179; *Duchy Pleadings,* I, 151–3; *L & P,* VIII, 496, No. 2; *Visitation of Lancashire, 1533,* 34.

archdeaconry, partly because the guilty were able to avoid ecclesiastical censure by annual compositions with the official of Chester. Smith had not been properly supervised by his superiors, and discipline was slack among laymen because they 'have not been accustomed to be reformed by inferior ordinaries as the bishop and the archdeacon'. There could be no improvement, in Beconsall's view, until the king cut through the administrative tangle, suspended the authority of the archdeacon and acted personally by royal supremacy.[1] The archdeaconry of Chester in the 1530s illustrates a central dilemma of ecclesiastical government in the north-west; the size of administrative areas made a devolution of power essential, but it then became difficult to superintend the work of possibly unreliable local officers.

The archdeaconry of Richmond, which included north Lancashire, was even more unwieldy than the archdeaconry of Chester. It stretched from the River Ribble in the south-west to the border of County Durham in the north-east, and contained some of the wildest country in England. Although Richmond lay in the diocese of York, the archdeaconry could not be ruled directly from the cathedral city, especially as it was almost impossible to cross the Pennines in winter. The twin problems of distance and terrain gave Richmond a unique independence, and from at least the mid twelfth century the archdeacon exercised all ordinary jurisdiction. The autonomy of Richmond was settled by an agreement between archbishop and archdeacon in 1331, which confirmed the archdeacon's authority over institutions to benefices, deprivations, grants of licences and dispensations, testamentary jurisdiction, visitations, excommunications and interdicts and the collection of clerical subsidies. In return the archdeacon merely recognised his bishop's general right of visitation, a right which geographical conditions meant would rarely be exercised.[2] Except for the strictly episcopal powers of ordination and confirmation, the archdeacon was master in his own house; he even possessed, alone of English archdeacons, the right to 'signify' unrepentant excommunicates to the secular arm for arrest.[3]

The powers of the archdeacon were matched by his income; a fourteenth-century account put the revenue at £469 18s 1d, although by 1541 this was said to have fallen to £171 6s 8d.[4] But Richmond

[1] *L & P*, VIII, 495, 496, Nos. 1 and 2.
[2] J. Raine, *Historians of the Church of York*, III, Rolls series, 3 vols. 248–50; A. H. Thompson, 'Diocesan organisation in the Middle Ages; archdeacons and rural deans', *Proceedings of the British Academy*, XXIX, 158; R. M. T. Hill, *The Labourer in the Vineyard*, Borthwick Papers, XXV, 6–10.
[3] F. D. Logan, *Excommunication and the Secular Arm in Medieval England*, 33, 176–9.
[4] CRO, EDA 3/1, fos. 10, 35v.

was still a rich prize, and between 1494 and 1541 it was held by a succession of non-residents: Christopher Urswick, an ambassador and Court patron, James Stanley, the immoral scion of a powerful family, Thomas Dalby, a northern administrator, Thomas Winter, bastard son of Wolsey and a mere student, and William Knight, a lawyer and career diplomat. The prestige and authority of the archdeacon made friction with his nominal overlord, the archbishop, likely, but this was avoided in the fifteenth century. The jurisdiction of the absentee archdeacon was nominally exercised by a vicar-general, but he too was often a non-resident pluralist, so the vicar-general of York was appointed as his deputy or commissary-general.[1] But although this move may have prevented conflict between York and Richmond, it negated the whole purpose of the original devolution of power from the cathedral city. The arrangement seems to have been abandoned in the early sixteenth century, and thereafter there was a good deal of trouble. In 1514 the officers of Archdeacon Dalby and Archbishop Bainbridge came into conflict over their respective rights, and when Bainbridge appealed to the king for help, Dalby appealed to the pope; a potentially serious crisis was only avoided by the archbishop's timely death.[2] There was further trouble in 1533 when Archbishop Edward Lee, always jealous of the rights of his see, claimed the power to examine ordination candidates from Richmond. Archdeacon Knight cited the traditional 'episcopal jurisdiction' of Richmond and appealed to Rome, while as in 1514 the archbishop appealed to the courts of the king.[3]

Although interpretation of the agreement of 1331 could raise difficulties, it is clear that for the people of Richmond the effective ecclesiastical authority was the archdeacon's deputy. A fourteenth-century account of the liberties of Richmond shows that the clergy and officials were answerable to the archdeacon, and could not be cited before the archbishop against their will.[4] But for the people of north Lancashire it made very little difference whether they were ruled from Richmond or York, since the two were almost equally inaccessible. The Pennines presented a formidable barrier to effective control from either centre, and the archdeaconry was commonly held to consist of two sections, 'citra moras' and 'ultra moras'.[5] It was therefore essential to delegate authority from Richmond, and as in Chester a large archdeaconry meant wide powers for the rural

[1] 'Richmond Registers', II, 15, 17–18; CRO, EDA 3/1, fo. 11.
[2] D. S. Chambers, *Cardinal Bainbridge in the Court of Rome, 1509–1514*, 19–20; *L & P*, I, 3007.
[3] *L & P*, VI, 1440, 1441, 1451, 1452.
[4] CRO, EDA 3/1, fo. 11v.   [5] 'Richmond Registers', I, 139.

deans.[1] But a potentially important link with the parishes was nullified, in Chester when the archdeacon took the Lancashire deaneries into his own hands, and in Richmond by the appointment of lesser men as deans. Between 1517 and 1531 the deanery of Amounderness was held by the curate of Caton, whose chapel lay in another deanery, and a little later the deans of Furness and Richmond were mere assistant chaplains.[2] Such men can have excited little fear among laymen and their fellow-clergy. To make matters worse, the officers of Richmond seem not to have held visitations, so that the work of the deans was not supervised. Rural deans were thus allowed far too much latitude, and early in the reign of Elizabeth they were conniving at offences and taking bribes.[3]

The inadequacy of the administration of the Church in the north-west was of little consequence in normal times, when at worst petty offences went undetected. But in the 1530s and after, Church and state were attempting to enforce religious change, and administrative weaknesses assumed a crucial importance. The Henrician government seems to have realised this, and when a statute of 1539 empowered the king to erect new dioceses by letters-patent the area was given attention. In 1539 Thomas Cromwell was anticipating the foundation of a new see based on the suppressed abbey at Fountains, of which Richmond would form a major part. A more comprehensive scheme was drawn up later, in which south Lancashire and the rest of the archdeaconry of Chester would form part of a new diocese of Chester, while north Lancashire and the rest of Richmond would be part of a Fountains see.[4] Perhaps the authorities were reluctant to divide the administration of Lancashire again, and so perpetuate the weak government of a county which had recently proved itself so dangerous in the Pilgrimage of Grace, for this second plan was also dropped. The position of William Knight as archdeacon of both Richmond and Chester must have drawn attention to the possibility of uniting the two archdeaconries into a diocese, and when Knight was promoted to the see of Bath and Wells the amalgamation took place. It is not surprising that Knight himself was not appointed to the new see, for it was wiser to keep a known conservative busy seeking heretics in Somerset, while a bishop of a more radical temper was needed to enforce reform in the difficult north-west.

In August 1541 William Knight, as archdeacon of Chester, and Rowland Lee, bishop of Lichfield, surrendered the archdeaconry of

[1] W. Dansey, *Horae Decanicae Rurales*, 2 vols. I, 118–19, II, 369–71.
[2] *Valor*, V, 219, 225, 227, 231; *VCH*, VII, 71; BIY, R/I/5, fo. 644v; *Richmond Wills*, ed. J. Raine, 21; LCL, RD/A/1A, fo. 62.
[3] See below, pp. 232–3.
[4] *L & P*, XIV(2), 427, 429.

Chester to the king, and Knight, as archdeacon of Richmond, and Edward Lee, archbishop of York, surrendered Richmond in the same way. The archdeaconries were then united by royal letters-patent into the new diocese of Chester, and John Bird, bishop of Bangor, was translated to the see.[1] Chester was originally placed in the province of Canterbury, but it was soon recognised that administrative logic demanded it should be within the northern province. In 1542 the diocese was transferred to the province of York, and Bishop Bird took his oath of obedience to Archbishop Lee.[2] Considerable administrative progress was thus made in 1541–2, but major difficulties still remained. The problems posed by the unwieldy dioceses of York and Lichfield had merely been repeated in the creation of the equally unwieldy diocese of Chester. The new diocese was 120 miles long at its longest point and 90 miles wide at its widest; it covered over 5,200 square miles, and was the third diocese of England in area.[3] The cathedral city was in the extreme south-west, so that the northern part of the diocese lay as far from the seat of its new bishop as from York, the seat of its old one.

Size alone was not a serious handicap in the two dioceses larger than Chester. In the diocese of York powerful archdeacons formed an effective link between the central administration and the parishes, while in Lincoln there was an episcopal commissary as well as an archdeacon in each archdeaconry. Chester's problems stemmed not only from its area, but from the inadequacy of its original endowment. At its foundation the see yielded a gross annual income of £473 4s 8d, and essential fees and pensions reduced the bishop's net revenue to only £369 4s 6½d.[4] Despite its size, the new see had one of the lowest episcopal incomes in England. The revenues were assessed, for taxation purposes, at £420 1s 8d, but the average gross income of the seventeen English sees in the *Valor Ecclesiasticus* was £1568. The bishop of Chester received less than any of his episcopal colleagues, except for the bishop of Rochester, whose diocese was less than one-tenth of the size of Chester.[5] The poverty of the see had an immediate and most unfortunate result. If a bishop had been appointed over the heads of the powerful archdeacons of Chester and Richmond, he could have exercised very little authority of his own.

[1] *L & P*, XVI, 1135, g. 4; T. Rymer, *Foedera*, 20 vols. XIV, 717–24.
[2] *L & P*, XVII, 28; BIY, Reg. Lee, R/I/28, fo. 138.
[3] P. Hughes, *The Reformation in England*, 3 vols. I, 32–4.
[4] CRO, EDA 3/1, fo. 35v.
[5] PRO E 334/4, fo. 145, E 334/7, fo. 121v. In 1575 the author of a project to raise money for the Crown in first-fruits by translating all the English bishops thought Chester and Rochester would have to be left vacant, as they were too poor to translate any bishop to them (J. Strype, *Annals of the Reformation*, 4 vols. II(1), 575–6).

So at the foundation of the see the jurisdiction of the archdeacons was extinguished and vested in the new bishop; thereafter the bishop could nominate two archdeacons and delegate to them as much or as little authority as he wished, but he had to pay each a salary of £50 a year.[1] But Bishop Bird simply could not afford to spend more than a quarter of his net income on stipends for archdeacons; no archdeacons were appointed, and an essential link in the ecclesiastical chain of command was missing.

The financial position of the see of Chester soon became very much worse, and it is ironical that the deterioration sprang from an attempt by Bishop Bird to increase his revenues. Late in 1545 or early in the following year, Bird petitioned the king that if, as it appeared, Manchester College was to be suppressed, the bishop himself might be 'preferred to the house, lands and tithes thereof, proportionately for the exchange of other lands as much in value, to the King's Grace's use'. After the establishment of a new college, Bird expected to profit by £73 0s 10d, so he intended, in exchange for Crown lands to the value of £11 13s 7½d, to grant to the king the episcopal manor of Weston in Derbyshire, worth £84 14s 5½d. The king was to pay the ex-warden of Manchester's pension, Bird's taxes were not to be increased and the bishop was to retain the patronage of the churches belonging to Weston, 'forasmuch as the said bishop hath very few promotions to give to his preachers and chaplains'. The advantages Bird hoped to secure are clear, for although he proposed the exchange of properties of equal value, lands and tithes in the rapidly growing town of Manchester would prove far more profitable than a manor in Derbyshire, 'which lieth above forty miles out of the said bishop's diocese, so that he cannot use the commodities thereof so well as of lands near'.[2]

Unfortunately for Bird and his diocese, the petition did not go unheeded, for although the bishop's plan was not accepted he had drawn attention to a valuable episcopal manor when the Crown was looking for Church lands. Bird and the chancellor of Augmentations were instructed to negotiate a transfer, and late in 1546 the bishop surrendered the manor of Weston and other property to the king. In return, the bishop received five appropriated rectories, together with the advowsons of eight other rectories and a licence to appropriate them when they became vacant.[3] The lands Bird surrendered were together worth £153 18s a year, and the bishop had to continue paying tenths on the properties as if he still owned them. In return

---

[1] Rymer, *Foedera*, XIV, 720.

[2] *L & P*, XXI(1), 967, printed in S. Hibbert-Ware, *History of the Foundations in Manchester*, 3 vols. II, 353–4.

[3] *L & P*, XXI(2), 183, 199, Nos. 135, 137, 574, 771, g. 10; CRO, EDA 3/1, fos. 53–58v.

the king gave five appropriated rectories guaranteed to yield £81 3s 0½d net, and an annual payment from the Crown of £83 9s 9d. Thus in the short term the bishop lost lands worth £153 18s and taxes worth £15 7s 9½d, or £169 5s 9½d, and gained £164 12s 9½d, amounting to an annual loss of less than £5.[1] The annual payment of £83 9s 9d, was in lieu of the other eight rectories, as yet still held by rectors, but as each one became vacant the bishop was to appropriate it, institute a vicarage with a stipend set by the king and retain the profits for himself. As each rectory came into the bishop's hands, the pension from the king was reduced by an amount equal to the profit Bird obtained. The total gross value of the eight rectories was £303 18s 6d in 1535, but after appropriation and the deduction of taxes, stipends for the vicars and other fees, they would produce, on the *Valor Ecclesiasticus* figures, a net income for the bishop of £99 16s 5d. The *Valor* for the north-west underestimated incomes by between a fifth and a quarter, and the king guaranteed that the rectories would bring in £111 4s 6d. Thus on the low estimates of 1535 in the long term the bishop would lose lands and taxes worth £169 5s 9½d and gain rectorial incomes of £81 3s 0½d plus £99 16s 5d, or £180 19s 5½d, thus making a profit on the transaction of £11 13s 8d. According to the king's revised and guaranteed figures of 1546, the bishop would lose £169 5s 9½d and gain £81 3s 0½d plus £111 4s 6d, or £192 7s 6½d, and so make a profit of £23 1s 9d. The exchange was not, as it has been called, a 'spoliation' of the see by the Crown, for though the king granted to Bird rectories which had not yet been appropriated, the Crown's considerable profit was not made at the bishop's expense.

The nominal value of the rectories Bird received was not, however, the same as the real income he obtained from them, especially in a period of severe inflation. When the exchange took place, four of the five rectories which came immediately into the bishop's hands were already burdened by long leases, one of which was not due to fall in until 1605[2], so that during the Tudor inflation revenue from the new rectories was fixed. To make matters worse, Bishop Bird himself granted new leases of these rectories, to follow the existing ones. The 70 year lease of Castleton which had begun in 1535 was to be followed by a 99 year lease, the 21 year lease of Weaverham from 1541 was to be followed by a 99 year lease, and a new lease for 99 years was to follow the existing lease of Bowdon made in 1546. In

---

[1] This discussion is based on an account of the income of the see at its foundation (CRO, EDA 3/1, fo. 35v), the details of the exchange (ibid. fos. 53–58v), and the 1535 valuation of the benefices granted to the bishop by the king (*Valor*, III and V). Similar exchanges were imposed on other bishops.

[2] The following discussion is based on the leases in CRO, EDA 3/1, fos. 110–123.

each case, the rents in the new leases were no higher than those in the earlier grants. Bird was equally rash with the other eight rectories; those which came into his hands as incumbents died or resigned. As soon as the bishop gained possession of Mottram in 1547, he made consecutive leases of the rectory for 60 years and 92 years at the same rent, he granted long leases of Cottingham and Bradley to begin when the rectories passed to the see of Chester, and he sanctioned long leases by the existing rectors of Chipping and Ribchester. The rents demanded by Bird were not low by the standards of the 1540s, but the leases were extremely long; the bishop's chancellor, George Wilmesley, secured four leases totalling 368 years.[1] The revenues from the new rectories were thus in many cases fixed for many years, and consecutive leases could fix rents for a century and a half. If the leases ran their full courses, Bowden's rent could not be increased until 1685, Mottram's until 1699 and Castleton's until 1704. The see had been poorly endowed in 1541, and Bird's leases almost crippled the finances of the diocese. By 1553 Bishop Bird owed the Crown £1,087 18s 0½d in unpaid tenths and subsidies, and although the revenues of the see were temporarily sequestered it was obvious that the debt could never be paid and Bird's successor was released from it.[2]

The finances of the see were thus totally inadequate, and this had serious implications for the administration of the diocese. We have already seen that Bishop Bird was unable to appoint archdeacons, the 'oculi episcopi'. Much of a bishop's routine work was normally delegated to archdeacons, who formed links betweeen the cathedral city and the parishes, and by their annual visitations kept a check on clergy and laity. In the diocese of Lincoln, which before the reconstruction of 1541 was perhaps half as large again as Chester, there had been eight archdeaconries, each supervised by both an archdeacon and a bishop's commissary.[3] But Bishop Bird ruled his diocese only through a chancellor at Chester, to whom he paid £10, and a commissary at Richmond with a salary of 10 marks.[4] The chancellor, as vicar-general and official principal, was responsible for the exercise of the bishop's spiritual jursidiction over the whole diocese, and for holding the consistory court at Chester.[5] The commissary of Richmond held another consistory at Richmond, and

---

[1] I have discussed these rents and leases in detail in 'A mid-Tudor ecclesiastical official: the curious career of George Wilmesley', *THSLC*, CXXII, 16–17.
[2] PRO, DL 42/96, fos. 83–83v; *CPR*, Philip and Mary, I, 389.
[3] M. Bowker, *The Secular Clergy in the Diocese of Lincoln, 1495–1520*, 6, 30–1.
[4] CRO, EDA 3/1, fo. 35v.
[5] The patent for Bird's chancellor does not survive, but it was almost certainly the same as the first two extant patents, for 1562 and 1587 (CRO, EDA 2/2, fos. 48–49v, 52–53).

seems to have had a jurisdiction within the archdeaconry concurrent with that of the chancellor.[1]

The first of the Richmond commissaries was Robert Leyburne, a prominent local incumbent, but he held office for a short time only and was replaced in 1544 by Miles Huddleston, LL.B.[2] Huddleston was rector of Whittington in north Lancashire, where his family held the manor and patronage of the rectory, and his influence secured other benefices with a royal licence for non-residence.[3] As a man with such widespread interests, he was often away from Richmond, and does not appear to have been a conscientious commissary. The Richmond consistory was normally presided over by a mere local chaplain, Thomas Bland, who was Huddleston's curate at Whittington. There is no evidence that Bland had any formal legal training, but the patronage of Huddleston secured for him an array of minor, though influential, posts. As well as being deputy to the commissary, Bland was rural dean of Richmond; in 1550 he acquired the deaneries of Kendal, Lonsdale and Catterick, and later he succeeded his master as rector of Whittington.[4] The administration of the massive archdeaconry of Richmond was thus in the hands of a comparatively lowly official, whose later career showed that he was not trustworthy,[5] and who, because of the distance between Richmond and Chester, enjoyed considerable independence from his diocesan superiors.

The recognition of the special problems of the diocese of Chester by giving it, unlike most English dioceses, two consistory courts was, however, of little help to the people of the western deaneries. From north Lancashire and south Cumberland and Westmorland, travel to Richmond was as unattractive a prospect as travel to Chester. The commissary cannot have kept in touch with events in parishes west of the Pennines, and very few Lancashire litigants went to the Richmond consistory. Fewer than 10% of the cases before the consistory in the 1540s originated in Lancashire, and fewer than 5% of the surviving Tudor cause papers concern cases from this county.[6] It was, in fact, easier for north-Lancashire

---

[1] I wish to thank Mr J. Addy for introducing me to the early records of the commissaries, and for several useful discussions. Although the commissary seems to have achieved some independence later, there can be no doubt that in the sixteenth century the chancellor's jurisdiction extended into Richmond: (i) chancellors' patents explicitly grant authority over the *whole* diocese, and (ii) the Chester consistory, under the chancellor, heard cases which originated in Richmond, including some which involved the commissary.

[2] LCL, RD/A/1A, fos. 15v, 36v.

[3] *VCH*, VIII, 245, 251; *L & P*, XI, 202, g. 8.

[4] LCL, RD/A/1A, *passim*; CRO, EDR 6, pp. 53–5, EDV 2/4, fo. 27.

[5] See below, p. 257.

[6] LCL, RD/A/1A, *passim*, RD/AC/1–6, *passim*.

litigants to travel to the consistory at Chester, so that rather more of their cases went to the chancellor than to the commissary. But the distance involved meant that few cases from the area went even to Chester.[1] It is clear that the foundation of the see of Chester did little to increase ecclesiastical control over the large and barren parishes of northern Lancashire, for there neither the chancellor nor the commissary could exercise effective authority.

The southern section of the diocese was probably better governed than Richmond, but there too there were weaknesses, and the poverty of the see may have influenced the structure of the central administration. It is true that from the fifteenth century there was a tendency in several dioceses to combine the three offices of vicar-general, official principal and commissary-general and grant them to one man. But it may have been Bishop Bird's need to limit his salary bill which prompted him to nominate a chancellor to fulfil these functions.[2] Bird's chancellor was George Wilmesley, an ambitious and grasping bastard member of an influential local family and half-brother of Edmund Bonner. In 1544 Wilmesley added to his stock of offices by purchasing from the holder the fourth major diocesan post, that of registrar, for £114, but the original holder must have regretted the deal for he tried to regain his position by violence.[3] Wilmesley was able to establish a monopoly of the administration of the diocese, and although he appointed deputies to assist him they were his officers rather than the bishop's. The chancellor used his position to speculate in ecclesiastical offices and revenues; he secured leases of four episcopal rectories, the advowsons of four rectories and an archdeaconry, the lease of the tithes of at least one other rectory and the next presentation to at least one vicarage. He leased out the profits of one of his offices, he sub-let one of his rectories and he sold the leases of two others. Wilmesley needed these revenues to support his growing family, for he fathered seven children by three different women.[4] The central administration of the diocese was in the hands of a man whose main interest lay in providing for a family he ought not to have had, but the institutional aspects of his position were more important than the personal. As well as the four main diocesan offices, he held three rural deaneries,

---

[1] The Chester consistory act books give the parishes of litigants only in tithe suits; between October 1541 and December 1558 the consistory heard 112 tithe cases from the 32 parishes of the Lancashire portion of the archdeaconry of Chester, but only 17 causes from the 26 Lancashire parishes in the archdeaconry of Richmond (CRO, EDC 1/10–15, *passim*).

[2] CRO, EDR 6, p. 47, EDC 1/10, fos. 146v, 192, 196v.

[3] CRO, EDA 3/1, fos. 103v–104v; PRO, Req. 2/14/91.

[4] Haigh, 'Mid–Tudor ecclesiastical official', 15–18.

and he had to fulfil the duties of archdeacon of Chester as well. Whereas in other dioceses a new incumbent was instituted by the vicar-general and inducted by the archdeacon, in Chester the chancellor performed both tasks. Wilmesley's wide responsibilities meant that he was unable to give the diocese the close supervision necessary if the absence of archdeacons was not to be a serious flaw in the ecclesiastical structure.

Bishop Bird seems to have been well aware of the deficiencies of his diocesan administration, but there was little he could do without help. His control of the diocese was severely limited by the location of his cathedral city, and as the property of the see consisted almost entirely of rectories Bird had no string of episcopal manors to use as local bases. In 1545–6, therefore, Bird petitioned the king for assistance. He asked that if Manchester College could be spared from suppression the present warden might be pensioned off and the bishop himself made warden. Bird gave four reasons for his request: that 'the country thereabouts is populous and much destitute of preachers', that he 'hath no house of residence within his large and ample diocese but alonely his house at Chester', that from Chester he could not 'execute his office and duty, implanting virtue and suppressing vicious living', and that the people 'have used to come far from thence to Chester for confirmation of their children and other divers matters pertaining to the bishop's office'.[1] Bishop Bird hoped to use Manchester College as a second administrative centre, and the good sense of his proposal was seen later in the century. In 1557–8 Bishop Scott used the college as a base for his attack on Lancashire heresy, and in the 1580s Bishop Chadderton held the wardenry of the college and used Manchester as the bridgehead of his drive against recusancy.[2] In 1546, however, the Crown found the revenues of the college more attractive than its administrative possibilities.

Bishop Bird did, however, make what could have been a useful contribution towards the maintenance of links between the cathedral city and the parishes. It has already been noted that the size of the archdeaconries of Richmond and Chester led to an unusually wide authority for the rural deans, and Bird developed the role of the deans as local administrators. A rural dean's patent issued by him in 1550 granted authority to proceed in all disciplinary cases except simony and heresy, to prove wills, except for those of knights and priests, where the estate of the deceased was worth less than £40, and

---

[1] Hibbert–Ware, *History of the Foundations*, II, 353–4.
[2] R. Hollingworth, *Mancuniensis*, ed. W. Willis, 79; Hibbert–Ware, *History of the Foundations*, I, 81; F. Peck, *Desiderata Curiosa*, 110.

to collect synodals and procurations.[1] It is difficult to trace the work of the deans in the middle of the century, but in the reign of Elizabeth they can be found investigating doubtful wills, excommunicating, imposing and commuting penances and holding their own visitations and correction courts.[2] But the rural deans were at best imperfect links between the bishop and his flock. The deaneries of Lancashire were far too large for close supervision to be possible; though the two counties covered an equal area, Essex had thirteen deaneries and Lancashire only eight, two of them also covering many parishes in other counties. Pluralism made the areas of individual jurisdiction even larger, and while the chancellor of Chester held three deaneries the deputy-commissary of Richmond held four. Unsuitable men were often appointed to the office; rural deans were often mere assistant chaplains, and in 1558 the dean of Warrington was Thomas Kirkby, the thoroughly disreputable ex-curate of Halsall.[3] By 1571, as we shall see, the rural deans of Lancashire were a sorry crew, who did little to enforce the will of the bishop.

The deans were merely the advance guard of the disciplinary forces of the Church, and the heavy artillery was provided by the ecclesiastical courts. The records of the court of the archdeacon of Chester, which became the diocesan consistory in 1541, are rather patchy for the years 1502 to 1529, but thereafter they seem fairly full, and it is possible to construct an account of their operation in the first half of the century. Although the position was not nearly so serious as it was to become in the reign of Elizabeth, the evidence suggests that even earlier the Church found it difficult to discipline the laity. In particular, it was impossible to enforce the attendance of all those cited to appear at court. In 1531, for example, two sisters from Whalley who had refused to give a mortuary failed to attend the court when summoned, and had to be suspended from receiving the sacraments. In the same year Margaret Osbaldeston of Blackburn was ordered to answer for her failure to pay a mortuary on her late husband, but she did not appear before the court and was declared contumacious, though she later submitted and was absolved.[4]

Those who flouted the authority of the court in this way were not anti-clericals or opponents of ecclesiastical jurisdiction, and clergy as well as laymen resisted. In 1539–40 John Trafford, priest, tried a variety of expedients to escape the clutches of the archdeacon's court; twice he failed to appear and was suspended from the

[1] CRO, EDR 6, pp. 53–5.
[2] CRO, EDC 2/7, fo. 45, 2/8, fos. 273v–274, EDC 1/30, fo. 359, EDA 2/2, fo. 198.
[3] PRO, DL 44/36; *Church Goods*, III, 10; CRO, EDC 1/15, fo. 136; see also above, p. 6 and below, pp. 35–6.
[4] CRO, EDC 1/4, fos. 13v, 16v, 18, 20v, 23, 25v, 29v, 37.

14

celebration of the sacraments until he submitted, once he produced some sort of patent of exemption which the court refused to recognise, and finally he defeated the officials by refusing to submit to a third suspension.[1] It was often a witness rather than the defendant who proved uncooperative, and this could lead to much difficulty. In 1545 George Wolset's tithe suit against eleven of his parishioners ground to a halt when a witness failed to present himself before the consistory. The chancellor of Chester wrote to warn Wolset to ensure the attendance of his witness, but still the man did not turn up and the case had to be dropped. Three years later Elizabeth Traves of Prestwich cited Francis Buckley in a paternity case, and called the curate of Oldham, who had baptised the child, to give evidence. Edward Hall, the curate, did not attend the consistory but sent a written testimony, and later his rector had to write to the deputy-registrar to apologise for the curate's temerity.[2] In 1556 Isabel Holden of Church was unable to persuade three of her witnesses, including her curate, to go to Chester without the issue of a citation mandate.[3] Those who wished to avoid a journey to Chester might concoct plausible excuses, but sometimes the stories were checked. In 1537 Laurence Ainsworth of Oswaldtwistle was summoned before the court but sent a message that he was too ill to appear. Later two local gentlemen signed a declaration that he had been seen, fit and well, and 'so will all the country thereabouts testify, that of truth the said Laurence is not grieved with any manner of sickness, but that he may well labour'.[4]

It was probably the time and trouble involved in litigation which discouraged men from appearing before the courts. Thurstan Arrowsmith was prepared to travel to Chester to defend himself before the archdeacon's court in 1534, but when the plaintiff appealed against the official's decision to the bishop's consistory the journey to Lichfield was too much for Arrowsmith and he suffered excommunication rather than submit.[5] After 1541, litigants from as far away as Cartmel and Kirkby Ireleth were taking their suits to Chester, and over such distances attendance was extremely difficult to enforce. During her defamation cause before the consistory, Isabel Holden had to attend the court on three occasions; she later claimed from the defendants £1 'for my costs and my witnesses coming to Chester at two sundry times at 10s each time', and a further 10s 'for my costs coming to Chester time of the sentence'. This £1 10s just for

---

[1] *Ibid.* 1/9, fos. 188, 190, 193, 1/10, fos. 4, 9, 23.
[2] *Ibid.* 1/11, fos. 140, 172v, 173/1, 1/12, fo. 90/1.
[3] BIY, R VII, G 684; CRO, EDC 1/14, fo. 120.
[4] CRO, EDC 1/8, fo. 175/1.
[5] Lich. RO, B/C/2/3, fos. 250, 251.

travelling represented six months' wages for a skilled worker in Chester forty years later.[1] Here lay the real danger for the ecclesiastical courts when they served such large areas, for the sanctions which could be imposed to enforce attendance – suspension and excommunication – might be less onerous than a journey to the court.

There seems to have been a fear that the authority of the consistory was being eroded, and an awareness that disobedience to its orders would lead to a decline in respect. In 1550 a Lancashire gentleman urged an official of the consistory to enquire into the failure of a defendant to obey the court: 'I heartily desire [you to] cause this matter to be looked upon, or else your court will be but small regarded if such as ye commanded be not performed.'[2] The clergy may have doubted the ability of the court to discipline their parishioners. In 1529 Ralph Lynney, the abbot of Whalley's proctor for Blackburn parish, found it necessary to remind the officers of the court that a parishioner had been cited to appear, and to ask them to 'lay into him for withholding his tenth corns by the space of two years last passed'.[3] Such reactions are not surprising, for some held the court in contempt. Katherine Mollineux of Hulton in Dean sued her husband, Henry, in 1552 for maintenance after he had deserted her, but he did not attend the court when it was ordered that he should pay the money owing. Katherine then sent two honest men to her husband to require other money which was awarded her by the court for her finding', but Henry was in no mood to pay and 'did make answer that he would give her none, neither at her desire nor by no Church commandment, for he neither set by them nor by her in this matter'. When this was reported to the consistory Henry was excommunicated, but he soon submitted.[4]

The influence of a local gentleman could be more effective than fear of the sanctions of the Church. In 1550 a large number of witnesses from Wigan were called to testify on the characters of the witnesses appearing for James Winstanley, gentleman, in a testamentary suit. The court heard many allegations that Winstanley's witnesses were all his servants or tenants, and had given false evidence through fear or bribery.[5] It was said, for example, that William Rainford was 'such that dare not say or depose any things against James Winstanley his master', that Margery Grey 'did

[1] BIY, R VII, G 329; R. H. Morris, *Chester in the Plantagenet and Tudor Reigns*, 367–8.

[2] CRO, EDC 1/12, fo. 180/1.

[3] CRO, EDC 2/1, fo. 41/1.

[4] CRO, EDC 1/12, fos. 180/1, 185, 190v, 199v.

[5] See the numerous depositions in CRO, EDC 2/4, pp. 242–56, 266–78.

16

depose against her conscience for the profit of James Winstanley' because 'being a poor woman she might lightly be hired or corrupted for a little reward', and that Margaret Orrell 'had a pair of shoes of Mr Winstanley for bearing record and witness in this matter, and she trusted to have better gift of him'. A similar case came before the consistory three months later, when it was pointed out that, of the witnesses Sir John Byron had produced in a tithe suit, seven were his servants, one was related to him, another was his deputy steward at Rochdale, another was brother to one of his servants and two more had sub-leases of tithe from him. It was alleged that all were 'such persons as would be corrupted to say contrary to the truth'.[1] The evidence in these cases may have been false, but the unanimity of the deponents, with no obvious signs of collusion, is suggestive.

In most cases of refusal to obey the court, suspension or excommunication sufficed to bring the recalcitrant to heel, but if this was not enough there was little the Church could do. In a sparsely populated area with poor communications, excommunication could easily be evaded, and it was a sanction which held few terrors for the indifferent. In cases of serious disobedience the consistory might invoke the cumbersome machinery of signification, but in a diocese which covered several counties and jurisdictions this was a long and complicated process which usually failed to produce results. The courts therefore 'signified' offenders very infrequently, and excommunicates usually went unmolested.[2] In Lancashire the courts were many miles from the parish of the accused, and the necessary local officers did not exist or were ineffective, so that the Church could only enforce its discipline upon those who voluntarily submitted to it.

This meant that there were always men who were frequently in trouble, but whom the Church could not control. In 1532 John Ridehalgh was sued for non-payment of tithe by the abbot of Whalley, but the abbot was unable to get satisfaction from Ridehalgh at the archdeacon's court in Chester, and began an action in the court of the Duchy of Lancaster. In the awe-inspiring surroundings of a royal court, Ridehalgh lost his confidence and agreed to ask the abbot's pardon for his 'lutherous demeanour', but once away from the court he again plucked up his courage and refused payment. The abbot cited him before the archdeacon's court again in 1534, but Ridehalgh refused to appear and was suspended from entering church.[3]

[1] *Ibid.* pp. 327–31.
[2] See below, pp. 235–6, for a fuller discussion of the process of signification.
[3] CRO, EDC 1/5, fo. 63, 1/7, fos. 19, 21, 25v, 33v, 37, 43v; *Duchy Pleadings*, II, 32–3. 'Lutherous' was presumably derived from Luther's attack on the Church, and

We hear no more of him, and there is no sign that he ever submitted. James Hartley of Burnley, who seems to have been something of a sea-lawyer, was another vigorous resister of payments to the Church. In 1540 he was one of a group of men who refused to pay the usual 4d mortuary, and he was taken before the Chester court by the lessee of Whalley rectory. It was said that the payment had never before been contested, but when the case went against him Hartley appealed to the archbishop's court at York.[1] Between 1544 and 1546 Hartley was involved in a long conflict with the vicar of Whalley over dues, and when the vicar made no progress in the Church courts he took his suit to the Duchy.[2] In 1549 Hartley was again in trouble for failure to pay tithe, and his final appearance in the episcopal consistory was in 1557, also in a tithe suit.[3]

The central weakness of the ecclesiastical courts was that they depended, for the detection of offenders and the enforcement of decrees, on the cooperation of local clergy and laity. We shall see that the parish priests were often of poor quality and, as many depended for their livelihood on voluntary benefactions from parishioners, they were therefore not eager to offend. The churchwardens were even less effective instruments, for the office was onerous and unpopular. At Woodplumpton chapel in 1606 and 1607 the three men elected as wardens hired deputies to act for them, and in both years the curate had to serve as a warden though the clergy were exempt from the office.[4] Though wardens were in theory officers of the Church, they were in fact controlled by the local gentry. The nomination of churchwardens in Prescot was firmly in the hands of the gentry in the first half of the sixteenth century, and an attempted reform by the bishop of Chester in 1555 merely institutionalised gentry control. By the early seventeenth century there were more than twenty closed vestries on the Prescot model in north Lancashire alone.[5] A Puritan petition of 1590 summed up a state of affairs which had existed for many years: the wardens were chosen 'by the singular nomination of the gentlemen and better sort of every town, without the consent of the pastor', so that they were 'of the meanest

seems to have covered all forms of anticlericalism. Its use shows an awareness of heretical currents of thought, but perhaps also that defiance of the Church was sufficiently unusual to warrant such a description.

[1] CRO, EDC 1/10, fos. 3–42, *passim*, EDC 2/2, fos. 347, 369; BIY, R VII, G 297.
[2] CRO, EDC 1/11, fos. 47–118, *passim*, EDC 2/3, fo. 25; PRO, DL 3/14, P. 4.
[3] CRO, EDC 1/12, fos. 154, 157v, 1/14, fo. 273.
[4] G. H. Tupling, 'Parish books', *TLCAS*, LXII, 16–17.
[5] Bailey, 'Churchwardens' accounts of Prescot', I, 138–9; CRO, EDA 2/1, fos. 406v–407v; Tupling, 'Parish books', 13.

and lewdest sort of the people, and therefore most fit to serve the humour of the gentry and multitude'. If the wardens dared to make presentments at visitation, the gentry would 'remove any such from the office and put another in his place, that neither can nor will give notice of their offences'. Churchwardens were often mistreated 'at the hands of those that stand in danger of the laws', while parishioners refused to finance the work of the wardens.[1]

The Church could not rely on its own officers and institutions to maintain discipline, and had to turn to laymen for assistance. It was often local gentlemen rather than priests who reported offences to the courts,[2] lay rather than clerical commissions conducted enquiries for the consistory,[3] and lay arbitrators were used in disputes even when one of the participants was a priest.[4] The officers of the diocese of Chester were unable to perform their duties unaided, and in 1543 and 1550 royal commissions containing a large majority of laymen were appointed to deal with matters which were normally the concern of episcopal visitations.[5] In a number of cases priests were unable to bring the laity to heel in the ecclesiastical courts, and had to turn to the secular power. In 1532 the abbot of Whalley sued a number of men from Great Marsden in the official's court at Chester, but in the following year he had to take the case to the Duchy.[6] The rector of Chipping fought a tithe case in the bishop's consistory, but when he had made no progress after four years of litigation it was not surprising that he transferred his efforts to the Duchy court in 1547.[7] At about the same time, the vicar of Whalley had trouble with the chapelry of Colne but after two years he, too, dropped his case in the consistory and went to the Duchy court.[8] However, as will be seen, the secular administration in Lancashire was only slightly more effective than the ecclesiastical. Neither Church nor state possessed the machinery necessary if religious change was to be enforced in the county.

---

[1] *State Civil and Ecclesiastical*, 9–10.
[2] e.g. CRO, EDC 1/8, fos. 175/1–1v, 1/12, fo. 180/1.
[3] e.g. CRO, EDC 1/15, fos. 99–102v.
[4] e.g. Lich. RO, B/C/2/3, fo. 205; CRO, EDC 1/5, fo. 153.
[5] CRO, EDA 12/1, *passim*; PRO, DL 42/96, fo. 33v.
[6] CRO, EDC 1/5, fo. 63; *Duchy Pleadings*, II, 32–3.
[7] CRO, EDC 1/10, fos. 183v *et seqq*; EDC 1/11, fo. 173/1; *Duchy Pleadings*, II, 211.
[8] CRO, EDC 1/11, fo. 47; *Ducatus Lancastriae*, ed. R. J. Harper *et al.* 3 vols. I, 183.

Lancashire parishes and their incumbents

Lancashire was, in the sixteenth century, among the very poorest of the counties of England. In 1489 William Paston thought 'that there be gentlemen of as great substance that they be able to buy all Lancashire',[1] and he was not alone in his low estimation of the area's wealth. The earl of Derby wrote in 1536 that the people were 'very poor and of small ability', and in 1557 he drew attention to the 'poor estate' of the shire.[2] Lancashire gentry were assumed to be less prosperous than their southern counterparts. When, in 1549, Alice Radcliffe's daughter refused to allow Sir Andrew Windsor to marry her off to a non-Lancastrian, Windsor wrote angrily to her mother that 'she should have lived better with any of them that I intended to marry her to the worst day of the year than she shall do with him that you hear say she shall be married to in the best'.[3] It is possible to provide some statistical confirmation for these views. Recent studies of the geographical distribution of wealth in England have suggested that in 1334, 1503, 1515 and 1636, Lancashire was either the poorest or the second poorest of all English counties. Even at the Hearth Tax survey of 1662 Lancashire was thirtieth out of forty areas by wealth in proportion to size.[4] Though one may doubt the validity of some of the methods used and the accuracy of the tax assessments which provided the bases for this work, the agreement of four scholars and five tax-lists seems convincing.

The poverty of the county had serious implications for the practice of religion. Lancashiremen were not sufficiently wealthy to maintain the fabric of their churches, and in 1554–5 sixteen of the thirty-one churches visited by the chancellor of the diocese were in

[1] A. F. Pollard, *The Reign of Henry VII from Contemporary Sources*, 3 vols. I, 67.
[2] *Derby Correspondence*, 26; J. Strype, *Ecclesiastical Memorials*, 3 vols. III(2), 90.
[3] *Kenyon MSS*, 3.
[4] E. J. Buckatzsch, 'The geographical distribution of wealth in England, 1086–1843', *Economic History Review*, 2nd series, III, 187; R. S. Schofield, 'The geographical distribution of wealth in England, 1334–1649', *Economic History Review*, 2nd series, XVIII, 504; H. C. Darby, ed., *Historical Geography of England before A.D. 1800*, 438; A. Everitt, *Change in the Provinces*, Leicester University Dept. of English Local History, Occasional Papers, 2nd series, I, 54–5.

need of repair.[1] The poor state of Lancashire churches caused concern even in government circles, and a series of commissions investigated the problem. In 1543 a royal commission which dealt with south-Lancashire churches found that five needed major renovation, and in 1550 another commission was appointed to raise contributions for the repair of local churches.[2] In 1555 the queen deputed four Duchy officers to enquire into the state of one Lancashire church, and arranged for stone from Furness Abbey to be used to rebuild another.[3] Once a church had fallen into disrepair it was difficult to raise enough money for improvements. Richard Standish left £40 'to the new making' of Standish church in 1535, but the sum was clearly insufficient and the work had not been done by 1543, when the fabric was 'in great ruin and decay'. The nave and chancel were still in poor condition in 1554, and although in 1555 Dr Richard Standish left £20 for renovation, thereafter things grew worse. It was reported in 1578 that 'their church is fallen down to the ground and hath been divers years', but it was not until 1584 that a parish meeting agreed on levies to finance reconstruction and even then there was a good deal of resistance.[4]

Clergy and churchwardens were harried by royal and diocesan officials to improve their church fabric, and money was often raised by selling church property. When Bishop Bird visited the deanery of Amounderness in 1548 he found that the wardens of two churches had recently sold plate to pay for repairs, and two more churches had pawned chalices for the same purpose. By 1552, presumably after pressure from the Duchy commissioners of 1550, a number of churches in Warrington deanery had made sales, usually of bells and chalices, to finance rebuilding.[5] This tendency to choose between church fabric and 'church goods', together with the poverty of the region, left the churches badly provided with items needed for the liturgy, and in 1550 it was found that 'the vestments and ornaments of the chantries were very little'.[6] If we assume that vestments, a cope, a chalice, an altarcloth, bells and a hand bell were the minimum required for pre-Reformation services,[7] the inventories of

---

[1] CRO, EDV 1/1, *passim*.
[2] CRO, EDA 12/1, *passim*, EDC 5, 1550; PRO, DL 42/96, fo. 33v.
[3] *Ibid.* fos. 111–111v, 121–121v.
[4] *Calendar of Standish Deeds, 1230–1575*, ed. T. C. Porteus, No. 221; T. C. Porteus, *History of the Parish of Standish*, 56–7; CRO, EDA 12/1, p. 14, EDV 1/1, fo. 145, EDC 1/25, fos. 103, 199v; BIY, R VI, A 7, fo. 58.
[5] PRO, SP 10/3/4; *Church Goods*, II, 91, 94, 107, 111, 114.
[6] *Lancs. Chantries*, I, 22.
[7] Other items essential for services, such as pixes, candlesticks, etc., are excluded from this analysis as they were often of small value and so were usually omitted from the lists.

1552 indicate that fewer than half the parish churches and 5% of the chapels had what was needed for the celebration of masses. Lancashire churches were much less well provided for than were churches in other areas. In the inventories for both Lancashire and the East Riding, 27 items of liturgical use occur but of these 16 occur noticeably more often in the East Riding lists and only 8 items occur less often. Similarly, the extant lists for Bedfordshire have 21 items in common with the Lancashire survey, of which 13 occur more often in Bedfordshire and only 2 less often.[1]

Not only were Lancashire churches less well maintained and well furnished than those elsewhere, there were even fewer of them. In the late medieval period Lancashire was poor partly because it was among the least densely populated of English counties.[2] If the population was small only a limited number of parish churches was needed, while each parish had to cover a wide area to draw in sufficient revenue to support a church and priests. There were therefore only 56 parishes in Lancashire by 1291, and thereafter the parochial structure of the county remained almost unchanged until the Civil War. In 1535 only Westmorland and Rutland contained fewer parishes than Lancashire, so that the county's parishes were very much larger than those elsewhere. Fourteen counties in the Midlands and the south-east had parishes which averaged 4 square miles or less in area, and even parishes in poor shires such as Devon, Cornwall and Shropshire averaged between 7 and 9 square miles. But the average Lancashire parish covered 33 square miles, seven or eight times the national average, and Northumberland was the only county with larger parishes.[3] However although by the sixteenth century Lancashire was still poor, it was no longer thinly populated. A survey conducted by the bishop of Chester in 1563 indicates that there were 19,000 households in the county, and on the assumption that an average household consisted of five members the population must have been about 95,000. Between 1377 and 1563 the county population may have multiplied by over two and a half times and, as only one new parish was added in the meantime, the average parish population increased from 630 to 1,700.[4] The population of parishes in other parts of England was very much lower than this in the early

---

[1] Calculations based on *Church Goods*, I–III, *Inventories of Church Goods for the Counties of York, Durham and Northumberland*, and *Edwardian Inventories for Bedfordshire*. For the accuracy of the Lancashire lists see Haigh, 'Reformation in Lancashire', 71–2, 74–5.

[2] J. C. Russell, *British Medieval Population*, 53–4, 312–13.

[3] My figures are based on the map in Hughes, *Reformation in England*, I, 35.

[4] BM, Harleian MS 594, fos. 101–108. The survey appears accurate, as parish totals are rarely given in round numbers and a survey of 1603 implies a similar number (B. Magee, *The English Recusants*, 83).

sixteenth century, an average of 412 in the diocese of York, 298 in the diocese of Ely, 294 in the diocese of Canterbury and only 167 in Salisbury diocese.[1]

The reason for Lancashire's large parishes had thus disappeared by the sixteenth century, and their high average population now meant that incumbents received correspondingly high incomes from tithe. Peter Heath has estimated that in 1535 three-quarters of English livings were worth less than £15 a year and about half less than £10; in Lancashire, however, the proportions were under half and less than a third respectively. The average income of Lancashire rectors and vicars in 1535 was £22 16s 5d, whereas the average revenue of Essex incumbents, in an area much richer but with only small parishes, was £13 11s 7d. Lancashire rectors received an average of £34 8s 5d, whereas in Warwickshire the average rectorial income was £11 8s, and the contrasts are even more impressive because the *Valor* seriously under-estimated Lancashire incomes.[2] Even in the poorer north of the county, that portion in the archdeaconry of Richmond, the average income of rectors was £17 6s 6d in 1524, whereas two years later the average in the diocese of Lincoln was £12 13s 8½d.[3]

The revenues yielded by parochial livings remained high despite the impact of unusually heavy appropriation. Over England as a whole about one-third of all benefices were appropriated; in Lancashire as many as 56% of the parishes had appropriated rectories. The incomes available for incumbents were seriously reduced by appropriation, and though the average income of the rectors of the county was £34 8s 5d the vicars received only £12 9s 4d. The revenue from Whalley rectory was £91 6s 8d but Whalley abbey paid its vicar only £6 3s 4½d, and though the abbey received £74 6s 8d from Blackburn rectory the vicar's stipend was only £8 1s 6d.[4] Some vicars suffered real hardship, largely as a result of inflation and the size of their parishes. In 1540 the Duchy of Lancaster paid the vicar of Ormskirk a salary of £10, but this had been fixed two hundred years earlier. It was pointed out that the parish embraced eleven separate hamlets with over 2,000 communicants, so that the vicar had to pay a curate out of his own small income; even the Duchy Council had to admit

---

[1] My calculations are based on Hughes, *Reformation in England*, I, 32, 34. His figures may be questioned, but only a huge error-rate would invalidate the contrast.

[2] *Valor*, V, 219–27, 230–2, 259–60, 262–3, 267–8; P. Heath, *The English Parish Clergy on the Eve of the Reformation*, 173; J. E. Oxley, *The Reformation in Essex*, 279; P. A. Bill, *Warwickshire Parish Clergy in the Later Middle Ages*, Dugdale Society, Occasional Papers, XVII, 5; Haigh, *Lancs. Monasteries*, 37–8.

[3] PRO, E 36/61, pp. 8–10; Bowker, *Secular Clergy*, 139.

[4] C. Hill, *Economic Problems of the Church*, 144–5; *Valor*, V, 229–30.

that 'the said vicarage is too little for the living of two persons'.[1]
Lancashire vicars, however, like the rectors of the county, received
incomes higher than those of their southern counterparts. In the mid
1520s the average income of north-Lancashire vicars was £13 4s 8d,
whereas in the diocese of Lincoln the average was only £9 9s 2d; a
decade later Lancashire vicars were receiving an average of £12 9s 4d
as against £9 yielded by vicarages in Warwickshire.

With a few exceptions Lancashire benefices were well worth
having, and there was always a good deal of demand for them. On
the very day that William Clayton, rector of Ribchester, died in
1532, Thomas Bedyll wrote to Thomas Cromwell to tell him of the
vacancy, and though he modestly pointed out that he was new to the
royal service and did not expect the benefice for himself he clearly
had hopes in that direction. At this time Edmund Bonner was in
Bologna about the king's affairs, but he too was interested in the
rectory and thanked Cromwell for mentioning his name to Henry.[2]
In 1534 the Lancastrian Robert Farington asked Cromwell to help
him obtain the rectory of Eccleston, and two years later he was again
hinting for some similar promotion.[3] Wealthier men found benefices
easier to obtain; young Thomas Wingfield's father bought the next
presentation to Warrington for his son, while John Stringer, a
pluralist and lately almoner to the duke of Richmond, bought the
next presentation to the rich rectory of Warton and presented
himself.[4] Others sailed close to simony in their efforts to secure a
Lancashire benefice, and it was not unusual for a would-be incumbent to promise a lease of tithes on favourable terms to the patron.
Edward Keble gave Sir Thomas Butler, the patron, a lease of the
rectory of Warrington before he was ever presented, and after Butler
duly made the presentation Keble refused to honour the lease on the
grounds that he had had no rights in the rectory when he made it.[5]
Richard Moody and Edward Standish worked through an intermediary; in 1559 Moody signed a bond promising Robert Shaw a
lease of the tithes of Standish should he become rector, in the same
year Moody was presented to the rectory by Edward Standish, and
in 1560 Moody made a lease to Shaw who immediately transferred
his rights to the patron.[6]

Many Lancashire benefices were not open to outside competition,
for one-third of the patronage was in the hands of local families in
1530 and this had risen to almost half by 1560.[7] Local patrons often

[1] *Ibid.* 223; PRO, DL 5/6, fos. 226–226v.   [2] *L & P*, V, 1427, 1658.
[3] *Ibid.* VII, 652, X, 85.   [4] *VCH*, III, 311; *Duchy Pleadings*, II, 154.
[5] *Ibid.* 120.   [6] *Calendar of Standish Deeds*, Nos. 423, 424.
[7] Figures from *VCH*, III–VIII, *passim*. By the end of the century laymen presented to over half the benefices in the county (*Kenyon MSS*, 7–13).

presented their relatives and friends. Between 1462 and 1557 the rectory of Sefton was held by five successive members of the Mollineux family which, as lords of Sefton, held the advowson. The rectory of Halsall was held by members of the patron's family from 1495 until 1571, the rectory of Prestwich followed the same course throughout the fifteenth and sixteenth centuries, and between 1520 and 1552 three of the four rectors of Standish were related to the patron.[1] Incumbents did not always wait until the patron's protégé came of age before dying, so minors were sometimes presented to family benefices. Hugh Halsall was presented to the family living in 1495, but seven years later he had to secure a dispensation for having been ordained and instituted before reaching the canonical age. His successor, Richard Halsall, was probably also a minor, for although he was presented to the rectory in 1513 he did not take his B.A. until 1520 and was not ordained until 1523.[2] George West, a mere child, was presented by his father to the wardenry of Manchester College in 1516, but when his father died he refused to proceed to holy orders and resigned the benefice.[3]

When outsiders had to invest heavily to acquire a Lancashire benefice, and when incumbents were sometimes the sons of the manor house, it is not surprising that rectors and vicars tried to extract the maximum revenue from their parishioners. There is some evidence that conflicts over tithe resulted as much from the clergy demanding too much as from the people offering too little. In the parish of Winwick it had long been customary for the people to pay the tithe of corn in kind, but for hay they paid a fixed sum of 3d for each acre under cultivation, until in 1544 the rector tried to enforce payment in kind on the hay harvest. Similarly, in 1551 the vicar of Prescot tried to impose a wool tithe in kind in place of the usual cash payment.[4] The vicar of Ormskirk and the rector of Prestwich tried in 1557 to enforce tithe on the produce of lands only recently reclaimed from the moor, though such land was legally exempt from tithe.[5] As the act books of the Chester consistory record only the progress of a case through its legal processes, and we can discover the origins of a suit only if the cause papers survive or evidence was entered in the depositions books, it is impossible to estimate the proportion of cases which resulted from excessive demands by incumbents. It is likely, however, that the pressures of

---

[1] *VCH*, III, 63, 189, V, 72–3, VI, 188.
[2] *Ibid.* III, 189; Lich. RO, Reg. Arundel, B/A/1/13, fo. 249v; Ordination Reg. B/A/1/14, II, December 1523; *Register of the University of Oxford*, ed. C. W. Boase, I, 113.
[3] *VCH*, IV, 195.
[4] CRO, EDC 2/3, fos. 20–20v, EDC 2/5, fos. 26v–30v.
[5] *Ibid.* 2/6, fos. 117v–119v, 134v–136v.

inflation and the resulting efforts of incumbents to increase their receipts, contributed to the increase in tithe suits from south Lancashire from 22 in the 1530s to 52 in the 1540s.[1]

Lancashire benefices, then, were lucrative prizes which were exploited to the full by those fortunate enough to secure them. Their profitability made them attractive to men of influence and standing, and some of the richest benefices were held by a succession of notables. The rectory of Winwick was an extreme example, with its bait of a net income before tax of £102 9s 8d, and it was probably the richest rectory in England. From 1495 until 1515 it was held by James Stanley, brother of the earl of Derby, archdeacon of Richmond, warden of Manchester and a considerable pluralist. Stanley was succeeded by Thomas Larke, Wolsey's secretary, archdeacon of Sudbury and then of Norwich, and master of Trinity Hall in Cambridge; in 1525 he passed on the benefice to his master's bastard son, who held an impressive array of preferments while still a student. The next rector was William Boleyn, uncle of Anne Boleyn and archdeacon of Winchester, and on his death in 1552 the rectory passed to Thomas Stanley, a relative of the earl of Derby and bishop of Sodor and Man.[2] Rich benefices went to men of influence, men powerful enough to obtain other wealthy benefices too, so that the best prizes in Lancashire went to pluralists. At the beginning of each decade from 1490 until 1550, pluralists held between five and eight, usually six or seven, of the ten richest benefices in the county, and between twelve and fourteen of the twenty richest. By 1550 the average yield of the benefices held by pluralists in the deanery of Leyland was £46 16s 6d, while the average yield of the remaining livings was £22 15s 1d. Thus pluralism in Lancashire was not the result of the poverty of livings and the need to combine them, but the result of the wealth of livings and the ambition of influential men. Edward Mollineux, a member of one of the most powerful families in the county, held three of the richest Lancashire rectories and one average vicarage in 1535, and they brought in a total revenue of £137 11s 10d. But Mollineux had nothing to recommend him but his connections; he did not hold a university degree, he spent much of his time in litigation, he used force and deceit in his financial dealings and was a thoroughly disreputable character.[3]

---

[1] Figures from CRO, EDC 1/4–12, *passim*. Cf. Heath, *English Parish Clergy*, 192.

[2] These details and those following are based on the *Valor* and the lists of Lancashire pluralist incumbents in Haigh, 'Reformation in Lancashire', App. A.

[3] *Valor*, V, 221, 223, 227, 232; LRO, DDBl/24/3, 24/5, 42/174, 54/1, 55/51–4; PRO, Sta. Cha. 2/5/51; *Lancashire and Cheshire Cases in the Court of Star Chamber*, ed. R. Stewart-Brown, 75.

Lancashire parishes and their incumbents

The wealthiest livings in Lancashire went consistently to those who had already secured for themselves a considerable income from the Church. Richard Dudley held the rectory of Walton from 1506 until 1528 and the rectory of Warton between 1508 and 1528, and together they gave him, according to the *Valor*, £144 6s 11d each year. At the same time he held the precentorship of Salisbury, prebends or canonries at London, Chichester, Lincoln, York and Sarum, and six minor benefices. Dudley was succeeded at Warton by Brian Higden, who during his tenure of the benefice was dean and vicar-general of York, prebendary of Lincoln, London and York, and chancellor of the council of Henry Fitzroy. While Richard Gwent held the rectory of Warrington, between 1536 and 1543, he also held the archdeaconries of London, Brecon and Huntingdon, prebends at Lichfield, Lincoln, Llandaff, St David's and London, together with parochial livings and the deanery of the Arches. As its rectories and vicarages were so alluring, Lancashire attracted more than its share of pluralists and absentees. Between 1490 and 1520 the rate of pluralism among county incumbents increased from 23% to 30%, and by 1550 exactly one-third of rectors and vicars were pluralists.[1] Mrs Bowker found that in the diocese of Lincoln 22% of the parishes visited between 1514 and 1520 had non-resident incumbents, but that only one-third of those who gave reasons for their absence ascribed it to pluralism.[2] Lancashire's large parishes provided the high incomes which attracted those priests with the influence which could secure more than one benefice, so that the county had a high proportion of pluralists. But a violent, backward area, far from the intellectual and social centres of England, could not induce these men to reside in their cures.

Despite the extent of pluralism, and presumably, therefore, of non-residence, the ecclesiastical authorities only rarely proceeded against the guilty. Those men who were powerful enough to secure a rich Lancashire benefice and other livings besides were probably sufficiently influential to obtain a dispensation for non-residence, while after the Pluralities Act of 1529 those important enough to be Lancashire pluralists were likely to fall within the categories allowed by the statute to hold more than one benefice. Diocesan officials seem to have acted only in cases where neglect was thought to have resulted from non-residence. In 1555 the absentee rector of Eccleston was in trouble for failure to provide a curate, and two years later the vicar of Rochdale was proceeded against for non-residence and

[1] Figures based on the lists of incumbents in *VCH*, III–VIII, *passim*, compared with the accounts of careers given in Haigh, 'Reformation in Lancashire', App. A.
[2] M. Bowker, 'Non-residence in Lincoln diocese in the early sixteenth century', *J Eccl. Hist.* XV, 42, 45, 47.

negligence, and was deprived when it was found that the people had had no parish priest for a month.[1] With the exception of these cases, no records survive of pressure against absentees in the reigns of the first four Tudors, and the diocesan authorities at Lichfield, York and Chester seem to have compiled none of the lists of absentees which Mrs Bowker found so useful at Lincoln. But the officers of the diocese of Chester were well aware of the extent of non-residence, for the visitation call books normally omit the names of absentee incumbents and call the senior resident priest 'curatus'.[2]

The official view was that the non-residence of incumbents led to neglect in the parishes. In 1426, when the parish church of Manchester was made collegiate, the papal confirmation asserted that rectors had usually been absent and 'the cure of souls has been discharged for the most part by other priests, and from this cause has ensued neglect of the pastoral charge'. It was hoped that the foundation of the college would 'preclude such dangers and scandals '.[3] In fact, there is very little evidence of real neglect resulting from the absence of incumbents, since in most Lancashire parishes there were two or three assistants who could carry the burden of pastoral care. Further, it will be shown that about one-third of the people of the county attended the services of a chaplain at a chapel of ease, rather than those of an incumbent at a parish church. The absence of a rector or vicar was thus of little consequence, and the absenteeism of assistant clergy was of much greater significance. In 1526 the abbot of Whalley had to cite two priests before the Lichfield consistory for persistent failure to celebrate the sacraments at a local chapel. In 1535 the people of Pendle complained that the curate of their chapel was always away and never heard confession, and they had him suspended and replaced for his neglect.[4] The chaplains and assistants were the main providers of services in Lancashire, and it is possible that the ecclesiastical authorities did not proceed against pluralists and non-residents because they knew that no neglect resulted.

Even if outright neglect did not follow, it is possible that non-residence meant that parishes were left to be served by priests of lower quality than their incumbents. It is, for example, certainly true that many more incumbents than assistants were university

---

[1] CRO, EDV 1/1, fos. 41v, 147, EDC 1/14, fo. 261; F. R. Raines, *Vicars of Rochdale*, I, CS, NS, I, 39–40.

[2] e.g. CRO, EDV 1/1, fos. 32v, 33, 37, 45v.

[3] Confirmation printed in full in J. Moyes, 'The collegiation of Manchester church', *TLCAS*, XXIV, 11–20.

[4] Lich. RO, B/C/2/1, fos. 84, 94, 97v, 102, 113, 117v, 126, 129v, 135, 139; *Whalley Act Book*, 176, 191, 196.

graduates. In 1548 20 of the 54 Lancashire rectors and vicars were graduates, but only 1 out of more than 350 assistants had a degree.[1] Non-residence thus seems to have deprived parishioners of the graduate pastors they might otherwise have had, and left them with only non-graduate curates. Those incumbents who had degrees were rarely of any benefit to their people, for graduates often had enough influence to secure more than one benefice and so were often absentees. In 1500 83% of Lancashire graduate incumbents were absentees, as against 10% of the non-graduate rectors and vicars, and though there was some improvement later, the number of graduate incumbents who were non-residents never fell below 63% of the total in the first half of the sixteenth century.[2] This meant that only a very small proportion of parishes were ever served by *resident* graduate incumbents, only 2% in 1500, rising to 12% in 1540, though the latter was an unusually good year. Several scholars have provided calculations of the proportions of incumbents in different areas who held degrees, but when so many graduate clergy were absentees such qualifications brought few advantages to parishioners.

Pluralism and absenteeism, however, were not depriving Lancashire of its graduate incumbents, since it is unlikely that well-qualified men would have taken benefices in the county if residence had been enforced. If Lancashire could not attract its incumbents to reside, it would be unlikely to attract graduates to take its benefices if residence were to be a condition of presentation. It is clear, for example, that Lancashire graduate incumbents were more likely to be non-resident than those of other areas. In the diocese of Lincoln, 35% of all absentees were graduates in the early years of the century, but in Lancashire in 1510 half of the non-residents had university degrees.[3] As one would expect, graduate absenteeism becomes higher the further one moves from the university towns and the capital. In 1520 less than a fifth of Lancashire graduate incumbents resided, and this suggests that if residence had been enforced the county would have had only a small number of university men among its incumbents.

Lancashire thus had the worst of all possible worlds, with a number of rich benefices to attract the ambitious but social conditions which dissuaded them from residence. This does not seem, however, to have had any marked effect on the quality of the clergy

[1] Names of assistants were taken from CRO, EDV 2/3–4, and compared with 'alumni' lists.
[2] We have no official lists of absentees; a pluralist is counted as absent if it was physically impossible for him to serve his benefices simultaneously, so the standard applied here is of necessity stricter than that of canon law.
[3] Bowker, *Secular Clergy*, 97; the Lancashire figure is based on the lists of graduates and pluralists in App. A of my thesis.

who actually served in the parishes. Mrs Bowker found in the diocese of Lincoln that only a very small number of priests were in trouble for personal offences or neglect of their duties, and that there were no perceptible differences between the behaviour of the beneficed and the unbeneficed clergy.[1] The same was true in Lancashire, where such small numbers of priests were disciplined in the Church courts that any attempt to distinguish between categories carries no significance. In the 1530s only ten south-Lancashire priests were prosecuted in the archdeacon of Chester's court, and three of them were beneficed,[2] but if this shows anything it is that the beneficed were more likely to offend, or to have their offences detected, than the assistants. It is thus difficult to see any of the dire consequences which are assumed to have followed from non-residence, for the beneficed men were no better behaved than the assistants, and the well qualified would not have resided in Lancashire whatever was done. If residence had been enforced, the stipends which had gone to absentees would have been paid to the men who actually served the cures, the curates. The personnel serving the parishes would not have changed, merely their standard of living.[3]

The parochial structure of Lancashire, which gave the county only a small number of incumbents, drawn from social groups with power and influence but who were often non-residents, does not seem to have been a major disadvantage in normal circumstances. But by the 1530s and after, the circumstances were no longer normal. Men whose connections and education might have made them useful instruments of reform did not reside in their benefices. The size of the parishes made it impossible for even the resident incumbents to supervise the lives and beliefs of their parishioners, so that the gulf between the hierarchy and the laity was widened. Control of the Church at the local level in the period of the Reformation was to be in the hands of poorly-educated assistant clergy, who were difficult to discipline and who had no contact with the reformist ideas of the capital and the university towns.

[1] Bowker, *Secular Clergy*, 107–16.
[2] Figures from CRO, EDC 1/4–9, *passim*.
[3] My conclusions here are the same as those of Mrs Bowker, but were reached independently.

3

Chapels, chaplains and chantrists

The fundamental geographical feature of the Church in Lancashire
was the size of its parishes. We have seen how this influenced the
incomes of rectors and vicars, and therefore the whole character of
the beneficed clergy. But the significance of parish size extends still
further. Most parishes in southern England were co-extensive with
the manor and contained only single townships, but in Lancashire
four-fifths of the parishes had three or more townships and the huge
parish of Whalley had no fewer than thirty.[1] This meant that most
Lancashiremen lived far from their parish churches. In 1540 the
people of Ormskirk told the Duchy Council that there were eleven
townships in their parish, and 'some of them extend four, five or six
miles from the said parish church'. Dean chapel was raised to the
status of a parish church in the following year because it lay eight
miles from its parish church at Eccles.[2] Such distances between
outlying townships and parish churches led, as population increased,
to the building of chapels for the convenience of the inhabitants of
the parochial fringes. By the end of the fifteenth century there were
61 chapels in the county, and by 1548 a further 38 had been added.
In the middle of the sixteenth century there were about 100 chapels
to 58 parish churches, and the bishop of Chester's census of 1563
suggests that almost 6,000 of the 19,000 households in Lancashire
were attached to chapels of ease rather than to parish churches.[3]
The peculiarity of the county was recognised by the bishops at
the Hampton Court conference: 'In Lancashire and in the shires
adjoining there are many parsonages of very large extent which
have divers chapels under them, whereunto as many householders
do appertain as to the most parishes in England southward.'[4]

When local people attended a chapel rather than a parish church,
they naturally lost contact with their rector or vicar, who came to
have only a nominal oversight of their spiritual welfare. The incum-

[1] A. H. Thompson, *Parish History and Records*, 8; G. H. Tupling, 'Pre-Reformation parishes and chapelries of Lancashire', *TLCAS*, LXVII, 7.
[2] PRO, DL 5/6, fo. 226v; *L & P*, XVI, 1391, g. 41.
[3] Tupling, 'Pre-Reformation parishes and chapelries', 12–16; BM, Harleian MS
594, fos. 101–108.
[4] R. G. Usher, *The Reconstruction of the English Church*, 2 vols. II, 333.

bent could not act as a real link between bishop and people, and the isolation of local affairs from the diocesan administration was increased. When the people's allegiance was directed towards a chapel that chapel acquired, in the eyes of those who frequented it, a certain independence, and there was resentment of any interference by the incumbent and wardens of the parish church. There was a running battle between the people of the chapelry at Farnworth and their mother church at Prescot over the financing of repairs to the parish church. This led to three lawsuits in the 1520s and a major crisis in 1555, when the bishop had to intervene and enforce a settlement so that essential repairs could be carried out.[1] At Burnley in 1553 the people claimed that their chapel was a parish church in its own right, rather than a daughter-chapel of Whalley parish. The people of Oldham tried in 1558 to escape from the financial implications of dependence on Prestwich parish church, and the bishop had to threaten them with an interdict or even the suppression of their chapel before they would submit.[2]

A chapel was much more likely to fall under the dominant influence of the local gentry than was a parish church, especially if the chapel was struggling for independence from the incumbent. A rector or vicar might find life difficult if he came into conflict with the leaders of the local community, but his allegiance was to the bishop, who alone could deprive him. His income came from tithes or a stipend from an appropriator and was enforceable at law, but many chaplains, as we shall see, depended for their livings on the generosity of the gentry or collections among the local people. It is not surprising that those who financed a chapel expected to control its affairs. In 1525 Thomas Langton would not allow any priest nominated by the abbot of Whalley to serve Lawe chapel. At Colne in 1544 the leading members of the community tried to exclude the vicar of Whalley from their chapel by locking the doors against him and organising a boycott of his masses, and they were able to gain the support of their curate.[3] Curates of chapels had little choice but to follow the dictates of local opinion, and when governments were trying to alter the religious beliefs of the people there would be no change unless local opinion desired it.

The small number of parishes and the large number of chapels meant that the beneficed clergy formed only a small proportion of the serving clergy. There were over 400 priests in the county in

[1] Bailey, 'Churchwardens' accounts of Prescot', I, 142–3, 179–81; CRO, EDC 1/3, fo. 28, 2/1, fo. 6, EDV 1/1, fo. 142, EDA 2/1, fos. 406v–407v.
[2] *Duchy Pleadings*, III, 158–9; J. Booker, *Memorials of the Church in Prestwich*, 257–9; F. Gastrell, *Notitia Cestriensis*, II, 112.
[3] *Duchy Pleadings*, I, 154; CRO, EDC 2/3, fos. 25–32v.

1548, but only 29 vicarages and 25 rectories; 7½% of the clergy were parochial incumbents.[1] The bulk of the pastoral work of Lancashire therefore fell onto the shoulders of two groups of priests, the chantrists and the assistant chaplains. Miss Wood-Legh found that as a rule chantry priests did not fulfil any useful social functions and tended to say their masses in private.[2] But in Lancashire there were almost twice as many chantry priests as there were incumbents, and the services of the chantrists were essential to the life of the Church. Many chantry priests served chapels at which there was no other priest, and the 4,000 communicants who attended Liverpool chapel would have had no regular services without the clergy of the four chantries endowed there. At Rufford the people were often completely dependent on their four chantrists; it was reported that the chapel was

in the parish of Croston and distant from the parish church four miles, and one arm of the sea betwixt the said chapel and the parish church, so that often and many times the tide will be so high that no man can pass betwixt by the space of four days, by occasion whereof the said priest with other his fellows be enforced to minister sacraments and sacramentals to the inhabitants adjoining.[3]

Chantrists were not only used in chapels, for some rectors and vicars had so many parishioners that they were unable to serve the cure properly without the assistance of chantry priests at the parish church.[4] Of the 91 foundations they discussed, the chantry commissioners of Henry VIII and Edward VI thought that 21 were necessary to provide clergy for chapels or to assist incumbents, while 1 of these and 9 others provided schoolmasters. At least one-third of the chantries played a useful social role, and their importance is suggested by the fact that at least eight chapels fell into decay once there were no longer chantry priests to serve them.[5]

   The contribution of the chantrists was not reflected in their remuneration, however, for they were extremely poorly paid. On the basis of the accounts of two chantrists, Peter Heath calculated that in the 1520s a priest needed an income of almost £6 to support himself, although he might manage on £4 if he lived in a vicarage or rectory with the incumbent.[6] Almost all the Lancashire chantrists received less than this, and some were clearly in dire poverty. In 1546 Robert Wright, the chantrist at Warrington, had the meagre revenue of £1 1s 8d, John Kay of Padiham was paid £1 6s 6d and Hugh Watmough

[1] Figures from CRO, EDV 2/4, fos. 1–11, 26v–37v.
[2] K. Wood-Legh, *Perpetual Chantries in Great Britain*, 275.
[3] *Lancs. Chantries*, I, 83–9, 162.
[4] e.g. at Eccles, *ibid.* I, 137–8.   [5] Haigh, 'Reformation in Lancashire', 85–6.
[6] Heath, *English Parish Clergy*, 22–4.

at Holme had £1 10s 4d.[1] In 1535 the average income of the 81
Lancashire chantrists given in the *Valor* was £3 19s 3d, and although
the chantry returns of 1546 gave an average revenue of £4 14s 3d this
covered the total receipts of the chantry rather than the income of
each of the 93 priests.[2] Chantry priests in England and Wales normally received about £5, but almost two-thirds of the Lancashire
chantrists had less than £5 and more than a third had less than
£4.[3] Certainly the Lancashire figures are lower even than those for
other areas which might be expected to have been poor. In the 1540s
the average revenue of the Lancashire chantries was £4 14s 3d and
63% of the priests received less than £5, whereas the comparable
figures for Yorkshire are £4 17s 8d and 54%, for Cornwall £5 8s 3d
and 39%, and for Devon and Exeter £5 12s 4d and only 24%.[4] It was
presumably the poverty of Lancashire chantries which caused the
vacancy of three of them in 1546 and four in 1548, while others were
held by pluralists and absentees.[5]

In 1548 rectors, vicars, chantrists and endowed stipendiaries
formed only 36% of the clergy of Lancashire, and there remained
almost 230 priests who were merely curates and chaplains.[6] The
incomes of the assistants were very uncertain. A clergy list for the
archdeaconry of Chester in 1541 gives the names of 135 assistants in
south Lancashire, with an indication of how they obtained an
income. There were 33 who were paid by their parochial incumbent,
6 by groups of local men, and no fewer than 70 were financed by
individual gentlemen. The remaining 26 were dependent on the
offerings of the people, with such comments as 'vivit de stipite' set
beside their names.[7] This situation persisted until at least the middle
of the seventeenth century, when almost half the chapels in Lancashire had no settled endowment and the clergy depended on voluntary contributions.[8] Such sources naturally produced very low in-

---

[1] *Lancs. Chantries*, II, 240, 242, 252.
[2] In 1546 the revenue of the Derby chantry at Lathom was almost £17, but the
foundation included an almshouse and the chantrist probably had no more than the
£4 6s 8d given in 1535. The same figures for the similar Gardiner chantry at Lancaster
were £11 6s 10d and £5 0s 10d.
[3] Wood-Legh, *Perpetual Chantries*, 203, 207; *Lancs. Chantries, passim.*
[4] My figures are drawn from *Lancs. Chantries, Yorkshire Chantry Surveys, Chantry
Certificates for Cornwall*, and *Chantry Certificates for Devon and the City of Exeter.*
[5] *Lancs. Chantries*, I, 78, 177, 199, II, 236. A Wigan chantrist held an Essex vicarage
in the 1520s and a Parbold chantry priest served a cure in Somerset (*Duchy Pleadings*,
I, 102, 149). In the 1530s a Preston chantrist leased out his chapel and allowed it to fall
into ruins while he was absent (*Lancs. Chantries*, II, 208–9; *Ducatus Lancastriae*, I, 140).
[6] CRO, EDV 2/4, fos. 1–11, 26v–37v; *Lancs. Chantries, passim.*
[7] *Clergy List, passim.*
[8] D. Lambert, 'The lower clergy of the Anglican Church in Lancashire, 1558–1642',
University of Liverpool M.A. thesis, 1964, 12–13.

comes; there were just over 100 north-Lancashire assistants in 1524, when 19 of them received less than £1 each year and the average income was £2 9s 6d.[1] In the diocese of Lincoln, which was large enough to provide us with a fair cross-section of England, the average income of curates and assistants in the 1520s was £5 3s 2d, a little over twice as much as their north-Lancashire contemporaries.[2] The payments received by the assistant clergy were totally inadequate; in 1538 Archbishop Lee of York regarded £5 6s 8d as too small a payment for a priest to serve a cure, though in 1524 only 5 of the 105 unbeneficed clergy in north Lancashire received this sum or more.[3]

It must therefore be clear that if the lower clergy of the county were not to starve, they would have to supplement their stipends and the offerings they received, and many were forced to use their wits to earn a dishonest penny. In 1471 the chantry priests of Eccles were taking the whole revenues of their appropriated churches at Beetham and Slaidburn, including the stipends which ought to have gone to vicars.[4] In the 1520s Henry Standanought, who had been ordained in 1516 but had not yet secured a benefice or a chantry, tried to ease his lot by cheating Hugh Rigby out of his chantry at Douglas.[5] Robert Fazakerley, curate of Walton in 1530, was supplementing his income from dues which ought to have gone to the rector of the neighbouring parish of Sefton.[6] Most successful of all was Thomas Kirkby, curate of Halsall in 1530. While the rector was a student at Oxford, Kirkby seized the tithes and temporal possessions of the rectory for himself. His parishioners complained that he was frequently involved in litigation, and in the year of the complaint he was plaintiff in a dispute over lands at Lancaster. But these were the least of his sins. When any of his parishioners seemed likely to die, Kirkby would visit them and warn them to remember their 'ghostly father' in their wills, so that he obtained a number of legacies. To ensure that his people grasped the point, Kirkby would preach that those who did not leave mortuaries were damned, and the souls of the dead of the parish were 'burning in pain of purgatory or hell'.[7] The parishioners were provoked to take action against their curate, and Kirkby alleged that the servants of the lord of the manor led a group which chased the priest into the next parish and later set fire to

---

[1] PRO, E 36/61, pp. 20–7.
[2] Bowker, *Secular Clergy*, 103, 144.
[3] *L & P*, XIII(1), 94; PRO, E 36/61, pp. 20–7.
[4] *Calendar of Papal Registers*, XII, 258, 369.
[5] Lich. RO, B/A/1/14, II, September 1516; *Duchy Pleadings*, I, 147.
[6] CRO, EDC 1/4, fos. 30v, 34, 37v, 40, 43.
[7] *Duchy Pleadings*, I, 198–9; PRO, PL 15/4, m. 1.

his bedroom in an attempt to burn him to death. Kirkby's career, however, still had some years to run, and in 1550 he was said to have acquired lands by embezzlement and the forgery of deeds; certainly he accumulated at least eighteen parcels of land, which he rented out to tenants.[1]

There were other ways besides crime by which priests might improve their living standards. Thomas Kirkby of Halsall also tried his hand at trade, and Richard Mercer, the curate of Harwood, was a sheep-merchant. In 1528 Stephen Smith, the curate of Rossendale, was one of three men fined 'quia sunt communes le forestallers of the market in emendanda lana, ad nocumentum vicinorum et ad maximum detramentum fori domini regis de Bury'.[2] Some priests were involved in the renting and farming of land. Two Pendle priests held lands jointly in 1532, and three years later the curate of Burnley took over reclaimed moorland. John Foster, a former monk of Whalley, was farming on the abbey site soon after the suppression, and another ex-monk, Richard Wood, owned a large block of land in Accrington while he was chantrist at Great Harwood.[3] The most obvious way in which assistants could supplement their earnings was by saying masses for the dead, but in a comparatively poor county, where only a minority could afford more than a few masses, the extra income which such sources could provide for each priest was limited. When Lord Mounteagle died in 1523, he left money for 30 priests to pray for his soul, but 80 turned up to the funeral hoping to receive the fee.[4]

It was clearly not the incomes of curates and assistants which attracted young Lancastrians to ordination, for most ordinands could anticipate only a life of hardship. A vicarage or a rectory must have been the ambition of all local ordinands, but only a handful gained one. Lancashire benefices were far too valuable pieces of patronage to waste on local nonentities, and for the vast majority of Lancashire-born priests, without ties to patrons by birth or service, opportunities for promotion were very limited. There were 234 men ordained priest at York or Lichfield between 1523 and 1527 on the titles of Lancashire monasteries, and almost all of them must have been local men, but only 7 ever became rectors or vicars in the county or fellows of Manchester College, and only 7 more became chantrists.[5] Similarly, 41 men were ordained at York during 1533–7

---

[1] PRO, DL 3/21, K 5, 3/57, U 2; LRO, DDCl/591.

[2] *Duchy Pleadings*, I, 200; *CCR*, III, 64, 318.

[3] *CCR*, II, 106–7, 119, III, 109–10; *Whalley Coucher Book*, 1177.

[4] *L & P*, IV(1), 235.

[5] Ordinations from BIY, Reg. Wolsey, R/I/27, fos. 198–214v; Lich. RO, B/A/1/14, II, Feb. 1523–Dec. 1527. For a list of those who gained promotion and a proof that

on Lancashire titles, only one of whom gained a benefice in the county, and of 82 local men ordained priest at Chester in the period 1543–7 4 gained vicarages and one a chantry.[1] The incumbents of Lancashire were not, as a rule, drawn from among local ordinands or from the ranks of those already serving as assistants. Of approximately 115 institutions to Lancashire benefices between 1530 and 1560, only 18 were of men who had hitherto been chaplains or chantrists in the county.[2] Only 3 of the 18 were instituted before 1553, and the rest were concentrated in a few years in which there was a shortage of clergy and more vacant benefices than was usual. The lower clergy could not hope to work themselves up through the ranks, and they achieved promotion only in exceptional circumstances.

Service in the Church in Lancashire represented a poor prospect for the newly ordained. There were few beneficed positions, which only rarely went to serving priests, and the assistants were very badly paid. There was thus a strong disincentive for priests to work in the county, and there is evidence of extensive emigration by native-born clergy. Only 46, almost 20%, of the 234 Lancastrians ordained priest at York or Lichfield between 1523 and 1527 ever became serving priests in their own county.[3] As many as 80% of Lancashire-born priests, perhaps 40 each year, were leaving the county, soon after their ordination, in search of more profitable posts elsewhere. It is true that this calculation has some obvious weaknesses. Some priests must have remained in the county as private chaplains, who were not recorded in the visitation call lists or the clerical subsidy assessments on which our knowledge of assistant priests is based. But chaplaincies were lowly posts, attractive only to those who wished to go into semi-retirement,[4] while few of the Lancashire gentry were sufficiently prosperous to afford a chapel and a chaplain, so that the number of priests who served in this way would not materially affect the conclusion. The state of the evidence provides a more serious criticism, for the lists of clergy are scarce and incomplete until 1541, fourteen years after the last ordination studied, and some may have died in the meantime. Later figures confirm the

most of those ordained on Lancashire titles were local men, see Haigh, 'Reformation in Lancashire', 126n, 128n.

[1] Ordinations from BIY, Reg. Lee, R/I/28, fos. 185v–97v; *Ordination Reg.* 42–80. Those promoted are listed in my thesis, pp. 126n, 127n.

[2] Institutions from CRO, EDA 1/1, *passim*; *VCH*, III–VIII, *passim*. The eighteen, with their early offices and later posts, are listed in App. B of my thesis.

[3] For ordinations, see p. 36, n. 5. Those who served in the county are listed in App. C of my thesis.

[4] Thus the case of Ralph Lynney, who resigned the vicarage of Blackburn on a pension at the age of 62 in 1555, and went to become chaplain to Sir John Byron (*VCH*, VI, 241; CRO, EDC 2/5, fos. 108–109).

proportions already suggested. Of the Lancastrians ordained priest at York 1533–7, and those ordained at Chester 1543–7, 17% and 25% respectively later served in their own county, and most of the others presumably went elsewhere.[1]

It is possible to substantiate the argument by a completely different type of calculation. In order to maintain its usual clerical labour force of a little over 400 priests, Lancashire needed to recruit about twelve new parish clergy each year to take the places of those who died.[2] But in the decade 1518–27, the last for which complete ordination lists are available for both dioceses, an average of 49 men each year were ordained into the secular priesthood from Lancashire.[3] The county was thus producing 49 men to fill a dozen vacancies, so that there ought to have been not only enough priests to serve the area adequately, but even a surplus. Despite the end of monastic titles, the level of ordinations from Lancashire remained high in the 1540s, when an average of seventeen Lancastrians a year were priested at Chester.[4] We shall see, however, that there was a shortage of clergy in the county, and this can only have been due to a high level of emigration. A realisation of the limited career prospects offered in Lancashire was not confined to ordinands, for there is also evidence of emigration to greener pastures by the serving assistant clergy. South Lancashire had 144 priests serving in 1541, yet by 1548 38, or 26%, of them had disappeared and only 7 are known to have died in the meantime.[5] It appears that early Tudor Lancashire was playing modern Ireland to the pre-Reformation Church, providing large numbers of clergy who moved to serve in other areas.

It is possible to give a few individual examples of this general trend. Richard Thornton of Goosnargh in the parish of Kirkham was ordained priest at York in 1505, and after serving for a short time as a chaplain in the earl of Derby's foundation he moved to more promising counties and worked in various places in the dioceses of Lincoln and London. Hugh Brown was a monk of Furness, but after the suppression of his house he went south and became a

[1] The totals were 7 out of 41 in the York group, and 19 out of 82 at Chester. Ordinations from BIY, Reg. Lee, R/I/28, fos. 185v–197v; *Ordination Reg.* 42–80. Those who served in the county are listed in Apps. D and E of my thesis.
[2] This is based on the death-rate of priests between 1541 and 1548, and between 1548 and 1554, as in Haigh, 'Reformation in Lancashire', 127–8.
[3] Lich. RO, B/A/1/14, II, Feb. 1518–Dec. 1527; BIY, Reg. Wolsey, R/I/27, fos. 179–214v.
[4] *Ordination Reg.* 31–80. Those from the diocese of Chester ordained on the titles of Lancashire gentlemen are assumed to have been Lancastrians.
[5] Figures from a comparison of *Clergy List* with CRO, EDV 2/4 and parish registers. Only parishes with names for both 1541 and 1548 are included.

chaplain in Cambridgeshire.[1] John Estgate was ordained as a monk of Whalley in 1536, and when his abbey was suppressed he lived in his native Blackburn, but by 1546 he had still not found satisfactory employment and he moved to Billericay in Essex. Some time before 1551 Thomas Leyland, who had been an assistant at Prescot, gave up his post and went to Ely.[2] Finally, Richard Brettan of Preston was ordained up to the rank of deacon at Chester in 1546–7, and he proceeded to the priesthood later in another diocese, after ordinations at Chester had ceased. His first post was as domestic chaplain to Sir Richard Houghton, but he seems to have regarded this and other local opportunities as inadequate, for in 1554 he gave up his appointment, secured a testimonial from the common council of Preston and went 'unto the south parts'.[3]

It was a serious disadvantage to the Church in Lancashire that it was losing a substantial proportion of its ordinands and assistants, but the position was even worse than this because the exodus was primarily of the better-educated and ambitious. Those Lancastrians with ability and qualifications could not be attracted to remain in their home county, where incomes were low and prospects poor, and when a local man went to the university it was unlikely that he would return to serve in Lancashire. Of those who are known to have entered Brasenose College, Oxford, in the reigns of Henry VIII, Edward VI and Mary, 60 were of Lancashire origin, and at least 32 of them entered the priesthood, but only 2 of them ever served in Lancashire and both were absentee pluralists.[4] There is some evidence that the emigration of university men was greater from the north-west than from other parts of England. In the 1540s the archbishop of Canterbury's faculty office issued dispensations to thirteen scholars from the diocese of Chester for them to be ordained in other dioceses. Not one of the thirteen was to work in Lancashire, and almost as many dispensations were granted to Chester men as to natives of all the other dioceses put together.[5] Those who secured the university education which might gain for them promotion within the Church chose not to return to their own county. Of all the many Lancastrians who must have taken degrees at Oxford or Cambridge during the period, only fifteen held benefices in the county between 1490 and 1560. Six of the fifteen were closely related

[1] *An Episcopal Court Book for the Diocese of Lincoln*, ed. M. Bowker, 124–6; T. A. Beck, *Annales Furnesiensis*, App. IX.
[2] BIY, Reg. Lee, R/I/28, fo. 196v; *Duchy Pleadings*, III, 82; CRO, EDC 2/5, fo. 24.
[3] *Ordination Reg.* 69, 70, 76; LRO, DDCl/1054.
[4] Figures from *Brasenose College Reg.* 1–28. The two were Edward Morecroft and John Woolton. John Standish was presented to Wigan, but ineffectively.
[5] *FOR*, 229, 230, 233, 236, 251, 262, 263, 274, 275, 282, 289, 290.

to the patrons of their benefices, four more came from families important enough to secure presentations anywhere, and twelve were in any case pluralists and non-residents.[1] Except for the few with influential connections, the avenue to promotion lay outside Lancashire, and Lancashire-born graduates therefore showed little inclination to begin their ecclesiastical careers by service in their own county.

Since the Church in Lancashire was unable to retain the services of many of its native clergy, and especially of the able men, it is unlikely that it was successful in attracting clergy from other areas. In an attempt to trace the origins of the serving clergy, a study has been made of the ordinations of two groups of priests, the 45 who appeared in the deanery of Blackburn at the ordination of 1548, and the 38 who appeared in the deanery of Leyland at the same visitation. Despite the fact that there are no ordination records for the diocese of York for the years 1511–12 and 1528–31, and none for the diocese of Lichfield for the years 1532–41, and the probability that local men were sometimes ordained in other dioceses, it was found that 28 of the Blackburn group, or 62%, and 20 of the Leyland group, or 53%, were ordained at Lichfield, York or Chester, on the titles of Lancashire monasteries or of Lancashire gentlemen.[2] The true proportion of local men among the clergy, especially in view of the long break in the Lichfield records, was certainly very much larger, and there can be no doubt that the Church in Lancashire was staffed almost entirely by natives of the county.

Although it is impossible to trace the precise origins of more than a handful of the parish clergy, it is also clear that the assistant clergy were often serving in the parishes in which they had been born. The York ordination lists give the home parish of each acolyte ordained, so that it is possible to trace the birthplaces of serving priests if they had been ordained acolyte by the archbishop or one of his suffragans. Richard Hudson, for example, came from Warton parish, and in 1511 he was ordained on a title from the nearby priory of Cartmel; he was presented to a chantry at Warton in about 1520, and he was still there in 1524 and 1535.[3] Thomas Dicconson of Aldingham was ordained priest on a Conishead title in 1513; he was an assistant in the neighbouring parish of Urswick in 1524, but he later returned to his native parish and appeared at visitations there in 1548 and

---

[1] Figures from a comparison of lists of incumbents in *VCH*, III–VIII, with 'alumni' lists. The 15 are the only locally-born graduate incumbents.

[2] CRO, EDV 2/4, fos. 5–6, 10–12. These men are listed, with their ordinations, in App. F of my thesis.

[3] BIY, Reg. Bainbridge, R/I/26, fos. 108, 114v; PRO, DL 43/5/15, E 36/61, p. 24; *Valor*, V, 268.

1554.[1] Richard Kelver was also from Aldingham, and after ordination he served as curate there, at least between 1524 and1548.[2] Laurence Galter came from Kirkham, and thirty years after his ordination he was serving in the same parish.[3] These examples are all from north Lancashire, but the chance survival of a slip of paper in a Lichfield ordination register enables us to trace the origins and career of Edward Norham; he was born in the parish of Whalley, ordained priest in 1524 on a title from the abbey, and until he died in 1565 he served as an assistant at Great Harwood, one of the chapels of Whalley.[4]

Most of the educated clergy left Lancashire, and the county could not attract outsiders, so the Church was served by a rump of poorly-paid men who could hope to secure nothing better elsewhere. Emigration without compensatory immigration insulated the county from intellectual movements within the Church, and left the parishes to be served by the dregs of the clerical proletariat. Among the assistant clergy, on whom the main burden of pastoral care fell, university degrees were a rarity; in 1548 only one of the 360 unbeneficed clergy was a graduate, and he was master of the grammar school in Manchester.[5] The education of the serving clergy therefore took place at lesser institutions than universities. The intense parochialism of Tudor Lancashiremen,[6] and the fact that many of the priests spent their lives in the same parishes, suggest that only a small minority received their education outside the county. But in the early sixteenth century educational provision in Lancashire was extremely meagre. Only five schools had been established by 1500, and there were only fifteen by 1530 and nineteen by 1540, to serve an area of over 1,800 square miles. The rush of foundations in the first half of the century, and especially the establishment of over forty more in the second half, merely indicates how inadequate the existing schools were seen to be.[7] The original statutes of Manchester Grammar School noted that Bishop Oldham, the founder, realised that the children of Lancashire

hath lacked and wanted in the same, as well for great poverty of the common people there, as also by cause of long time passed the teaching, bringing up

[1] BIY, R/I/26, fos. 121, 123; PRO, E 36/61, p. 26; CRO, EDV 2/4, fo. 30v, EDV 1/1, fo. 65.

[2] BIY, R/I/26, fos. 123v, 125v; PRO, E 36/61, p. 26; CRO, EDV 2/4, fo. 30v.

[3] BIY, Reg. Wolsey, R/I/27, fo. 198; CRO, EDV 2/4, fo. 26v, EDV 1/1, fo. 45.

[4] Lich. RO, B/A/1/14, II, May 1524 and loose leaf inserted there; CRO, EDV 2/4, fo. 10, EDV 1/1, fo. 34; *Great Harwood Reg.* 286.

[5] The clergy in CRO, EDV 2/4 were compared with the 'alumni' lists.

[6] See below, pp. 89–91.

[7] Figures based on the tables in P. J. Wallis, 'A preliminary register of old schools in Lancashire and Cheshire', *THSLC*, CXX, 10–17.

of young children to school, to learning of grammar, hath not been taught there, for lack of sufficient schoolmaster and usher there, so that the children in the same county, having pregnant wit, have been most part brought up rudely, idlely and not in virtue, cunning, erudition, literature and good manners.[1]

Similarly, the foundation indenture of Warrington Grammar School mentioned the scarcity in Lancashire of schools where the sons of gentlemen 'might learn grammar to the intent that they might the better learn to know Almighty God'.[2]

The number of schools was small, and the quality of the education they gave cannot have been high. In the 1540s the single master at Blackburn had 140 pupils and a stipend of only £4 7s 4d, and in 1554 the master at Lancaster taught 104 pupils for 5 marks.[3] Where the schools were so large and the stipends so small, teachers of ability cannot have been attracted. Roger Lewyns, who was paid to act as chantry priest and schoolmaster at Preston in 1528, did not bother to keep a school at all. Richard Taylor, master at Warrington from 1526 to 1569, and so an extremely important influence on Lancashire education, was a violent, quarrelsome and disobedient priest, whom the Church courts could not control, while Nicholas Bannester, schoolmaster at Preston by 1535, was described as 'an un-learned priest' in 1561.[4] Even a high stipend could not secure men of quality; Bishop Smith decreed in 1507 that the master of his new school at Farnworth was to be a graduate, but the annual salary of £10 was apparently insufficient and the three known masters between 1542 and 1563 were certainly not graduates.[5] Adequate schoolmasters might have been found, yet too many of them had more to do than teach schoolboys, for ten schools were linked to chantry foundations and at eight of them the chantry priest was also the master.[6]

The educational resources of the county were not restricted to these formally constituted schools, and there were other, less official, establishments. At Dalton a priest named William Rede was keeping a school in 1537, and at about the same time John Henshaw, priest, was teaching at Hawkshead. In the 1540s Lord Mounteagle used his chaplain at Hornby to teach the local children.[7] Further south,

[1] Hibbert-Ware, *History of the Foundations*, III, 21.   [2] *Lancs. Chantries*, I, 58.
[3] G. A. Stocks, *Records of Blackburn Grammar School*, CS, NS, LXVI–VIII, x; PRO, DL 5/10, fo. 270v, DL 1/37, C. 16.
[4] PRO, DL 3/17, L. 6; *Lancs. Chantries*, I, 58, 60; *Ducatus Lancastriae*, I, 186; CRO, EDC 1/14, fos. 12v, 51; *Valor*, V, 263; *VCH*, II, 571; PRO, SP 12/11/45.
[5] R. Churton, *Lives of Smith and Sutton*, 236; *VCH*, II, 589; *Farnworth Reg.* 11; *Ducatus Lancastriae*, II, 246–7; CRO, EDV 1/3, fo. 33.
[6] *Lancs. Chantries, passim.*
[7] PRO, SP 1/75, fo. 63, SP 1/118, fo. 9v (*L & P*, VI, 287; XII(1), 842), PL 25/15, m. 19d; *Lancs. Chantries*, II, 236; BIY, Reg. Sede Vacante, R/I/5, fo. 644v.

Stephen Ellis, clerk, had a school at Pendle in 1532, and in 1556 the people of Huyton agreed among themselves to collect £6 each year to pay one of the local chaplains for running a school.[1] Schools such as these, in numbers which we could not begin to assess, shared the characteristics of the chantry schools; they were kept by men with no known academic training who had other duties as well as their teaching. The parish clergy of Lancashire were presumably educated at schools such as these; we know, for example, that William Thomson, rector of Ashton 1535–53, attended an informal school kept by the chantry-priest at Standish, and that the rascally Thomas Kirkby was educated at a school near his home.[2]

The educational standards of the Lancashire clergy were too low for the major task the Reformation was to impose upon them. Certainly contemporaries thought little of the intellectual attainments of the local priesthood. George Marsh, the Dean martyr, referred to Lancashire priests as men 'whose mouths it was a thing easy to stop; for the priests (which is much to be lamented) be not always the greatest clerks and the best learned in the law of God. At their departing they either agreed with me or had nothing to say against me.'[3] Such gentle irony was, if Archbishop Lee's comments twenty years earlier can be trusted, dangerously near the truth. Lee issued, in 1535, two short tracts on the royal supremacy to the clergy of his diocese, which included north Lancashire, but feared that

doubtless many of our curates can scant perceive it. Many benefices be so exile, of £4, £5, £6, that no learned man would take them, and therefore we be fain to take such as be presented, so they be honest of conversation and can competently understand that they read and minister sacraments and sacramentals, observing the due form and rite, although otherwise they be not all perfect but must resort for counsel. And in all my diocese I do not know secular priests that can preach, any number necessary for such a diocese, truly not twelve, and they that have the best benefices be not here resident.[4]

As an analysis of the economic and educational position of the clergy in Lancashire, Lee's views cannot be faulted. The few notable preachers who held benefices in the county, such as Simon Mathew, vicar of Prescot, were invariably absentees, and one of the few men who did preach, William Rede of Dalton, was silenced by the archdeacon of Richmond's commissary.[5] Even the vicar of Whalley,

---

[1] *CCR*, II, 106; LRO, DDM/33/1; CRO, EDV 2/4, fo. 2v.
[2] *L & C Wills*, I, 92; *Lancs. Chantries*, II, 180; PRO, DL 3/57, U. 2.
[3] J. Foxe, *Acts and Monuments*, ed. J. Pratt, 8 vols. VII, 46.
[4] BM, Cotton MS Cleopatra E. VI, fo. 243 (*L & P*, VII, 936).
[5] Strype, *Ecclesiastical Memorials*, I(1), 265; *VCH*, III, 344; PRO, SP 1/118, fo. 9v (*L & P*, XII(1), 842).

an Oxford B.D., used to 'bid the beads' in the pulpit rather than preach, and the first bishop of Chester soon blamed the ignorance of the people of his diocese on 'lack of doctrine and preaching'.[1] The Crown was well aware of the shortage of preachers in Lancashire. After the collapse of the Pilgrimage of Grace the king planned to send 'certain discreet, learned and great personages to teach and preach the word of God sincerely', for it was thought that lack of such instruction had been the cause of the rising.[2]

There was certainly a severe shortage of educated and able clergy in Lancashire, and there is even evidence that it was not possible to recruit an adequate supply of the less able. Despite the large numbers of men ordained from the county, emigration reduced the clerical labour supply alarmingly. If we assume that in large Lancashire parishes 3 priests were needed to serve a parish church, 2 a chapel and 1 a chantry, the 26 parishes of north Lancashire required 146 priests in the 1520s; the subsidy list of 1524, however, indicates that there were only 125.[3] The release of the monks and friars for parish service did little to improve the situation; the county as a whole needed 463 clergy in the 1540s, but the call book lists of 1548 give only 406.[4] It is usually suggested that there was at this time 1 priest for every 50 or 100 lay people, whereas in Lancashire the proportion was very much lower. When the clergy lists for 1548 are compared with the return of households of 1563, it is found that there was only 1 priest for every 234 laymen; in the densely populated deanery of Manchester the ratio was 1 to 310, and in the sparsely-populated deaneries of Furness and Lonsdale, 1 to 244.[5] This scarcity of priests may have been one of the reasons, as it had been in Durham a century before, why so many parishes were served by monks, and it also explains the ease with which the ex-monks were absorbed into the parochial clergy after the suppression.[6]

The nature and supply of the clerical labour force in Lancashire exercised a crucial influence on the religion of the area, and affected the way in which the Reformation took place. Large parishes and the

[1] CRO, EDC 2/3, fo. 32; PRO, SP 1/75, fo. 7 (*L & P*, XVI, 1377).
[2] *L & P*, XII(1), 302.
[3] PRO, E 36/61, pp. 8–10, 20–7.
[4] CRO, EDV 2/3–4, *passim*. The figure given includes estimates based on a 1554 return (EDV 1/1, *passim*) for the few parishes not listed in 1548.
[5] CRO, EDV 2/3–4, *passim*; BM, Harleian MS 594, fos. 101–108. Cf. S. T. Bindoff, *Tudor England*, 77; J. C. Russell, 'The clerical population of medieval England', *Traditio*, II, 179. The ratio for the county is confirmed with surprising exactness by a comparison between the population estimates given by the chantry commissioners for 24 parishes and the numbers of priests serving in them, 1:237.
[6] Haigh, *Lancs. Monasteries*, 3, 114–24; R. L. Storey, *Thomas Langley and the Bishopric of Durham*, 177, 181.

existence of so many chapels made it difficult for the ecclesiastical authorities to control the county, and this became increasingly significant as the Crown began to use the diocesan machinery to enforce religious change. It was a much more formidable task to enforce laws and detect offenders in Lancashire than in most other parts of England. Again, large parishes and many chapels depressed the supply of worthwhile preferments in the county, so that the educated clergy who might have brought reformist ideas to the north-west were not attracted. The poor quality and small numbers of the serving clergy meant that services were provided only intermittently in some areas, the people were inadequately instructed in the essentials of their faith and there was insufficient surveillance of the laity by the clergy. It is not surprising, therefore, that the conduct of both priests and laymen fell below the standards prescribed by canon law.

4

Priests and people: conduct and attitudes

When, in 1583, Lord Strange described his native county as 'this so unbridled and bad an handful of England', he was merely repeating a conventional view of the behaviour of Lancastrians. Among local men and outsiders Lancashiremen had a formidable reputation for theft, violence and sexual laxity. In 1547 Bishop Gardiner protested against the plan to have Erasmus' *Paraphrases* in every church, on the grounds that 'by the *Paraphrases* the keeping of a concubine is called but a light fault. And that were good for Lancashire.' Roger Holland, who had lived in London for some years and saw his home county through puritanical spectacles, thought in 1558 that 'in Lancashire their blindness and whoredom is overmuch more than may with chaste ears be heard'.[1] Royal officials shared such opinions, and tried to control the unusual sexual delinquency of Lancashiremen. In 1543 a royal commission sat at Wigan to examine cases of adultery among the senior gentry of the county and imposed heavy penalties on offenders. The Duchy appointed another powerful commission of laymen and ecclesiastics seven years later, to deal with 'detestable crimes and offences of adultery, incest, fornication and bawdry, much used in those parts'. The second commission also sat at Wigan, and called for evidence on 'all such enormities, fornications and adulteries'.[2] These efforts seem to have had little impact however, and in 1590 the Puritan clergy of the county were complaining of widespread laxity. In the following year the Council in the North claimed it could not maintain good order in Yorkshire because the people could not be insulated from the evil influence of Lancashire, where 'since the statute of Anno XVIII bastards have been more plentiful'.[3]

There is ample evidence that the complaints of contemporaries were far from exaggerated, and were true of all levels of society. The Duchy Council thought that 'such as being of noble blood which ought to be the light and example of virtue and goodness to other inferiors' were guilty of sexual lapses, and Roger Holland observed

[1] Peck, *Desiderata Curiosa*, 141; *Letters of Stephen Gardiner*, 386; Foxe, *Acts and Monuments*, VIII, 475.
[2] CRO, EDA 12/1, *passim*; PRO, DL 42/96, fo. 33v; CRO, EDC 5, 1550.
[3] *State Civil and Ecclesiastical*, 12; PRO, SP 12/240, fo. 292v.

that the gentry were 'not clear in these notable crimes'.[1] In 1535 Sir Richard Houghton was living openly with a mistress and he fathered at least six bastards, while Sir John Byron lived in adultery with a woman who was herself also married, and had several children by her.[2] Two Lancashire knights and three esquires were reported to Thomas Cromwell in 1535 as 'notable and slanderous livers' who kept concubines, and in 1543 nine major gentlemen, including an uncle of the earl of Derby and a former sheriff, were in trouble for adultery.[3] Sir John Atherton put his wife out of his house and had another woman in her place, and in 1551 the bishop of Chester was commissioned to divorce Atherton on the grounds of his wife's adultery.[4] Three of the most important men in north Lancashire were called before the consistory in 1555 for keeping concubines, while so many of the leading gentry of the county had bastard children that illegitimacy carried no social stigma.[5]

Marriage was treated very lightly among the higher social groups, though the case of Ralph Rishton was presumably an extreme example. In about 1530 nine-year-old Ralph married Ellen, daughter of Richard Towneley, who was a year his senior. Soon after the marriage Ralph was sent to be trained in arms at the house of Sir Ralph Ashton, but he began to cohabit with Ellen three years later and the child marriage was thus ratified. The couple lived together until 1544, when Ralph went off to the Scots Wars, but while her husband was away Ellen lost her sanity. When Ralph returned to Lancashire he seduced Elizabeth Parker, had his marriage with Ellen annulled by a commissary of the Chester consistory, and went through a form of marriage to Elizabeth at Clitheroe chapel in 1546. Ellen Towneley recovered her wits sufficiently to fight back, and in 1550 she sued Ralph for lands awarded to her by her marriage articles. Ralph and Elizabeth lived together quietly until 1552, when Ralph's father laid information against the couple before the vicar-general of the diocese, who reversed his commissary's earlier decision and ordered them to separate. Ellen died about 1555, but Elizabeth was unable to reclaim her erstwhile spouse for he had begun to live with Anne Stanley. When Anne was three months pregnant by Ralph, her mother put her into the custody of Sir

[1] PRO, DL 42/96, fo. 33v; Foxe, *Acts and Monuments*, VIII, 475.
[2] *Visitation of Lancashire, 1533*, 48; J. B. Watson, 'The Lancashire gentry, 1529–1558, with special reference to their public services', University of London M.A. thesis, 1959, 167, 363; *VCH*, IV, 285.
[3] *L & P*, VIII, 496, No. 2; CRO, EDA 12/1, pp. 3, 12.
[4] *Ducatus Lancastriae*, I, 183; Strype, *Ecclesiastical Memorials*, II(2), 203.
[5] CRO, EDC 1/14, fo. 68; Watson, 'Lancashire Gentry', 167–8.

Thomas Talbot, who tried to marry the girl to a certain John Rishton. Neither partner approved of the match and they refused to live together, so the marriage was annulled in 1560. Ralph Rishton then married Anne, but Elizabeth Parker, the second of his wives, did not regard her cause as lost. In 1571 she promoted a case before the Ecclesiastical Commission at York, in which she tried to prove that she was Ralph's lawful wife, and the whole tortuous story came out. The court ordered Ralph and Anne to separate pending a decision, but they failed to obey and Elizabeth's action seems to have failed. The conflicts did not even end with Ralph's death in 1573, for Elizabeth called herself his widow and sued his heirs for a portion of the estate.[1]

The instability of gentry marriages was in part the result of the early age of marriage. The Lancashire gentry class was small and patronage and connection were extremely important,[2] so families used their children to forge alliances and bind settlements. There survives among the sixteenth-century cause papers of the Chester consistory a large bundle containing details of marriages which were later contested on the grounds that the parties had been children at their weddings, and there is a number of similar cases in the depositions books.[3] Child marriages were, as in the case of Ralph Rishton and Ellen Towneley, quite likely to break down. When Adam and Jane Preesall married in 1481 he was aged ten and she was a year younger; they lived together for eight or nine years but then Jane went off with John Leigh, by whom she had a child. The marriage between Gilbert and Anne Gerard had collapsed by 1543, partly because they had been aged five and six at their wedding, when Gilbert had been held in the arms of a relation who had spoken the words of the service for him. Laurence and Anne Whittaker had been thirteen and eleven at the time of their marriage, which 'was made by compulsion of Sir John Towneley, knight, which was a great ruler in that country and no man durst say "nay" for fear of his displeasure'.[4]

It would be possible to quote large numbers of similar examples, and it is clear that child marriages were also common lower down the social scale. It may be that Lancashire was unusual in this respect, for Peter Laslett has argued that despite the Shakespearean examples

[1] LRO, DDTo/DD/1404, HH/150, DDPt/63; CRO, EDC 2/6, fos. 290–292v; BIY, R VII, HCAB 6, fos. 88–89v, 152, 162v; *Ducatus Lancastriae*, I, 246; III, 25, 58, 84.
[2] See below, pp. 89, 90, 107.
[3] CRO, EDC 5, Child Marriage Bundle; see especially EDC 2/7, abstracted by F. J. Furnival in *Child Marriages and Divorces*.
[4] CRO, EDC 1/15, fos. 98–98v, 100–101v, EDC 2/2, pp. 534, 553.

child marriages were rare in England.[1] He has suggested that the evidence of a Chester depositions book for 1561–6 indicates that such marriages were unusual rather than frequent. Laslett points out that the volume contains about 30 examples of child marriage, and concludes that as at least 10,000 weddings took place in the diocese during the period of the book young marriages formed only a small fraction of the total. But child marriage was not an offence, and the daughters of an Elizabethan bishop of Chester and a chancellor of the diocese were married at an early age.[2] The cases were not before the consistory because they had been detected and were to be dissolved, but because the parties had tired of them and wished them annulled. When a marriage proved unsuccessful the couple was able to escape from it by arguing that it had not been a free contract or that it had not been consummated. The 30 mentioned above did not constitute all the child marriages, merely those which had failed, and the vast majority never came before the courts. Although Laslett is certainly wrong in his suggestion that there were few child marriages in Lancashire, his other evidence does make it clear that the age of marriage in England generally was usually in the middle or late twenties, and the county palatine may thus have been an exception.

The social structure and geographical isolation of Lancashire encouraged child marriages, and it was among the gentry, where families had interests to safeguard and property to protect, that they were most common. The practice became established of allowing a child marriage on the understanding that if the relationship was not a happy one or if the families broke their connection, then the contract would be annulled. It was said in 1538 that the marriage between Kathleen Tatlock and Edmund Mollineux would never have taken place if the rector of Sefton, a Mollineux, had not said 'she should have him for the space of two years, and then if they could agree together it were well, and if not he promised her that she should be divorced again'.[3] Such attitudes were not conducive either to stable marriages among the gentry or to respect for the sacraments and institutions of the Church.

Lower down the social scale, where pressures towards early marriage were not so strong, fornication rather than adultery was the common failing. At a visitation of Manchester parish in 1554 only 2 individuals were accused of adultery but 84 were charged with fornication, and in a population of 5,000–7,000 these must have represented a substantial proportion of those neither too young for the offence nor already married. In the chapelry of Colne, with a

[1] P. Laslett, *The World We Have Lost*, 83–6.
[2] CRO, EDA 2/2, fos. 46, 314v.
[3] CRO, EDC 2/2, pp. 157–62. Several witnesses made the same point.

population of about 1,500, 23 couples were presented for fornication in 1557, but only one for adultery.[1] As there were clearly no strong social pressures against sexual laxity, it is probable that those reported formed only a small fraction of all offenders. Although the comparison involves several doubtful assumptions, it may be that irregularity was more widespread in Lancashire than in some other areas. The diocesan officers who visited the county found, on average, seven cases of adultery or fornication in each parish or chapelry in 1554, four cases in each in 1556 and four cases again in 1557. This compares with a visitation of the diocese of Lincoln in 1518–19 when officials discovered only one offence in every four parishes in Oxfordshire and only one in every seven parishes in Buckinghamshire. The population of a Lancashire parish or chapelry was two and a half times greater than that of a Lincoln parish, so that the incidence of detected sexual indiscipline was perhaps ten times higher in the north-west than in the south-Midlands.[2] We cannot assume that all visitations were carried out with equal thoroughness, but it is likely that the massive difference between the figures reflects a lesser, though nevertheless real, distinction between the counties.

Roger Holland thought that the sexual morals of Lancashire clergy were as low as those of the laity, and told Bishop Bonner in 1558 that 'I know some priests, very devout, my Lord, yet such as have six or seven children by four or five sundry women.' But Holland was making a propagandist point when accused of heresy, as well as insulting a bishop, for Bonner's own father was a Cheshire priest who had at least seven bastards by three different women and the bishop's half-brother, chancellor of the diocese of Chester, precisely equalled their father's achievement.[3] There is, in fact, very little evidence of clerical unchastity in Lancashire, and most of the examples we have are of those priests with common-law wives and acknowledged children who were perhaps an accepted part of the parochial scene. Alexander Thornton, chantry priest at Fernyhalgh, lived with the same woman at least between 1489 and 1514 and one

---

[1] CRO, EDV 1/1, fos. 120–124, 1/2, fos. 72–75. These are accusations rather than convictions, but not all those presented appeared for correction and the scrappy record makes it impossible to count convictions. None of those who appeared seems to have been innocent.

[2] Lancashire returns from CRO, EDV 1/1, fos. 120–155v, 169–174v, 1/2, fos. 33–42v, 65–82v. Lincoln figures calculated from Hughes, *Reformation in England*, I, 103. For ease and fairness of comparison, Lancashire chapelries are included as if they were parishes. For population figures, compare BM, Harleian MS 594, fos. 101–108, with Hughes, *Reformation in England*, I, 32.

[3] Foxe, *Acts and Monuments*, VIII, 475; Haigh, 'Mid-Tudor ecclesiastical official', 2, 17–18.

of his sons followed him into the Church, while the children of Gilbert Haydock, vicar of Rochdale, shared the same mother and were remembered in their father's will.[1] Henry Colley, an assistant at Prescot, set up house with Cecily Hitchmough, and Isabel Livesey 'was concubine to Sir Edmund Potter'. Ralph Parker had a ready-made household, for he had two children by a servant girl in his master's house.[2] We hear of very few priests involved in casual liaisons, though it is worth recording the case of Laurence Galter, chantrist at Goosnargh, who paid Ellen Taylor a mark to sleep with him and said 'as she liked that she should have another mark of him'.[3] It is only possible to be impressionistic on the parish clergy, as the consistory act books do not give the reasons for office prosecutions of priests, but it is noticeable that no priests were accused of sexual offences at any of the three pre-Elizabethan parish visitations which survive. The example of the Lancashire monks suggests that the level of clerical morality was comparatively high. In 1536 Layton and Legh reported 18% of the Lancashire religious they examined as guilty of some sort of sexual lapse, as against 24% of the monks in the diocese of York and 36% of those in the diocese of Norwich.[4] Perhaps a higher proportion of the secular clergy succumbed to temptation, but at least in comparison with the laity the priests of the county were successful in their adherence to the conventional moral code.

Tudor Lancashire was commonly accepted not only as one of the most immoral of the counties of England but also as one of the most violent. The upper gentry needed armed followers for protection in the endemic conflicts between families, and the requirements of defence against the Scots affected Lancashire as well as other parts of the north. The county was one of the traditional sources of recruitment for soldiers for the north, and from Flodden to Mary's wars Lancashire forces were extensively involved in every campaign. The major gentry always provided substantial contingents, and in 1544 fourteen of them each led about 100 men northwards. Perhaps the men of the north-west felt that they bore an unfair share of the burden, for in 1549 120 of them deserted from the army.[5] The musters held early in Elizabeth's reign show the extent to which

[1] *An Episcopal Court Book for the Diocese of Lincoln*, ed. M. Bowker, 126; Raines, *Vicars of Rochdale*, 38.

[2] *Prescot Records, 1447–1600*, ed. F. A. Bailey, 116, 118; CRO, EDC 2/8, fo. 60v; Foxe, *Acts and Monuments*, VIII, 564. Though Foxe calls Parker 'Parkinson', his circumstantial detail is so accurate that the story must have come from a reliable source.

[3] CRO, EDC 2/4, pp. 46–9.

[4] Haigh, *Lancs. Monasteries*, 26–7.

[5] *L & P*, XIX(1), 532; *Rutland MSS*, I, 35–6.

51

the palatinate was still a military society, with a higher proportion of soldiers in the population than any county except the untypical Middlesex.[1] Where there were trained soldiers, with the implement of warfare readily to hand, violence was common.

The council of the Duchy of Lancaster certainly thought the county was unusually violent. In 1482 the law officers noted that local disorders

hath caused the unrestful rule and governance of the said county, not only to the great impoverishment of the inhabitants within the same but also great hurt and loss is likely thereby to ensue to the king our sovereign lord in his livelihood there and the tenants occupying the same.

There had been no improvement by 1532, when commissions for each of the Lancashire hundreds were issued for the arrest of those guilty of murder, felony, retaining, forcible entry and other offences which 'hath not oftentimes been seen nor heard of' in other parts of the country.[2] The Council was right that large-scale and often organised violence was frequent, but was powerless to control it. Late in the reign of Henry VII John Lawrence assembled a mob of 300 men and broke into Lancaster gaol in an attempt to free two of his servants. Early in the next reign 500 Lancashiremen were indicted for riot, and county officers were ordered to implement new measures to keep the peace.[3] But in 1514 a cock-fight at Winwick was followed by a great riot in which Sir Thomas Gerard and 40 of his men attacked Thomas Butler and his followers with bows and arrows, swords and staves; only with the greatest difficulty was Sir John Southworth able to restore order between the two sides. This was only one of a series of brawls, and the area around Warrington and Winwick was constantly disrupted by fights between rival gentry families, the Butlers, the Leighs, the Gerards and the Bruches.[4]

Local officials could not control disorders, for it was often the most powerful who were responsible for them. Those at the top of the county hierarchy maintained their authority by violence and intimidation; there were complaints to the Duchy chancellor and to Wolsey himself in 1520–1 against the conduct of the earl of Derby and his men, and on one occasion the earl had sent 800 men under Sir Henry Keighley into Preston to eject a chantry priest against the will of the burgesses. When there were disturbances at Wigan early in the reign of Edward VI the mayor was unable to keep the peace and the Duchy Council had to arrange to proceed against

[1] *VCH*, II, 223; *Lancashire Lieutenancy*, ed. J. Harland, I, 34–61.
[2] PRO, DL 5/1, fo. 62, DL 42/95, fo. 128v.
[3] *Duchy Pleadings*, I, 45; PRO, DL 5/5, fos. 12, 15, DL 42/95, fos. 9–9v.
[4] *Duchy Pleadings*, I, 61–6; J. B. Watson, 'The Lancashire gentry and the public service, 1529–58', *TLCAS*, LXXIII, 14.

offenders.[1] Things were no better later in the century, and in 1581 there was a fracas during the assizes at Lancaster between retainers of Lord Strange and those of Lord Morley. Eight years later Sir Thomas Langton with 80 of his men besieged Thomas Houghton and 30 servants in Lea Hall, and Houghton was killed. The law was unable to deal with this conflict, and when a special session was held at Lancaster only three jurors dared to appear and no presentments were made. After two and a half years the earl of Derby proposed that the case should be dropped, as the principals were

so great in kindred and affinity and so stored with friends as if they should be burned in the hand I fear it will fall out to be a ceaseless and most dangerous quarrel betwixt the gentlemen that any county of Her Majesty's hath this many years contained.

The earl's advice was taken, and the affair was patched up with blood money.[2]

The clergy were, of course, sometimes involved in such violence. In 1518 John Osbaldeston, priest, was one of a group of men accused of ejecting Hugh Gartside from his lands by force. In the course of a mortuary dispute Edward Mollineux, the grasping rector of Sefton, waylaid John Cokeson on his way to market and captured 38 of his cattle. In 1537 George Huncott, a chaplain at Church, was fined for fighting and drawing blood, and in the late 1540s two Warrington priests were in trouble separately for attacking local men.[3] Priests, like laymen, were normally armed; in 1556 Robert Briddock, priest, bequeathed 'my best bow and arrows' to a relative, and in 1564 Thomas Primett, priest, saw no inconsistency in leaving a Bible and a sword to the same man. In 1558 the rector of Prestwich carried an armoury with him; he had 'a sword and a dagger such as he commonly rode with' and carried a 'pair of knives'.[4] Clerics, too, were as involved as laymen in those habits and institutions which gave rise to violence. In 1496 James Stanley, brother of the first earl of Derby and warden of Manchester College, was indicted at Tadcaster for retaining a long list of labourers and artisans, and in 1519 Edward Mollineux was poaching the retainers of others and making them his own men.[5]

Violence intruded not only into the lives of the clergy but into the churches, which were the centres of quarrelling as well as of

---

[1] *L & P*, III(2), 1923; PRO, DL 42/96, fo. 14v.

[2] *Survey and Account of the Estates of Hornby Castle*, 113; *VCH*, I, 374, VI, 292.

[3] *CCR*, II, 124, III, 31; *Lancashire and Cheshire Cases in the Court of Star Chamber*, 75; *Ducatus Lancastriae*, I, 186, 222.

[4] *L & C Wills*, III, 142; *Richmond Wills*, 172; *Duchy Pleadings*, III, 251.

[5] W. H. Dunham, *Lord Hastings' Indentured Retainers*, 84–5; LRO, DDBl/24/3.

3-2

worship. The church was the only place where enemies were almost certain to meet, and this is one reason why conflicts between families often revolved around ownership of a pew in a church or chapel.[1] As the isolated homestead was the normal social unit, it is probable that men had not learned the self-discipline necessary when two or three hundred met together. Violence was even more likely in the church than elsewhere, though it was usually confined to mere brawling, as at Holcombe chapel in 1509, or in Padiham chapel in 1531, or in the series of fights in Edenfield chapel in 1543.[2] Sometimes churches were the scenes of more important conflicts. In 1522 a mob of about 40 men pulled down a new aisle in Dean chapel, and two years later a conflict over the succession to an estate was fought out in Kirkby Ireleth church one Sunday morning. When Sir Thomas Butler's deputy sheriff tried to arrest Thomas Pomfret in his parish church at Leigh during the mass, the local people were so angry that the under-sheriff was attacked after the service by a mob of about 150.[3] At Billinge in 1539–40 a service in the chapel was disrupted by fighting, and the most serious of the affrays in Edenfield chapel in 1543 was an attack on Thurstan Booth during vespers, 'to the disturbance of divine service in the said chapel, so that his life would have been taken but for God and the good people being there present to help'.[4] Although he had already been bound over to keep the peace, in 1543 Thomas Talbot took bars from the churchyard at Church, used them to break down the chapel doors, and took away documents and armour stored inside.[5] Such cases were not confined to the first half of the century, and in 1575, for example, a conflict over the appointment of a curate at Leigh led to 'great misorders', and while the vicar was performing a service the people 'swarmed about him in the chancel like unto a swarm of bees'.[6]

Brawling and quarrelling were merely the most dramatic of the non-religious activities which took place in the churches. As local communities met together only in the churches, common problems were presumably discussed there, and this probably explains the large number of prosecutions for talking in church.[7] Some may have talked because they found the services tedious, and at Tottington in 1522 two men whiled away the time by playing cards during mass; Anglican services held attention no more successfully, and late in the

---

[1] e.g. at Chuch and Accrington (*Duchy Pleadings*, II, 105–6, 106–7).
[2] *CCR*, II, 108, III, 274, 333, 335, 336; see also III, 134, 142.
[3] *Duchy Pleadings*, I, 111, 116–19, II, 43–8.
[4] *Ducatus Lancastriae*, I, 159; *CCR*, III, 335–6.
[5] *Duchy Pleadings*, I, 116–19.
[6] *Lancs. Chantries*, II, 271.
[7] e.g. *Whalley Act Book*, 54, 55, 59–60, 139.

reign of Elizabeth a Richmondshire churchwarden was in trouble for gambling in church, 'after which the said church was lamentably consumed by fire'.[1] The church, a natural centre for trading, became almost a market on Sundays, and there were complaints about trading during the service at Sefton and Prescot in 1554, while at Croston the people chatted in the churchyard while mass was in progress.[2] In each parish the church was the centre of all official activity. In 1514 a confession in a forgery case was taken in Leyland church, in 1529 depositions on a boundary dispute were taken in Halsall church, and in 1533 the steward of Clitheroe published a royal decree in Colne chapel.[3] Chorley chapel and Kirkby Ireleth church were used as court houses, while Lord Mounteagle held his manorial courts in Hornby chapel and it was reported in 1590 that the chapel was only a place of worship 'but at such times as his lordship shall appoint'.[4]

As church buildings were used for many secular purposes, it is not surprising that they were regarded with no special awe. Thefts from churches were extremely common and, though the objects stolen were probably of small value and the thieves difficult to detect, we have record of a large number of such cases. In 1530 Robert Smith, a young scholar from Liverpool, broke into Tarleton chapel and stole property belonging to the chaplain; he was arrested and indicted, but pleaded his clergy and was imprisoned in the archdeacon of Chester's gaol at Tarporley.[5] In 1541 a group of men broke into Eccleston church at 'one of the clock after midnight' and stole money from a chest which had belonged to the late rector. Seven 'riotous persons' took a chalice and other plate from Farnworth chapel in 1544, and five years later Sir Richard Brereton complained that, among other lawless acts, his son had removed a chalice from Ellenbrook chapel. It was reported in 1552 that a bell had been 'embezzled' at St Helen's chapel, two chalices and a copper cross had disappeared from Childwall, and at Trinity chapel the churchwardens had been involved in some double-dealing over bells.[6] Under Edward VI parishioners sometimes helped themselves to property made redundant by the new prayer books. At Eccleston two altars, three 'magna candelabra' and a crucifix were stolen, while the wardens at Farnworth had a candle-stand cut up by

---

[1] *CCR*, III, 289; CRO, EDV 1/12b, fo. 26.

[2] CRO, EDV 1/1, fos. 141, 142, 145v. See also the complaints that such offences were common about 1590 in *State Civil and Ecclesiastical*, 2, 4.

[3] LRO, DDF/666, DDIn/49/9–10; *CCR*, I, 313.

[4] *Duchy Pleadings*, I, 116, II, 96; BIY, R VI, A 11, fo. 46.

[5] PRO, PL 20/10; Lich. RO, Reg. Blyth, B/A/1/14, fo. 66.

[6] *Duchy Pleadings*, II, 159; *Church Goods*, II, 63, 81, 85, 91; PRO, DL 3/25, B 15.

the local smith and sold the pieces as scrap metal for their own profit.[1]

Such thefts as these pale into insignificance beside the activities of an organised ring of church-robbers based on Middleton and Standish. The group, which was uncovered in 1535, operated mainly in Lancashire churches, and members raided churches and chapels at Burnley, Lytham, Haslingden, Caton, Singleton, Wyresdale, Cockerham, Rochdale and Prestwich. Their favourite haul was chalices, which they took to Hull or Penrith, well out of the county, to sell to gold and silversmiths. They also took vestments, which were altered for resale by one of their number, a vestment-maker, and money from altar boxes. Although Lancashire was the centre of their operations, they conducted forays into Yorkshire and Cheshire. The members of the group spent their off-duty hours at the house of a Middleton woman, 'which is a great receipter of thieves in buying of such things as they do steal', and with David Turner of Standish, another 'receipter of thieves', who seems to have guarded his friends' booty while they were away seeking new spoils.[2] They formed a well-organised gang of social outcasts, migrants, pedlars and crippled beggars, and their story affords a rare glimpse into the Lancashire underworld.

If church buildings were not respected, there is some evidence that the same was true of the priests who staffed them. Hugh Sneyd, vicar of Poulton, seems to have been unpopular among some of his female parishioners; the wife of a local gentleman increased the rent on lands he worked and threw him off when he could not pay, while another woman prevented him from using his tithe barn. During a dispute between the vicar of Whalley and the people of Colne in 1544, Nicholas Marsden called the vicar down from the pulpit 'for it were meeter for him to be in a swine sty'. In the following year a Manchester woman persistently called the warden of the collegiate church a 'whoremaster priest', and there survives a missal which contains disparaging manuscript notes on Richard Moody, curate of Standish.[3] A priest who was insulted could initiate a defamation suit in the ecclesiastical courts, and thirteen Lancashire clergy took parishioners before the court at Chester for slander in the 1530s and 1540s. Friction between priests and laymen may have been increasing, for the Chester court books have no slander actions by Lancaire priests until 1537 and though there were only three cases in the first half of the 1540s there were seven in the second half.[4]

[1] CRO, EDV 1/1, fos. 147–147v; *Duchy Pleadings*, III, 199–204.
[2] PRO, SP 2R, fos. 299–300.
[3] *L & P*, XIV(2), 582; CRO, EDC 2/3, fos. 25, 75v–76; Porteus, *History of the Parish of Standish*, 101.   [4] CRO, EDC 1/8–12, *passim*.

Priests and people: conduct and attitudes

Quarrels between clergy and laity sometimes erupted into violence. There were at least four examples of assaults on priests in 1526; in two cases chantry priests were driven out by force, and in the most serious conflict the rector of Bury was attacked in procession and again in his church. The curate of Padiham was dragged from the altar while celebrating mass in 1535, and a year later a chaplain was assaulted at Tottington. The curate of Urswick claimed in 1548 that he went in fear of his life, as he had twice been attacked with swords, bucklers, bills, clubs, daggers and other weapons.[1] Violence towards the clergy was not confined to Lancashire, however, and in a disorderly area priests naturally suffered as much as other men. Violent words and actions against priests are not necessarily examples of the 'anti-clericalism' historians find so convenient a concept, and there is no evidence that laymen attacked clergy *qua* clergy.

Priests found themselves assaulted because they were often involved in conflicts, usually over fees and dues. One of the most potent sources of trouble was probably the vexed question of mortuaries or, as they were called in Lancashire with grim accuracy, 'dead corpse presents'. The Hunne affair brought the problem into the limelight; if the views of members of parliament were at all representative, opinion had turned against what was seen as a particularly unpleasant form of fund-raising. There were certainly disputes over mortuaries in early Tudor Lancashire. In 1514 John Cokeson of Sefton refused to give a 'fat ox' to the rector as a mortuary for his late wife, arguing that she had died in the parish of Warrington, but the rector seized the ox and impounded Cokeson's cattle to teach him a lesson. There was apparently some argument at Lancaster in 1524 over mortuary customs, for in that year the vicar and four local men drew up a sliding scale of fees based on the wealth of the deceased person.[2] A more complicated dispute took place in 1526 when, it seems, the abbot of Whalley demanded mortuaries from Walton-le-dale for the first time, and took those who refused to pay before the bishop's consistory at Lichfield. Those who were cited resisted vigorously, and the case went on for seven months and eleven sessions of the court. Finally, the abbot's case was dismissed when the defendants produced a signed testimonial from 24 of their neighbours, to the effect that mortuaries had never been paid in their village.[3]

[1] *Duchy Pleadings*, I, 147, 151–3, III, 34–5; *CCR*, III, 54, 316; PRO, DL 3/17, L 6, PL 26/5/1.
[2] *Lancashire and Cheshire Cases in the Court of Star Chamber*, 75; BM, Additional MS 32105, No. 823.
[3] Lich. RO, B/C/2/1, *passim*; *De Houghton Deeds and Papers*, ed. J. H. Lumby, No. 1094.

It is usually suggested that mortuary conflicts were fairly common and were an expression of the laity's dislike of priests.[1] This may have been true in the south of England, but it was not so in Lancashire. Two of the cases cited resulted not from malicious refusal by parishioners but from attempts by clergy to obtain mortuaries to which they were not entitled, while the third was settled in an amicable manner. There appear to have been very few mortuary disputes in the county, and though the Chester court book for 1502–15 contains five mortuary cases from Cheshire, there were none from the Lancashire portion of the archdeaconry.[2] The Mortuaries Act of 1529 was designed to simplify and restrict the mortuary system, and so to remove one cause of friction between clergy and laity, but in Lancashire, where there had been no trouble, the statute merely created new difficulties and uncertainties. There were no mortuary cases from the county at Chester in the years immediately preceding the act, but in the year following it there were thirteen. These suits probably arose from differences of opinion over the interpretation and implementation of the statute, and the flood of litigation soon subsided.[3] The new legislation made serious inroads into the clergy's revenues, and between 1486 and 1535 receipts from mortuaries in the parish of Eccles fell from £6 16s to only £1.[4] It is therefore surprising that in the long term there was not more trouble, for only two Lancashire mortuary cases went to the Chester court between 1531 and 1560. Both involved technical questions not covered clearly by the act of 1529, and it seems that mortuaries were never an important source of conflict in Lancashire.[5]

The custom of exacting a tithe of all produce for the support of Church and clergy was a more fertile ground for dispute, and dissension over tithe seems to have been common in many parts of England. Although quarrels over tithing were nothing new, and had been raging in London for at least two centuries, there is some evidence that confrontations were becoming more frequent. South Lancashire produced only 5 tithe cases before the archdeacon's court at Chester between 1502 and 1515, but 22 in the 1530s. The Chester consistory heard 52 tithe suits from the whole of the county in the 1540s, but 77 in the 1550s. Not all these cases were between priests and laymen, however, for the suppression of the monasteries gave

[1] A. G. Dickens, *The English Reformation*, 91–3, 95. Professor Dickens quotes Chapuys' comment that 'nearly all the people here hate the priests'.
[2] CRO, EDC 1/1, fos. 9, 44, 53, 58.
[3] CRO, EDC 1/3–4, *passim*.
[4] LRO, DDIn/63/1–2.
[5] CRO, EDC 2/2, pp. 214–18, 1/10, *passim*; BIY, R VII, G 297.

the Crown a number of rectories and these were usually leased out to lay farmers. Thus although the Chester court dealt with more than twice as many tithe cases in the 1540s as in the 1530s, the number of cases involving priests remained stable while the number involving lay farmers multiplied by more than six times. The increase in tithe suits does not reflect an increase in conflicts between priests and their people. The incidence of tithe conflicts is easily exaggerated, but on average a tithe case went from any one Lancashire parish to the Chester consistory only once every eight years in the period 1541–59.[1]

The longer tithe cases, however, in which both sides refused to give in and parishioners were put to great expense and inconvenience, may have caused much bitterness. The abbot of Whalley, for example, fought a group of men from Marsden in Colne through the courts for more than two years. In April 1532 the abbot sued five men before the official at Chester and claimed that they had not paid tithe on corn and hay for two years. The five failed to appear in court and the official issued a suspension, but when the curate of Colne tried to read out the mandate the men snatched it from his hands and tore it up. Abbot Paslew then took the case to the Duchy court, and produced signed depositions from the most important men in Colne to counter the defendants' contention that the tithe had always been commuted for a cash payment. The court decided in favour of the abbot, but told Paslew that he would have to 'sue his remedy therein at the law spiritual, where the judgement hereof ought to be had, and not in this court'. But the Marsden men refused to submit and complained themselves to the Duchy court, alleging malicious prosecution by the abbot in the Church courts. They produced a document, purporting to come from a large number of Colne tenants, which appeared to support their claim of commutation, and when the abbot's proctor countered with a charter of 1333 they alleged it was a forgery. The Duchy council commissioned three Lancashire knights to hold local enquiries, and they found that all the signatures on the Colne document had been forged. Although they had no support from their neighbours, the five Marsden men still refused to submit, and Abbot Paslew had to ask the earl of Derby to intercede with the Duchy council on his behalf. Duchy officials again decided for the abbot, sent a decree to this effect to the official at Chester and ordered the five to beg Paslew's forgiveness, but again it was decided that payment of the tithe could only be enforced at Chester. The abbot accordingly reopened his suit at Chester in the Hilary term of 1534, and once more the defendants refused to appear,

---

[1] Figures from CRO, EDC 1/1–2, *passim*, 1/4–15, *passim*.

so the abbot informed the Duchy council that its orders had not been obeyed. The final outcome is not clear; the council issued a writ for the accused to appear after Easter, and as the Chester court book entries come to an end in July 1534 it is probable that payment was, finally, enforced.[1] This is one of the most determined efforts to avoid tithe of which record survives, and it is clear that the men involved were litigious rogues, ready to lie, cheat and forge to obtain the financial advantages of commutation. One of the most significant features of the case is the refusal of the other inhabitants of Marsden to support a claim which would have brought them profit, and it is unlikely that the dispute embittered relations between the people of Colne and Whalley Abbey.

Equally long and almost as complicated was the series of tithe suits fought by the rector of Chipping. In March 1542 George Wolset, the rector, began two tithe causes against six of his parishioners, and in May a further four defendants were added to the list. The Chipping men were determined not to succumb, and the suits continued until April 1545, when Wolset opened another case against eleven more parishioners. By mid-October the rector was in even deeper difficulties, for he had difficulty in persuading witnesses to support him, and in November he abandoned all hope of securing a decision at Chester and went to the Duchy court. There Wolset complained that the leading men of the parish had prevented his servants from collecting tithe, and had 'counselled nearly all the rest of the parishioners to stay their tithe corn and to stop all their dues to the Church, intending thereby to drive the plaintiff, being a stranger, out of the parish'. Even in the Duchy court the people of Chipping refused to abandon their fight, and they pawned church plate to finance 'our suit against Mr Dr Wolset, our parson'. If Wolset's testimony can be believed, and there is circumstantial evidence to support it, the parishioners were led by a handful of influential men who aimed 'to have the said parsonage to farm at such rent as they will'. It seems that the intrigues of the Sherburne family lay behind Wolset's troubles with his people. Richard Sherburne put up part of the money for a defence against the rector, and in 1548 he was causing additional problems for Wolset. At the neighbouring rectory of Ribchester, held also by Wolset, Sherburne encouraged two minstrels to burn down a house belonging to the priest, and tried to eject him from the benefice. In 1548, in fact, Wolset was forced to cut his losses and lease out the two rectories to local men at low

[1] CRO, EDC 1/5, fos. 63, 66v, 1/6, fo. 41, 1/7, fos. 19, 21, 22, 25v, 33v, 37, 43v; *Duchy Pleadings*, II, 31–9; PRO, DL 5/6, fos. 39–39v, 74–75, 75v–76; *Derby Correspondence*, 119.

rents.[1] Although it is true that the people of Chipping were easily turned against an absentee rector, the case does not show that tithe led to poor relations between incumbents and parishioners. Rather it shows how powerful families could use their influence to intimidate even a rector with Court connections.

Although tithing could lead to discord, its role in provoking resentment between priests and laymen may not have been significant. Tithe causes are, as we have seen, not always what they appear; some were occasioned by the ingenuity of swindlers, some were engineered by local gentry for their own ends,[2] and others were provoked by rapacious lay farmers trying to overthrow local usages. In 1543–4 the new lessees of the tithes of Eccles, Dean and Leigh each tried to enforce payments in kind for tithe which had previously been commuted, and when Sir John Byron, the farmer of Rochdale, made a similar attempt in 1548 he was solidly resisted by the people and the courts were kept busy for four years.[3] By the 1550s well over half the Lancashire tithe suits involved lay lessees rather than clerical rectors. The terseness of court-book entries makes it impossible to discover the origins of most quarrels, but the similarity of those which can be traced in detail is so striking that many others may have followed the same pattern. Tithe suits were not the product of resistance by parishioners to established tithing customs, but of disagreement over what constituted the custom. Those who refused payments did not do so from any quasi-heretical opposition to the principle of tithe or because they disliked clergy, but sometimes because of an honest disagreement and sometimes because they would cheat anyone, priest or layman.

Although it was often a lay lessee who provoked a dispute, cases were fought out in the Church courts and these may have taken the brunt of the people's acrimony. There was, however, a good deal of difference between anticlericalism (hatred of priests), and opposition to the Church courts (hatred of authority). There is no evidence that the ecclesiastical courts occasioned any more resistance than the secular, while the rising volume of instance business shows that laymen were quite prepared to use spiritual tribunals.[4] 'Ex officio' prosecutions may have caused more anger, but they formed only a small proportion of the business of the courts; between 1547 and

---

[1] CRO, EDC 1/10–11, *passim*, especially 1/11, fo. 173/1, EDA 3/1, fos. 114–16; *Ducatus Lancastriae*, I, 185; *Duchy Pleadings*, II, 211; PRO, DL 3/2, W 3, SP 10/3/4.
[2] As well as the Sherburne-Wolset case, see that promoted by Richard Towneley against the farmer of Whalley in 1546, Haigh, 'Reformation in Lancashire', 286–8.
[3] CRO, EDC 2/3, fos. 481–493, 495–499, 2/4, fos. 19v–20, 2/10, *passim*, EDC 1/12–13, *passim*.
[4] See below, p. 227.

1550 only 49 Lancashire office cases were heard at Chester, and even in 1564, when there was an unusually large number of office prosecutions, they formed only 16% of the total business of the consistory.[1] Except for the Lancashire speciality of sexual laxity, disobedience to the laws of the Church was not widespread, and can often be explained by local circumstances. The surviving act book of the abbot of Whalley's peculiar court for the exempt forest areas covers the years 1510–38, and during that period there were only 67 prosecutions for Sunday and feast-day working. One-third of the cases occurred in the first four years of the book, and 37 in the first decade.[2] The reason for this concentration in the early years is clear; in 1507 royal stewards began the disafforestation of the area, and new plots of land were granted out. Men were anxious to clear the land and make it productive as rapidly as possible, and the injunctions of the Church were temporarily forgotten. Similarly, the abbot's court heard only ten cases of tithe refusal in 29 years, but seven of these were in the first year of the act book; it would have taken some time to arrange the proper tithing of newly-cultivated lands, and disputes were almost inevitable.

There were many occasions of conflict between priests and laymen, but there is very little evidence of sustained antagonism between the two groups. If clergy were sometimes attacked and beaten, it was not because they were priests but because Lancashiremen were violent, towards priests or anyone else. If laymen tried to reduce their tithes it was because they disliked any form of taxation, and the Lancashire clergy themselves had a particularly poor record where taxes were concerned.[3] Men were irritated by the Church's courts and the Church's taxes, they might break the Church's laws and evade the duties they owed it, but only rarely did they flout its authority since it alone held the keys of heaven. General resistance to the jurisdiction of the Church was only possible when men were convinced that salvation could be attained without its intercession. But until at least the reign of Edward VI, Lancashiremen were almost completely orthodox and 'nulla salus extra ecclesiam' was not merely a doctrine, it was a veiled threat which prompted obedience.

[1] CRO, EDC 1/12, 1/17, *passim.*
[2] *Whalley Act Book, passim.*
[3] E. F. Jacob, *The Fifteenth Century*, 421–2; *L & P*, VII, 923, xviii.

5

Orthodox piety and practices

The churches of Lancashire were poorly provided for and often in disrepair, the resident clergy were invariably underpaid and usually ill educated, and the standards of behaviour which the Church prescribed were not always fulfilled. In its social habits the palatinate was, as we have seen, much behind counties in the south of England, and its religious development was equally retarded. The old faith in the south was losing its hold on the people, who were lapsing into the secularist anticlericalism which made the work of the Reformation Parliament possible, or were turning to the alternative faiths peddled by old Lollards or new Protestants. For Lancashire to be backward in this respect, however, meant that pre-Reformation Catholicism was still strong in the county, so that the early sixteenth century found the old Church not at its nadir but at its high point. There is little sign, it is true, of a deep spiritual life, but there was certainly a real enthusiasm for traditional practices. The Lancashire monasteries provide an apt illustration of this point; the spirituality and conduct of the religious may have been little better than in other parts of England, but there is a good deal of evidence that they were popular among local people who, when the monks were threatened, rose immediately to defend them.

Religion played a central role in the life of the community, and, as elsewhere, the focal point of popular piety was the sacramental system and especially the Eucharist. The consecrated host was treated with great reverence, and in the reign of Henry VII the curate of Bolton quelled a riot over tolls when he appeared carrying the host. In 1524 a brawl at Kirkby Ireleth was halted when a priest with a host placed himself between the combatants, and in 1530 a mob would have attacked Lytham priory in a property dispute had not two monks gone out to meet the crowd carrying a consecrated host.[1] The superstitions which surrounded the Eucharist were shared in Lancashire, and great importance was attached to the proper reception of communion. In 1529 Thomas Wetherby of Prescot remarked to his friends, 'How say ye by John Eccleston, that hath presumed to receive his Maker and hath not paid his offering

---

[1] *Duchy Pleadings*, I, 44, 116–19, 206–9.

penny?' Eccleston was highly indignant at this slur and retorted 'Say you that I presumed to receive my Maker, not paying my duties to God and Holy Church and especially my offering penny?' This insignificant charge of taking communion without first paying church dues was enough to spark off a defamation suit at Chester.[1] It was particularly important to communicate before death; in 1558 Richard Rothwell of Bolton received 'the blessed sacrament of the altar' on his death-bed, and William Bradshaw's wife asked two friends to persuade her dying husband 'to send for his ghostly father to receive the rites of the Church'.[2] The people of a church were always angry if their mass was interrupted, especially if the intervention came at the consecration. In 1535 an attempt by an under-sheriff to make an arrest in Leigh church at the consecration led to a riot, and when an apparitor tried to serve a mandate during mass at Church in 1555 he was pulled out of the way of the priest and abused by the congregation.[3] But such reverence for the host had an un-balancing effect on unstable minds, and 'at the time of the elevation of the body of our Lord Jesus Christ' the miller of Clitheroe would 'throw himself to the earth' and hide his face.[4]

Attendance at mass was of the greatest significance. When the bye-laws of Liverpool were codified in 1540–1, 'the priest of St John's altar' was instructed to provide an early mass for 'all lab-ourers and well-disposed people'. In 1555 a woman who was tem-porarily unable to attend her local chapel hired a priest to provide mass in her own home.[5] It naturally followed that those who could afford to do so employed a private chaplain, and the domestic chapel became increasingly common in Lancashire. In 1443 Thomas Law-rence of Warton was licensed to have an oratory, and in the following year Richard Clifton obtained a licence for a chaplain and masses at his oratories at Clifton and Westby. John Towneley had an oratory licence from the bishop of Lichfield in 1454, and in the succeeding years the archdeacon of Richmond gave similar licences to Nicholas Singleton, Robert Sherburne, John Skillicorne and John Claugh-ton.[6] In the sixteenth century some of the richer gentry had their own chapels. Robert Langley had a well-furnished chapel and a chaplain who continued to serve the family after his master's death in 1528. In 1532 the Scarisbrick family had a chapel with fourteen images and a

[1] CRO, EDC 2/1, fo. 6.
[2] *Ibid.* 2/6, fos. 171–171v, 177, 248v.
[3] *Duchy Pleadings*, II, 43–8; BIY, R VII, G 648.
[4] *CCR*, I, 58.
[5] *Liverpool Town Books*, ed. J. Twemlow, I, 3; BIY, R VII, G 648.
[6] 'Richmond Registers', II, Nos. 23, 106, 119a, 132, 133a, 136; Lich. RO, Reg. Boulers, B/A/1/11, fo. 72.

good supply of plate and vestments, and the bishop of Chester permitted Sir Thomas Langton to build an oratory in 1546. Thurstan Tildesley had chapels in his houses at Wardley and Myerscough by 1553, perhaps for the use of his brother, who had been a Carthusian at Sheen.[1]

As there was a shortage of clergy in Lancashire, domestic chaplains were less common than private chapels. In the first half of the sixteenth century only a dozen families are known to have had their own priests, who were often men who had retired from the parochial service. Instead, the gentry contributed towards the maintenance of the parish clergy, and in 1541 70 assistant priests in south Lancashire, more than half the total, were paid by individual gentlemen. Although men were often unwilling to pay their full tithes and other compulsory dues, they were prepared to make voluntary contributions towards clerical stipends. Groups of parishioners financed 6 priests in 1541, and another 26 had their livings from the free offerings of the whole parish.[2] In some townships the people imposed levies on themselves to support their clergy, and in 1534 the parishioners of Denton in Manchester agreed to an annual tax of 2½d per acre for the expenses of their chapel and the wages of a priest.[3] Large sums of money were devoted to the upkeep of the Church in Lancashire. Fifteenth-century England had seen a massive increase in bequests to churches, but Lancashire was, as usual, rather behind the rest of the country and an expansion in religious benefactions did not come until the Tudor period. In the years 1480 to 1540, 70% of all charitable benefactions went to religious causes, a higher proportion of the total than in any of the other nine areas studied by Professor Jordan. But what really distinguishes Lancashire from the rest of England is that this exceptional level of religious benefactions continued through the period 1540–60. While Norfolk gave 12% of its gifts to religion, Buckinghamshire 27% and even Yorkshire only 25%, 69% of Lancashire's charity went to religious uses.[4] It would be rash to argue that Lancastrians were more pious than their contemporaries, but their piety was more directed towards the institutional Church.

Investment in church building was particularly high, for although

[1] *L & C Wills*, I, 98–9, 102, 109, 112, 187, II, 18, 136–8, 253, IV, 35, 63; *De Houghton Deeds*, No. 1098; *L & P*, XV, 1032 (p. 548).
[2] *Clergy List, passim.*
[3] BM, Harleian MS 2112, fos. 164, 200.
[4] W. K. Jordan, *The Social Institutions of Lancashire*, CS, 3rd series, XI, 7, 75, 117; Jordan, *The Charities of Rural England*, 438–40; Jordan, *Philanthropy in England*, 253. Although a failure to take account of inflation makes Jordan's comparisons between different periods untrustworthy, comparisons between different areas at the same time are more reliable.

Lancashire church fabric was frequently in poor repair it is clear that construction was more attractive than routine maintenance. In the first half of the sixteenth century towers were built onto the churches at Ashton, Broughton and Leigh, side chapels were added at Whalley, Burnley, Garstang and Dean, there were considerable additions at Middleton, Blackburn and Eccles, lesser improvements at Bolton, Hawkshead and Kirkby Ireleth, and the parish churches of Bury, Sefton and St Michael's-on-Wyre were completely rebuilt. It is true that in the last case a new church was necessary because the old building had collapsed after years of neglect, but these examples represent a construction campaign of some intensity in a poor community.[1] Often we do not know how the new building was financed, but we can be sure that most of the money came from gentry families and other parishioners. A series of bequests from important local men made rebuilding possible at Eccles, the Ashton family was responsible for the alterations at Middleton, the people of Burnley raised the money for their new building, and between 1486 and 1518 various local interests added eight new chapels to the collegiate church in Manchester.[2] Sometimes it was the clergy who put up the money for rebuilding; the Cistercians of Whalley financed the extensions at Dean, and the rectors of Bury and Sefton made substantial contributions towards the costs of building in their own churches.[3]

Even more dramatic than the rebuilding of existing churches was the foundation of new chapels, an expensive undertaking. Between 1470 and 1548 about 46 new chapels were built in Lancashire, 38 of them after 1500. In less than eighty years the number of churches and parochial chapels was increased by almost half, and at least 10 of the chapels were financed by contributions from the local community.[4] At Goodshaw, seven miles from the parish church, the people built their own chapel about 1540, and they then collected another 20 marks to buy vestments and ornaments and provide for the wages of a priest. At Billinge, four miles from the parish church at Wigan, the people built a chapel at their own cost and maintained a priest and services from annual collections by the churchwardens.[5]

[1] Jordan, *Social Institutions of Lancashire*, 85f; *Duchy Pleadings*, I,111; W. Bennett, *History of Burnley*, II, 108; C. M. L. Bouch and G. P. Jones, *Economic and Social History of the Lake Counties, 1500–1830*, 30–1.
[2] *VCH*, IV, 355–6; *L & C Wills*, I, 15, 98, IV, 63; S. R. Glynne, *Notes on the Churches of Lancashire*, CS, NS, XXVII, 98; Bennet, *History of Burnley*, II, 108; Jordan, *Social Institutions of Lancashire*, 85.
[3] P. A. Whittle, *Bolton-le-Moors*, 321, 422; *VCH*, V, 125; *L & C Wills*, II, 263.
[4] Tupling, 'Pre-Reformation parishes and chapelries', 9, 12–16.
[5] *Duchy Pleadings*, III, 260–1; G. T. O. Bridgeman, *History of the Church and Manor of Wigan*, CS, NS, XV–XVIII, 750–1.

The growth of the textile industry in the hundred of Salford, and the expansion of agriculture in Blackburnshire after the disafforestation of 1507, led to greater prosperity in these two areas, and over half the chapels founded in the first half of the sixteenth century were in the south-east and east of the county.

The resources put into the established church reflect a commitment to the typical practices and beliefs of pre-Tridentine Catholicism. The cult of the saints and their images was particularly strong and attracted continuous investment. The chapel at Broughton had images of SS. Katherine, Margaret, James, Nicholas and Syth, which were repaired and repainted by local collection in 1512, and at Eccles and Dean in 1535 small sums were left to St Anthony and the Virgin. St Nicholas was the centre of some devotion at Leyland, and in 1528 Henry Farington left a shilling a year for candles before his image.[1] At Prescot there were eight collections each year between late November and late January for lights before the images of SS. Katherine, Stephen and Anthony; between 1528–9 and 1537–8 the sums raised totalled from £1 7s 6d to £1 12s 8d each year, and there was a slight increase in the donations over the period. From 1536 there was an extra collection, which usually raised over £1, 'for the St Mary candle', and in 1537–8 4s 1d was 'gathered in the parish to the painting of St George'. These donations were forbidden by the royal injunctions of 1538, and after 1539 there were no further gifts at Prescot.[2]

Another aspect of the cult of the saints was the adoration of relics, and Croston church had what was reputed to be the head of St Lawrence; part of the skull was apparently given to the dependent chapel at Chorley.[3] Holland priory had two silver reliquies, one of which contained 'a bone of St Thomas of Canterbury', who was the most popular of the saints in Lancashire. Despite the order deleting him from the calendar of saints to be remembered in England, Becket's name was not crossed from a missal in use at Broughton in the late 1530s; in 1548 his feast was still used in dating at the popular level and there was an altar to St Thomas the Martyr at Childwall.[4] The Virgin and saints were patrons of gilds; there was a 'Gild of the Blessed Mary' at Manchester in 1473, and though by 1501 it was the 'Gild or Brotherhood of our Blessed Lady and St George' it remained in being until at least 1540.[5] Devotion to the saints was also reflected

[1] F. C. Eeles, 'On a fifteenth-century York missal formerly used in Broughton', *Chetham Miscellanies*, NS, VI, 8; LRO, DDIn/63/2, DDF/644.
[2] *Prescot Accounts*, 11, 14, 16, 19, 20.
[3] Gastrell, *Notitia Cestriensis*, II, 355–6; *VCH*, VI, 146.
[4] PRO, DL 41/11/37; *Tudor Royal Proclamations*, I, 275–6; Eeles, 'On a fifteenth-century York missal', 4; CRO, EDC 2/4, p. 41; *Lancs. Chantries*, I, 99.
[5] *Mamecestre*, 506; *Lancs. Chantries*, I, 41; PRO, C 1/952/19.

in the preambles of wills, and 19 of the 24 Lancashire wills surviving from the years 1520–40 bequeathed the soul of the testator to 'Our Lady St Mary and all the holy company of saints in heaven'.[1]

There are far fewer references to Christ in contemporary sources, and it would appear that, as Professor Dickens has suggested, men felt more comfortable with the saints than with an all-powerful God. In 1535, for example, while Elizabeth Booth of Standish lay dying, she feared 'lest I stand in jeopardy and danger of God' because she had not reported a marriage contract she had seen take place. If the sermons of Thomas Kirkby were typical of what was heard in the churches, then the sinners of Lancashire had good cause to fear their God.[2] But popular religion was in an important sense Christocentric in its stress on the Eucharist, the consecrated host and the cross. The monks of Burscough had a fragment of the 'true cross', and the splinter at Cartmel must have been a local talisman, for when the priory was suppressed the parishioners petitioned to keep the relic.[3] The rood loft, with a crucifix at its centre, was the most common decoration in the churches; even at the visitations of 1554 and 1557, after the disruptions of the Edwardian years, only three Lancashire churches did not possess a crucifix. The people of Kirkham had their rood loft repaired in 1547, and in the same year a rood loft was added to Broughton chapel for the first time. After their rood had been removed under Edward VI, the parishioners of Cockerham were quick to have another made in the next reign.[4]

The most distinctive feature of popular religion was its preoccupation with death and the ensuring of salvation. This explains the detailed provisions for prayers found in most wills, for the period to be spent in purgatory depended, in part, on the arrangement of masses and prayers. In 1522 Sir Piers Legh, knight and priest, went into minute details: £20 was to be used for masses and alms on the day of burial, and within a month of this 100 priests were to say one mass each, all on the same day, in the form of 20 masses of Jesus, 20 of the Five Wounds, 20 of Our Lady, 20 of the Holy Ghost, 10 of the Trinity and 10 requiem masses. Six years later Henry Farington instructed that the profits of certain lands should go to the priest of the chantry of St Nicholas in Leyland church, that 30 priests were to say a trental for him on St Barnabas' day, that the parish clerk was to

[1] From *L & C Wills*, I–VI, *passim*; *Richmond Wills*, *passim*. For the reasons why so few wills survive and why they provide only a biased sample of the testaments made, see below, p. 70 n.

[2] CRO, EDC 2/2, p. 52; see above, p. 35.

[3] PRO, DL 41/11/36, DL 41/12/11, No. 21.

[4] CRO, EDV 1/1, fo. 147, 1/2, fos. 41v, 42; PRO, SP 10/3/4; Foxe, *Acts and Monuments*, VI, 564.

ring the church bells the day before the trental, that the curate was to receive 8d each year for prayers for his soul every Sunday, and that money was to be used to buy bread, wine and candles for St Nicholas' chapel. Geoffrey Legh, the third son of Sir Piers, made his will in 1546, but it was very similar to his father's 24 years earlier; on the day of the funeral he wanted a trental of requiem masses with 'dirige' and commendations, together with five masses of the Five Wounds, one of the name of Jesus, and another of All Saints. A month later he wanted a requiem with 'dirige' and fifteen other masses to be said in the same church. Poorer men could make equally full provisions if they had no wives and children to think of. The will of William Plumtre, priest, in 1545 was almost wholly concerned with charity and prayers; he left 10s to the church in which he was buried for prayers, half a mark to the Butler chapel at Warrington, 10s to the poor of Warrington and the same to 'my poor neighbours in Hockerton and Southwell', his books to his brother and fellow priests, £4 13s 4d a year for four years for a priest to pray for his soul and those of Sir Thomas and Lady Margaret Butler, his late master and mistress, and all Christians, while at his funeral he wished to have 'St Gregory's trental with "placebo", "dirige" and Commendations'.[1]

Prayers might be requested in other ways; in 1520 a cross was erected in Burnley with an inscription asking for prayers for the soul of John Foldys, a local priest, and after the death of Richard Delves, rector of Warrington, a plaque was placed in his church in 1527 asking for prayers 'of your charity'. A similar plaque was set up for Margaret Bulkeley in 1528, and in 1562 Thomas Leyland asked for an inscription on his tombstone requesting prayers for his soul.[2] Though prayers for the dead fell into disrepute elsewhere and injunctions forbade such prayers, they were requested in Lancashire well into the reign of Elizabeth. In 1572 George Trafford asked that the local poor be given money to pray for his soul and that a priest should say mass for him 'if God's laws be consonant that it so may be', and in 1575 John Braddyll, a Duchy official, asked for prayers for himself, his wife and his friends.[3] Of the printed wills from the 1520s, 11 out of 14 contain requests for prayers, as do 9 of the 10 from the 1530s, and 9 of the 15 from the 1540s. Thereafter the proportion falls considerably, to 17 out of 43 in the 1550s and 6 out of 27 in the 1560s. But it should be remembered that the surviving

[1] *L & C Wills*, VI, 34–5; LRO, DDF/644; *Lancs. Chantries*, I, 72–3; BIY, Reg. Holgate, R/I/29, fos. 75v–76v.
[2] *Palatine Note Book*, 4 vols. IV, 244; Gastrell, *Notitia Cestriensis*, II, 232; *Lancs. Chantries*, I, 110; *L & C Wills*, I, 163.
[3] *Ibid.* II, 107, 158.

69

wills are heavily weighted in a secularist and 'protestant' direction, and requests for prayers must have been far more common than the surviving sample suggests.[1] Even in the more advanced south-east of the county, prayers for the dead were a part of community life; in 1556 two men called at a house in Manchester on business, and were invited in to pray for the soul of the man whose body lay there 'as is the custom in the county of Lancaster'.[2]

Except for a general request for prayers, the cheapest and most popular form of prayer for the dead was the trental, or series of 30 masses, from which special benefits were expected. Those who could afford no more usually asked for a trental, and between 1520 and 1540 about half of those who left money for prayers specified a trental. Richer men, like Hamlet Harrington in 1527 and Robert Langley in 1528, might ask for more than one trental, while the poor trusted that one day their children might provide one or asked for half a trental.[3] The purchase of trentals began to die out in the 1540s, and the last known Lancashire trentals were requested in 1556 and 1558, but these were late dates for an essentially medieval practice. Those who could not afford more elaborate provisions on a long-term basis might leave money for an obit, or prayer said on the anniversary of the donor's death; by 1545 £5 2s 11d had been left to Manchester College for this purpose, and such a bequest was made in that year.[4] Another, though more expensive, means of securing annual prayers was to obtain letters of confraternity from a religious house, which were usually issued in return for gifts to the institution and entitled the recipient to inclusion on the obit roll and an annual mass. Between 1450 and 1531 Durham priory made fifteen confraternity grants to Lancashiremen and their wives, presumably for services to the daughter house at Lytham. In 1507 the second earl of Derby and his wife were given letters by the monks of Ely cathedral, and in 1526 members of the Moore family of Liverpool were affiliated as benefactors of Sheen Charterhouse.[5]

---

[1] The wills which survive are almost entirely those proved at Chester rather than at Richmond or before the rural deans, that is they are mainly from those who left estates worth over £40 and from knights and priests, and they are from the south of the county. Of 109 wills studied, only 17 are not those of knights, priests, gentry or prosperous merchants, and only 28 are from the three northern hundreds. The upper ranks of society in the south of the county were those most likely to come into contact with outside ideas, so that the extant wills are more likely to be non-traditional in temper than a random sample of all wills would be. So few wills survive because the majority were proved by rural deans and are lost.

[2] *Duchy Pleadings*, III, 195.

[3] *L & C Wills*, I, 31–2, II, 203, VI, 63; *Richmond Wills*, 14.

[4] *Lancs. Chantries*, I, 23; *L & C Wills*, II, 63.

[5] *Durham Obituary Roll*, ed. J. Raine, 111–120; LRO, DDK/2/16; *Calendar of Moore MSS*, ed. J. Brownhill, No. 225.

Orthodox piety and practices

For the moderately rich, one of the best ways of ensuring a steady stream of masses and prayers after death was to leave a fixed sum to be paid to a priest over a term of years in return for daily masses, thus constituting a form of temporary chantry. Particularly in the 1520s and 1530s, a number of Lancastrians made this sort of provision, leaving about £4 a year for terms ranging from one to ten years. Four of the fifteen Lancashire wills from the 1520s and three of the ten from the 1530s established temporary chantries, and although only one is known from the 1540s two more were founded in the last years of the next decade. In 1567 Sir John Byron left £10 a year for ten years for a priest to say mass for his soul, though he had the foresight to make alternative arrangements if the law prevented the fulfilment of the terms of his will.[1] But for those who could afford to make it, by far the most satisfactory provision was a chantry, an endowment, usually in land, which yielded an income in perpetuity for a priest to say masses for the souls of the founder and those nominated by him. There is, however, much evidence that by the early Tudor period the institution of endowed prayers was in disrepute, either from disbelief in their efficacy or from distrust of the ability of the clergy to fulfil their obligations under charters of foundation. It remained common practice to leave money for prayers, but the endowment of chantries on a large scale was clearly a thing of the past in most parts of England. At least two counties were exceptions to this general rule. One was Yorkshire, where about 97 chantries, a quarter of the total, were founded after 1480, and the other was Lancashire.[2]

The poverty of the county had retarded the rate of foundation, and only 14 of the 77 chantries with known dates of foundation were established in the fourteenth century. In the fifteenth century new endowments in Lancashire increased to 29, while in other parts of the country the foundation-rate declined from the peak of the previous century. But near the end of the century, when at least in comparison with former years the wealth of the palatinate began to increase, the rate of foundation in Lancashire accelerated. Eight chantries were established in the 1490s, seven in the first decade of the new century, eleven in the second and ten in the 1520s; in this third decade almost £2,000 was given by Lancashire benefactors to chantries, a massive sum when the flow of endowments had almost dried up elsewhere. Over half the foundations which can be dated with

[1] *L & C Wills*, v, 133–6.
[2] Dickens, *English Reformation*, 207–8; Jordan, *Philanthropy in England*, 306; Jordan, *Charities of Rural England*, 366.

some accuracy were made after 1490.[1] Just as the greater prosperity of the county made possible the rebuilding of churches and
the establishment of new schools and chapels, so a form of piety
which had been beyond the reach of all but a handful of illustrious
families became possible for others; about half the post-1490 foundations were made by laymen and women of only moderate status.
Lancashire founded chantries to the end; three were endowed in the
1530s, and though there were no new chantries-proper in the next
decade, three of the five datable stipendiary foundations were made
in the 1540s.

As the foundation of chantries continued until such a late date,
Lancashire acquired an unusually large number of them. There were
91 chantry and stipendiary foundations in the county by the 1540s,
but only 65 in Essex, a county of equal size, 106 in the diocese of
Coventry and Lichfield, more than twice the size of Lancashire, 72
in the diocese of Salisbury, one and a half times the size of the
palatinate, and 60 in the diocese of Norwich, almost twice as large as
Lancashire.[2] The late foundation of many chantries influenced their
character. By the later part of the fifteenth century it had become
customary to link the foundation of a chantry with something of
more general benefit, such as a school or an almshouse.[3] A high
proportion of Lancashire chantries had an additional function of this
sort; nine of the chantries and one of the stipendiary foundations
were linked to schools, and two more were linked to almshouses.
Edward, Lord Mounteagle, planned a chantry hospital at Hornby in
1523, but his will was never fulfilled. At two chantries in Warrington
and two in Manchester, and at the chantries at Eccles and Holinfare,
the incumbents were bound to give alms to the poor. All eleven
stipendiaries and the priests of four chantries were bound by their
foundation charters to say mass for the local people, and six more
chantrists were bound to assist the parochial clergy. In all, the eleven
stipendiaries and 38 of the chantrists had some important function
other than merely celebrating masses for their founders.[4] It is a
reflection of the poor provision of parochial clergy in Lancashire that
so many chantrists had additional tasks, and this shortage is one of
the reasons why there were so many foundations once the county
could afford them.

If the rebuilding of churches and the foundation of chapels and
chantries provide barometers of the attachment of Lancastrians to

[1] The Lancashire figures are based on *Lancs. Chantries, passim*, corrected where
necessary by *VCH*. See also Jordan, *Social Institutions of Lancashire*, 77.
[2] Haigh, 'Reformation in Lancashire', 217–18; Oxley, *Reformation in Essex*, 63;
G. H. Cook, *Medieval Chantries and Chantry Chapels*, 22.
[3] Jordan, *Philanthropy in England*, 306.
[4] *Lancs. Chantries, passim.*

the established religion, the number of men willing to enter the service of the Church at any time represents another guide. Over the rest of the country the population of the monasteries was falling in the decades before their suppression, and as for the secular clergy, episcopal registers suggest that fewer and fewer men were offering themselves for ordination. But in Lancashire, the monasteries were able to attract new recruits until their fall. While the membership of the Premonstratensian Order was falling, the population of the house at Cockersand increased. There had been only thirteen canons in 1381, but by 1488 there were seventeen canons and two novices, by 1497 there were twenty canons and two more novices, and by 1536 the abbey had a complement of twenty-three professed canons. With two more arriving after 1536, the number of canons had doubled in 150 years, and risen by nine in half a century.[1] On a much smaller scale the same thing was happening in priories in the south of the county; in 1517 Holland had four monks and Burscough five, but seven years later the numbers were five and seven, which were maintained until 1536.[2] Though we can give no realistic estimates of their staffs, other local houses were attracting significant numbers of recruits until the suppression. Between 1508 and 1521 23 new monks were ordained at York from Furness Abbey, and between 1510 and 1536 23 Whalley monks were ordained at York or Lichfield. A Whalley monk was ordained in 1534 and another in 1535, two Cartmel canons were ordained in 1535, and three Cockersand canons were ordained in 1536.[3] If all the canons were professed at the canonical age of 24, in 1536 five of the ten canons of Cartmel and eleven of the twenty-one at Cockersand whose ages were recorded, had taken their final vows within the previous ten years, and at Cockersand nine of them within the previous five years.[4]

Figures for the secular clergy are more difficult to verify, but until the suppression of the monasteries made clerical life less attractive, large numbers were being ordained from Lancashire. There were fluctuations from year to year, but the general level of ordinations remained high; for the four following five-year periods after 1508, the numbers of Lancashiremen priested at York and Lichfield were 202, 242, 258 and 234.[5] In both dioceses there was a peak in the early

[1] General trends from D. Knowles and R. N. Hadcock, *Medieval Religious Houses: England and Wales*, 491, 494; Haigh, *Lancs. Monasteries*, 13.

[2] Lich. RO, B/V/1/1, pp. 5, 8, Part 2, p. 28.

[3] Figures from BIY, Regs. Sede Vacante, Bainbridge, Wolsey, Lee; Lich. RO, B/A/1/14, II.

[4] PRO, DL 43/4/12, DL 43/5/4.

[5] These figures and those following are calculated from York and Lichfield registers, as above, n. 3.

1520s, with 48 Lancashire priests ordained at Lichfield in 1522 and 32 in 1523, while at York 27 were ordained in 1524 and 35 in 1525. Recruitment from Lancashire was high compared with other areas. An annual average of 47 Lancastrians were priested between 1508 and 1527, whereas the diocese of Lincoln, four times larger and including the university of Oxford, produced an average of only 104 between 1496 and 1520. Ordinations to the priesthood in the diocese of Exeter, twice the size of Lancashire, averaged 63 a year between 1505 and 1519 and only 34 between 1520 and 1539.[1] Lancashire was still a poor county, and even a meagre living in the Church was attractive to some, while ordination provided an escape route out of the palatinate into secure employment elsewhere. The new buildings and endowments improved clerical opportunities in the county, especially in the parishes south of the Ribble, where the 1541 staff of 244 had risen to 287 by 1548. If ordinations were falling in other parts of England, the parochial clergy must have been declining in numbers, but in south Lancashire the complement was increasing.[2]

It would be difficult to argue and impossible to prove that early Tudor Lancashire was any more pious than the rest of England. But our discussion of conventional popular religion suggests that the tenets and practices of late-medieval Catholicism still retained their hold in the county while disillusionment was spreading in the south. In Lancashire, men were now prepared to invest large sums in the official Church, so that the institutional expression of traditional religion was becoming stronger. This devotion to orthodox religion was belated, just as the Church in Lancashire had been retarded throughout its history. There were no monasteries in the county until the foundation of a small alien priory in 1084, the first native house was not established until 1127, and it was not until the end of the twelfth century that monasteries were founded in any number. Whalley Abbey did not transfer into the county until 1296, and there was no independent Benedictine house until 1319. Provision for the laity was equally slight; the number of parish churches remained almost unchanged between 1296 and 1541, and there were only 118 churches and chapels by 1500 to serve almost 1,900 square miles. This meant, in the crudest terms, that there was a massive backlog to make up in the early sixteenth century. In the reign of Henry VIII, however, increasing wealth made it possible for Lancashiremen to

---

[1] Calculated from Bowker, *Secular Clergy*, 38; A. A. Mumford, *Hugh Oldham, 1452–1519*, 104; D. H. Pill, 'The administration of the diocese of Exeter under Bishop Veysey', *Transactions of the Devonshire Association*, XCVIII, 269–71. The first Exeter figure includes religious.
[2] Haigh, 'Reformation in Lancashire', 227 and n; CRO, EDV 2/3, *passim*; 2/4, *passim*. The staff of the northern parishes remained stable at 125 from 1524 to 1548, though at the latter date 11 of the clergy were ex-monks.

provide the buildings, ornaments and endowments which their Church had lacked, while also securing prayers for their souls. The ability to provide benefactions coincided with the delayed development of Catholic orthodoxy, making Lancashire's loyalty to the established Church that much more conspicuous.

The growth of the textile industry will be discussed in detail later, and it is sufficient here to remark that it expanded considerably in the first half of the sixteenth century. Industrial development was not confined to cloth; the scale of the coal industry increased, with mines centred on Wigan, St Helen's and Manchester. Leland reported that 'Bradshaw hath found much cannel like sea coal in his ground very profitable to him', and that there were 'cannel and coal pits in divers parts of Derbyshire'.[1] In agriculture, there is evidence of a move towards mixed farming, and there was a vigorous onslaught on wastes, forests and moors; especially in Blackburnshire, the period saw the rise rather than the decline of the peasant farmer.[2] In the south of England, new wealth was devoted to secular purposes, municipal improvements, provision for the poor and educational improvements,[3] and also to the purchase of vernacular Bibles and heretical books. But the rising prosperity of Lancashire was directed towards the building of chapels, the repair of churches, the foundation of chantries and the payment of priests, thereby making the clerical life more attractive. Lancashire and the south shared their growing prosperity, but it reinforced their religious differences; in the former, benefactions made orthodox piety even stronger, while southerners were so disillusioned with traditional Catholicism that they put their money to alternative uses.

[1] J. Leland, *Itinerary in England*, ed. L. Toulmin Smith, 5 vols. V, 41, 43. 'Derbyshire' was, of course, West Derby hundred.
[2] J. Thirsk, ed. *Agrarian History of England and Wales*, IV, 89; B. G. Blackwood, 'Lancashire cavaliers and their tenants', *THSLC*, CXVII, 18; M. Brigg, 'The Forest of Pendle in the seventeenth century', *THSLC*, CXIII, 68, 72; G. H. Tupling, *Economic History of Rossendale*, CS, NS, LXXXVI, 43–6, 91–2.
[3] See the tables in Jordan, *Philanthropy in England*, 368, and *Charities of Rural England*, 438–9.

6

Lancashire, Lollards and Protestants

The records of the northern province yield very little evidence of local heresy in the 150 years before the Reformation, and there is certainly no sign of a continuing heretical tradition. A handful of priests was prosecuted in the diocese of Durham in 1402–3 and they may have been members of a small Lollard group in Newcastle, but they seem to have had no lasting influence. In the diocese of Carlisle the only known pre-Reformation heretic had taken part in the Old-castle rising in 1414 and caused a little trouble thereafter. In the diocese of York there were only one or two recorded cases in the fifteenth century, and the first known Tudor heretic, Roger Gargrave of Wakefield, was not a home-grown northern Lollard. He had travelled in the diocese of Lincoln, which had a long history of heresy, and he had acquired at least one of his heterodox views from a Lincolnshire priest. After Gargrave, there is no further trace of heresy in York diocese until 1528, when one of those detected was a Dutchman and the others were sailors from Hull who had seen Lutheranism in action in Germany.[1] In those parts of the dioceses of York and Lichfield which later became the diocese of Chester, there is no evidence of heresy between 1413 (when a Warrington friar with London connections helped Oldcastle to escape from the Tower) and 1503.

It would be impossible to prove that Lancashire was unaffected by heresy until the 1530s, for negative arguments are never entirely convincing. One can never be sure whether the apparent paucity of heretics in mid fifteenth-century England was the result of lack of heresy, lack of persecution or merely lack of records. For periods before the sixteenth century, episcopal registers are usually the only sources for the work of the Church courts, but registers were selective compilations and were often formulary books rather than records of the acts of the bishops. Some heresy cases documented in surviving court books were not entered into bishops' registers.[2] Thus it is only possible to assert an absence of substantial heresy if there is

---

[1] J. A. F. Thomson, *The Later Lollards, 1414–1520*, 192, 194; BIY, Reg. Bainbridge, R/I/26, fos. 75–76; A. G. Dickens, *Lollards and Protestants in the Diocese of York*, 17–18, 24–7.
[2] A. G. Dickens, 'Heresy and the origins of English Protestantism', *Britain and the Netherlands*, ed. J. S. Bromley and E. H. Kossman, II, 50–1.

at least a representative selection of all the classes of records in which heresy cases might appear. The sources which cover Lancashire, for the courts at Lichfield, York, Chester and Richmond, fulfil this criterion, and they make it clear that heterodox ideas were the prerogative of a few isolated individuals rather than of established Lollard communities.

For north Lancashire, it is true that there is a serious gap between the end of the extant registers of the archdeacons of Richmond in 1477 and the first of the records of the Richmond consistory in 1541. But there survives a complete series of archiepiscopal registers at York, together with consistory court books and cause papers. The act books of the court of audience do not begin until 1534, but although some York heresy cases were heard in the consistory[1] there is no record of any Lancashire cases in the consistory records or in the audience act books. In all these sources, the earliest heresy case in the archdeaconry, and one which was in any case outside Lancashire, was that of Stephen Sadler of Kendal in 1536.[2] Kendal was important in the wool, cloth and grain trades of the north, but the rest of Richmond was isolated from the rest of England and Professor Dickens has noted that the archdeaconry was, for 'obvious geographical and social reasons', 'little touched by heretical currents of thought'.[3]

For south Lancashire, the Lichfield registers are complete, we have a consistory act book from the 1470s, and the court books are almost complete from 1524. Lichfield had no separate court of audience and, except for one case which was heard partly in the consistory, all known heresy proceedings were by special commission of the bishop.[4] Such commissions would have no permanent court records, so it is probable that trials were normally entered in the bishops' registers. Thus although the great prosecution of Coventry and Birmingham heretics in 1511–12 was sufficiently important to have a court book of its own, details of the case were copied into Blyth's register.[5] It is true that the burning of the 'seven godly martyrs' from Coventry in 1519 is not mentioned in the register, but entries were made in the 1511 act book and in any case it was much less important to record the names of those who were burned than the names of those who recanted and might later relapse.[6] Thus if any Lancashire heretics were detected, some mention of them ought

[1] Dickens, *Lollards and Protestants*, 241.
[2] BIY, Reg. Lee, R/I/28, fos. 105–105v.
[3] Dickens, *Lollards and Protestants*, 2.
[4] Lich. RO, Reg. Blyth, B/A/1/14, fos. 51–52, 72, Reg. Hales, B/A/1/12, fos. 166–169v.
[5] Lich. RO, B/C/13, *passim*, B/A/1/14, fos. 98–100.
[6] Foxe, *Acts and Monuments*, IV, 557; Lich. RO, B/C/13, fo. 9.

to appear either in the episcopal registers or in the consistory act books, but though there were many from other parts of the diocese of Lichfield there was only one heresy case from Lancashire. The Lichfield sources can be supplemented by the records of the archdeacons of Chester; the registers begin in 1520, and except for the years 1515–23 and 1526–8 the archidiaconal court books are complete from 1502, but they contain no heresy cases. After the see of Chester was founded in 1541, heresy cases ought to have been heard either in the consistory or at the visitation correction court, as they were to be under Mary, but the series of act books contains no record of heresy until the 1550s.

Official documents, it must be admitted, record only those matters which were known to the authorities, and the number of heresy prosecutions in any period reflects not only the extent of heresy but also the vigour of episcopal campaigns against it and the willingness of clergy and churchwardens to make presentations. In view of what has been said on the inadequacy of ecclesiastical control over Lancashire, it is possible that diocesan officials knew little of what went on in the county. But in the early sixteenth century, authority was obsessed with the danger of heresy, and it will be argued below that at the parish level both clergy and laity hated heresy. We may assume, therefore, that the detection-rate for heretics was high, so that the small number of recorded heretics constituted a high proportion of the total. Before the reign of Mary only one known Lancashire heretic was brought to trial in his own diocese, before the dean and a canon of Lichfield in 1503. John Shepherd of Bolton, 'detected, defamed, accused and noised' as guilty of heresy, admitting holding 'divers articles and opinions erroneous and against the faith of Holy Church'. He submitted himself to the court and swore not to 'declare nor teach' any heresy nor to consort with heretics.[1] This is all the record tells us, and it would be unwise to lay much stress on the precise terms of the submission as the statement is brief and impersonal, full of official formulae rather than details of Shepherd's case. He was probably detected at the visitation of the archdeaconry of Chester which took place in 1502–3,[2] and if there was a Lollard group of any size in Bolton, other members would surely have been discovered. Heretics who recanted, as Shepherd did, were usually expected to prove their sincerity by reporting any heterodox acquaintances, but there is no sign that the Bolton man ever did so. If there was an heretical community in Bolton, there is no further trace of it until the 1550s, and by then its members were of an Anglican rather than a Lollard cast of mind.[3]

[1] Lich. RO, Reg. Blyth, B/A/1/14, fo. 72.
[2] CRO, EDC 1/1, fo. 77; *Duchy Pleadings*, I, 20.   [3] See below, pp. 185–8.

It seems certain that Lollardy never established itself firmly enough in Lancashire to leave more than the merest trace in the records. We must ask, therefore, why the county remained almost immune from its influence when areas equally far from the original Lollard centres were penetrated. Lollardy was first established among the lower classes of England when the academic Wycliffites left Oxford and formed conventicles in the small towns and villages of the south-east in which they settled. When the episcopal campaign against heresy and the failure of the Oldcastle rising stripped the movement of its leaders and its political objectives, Lollardy became a proletarian religion surviving in small pockets of the districts in which it had first been popularised. Thereafter, the heresy was spread among artisans and tradesmen by the more mobile elements in society, the wool-dealers and leather-sellers who provided village communities with their main links with the outside world.[1] From its centres in the Chilterns, London, Essex and the weaving towns of south-west Kent, heresy spread north and west until by the early sixteenth century Lollard groups could be found in all the English dioceses south of York.[2] By the late fifteenth century Lollardy had established itself in some strength in the Coventry area, and in 1488 a heretic was found as far to the north-west as Ashbourne, just north of Derby.[3]

But although heresy was strong in Coventry and Birmingham by 1511–12, Lollardy does not seem to have spread much further west or north. There were one or two cases on the Welsh borders, but the Shropshire curate who preached against fasting in 1528 had been under the influence not of Lollardy but of 'secte Lutheriane' and especially George Constantine.[4] In the diocese of Lichfield, the only known heresy cases detected north of Coventry were those at Ashbourne and Bolton. In the east of England, too, the expansion of Lollardy was restricted, and there is very little evidence of heresy moving from the dioceses of Lincoln and Norwich into Yorkshire until late in the 1520s. Even thereafter, the Yorkshire heretics were not members of Lollard groups but individuals who had come into contact with dissentient views in other parts of the country, including a sailor from Hull, two tailors who had worked in London and Colchester, and a Dewsbury man who had acquired his heresy in

---

[1] J. F. Davis, 'Lollard survival and the textile industry in the south-east of England', *Studies in Church History*, ed. G. J. Cuming, III, 194–7; Dickens, *English Reformation*, 24–5; Thomson, *Later Lollards*, 2.

[2] *Ibid.* 173–91; Dickens, 'Heresy and the origins of English Protestantism', 51–7.

[3] Lich. RO, Reg. Hales, B/A/1/12, fos. 166–169v.

[4] Lich. RO, Reg. Blyth, B/A/1/14, fos. 51–52.

Suffolk. Other heretics detected in Yorkshire were not local men at all, but at least three Dutchmen, a Northumbrian, and a Londoner whose only links with the county were by origin, and through occasional visits to his family.[1]

The obvious reason for the failure of heresy to penetrate the north-west is the simple geographical one; the area was at the opposite corner of England from the old Lollard centres, and contact between the two was disrupted by the Derbyshire Peaks and the Pennine chain. Particular stress has been laid on the role of highly mobile cloth-workers in the dissemination of Lollardy, but their importance was confined almost entirely to the south-east. From the middle of the fifteenth century the independent weaver in Kent was being depressed to the status of a wage-earner, employed by a clothier who had his own spinners, weavers, shearmen and fullers. Such wage-earning weavers had no fixed capital in looms to tie them to their villages, and they hawked their skills from employer to employer.[2] But until very late in the sixteenth century, the structure of the Lancashire textile industry was much more primitive. The vast majority of clothiers in the county were small men who worked at home with their families, owning one loom and a spinning wheel, and they almost always worked a small farm too.[3] As late as 1577 the weavers of Lancashire were petitioning against the restriction of middlemen, arguing that they themselves were 'poor cottagers whose ability will not stretch neither to buy any substance of wools to maintain work and labour, nor yet to fetch the same'.[4] The weavers of Lancashire were not mobile heresy-carriers, but sedentary workers tied to their villages by the lands and looms which gave them an independence they would not willingly abandon. Heretical weavers were not attracted into the county from the south because there was no employment for a wage-labourer who did not have his own loom.[5]

In the south-east of England the middlemen, who sold the wool and bought the cloth, had contacts in the villages of Kent and East

[1] Dickens, *Lollards and Protestants*, 17–21, 24–6, 30–7, 48–50.
[2] Davis, 'Lollard survival and the textile industry', 198–200. For other areas see R. B. Westerfield, *Middlemen in English Business*, 275–6, 292.
[3] N. Lowe, *Lancashire Textile Industry in the Sixteenth Century*, 20–1, 27–34.
[4] PRO, SP 12/117/38. This was an attempt to prevent the enforcement of the 1552 act which restricted the activities of the broggers essential to small weavers. The clothiers of Lancashire and Yorkshire had tried to get exemption from the act in 1562 (P. J. Bowden, *Wool Trade in Tudor and Stuart England*, 119).
[5] Although Professor Dickens has stressed the role of weavers in carrying heresy into Yorkshire, the structure of the West Riding cloth industry was very much like that of Lancashire, and the Halifax weavers were exempted from the act against middlemen (H. Heaton, *The Yorkshire Woollen and Worsted Industries*, 2nd edn. 92–3).

Anglia, and also in London, and formed obvious links between Lollard groups.[1] But the contacts created by Lancashire dealers were rather different. The flax and linen yarn used by county weavers came mainly from Ireland, while wool came predominantly from Lancashire itself and was supplemented by wool from Yorkshire and Ireland.[2] The wool and yarn broggers who brought the weavers their raw material had no contact with heresy, and the cloth-dealers who bought the finished product had no notable heretical connections either. One or two Lancashire clothiers took their wares to Southampton, but until the reign of Elizabeth their occurrence in the cloth records of the port is a rarity. Later in the century Lancashire cloth was sold all over England, but in the early years the industry was not large enough to need such widespread markets, and cloth went to markets in Lancashire or to Halifax, Beverley and occasionally Hull. The first known sale of Lancashire cloth outside the county was not until 1535 in Herefordshire, and the first recorded sale in London was in 1543.[3] Thus the north–south trading contacts which might have brought heresy into Lancashire did not exist until the 1530s; instead the lines of communication ran west–east.

The isolation of Lancashire from the main centres of heretical activity is further illustrated by the example of the secret book trade of the 'Christian Brethren'. The trade was conducted between men who knew and trusted each other in the back-rooms of houses and inns in London and the ports of the south coast, and the only entry was by introduction. Even if they had known of such an organisation, Lancashiremen could not have broken into it. The trade took books inland to old Lollard centres such as Steeple Bumpstead, Colchester and Bury St Edmunds, but to go further north was to court disaster; when George Constantine tried to extend the trade only as far as Whitchurch, the result was a heresy prosecution.[4] The considerable coastal trade between London and Rye, King's Lynn, Colchester and Exeter provided a ready-made distribution network for heretical books, but Lancashire's sea links with Cumbria and Ireland brought no such opportunities.[5]

---

[1] Davis, 'Lollard survival and the textile industry', 191, 194.

[2] Lowe, *Lancashire Textile Industry*, 7–12; A. K. Longfield, *Anglo-Irish Trade in the Sixteenth Century*, 77–8, 88–90; Bowden, *Wool Trade in Tudor and Stuart England*, 71.

[3] B. C. Jones, 'Westmorland packhorsemen in Southampton', *Transactions of the Cumberland and Westmorland Antiquarian and Archaeological Society*, NS, LXIX, 67–8; Lowe, *Lancashire Textile Industry*, 58–64; CRO, EDC 2/7, fos. 4v, 10v.

[4] E. G. Rupp, *Studies in the Making of the English Protestant Tradition*, 6–14; Lich. RO, Reg. Blyth, B/A/1/14, fos. 51–52.

[5] Davis, 'Lollard survival and the textile industry', 195. Even in the 17th century there was very little trade between the ports of the north-west and those of the south-east (T. S. Willan, *The English Coasting Trade, 1600–1750*, 111, 167, 184).

Lancashire had little to attract outsiders. Some merchants travelled from other areas to the county's markets, and in 1529, for example, a Leicester man bought cattle at Lancaster fair to drive back to his own town. But until late in the century, when Manchester and Rochdale became important trading centres, the range of influence of Lancashire markets was probably as restricted as that of Preston, used almost exclusively by those living within seven miles of it.[1] There were no employment opportunities for outsiders in the cloth industry and Lancashire wage-rates were low,[2] so that migration was away from rather than towards the county. Robert Slater and John Hargreaves gave up their lands in Clitheroe and headed south, to Southampton and Ely respectively, and in 1554 John Pennington of Wigan left his wife and went off to London. It was found in 1569 that a Childwall woman had been seeking consolation elsewhere since her husband 'went to service to London because he had very little living at home'.[3] The Elizabethan records of several of the London companies show that by the middle of the reign Lancashire was one of the two or three counties which provided the largest numbers of apprentices.[4] Such men left one of the poorest counties of England in search of better lives elsewhere, and they left for good. A steady stream of Lancastrians went to the capital to make their fortunes and several were successful, but though many remembered the county of their birth in their wills, few ever returned.[5]

It is thus easy to see how the transmission of Lollardy into Lancashire by its usual lay emissaries was impeded, but by the middle of the reign of Henry VIII, of course, Lollardy was not the only brand of heresy, and laymen were not the only carriers. The anticlericalism of Lollardy had made it unattractive to priests, but by the late 1520s the new Lutheranism, with its strong academic background, was gaining influence in the clerical ranks. It was not long before this was reflected in Lancashire, albeit on a very small scale. In March 1533 the archdeacon of Richmond's vicar-general ordered 'Sir William, parish priest of Dalton' to surrender a book called *Unio Dissidentium* to the abbot of Furness, who would forward it to the vicar-general. The volume was a collection of texts favourable to the new theology, and it had been banned by the

---

[1] PRO, DL 3/5, H 12; H. B. Rogers, 'The market area of Preston in the sixteenth and seventeenth centuries', *Geographical Studies*, III(1), 51–2.

[2] Thus compare wages in Lancashire and Devon in 1595: millers 48s 0d and 62s 0d per annum; female servants 10s 0d and 18s 0d per annum; most tradesmen 8d and 12d per day (*Tudor Royal Proclamations*, III, 149–51).

[3] *CCR*, I, 154–5, 423; CRO, EDV 1/1, fo. 139, EDC 2/8, fo. 275.

[4] I owe this information to a pupil, Miss Anne Scarth, who has worked through the records of the Stationers, Carpenters, Skinners and Scriveners.

[5] Jordan, *Social Institutions of Lancashire*, 98–102.

ecclesiastical authorities.[1] Four years later a friar living at Furness sent Thomas Cromwell a report on the religious state of the area and among the priests he mentioned was William Rede, by then school-master at Dalton and clearly our 'Sir William'. Rede had preached against the authority of the pope and had condemned conservative clergy – foolish things to do in those parts. He had also drawn attention to his advanced opinions by teaching his scholars from Erasmus' *Paraphrases*; his radical views led to his dismissal from the school, and thereafter he disappears from view.[2] How Rede and his heretical book got to Dalton in Furness is not clear; he had not been there in 1524, he was not ordained at York or Lichfield, and though he was certainly an educated man he is not known to have attended a university.

It must have been from Rede that John Henshaw, also of Dalton parish, received his heterodox ideas.[3] In 1533 it was said that Henshaw was in touch with 'suspect persons' and 'evil opinions', which he had apparently been teaching, and he was made to swear an oath before the chancellor of York that he would reform. His offences, whatever they were, were not thought to be dangerous, since the vicar-general became his surety for good behaviour, the abbot of Furness provided him with food and lodging for a period, and his wish to enter the priesthood was respected. By December 1536 he was serving as priest and schoolmaster at Hawkshead in Dalton parish, where he taught that images were of no value. At Henshaw's suggestion a pupil mocked the images in the chapel, seized a sword from the image of St George and broke it over the saint's head, shouting 'Let me see how now thou canst fight again'. The scholar disappeared, but Henshaw was indicted before the king's justices at Lancaster in August 1537. As far as is known, no action was taken against the erring schoolmaster at the assizes, nor was he tried for heresy at York, and he may have been saved by changes in official policy on images. By 1539 at least he was back at Hawkshead and he seems not to have relinquished his advanced views, for he tried to help a young married man to be ordained.[4]

Rede and Henshaw were the only two clerical 'heretics' known to have worked in Lancashire before the reign of Edward VI. William

---

[1] PRO, SP 1/75, fo. 63 (*L & P*, VI, 287); Strype, *Ecclesiastical Memorials*, I(1), 118, 254, I(2), 64–5.
[2] PRO, SP 1/118, fo. 9 (*L & P*, XII(1), 842).
[3] The two men were mentioned in the same letter; also, for the only two known north-Lancashire heretics to have been in the same isolated parish by coincidence alone is most unlikely.
[4] PRO, SP 1/75, fo. 63; BIY, Reg. Lee, R/I/28, fos. 195, 196v; PRO, PL 25/15, m. 19d; CRO, EDC 2/4, fo. 30v.

Rede's only offence was possession of a banned book, and in 1537 it was his opponents at Dalton, not he, who were breaking the law. Henshaw criticised images only two years before royal injunctions ordered the clergy to preach against their veneration, and he may have been questioning only the grosser superstitions which surrounded images. Either the two men were not dangerous or the Church authorities were unbelievably lax, for the only action taken against Rede was the confiscation of his book, while Henshaw was ordained after he had been spreading 'evil opinions', and no punishment seems to have been meted out for the image-breaking episode. Ecclesiastical officials did not find such hints of heresy disturbing, and this complacency was only possible where heresy posed no major threat. Rede and Henshaw did not manage to establish a community of heretics at Dalton, and the parish remained as conservative as the rest of northern Lancashire.

We are still left, then, with very little evidence of Lancashire heresy, but one way in which local men did acquire heterodox views was by leaving the county. The contrast between Lancashire and much of southern England is illustrated by the fact that, by and large, all who remained in the county remained orthodox, while several of those who left became heretics. There were two main routes into heresy, one to Lollardy via trade and the other to Lutheranism via learning. John Atkinson, a native of Garstang, was apprenticed to a painter in Coventry, and he was attracted by personal contacts with Lollard tradesmen into an heretical circle in the town. He was brought to trial in 1511, and though the court record gives a full account of his movements there is no sign that he had ever returned to Lancashire.[1] Robert Singleton of Single Hall was apparently converted during his studies at both Oxford and Cambridge. He became chaplain to Anne Boleyn, an agent of Thomas Cromwell in Dover, and by 1543 he was working among the heretics of Kent. In 1543 Singleton was forced to recant his heresies and in the following year he was executed, ostensibly for treason. He had been vicar of Preston since his presentation as a boy in 1516, but after his university career he worked in London and Kent and had a dispensation for absence from Preston. Although Singleton seems to have been Lancashire's first Protestant martyr, he contributed nothing to the religion of his own county.[2]

If a Lancashire-born emigré such as Atkinson or Singleton did become a heretic, he had one more reason for not returning to the county. Professor Dickens has argued that one of the reasons why so

---

[1] Lich. RO, B/C/13, fos. 2, 5, 7.
[2] I have discussed his career in detail in 'Reformation in Lancashire', 252–6. *DNB* is clearly wrong in calling him a 'Roman Catholic divine'.

few heretics were detected in the diocese of York was the natural sympathy of the laity for any man opposed to the priesthood, which helped in evading arrest.[1] In Lancashire, on the contrary, heretics faced recrimination and danger. The clergy were usually local men working in the parishes of their birth, and there was no marked antipathy towards them. The considerable attachment to and invest- ment in the pious practices of conventional religion made heretics unpopular, for in Lancashire they were seen as men who attacked images, rood and altars.[2] 'Lutherous' was used as a term of abuse in the 1530s for those with anti-clerical leanings, and the slightest imputation of heresy was bitterly resented; in 1537 Thomas Hoskyn was accused by his wife's cousin of refusing to have his child christened, and he retaliated immediately with a slander suit.[3] Among the common people false charges of heresy were made against those who had offended the community. In 1520 the people of Clitheroe complained at their halmote court that the miller, Nicholas Ranfurth, had been demanding excessive tolls, and added that 'the said Nicholas behaves as if he were heretic and fanatic, and he is deemed among his neighbours not to hold the Catholic faith'. Ranfurth's only religious failing was, in fact, an over-eager piety, and the court thought little of the accusation. The Duchy auditor was consulted on the tolls and the miller was fined half a mark, but there was no further mention of heresy and the ecclesiastical authorities were not called in.[4]

When there really were heretics in Lancashire, in the reign of Mary, they were very soon denounced. Geoffrey Hurst did not attend church in 1553–4, which prompted his neighbours to call him 'heretic and Lollard' and report him to officials; he had to flee from the county. By 1554 George Marsh had not lived in Lancashire for three or four years, and he made only occasional visits to see his family, but it was on one of these that he was delated to a local justice and arrested.[5] The hostility of the people made northern England a dangerous place for radicals. On the other side of the Pennines, the Freez brothers fled to York in 1546 to escape persecution in London, but they were immediately arrested in their home town, and under Mary a Suffolk man visiting Scarborough was picked up as a heretic.[6] Lancashiremen were willing to report heresy, and the authorities were willing to act. The earl of Derby had no sympathy for religious deviance; he voted against most of the reformist

---

[1] Dickens, *Lollards and Protestants*, 243.
[2] Foxe, *Acts and Monuments*, VIII, 565–6.
[3] *Duchy Pleadings*, II, 32; CRO, EDC 2/2, p. 138. [4] *CCR*, I, 58.
[5] Foxe, *Acts and Monuments*, VIII, 562, VII, 39–40, 45.
[6] Dickens, *Lollards and Protestants*, 30–2, 230, 246.

legislation under Edward VI, and in 1554 an anti-Lutheran tract was dedicated to him.[1] The commission of the peace was composed predominantly of conservatives, some of whom were active in the pursuit of heresy under Mary, and even in 1564 19 of the 25 J.P.s were reported as 'unfavourable' towards the new religion.[2] If heretics kept away from Lancashire they were wise, for in the county they would not have remained free for long.

Before the middle of the century fear and hatred of heresy was directed not against local deviants, for there were none or they were too few to provoke concern, but against those who guided policy in London. In 1533 a priest from Croston was lamenting the fact that the faith was under attack from the king, who would 'put down the order of priests and destroy the sacrament', and this, he thought, would lead to rebellion in the north.[3] In 1536 the Lancashire rebels complained that the Church was 'piteously and abominably confounded' by 'certain heretics in our time', and asserted that 'heretics' among the king's advisers had 'procured and purposed against the commonwealth certain acts of law under the colour of Parliament, which, put in execution, the estate of Poverty can no longer bear nor suffer'.[4] This suggests that men felt isolated and out of sympathy with the government and the capital, and to an extent this was because Lancashire avoided the contamination of heresy. It will be suggested later that the county fought the Reformation more vigorously and with greater success than did any other part of England. The peculiarity of the area thus has to be explained, and although Professor Dickens has warned against exaggeration of the differences between north and south, some of the reasons seem clear: Lancashire was relatively isolated, and therefore it was relatively backward.

[1] *Journals of the House of Lords*, I, 331, 384, 401, 421; Strype, *Ecclesiastical Memorials*, III(1), 266–7.

[2] See below, pp. 191–2, 213.

[3] *L & P*, VI, 964, printed in H. Ellis, *Original Letters*, 1st series, II, 43.

[4] *Derby Correspondence*, 47–8, 51–2.

7

The county community and the outside world

Early Tudor Lancashire was cut off from the mainstream of English life. Geographically, the county was far from London and the major ports, and England's main north–south artery lay on the opposite side of the Pennines. Except for the Isle of Man, which interested few but the earl of Derby, and Ireland, which exercised a wholly conservative influence, Lancashire was not on the road to anywhere. Soldiers on their way to Ireland embarked at Chester rather than at Liverpool until well into the reign of Elizabeth.[1] Trade links with the south were not strong until towards the end of the century; in 1561–2 Devon sent more cloth-merchants to London than did Lancashire, and Gloucestershire sent four times as many.[2] Commercial contacts were usually with other northerners, or with the Scots and Irish, and military contacts were with the same groups; Lancashire soldiers always went north against the Scots rather than to the Continent. With its own structures of government in the Duchy and the palatinate, Lancashire was not quite part of England. Even a hardened traveller like Camden was troubled 'with a kind of dread' as he approached the county boundary, but he pressed on 'trusting in the divine assistance'.[3]

Lancashire gentlemen might occasionally be taken to the capital by their duties in local government or as members of Parliament, but contacts of this kind involved only small numbers. In any case, it is clear that the Crown and its officers normally dealt with justices of the peace through the earl of Derby, and over half of Lancashire's handful of parliamentary seats were regularly held by outsiders.[4] Very few gentlemen made the transition from local service to national politics, and Sir Thomas Holcroft, a protégé of Somerset, was the only example in the first half of the century. Between 1529 and 1558 the county provided only two of the palatinate and Duchy legal officers, and even under Elizabeth only two of the twenty-two palatinate justices were local men.[5] The earl of Derby,

[1] R. Muir, *History of Liverpool,* 68, 76.
[2] G. D. Ramsay, 'The distribution of the cloth industry in 1561–2', *EHR,* LVII, 362.   [3] J. Parkes, *Travel in England in the Seventeenth Century,* 300.
[4] Watson, 'Lancashire gentry and the public service', 35.
[5] *Ibid.* 25; R. Somerville, *History of the Duchy of Lancaster, 1265–1603,* 470–1, 473–4.

one of the richest and most powerful peers in the kingdom, was consistently excluded from the councils of government. It is true that the third earl was belatedly admitted to the Privy Council in August 1551, but he was explicitly forbidden to attend meetings unless summoned and the appointment was merely a sop to his injured pride after he had been commanded to renounce the title of king of Man.[1]

In the first half of the century the Lancashire textile industry had not yet integrated the county into the economic structure of England. Cloth manufacturing in the county was considered small-scale, backward and in need of assistance, and was generally exempted from restrictive legislation. Its organisation in the county remained primitive and its markets predominantly northern, until the precocious growth of the cloth towns in the middle and later years of the century expanded production and exports.[2] The traditionalist outlook of the industry in Lancashire is illustrated by the religion of those who worked in it, for though a few weavers were Protestants by the 1550s the county produced no Humphrey Monmouth or Richard Hilles. Adam Byrom of Salford was one of the most successful of the pre-Elizabethan merchants, dealing mainly in wool but also importing iron from Spain, yet when he made his will in 1556 it was couched in terms as conservative as his mother's had been thirty years before. Ellis Hall of Manchester made a fortune in the cloth trade in the reign of Edward VI, but he was no radical in religion; he had a vision of the Five Wounds, and when the Elizabethan settlement was imposed he refused to attend Anglican services.[3]

The sea trade of Lancashire did not assist contact with more advanced areas. Liverpool had only thirteen vessels and 200 seamen in 1557, and by 1565, after an outbreak of plague, there were only twelve ships, all of less than 40 tons, and 80 sailors to man them. Liverpool traded with only a few ports, all in Catholic areas, especially Dublin, Bilbao and Lisbon.[4] Dalton, in the north of the county, was even smaller, and we know only of isolated cargoes entering or leaving; the trade of the port was entirely coastal, with Chester, Scotland and Ireland, though occasionally ships arrived

[1] *APC*, III, 328–9; *CSPF*, I, 119–20.
[2] B. Hewart, 'The cloth trade in the north of England in the sixteenth and seventeenth centuries', *Economic Journal*, X, 21–3; *VCH*, II, 561; A. P. Wadsworth and J. de L. Mann, *The Cotton Trade and Industrial Lancashire, 1600–1780*, 5–9; J. J. Bagley, 'Matthew Markland, a Wigan mercer', *TLCAS*, LXVIII, 61–2, 68; Lowe, *Lancashire Textile Industry*, 58–80.
[3] *L & C Wills*, I, 44, II, 180; see below, p. 144.
[4] Muir, *History of Liverpool*, 66, 68–9, 84; *Chester Customs Accounts, 1301–1566*, ed. K. P. Wilson, 84–90.

from Bristol and Cornwall.[1] The much more significant port of Chester handled most of Lancashire's trade, but there was no regular coasting traffic to London, and Chester dealt mainly with the ports of Catholic Ireland, Spain and France. The first port book of 1565–6 shows that Chester ships took small quantities of Lancashire cloth only to Bordeaux, La Rochelle and the Biscayan ports.[2] Lancashire had no Newcastle or Hull, with established coal and grain links with London and trade with the Protestants of Germany, Scandinavia and the Low Countries – contacts which were so important in introducing reformist ideas to the east coast of England.

Lack of contact with other areas forced county society to be introspective and self-sufficient. Lancashiremen appear to have had little interest in what went on outside their own shire; only 2% of the county's charitable bequests between 1480 and 1660 went to other areas; half of this was to Cheshire, and most of the gifts were made after 1610.[3] Only a handful of families looked to other counties for spouses for their children, and only the Stanleys did so regularly, but even that illustrious family was sometimes satisfied with Lancastrians such as Osbaldestons and Barlows. The heralds' visitations of 1533 and 1567 reveal very few non-Lancashire names among the pedigrees, and though occasionally a bride or groom was found in Cheshire, Yorkshire, Cumberland or Westmorland, this was extremely rare. Even between 1590 and 1640, 79% of all marriages made by justices of the peace or future justices were to girls from Lancashire or immediately adjacent counties.[4] This tendency towards local marriages and the relatively small number of gentry families enforced intermarriage if social inferiors were not to be admitted, so that all the major county families were related and the second rank of gentry consisted mainly of cadet branches of leading families. Marriages to relations were sometimes attempts to maintain estates intact without dispersal among heirs, and this was apparently the case in the Kirkby family in 1547 and the Towneleys in 1556. The ruling group in the county therefore formed a compact and interrelated coterie; the deputy-lieutenants of Tudor Lancashire came from a circle of no more than ten families, and they were all related.[5]

[1] Bouch and Jones, *Economic and Social History of the Lake Counties*, 118.
[2] D. M. Woodward, 'The foreign trade of Chester in the reign of Elizabeth I', University of Manchester M.A. thesis, 1965, 14–15, 102; *Chester Customs Acccounts*, 74–6, 82–4.
[3] Jordan, *Social Institutions of Lancashire*, 103.
[4] P. R. Long, 'The wealth of the magisterial class in Lancashire, *c.* 1590–1640', University of Manchester M.A. thesis, 1968, 10.
[5] Watson, 'Lancashire gentry, 1529–1558', 37; B. Coward, 'The lieutenancy of Lancashire and Cheshire in the sixteenth and early seventeenth centuries', *THSLC*, CXIX, 43.

Intermarriage within a small number of families meant that dispensations from affinity and consanguinity were frequently necessary. Between 1534 and 1535 the archbishop of Canterbury's faculty office issued over three hundred marriage dispensations, but although couples resident in the diocese of Lincoln claimed only 11 licences, those in Bath and Wells 6 and in London diocese 4, 67 dispensations were issued for the diocese of Lichfield and 65 for York, very many of them for persons with fairly common Lancashire names. On this evidence, at least, intermarriage seems to have been more common in Lancashire than elsewhere, while the number of dispensations recorded in these years suggests that the marriage patterns found among the gentry were followed by lower orders of society. The marriage of Richard Bold and Elizabeth Gerard, both of leading families, shows how complex the web of relationships could be; they had to obtain four separate dispensations, covering third and fourth and fourth and fourth degrees of consanguinity, and third and fourth and fourth and fourth degrees of affinity.[1] At a lesser level in society, marriages took place within a restricted geographical circle, and the way in which all those who counted in a small community were related is illustrated by the example of Queen Mary's Grammar School at Clitheroe in the second half of the century. The governors named in the foundation charter of 1554 were all interrelated, and all the Elizabethan governors, masters and tenants of the school lands were relatives. Even when outsiders with a university education came in, they were soon integrated into local society. The earliest known master, Robert Walbank, married the widow of one of the governors in 1573, and when he retired he was elected a governor himself and succeeded as master by his nephew, William, who married the grand-daughter of a governor.[2]

At all levels of society, family relationships bolstered community of interest, and except at times of extreme crisis the county presented a solid front to outsiders and outside influences. Even during the Pilgrimage of Grace, the county gentry retained some sort of unity. Few gentlemen are known to have joined the rebels, and when the county did divide it was between north and south, again emphasising the role of local influences; almost all the gentry who raised men to serve under the earl of Derby against the rebels were from south Lancashire.[3] Under Elizabeth, class and family loyalties proved stronger than either religious differences or allegiance to the Crown; conformist magistrates were willing to assist recusants, who were frequently their relations, while county leaders complained

[1] *FOR*, 1-40, 107-8.
[2] C. W. Stokes, *Queen Mary's Grammar School, Clitheroe*, 7-8, 27, 163-7, 199, 205.
[3] Haigh, *Lancs. Monasteries*, 80-1.

vociferously when Catholic gentlemen were removed from the commission of the peace and replaced by Protestants of inferior social status.[1]

Not only was Lancashire isolated from the rest of England, but communities were often isolated from each other within the county. Much of the county was difficult to farm, and there population was sparse. The Pennine spurs, the fells of Bowland and Rossendale and much of Lonsdale, with poor soil, difficult terrain and inadequate drainage, made intensive arable farming impossible, while on the Fylde coast and in the south-west the undrained mosses and wet land prompted pastoral agriculture.[2] Stock-farming naturally provided less employment than arable, and population density was low in these areas. The pattern of settlement was one of small, isolated hamlets and scattered homesteads, a tendency strengthened by the small landholding which made villages compact.[3] The parishes were too large and the distances between settled areas too great for the parish to have been a viable social unit, and society was broken up into smaller units centring on the chapel or small township. The geography of the county reinforced this structure; the marshes, the barren moorland and the many rivers which ran down from the Pennines divided the county into small sections. Many villages were separated from their parish churches by four or five miles of bad road, moorland and marshes, or by a river which was impassable in poor weather.[4]

This pattern of settlement had important effects on social structure and habits, and ultimately on the religious development of the area. Where small communities were the rule, the dominance of the local gentry was assured, and many hamlets were almost petty kingdoms. The isolation of townships made them economically and socially self-sufficient, and interference from outside was neither usual nor welcome. With its poor communications Lancashire was not easily influenced by change, and its history was always two or three steps behind that of the rest of England. The district had not been shired by Domesday, and there were no monasteries until the very end of the eleventh century, while thereafter foundation proceeded only very slowly. The establishment of grammar schools in any significant number did not begin until the movement was well

[1] PRO, SP 12/240, fos. 292–293v; BM, Cotton MS Titus B II, fos. 239–240.
[2] H. B. Rogers, 'Land use in Tudor Lancashire: the evidence of Final Concords, 1450–1558', *Publications of the Institute of British Geographers*, XXI, 85–8.
[3] G. H. Tupling, 'The causes of the Civil War in Lancashire', *TLCAS*, LXV, 2; Thirsk, *Agrarian History of England and Wales*, IV, 87–9; Bouch and Jones, *Economic and Social History of the Lake Counties*, 18–21.
[4] e.g. *Lancs. Chantries*, I, 162, II, 171, 174.

under way in other areas, and the foundation of chantries reached its peak a century after the rest of England. In the early sixteenth century, the monasteries in the south of England had ceased to be significant in the lives of local communities, but in Lancashire they still played an important role. The same may have been true of pre-Tridentine Catholicism in general; it is certainly true that in the towns of southern England many were increasingly critical of the old faith' and turned to the new Protestantism which was being preached, but in Lancashire there is little indication of a drift from orthodoxy.

Not only did heresy have great difficulty in reaching Lancashire, but county society was not the sort of seed-bed in which it could easily grow. With the sole exception of Manchester, the county's towns were small and weak. The pressures of the Scots in the fourteenth century, the long-term effects of plague, and the absence of extensive trade prevented the emergence of vigorous urban communities. Because of their poverty Lancaster and Preston did not send members to parliament between 1331 and 1529, while Liverpool and Wigan were unrepresented between 1307 and 1547.[1] At Liverpool the population was only 700 in 1565, and although this had reached 1,000 by 1590 it was still, apparently, below the level of 1346.[2] John Leland found Ribchester 'now a poor thing', in 1544 the four parliamentary boroughs were listed as 'decayed towns', and in 1557 Duchy officers reported that Lancaster was 'in great ruin and decay'.[3] Wigan, Preston and Lancaster were easily dominated by local gentry with their retained thugs, and the authority of the earl of Derby in Liverpool was rivalled only by that of the Duchy of Lancaster's chancellor.[4] The towns of Lancashire were neither thriving nor dynamic, but it was in an urban environment, and especially in a situation of growth and social change, that Protestantism flourished.

If the economic development of the Lancashire towns was retarded, so was that of its rural areas. The switch to mixed farming which was such an important feature of the agrarian history of early modern England was sluggish in Lancashire; little corn was produced for the market, cattle were still sold off to graziers from other areas for fattening, and the division of the cultivated area into innumerable small holdings made any change difficult.[5] William

---

[1] H. H. Strickland, *Lancashire Members of Parliament, 1290–1550*, 110–18.
[2] Muir, *History of Liverpool*, 66.
[3] Leland, *Itinerary in England*, II, 21; *L & P*, XIX(1), 25, No. 3; W. O. Roper, *Materials for the History of Lancaster*, 156.
[4] See e.g. Watson, 'Lancashire gentry and the public service', 33–4, 40.
[5] Thirsk, *Agrarian History of England and Wales*, IV, 3, 5, 9–10, 87–9.

Farington, an expansionist Lancashire gentleman, considerably en-
larged his estates, but he did so not to produce for the market but
to feed his family and a growing staff of servants. Farington commuted labour services on his estates in 1553, but other landlords
were less progressive; ploughing, harrowing, reaping and loading
services were exacted until the Civil War, and there is evidence of
an increased imposition of labour services towards the middle of the
seventeenth century.[1] A marked tendency to increase entry fines,
which was common in other parts of the north from at least the
middle of the sixteenth century, is not noticeable in Lancashire
until almost a century later.[2] These conservative features meant that
social relationships in rural Lancashire were relatively tranquil. In
the fifteenth century there had been a gradual fall in the number of
common fields, and this continued through the following century
until by the end of Elizabeth's reign the common fields covered
only a small proportion of the cultivated area, even in the lowlands.
Enclosure seems to have caused little dislocation; the number of
occupiers and the size of the fields in each township were both small,
so that agreement on enclosure was often possible and it took place
piecemeal and without conflict.[3] Enclosure in Lancashire did not
lead to the widespread grievances which characterised the Midlands
and East Anglia, and which probably contributed towards the
protestantisation of these areas.

Although it has been argued[4] that agrarian discontent was an
important motive for the Pilgrimage of Grace in at least some parts
of the north, there is very little evidence that this was true of
Lancashire. There was no serious unrest in the years before the
rising, and while enclosure was most common in the western lowlands the rebellion attracted most of its support from the eastern
uplands and the extreme north of the county. Where there was
hedge-breaking in the east, it followed rather than preceded the
Pilgrimage.[5] Although fields were enclosed, assarting of moss and

---

[1] A. J. Atherton, 'The estates of William Farington', University of Manchester
M.A. thesis, 1953, 50, 69–79, 120, 122–4; Long, 'Wealth of the magisterial class in
Lancashire', 113–16; H. L. Jones, 'The development of leasehold tenure in south
Lancashire', University of Manchester M.A. thesis, 1924, 6, 35–7, 42.
[2] Compare Long, 'Wealth of the magisterial class', 111–12, with R. B. Smith, 'A
study of landed income and social structure in the West Riding of Yorkshire, 1535–
1546', Leeds University Ph.D. thesis, 1962, 270–2; R. T. Spence, 'The Cliffords,
earls of Cumberland, 1579–1646', University of London Ph.D. thesis, 1959, 119.
[3] G. Youd, 'The common fields of Lancashire', *THSLC*, CXIII, 9–10, 34–5;
F. Walker, *The Historical Geography of South-West Lancashire*, 57; Tupling, *Economic
History of Rossendale*, 44–56.
[4] Especially by A. G. Dickens in *Studies in Church History*, IV.
[5] Youd, 'Common fields of Lancashire', 3; Haigh, *Lancs. Monasteries*, 64–7, 71,
81, 84; *CCR*, II, 123–4; Bennett, *History of Burnley*, II, 118–19.

moor increased both the cultivated area and the number of small-holders, and there is no sign that the small farmer was suffering in Tudor Lancashire at this time. Copyhold rents in Pendle Forest were the same in 1662 as they had been in 1507, when the forest lands were first granted out, and in south Lancashire customary tenure was so strong that it was only with the greatest difficulty that rents could be increased.[1] Further north, in Lonsdale hundred, tenant-right with its military ingredient helped to keep rents artificially low, while landlords had to bear in mind the need for good relations with their tenants, as they might need them for military service against the Scots. In the later seventeenth century a south-Lancashire royalist like William Blundell of Crosby could remain near the truth while painting an idyllic picture of conditions and social relationships in the countryside.[2]

The social structure of rural Lancashire changed as slowly as did the county's agriculture. In the first half of the sixteenth century local power in the north of England still depended on tenurial bonds with mesne tenants,[3] and there is ample evidence that feudal connections remained influential in Lancashire. The taking of an oath of fealty before the receipt of a tenancy was still common; the homage roll of the manor of Warrington gives the form of the oath which was taken, a list of tenants who did homage for lands held of Sir Thomas Butler between 1491 and 1517, and the payments of feudal relief for entry into tenancies. During these years homage was done on almost forty occasions, although the more important men, the Tildesleys, the Halsalls and the Athertons, had their homage commuted for a fee. This implies that homage was not enforced, but perhaps also that it was sufficiently meaningful for social equals to wish to avoid it, and it was not unknown for a Lancashire lord to distrain if homage was not done. The Warrington roll seems to have been drawn up by Butler's chaplain in part as a guide for the lord's heirs to the forms adopted, and there are notes on the document (in a later hand) of homage and relief on two occasions in 1563, and once in 1565.[4] The manor of Warrington merely provides the best of a

---

[1] Blackwood, 'Lancashire cavaliers and their tenants', 18; Brigg, 'Forest of Pendle in the seventeenth century', 68, 72ff.; Tupling, *Economic History of Rossendale*, 48, 91–2; Jones, 'Development of leasehold tenure', 24, 42, 44.

[2] E. Kerridge, *Agrarian Problems in the Sixteenth Century and After*, 43–4 and Lancashire references in 44n; Blackwood, 'Lancashire cavaliers and their tenants', 21, 24; *A Cavalier's Note Book*, ed. T. E. Gibson, 254–6, 260.

[3] M. E. James, 'The first earl of Cumberland and the decline of northern feudalism', *Northern History*, I, 48.

[4] 'Homage Roll of the manor of Warrington', ed. W. Beaumont, *Miscellanies relating to Lancashire and Cheshire, passim*; *Lancashire and Cheshire Cases in the Court of Star Chamber*, 50–1.

number of Lancashire examples; every mesne and customary tenant of the abbot of Furness also took an oath of fealty. The tenants of Furness were bound to provide military service for the abbey, and in 1525 an agreement between the abbot and the tenants of Low Furness stipulated that the tenants were to 'have in readiness threescore able men with harness'. At its suppression the abbey was entitled to military service from 850 men on its possessions in Lancashire, Cumberland and Yorkshire.[1]

The survival of feudal oaths and at least the commutation of feudal services was not unusual in Tudor England, but what makes the Lancashire case interesting is the length of time for which these customs endured. Early in the sixteenth century Sir Thomas Butler was extracting wardship from his tenants and was doing well out of sales of wardship and marriage, but by the reign of Elizabeth wardships belonging to mesne lords were very rare in England. In Lancashire, however, wardships were still being sold in the early seventeenth century; in 1607 Sir Richard Mollineux sold a wardship for £40, and in the mid 1620s Robert Blundell of Ince Blundell sold the wardship and marriage of two of his yeoman tenants.[2] It may be that the large number of child marriages in Lancashire was in part the product of the survival of wardship and marriage.

If feudal connections survived in Lancashire, bastard-feudal ones did so even more obviously, and many of the most powerful men in the county were in trouble for illegal retaining and mustering. A long series of complaints against the disorders created by the earl of Derby's retinue was sent to Wolsey in 1521, and the earl's vigorous use of armed men to maintain his domination of Lancashire may have had something to do with his suspected plots with the duke of Buckingham and others. In the early 1530s the third earl raised liveried men in Lancashire, ostensibly for use in the Isle of Man, and he refused to allow his men to serve the Crown under any other commander.[3] The county was disturbed in 1535 by conflicts between the retainers of rival magnates, with Sir Marmaduke Tunstall, Adam Hulton, and their men opposing Lord Mounteagle and his followers. There was little hope of restoring peace and order when the only men to whom the government could turn to deal with the emergency were Mounteagle and Tunstall, those responsible for the trouble.[4] In the early 1540s there were a number of

[1] T. West, *Antiquities of Furness*, liii, 97–8; PRO, SC 11/376.
[2] 'Homage Roll', esp. 24, 26, 28; J. Hurstfield, *The Queen's Wards*, 96–7; LRO, DDM/1/26, DDIn/53/93–4; Long, 'Wealth of the magisterial class', 66–7.
[3] *L & P*, III(2), 1923; J. J. Scarisbrick, *Henry VIII*, 164; *Derby Correspondence*, 117–18, 122–3.
[4] *L & P*, VIII, 984, 1008, 1029, 1030, 1046, 1108.

Lancashire prosecutions for retaining and unlawful assembly; at least six senior gentlemen were involved, who had been attempting to prevent their men wearing the king's livery and obeying the orders of royal stewards. In 1551 Sir John Southworth was committed to the Fleet prison by the Duchy court for unlawful assembly, and later Sir Richard Towneley and Sir Richard Sherburne, two of the most influential knights in the county, were in trouble for retaining. The offences of Towneley and Sherburne were particularly serious as they had given their liveries to copyhold tenants of the Crown.[1]

Lancashire was far from being the only county in England in which retaining and the violence it produced were common, but there is some evidence that the special circumstances of the county palatine made the problems more serious than elsewhere. In 1532 Duchy officers expressed the view that the disorders in Lancashire were so extensive that the like 'hath not oftentimes been seen nor heard of' in other parts, and in 1547 the Duchy Council thought there was more retaining in the palatinate than in the rest of England.[2] The county was outside the commission of the Council in the North, and rule was, as we shall see, to a considerable extent left in the hands of the earl of Derby. But his own position in the shire was partially dependent on retaining, so that it is unlikely that he did much to enforce the statutes against livery and maintenance. The Duchy Council did what it could to combat the problem; stewards of Duchy manors were several times ordered to ensure that the king's tenants wore no livery 'but only our badge the red rose', county commissions were issued for the arrest of offenders in 1532, and local commissioners were instructed to deal with retaining in Wigan in 1547 and Lancaster in 1557.[3] But the frequency of these efforts indicates that they had little success, and the Duchy Council was aware of some of the reasons for failure. A detailed analysis of the position in Lancashire was drawn up in December 1547, and it was suggested that the main reason for the unusual disorders in the county was the exemption of the inhabitants from attendance at the king's courts in Westminster. The king's writ and the processes of the royal courts did not run in the county, while sheriffs and other local officers were negligent and 'favourable' in the execution of palatinate writs. In the hope of remedy directions were given for improvements in the work of the assizes, and the proceedings of the quarter sessions were regulated. But there is no evidence that these

---

[1] *Duchy Pleadings*, II, 178–9, 185–6, 189–90; PRO, DL 5/9, fo. 170v, 5/10, fo. 88, 5/11, fo. 106v.

[2] PRO, DL 42/95, fo. 128v, DL 42/96, fos. 9–10.

[3] LRO, DDF/1233, 1235, 1236; PRO, DL 42/95, fo. 128v, 42/96, fo. 14v; Roper, *Materials for the History of Lancaster*, 156–7.

measures had any substantial effect, and the only method by which the problems of the county could be combatted with vigour, the inclusion of the county within the sphere of the Council in the North, was not adopted.[1]

The survival of feudal forms tended to keep authority in private hands and, as Dr Bossy has noted, where seigneurial powers remained extensive Catholicism tended to survive. This was partly because the influence of the conservative local gentry remained strong,[2] partly because the ability of the government to enforce change was thus limited, and partly because Protestantism was not likely to flourish in a semi-feudal society. Those parts of southern England which most readily accepted the new religion were the civilised and sophisticated towns, where men lived in close contact with one another and where traditional social patterns had been disrupted. But Lancashire remained partially insulated from the rest of England by attitude and geography, and economic and social change proceeded only slowly. Where traditional social structures and economic patterns faced, as we have seen, no challenge, there can have been no momentum towards religious change, and the stability of life must have produced a temper antipathetic towards any alteration in religion. Sir John Southworth, a leading county squire, spoke for many when he told Bishop Grindal that 'he will follow the faith of his fathers: he will die in the faith wherein he was baptised'.[3] The attempts of successive English governments to enforce religious change in Lancashire were unlikely to meet with great success.

[1] PRO, DL 42/96, fos. 9–10. See below, pp. 102–5, 136–7.
[2] J. Bossy, 'The character of Elizabethan Catholicism', *Past and Present*, XXI, 39, 41–2; Walker, *Historical Geography of South-West Lancashire*, 50, 66ff.
[3] *Remains of Archbishop Grindal*, ed. W. Nicholson, 305.

PART TWO

8

The enforcement of reform in the reign of Henry VIII

In the 1530s Henry VIII and Thomas Cromwell initiated a revolution in religion. The authority of the pope over the Church in England was replaced by that of the king as 'the only supreme head in earth of the Church of England'; traditional teachings on images, relics and pilgrimages were attacked and certain practices were abrogated; the people were taught the Creed, the Lord's Prayer and the Ten Commandments in English, and parts of the liturgy were put into the vernacular; English Bibles were placed in the churches and allowed to circulate freely; and an attempt was made to improve clerical education and morals.[1] There was bound to be strong resentment in many quarters, because the changes were interpreted as an assault on the very foundations of the faith. Henry himself was accused of heresy, and was said to be undermining the priesthood and the sacraments.[2] The friars were saying:

Oh father (or sister), what a world is this; it was not so in your father's days. Ye may see here a parlous world. They will have no pilgrimages; they will not we should pray to saints or fast, or do any good deeds; Our Lord have mercy on us. I will live as my forefathers have done, and I am sure your father and friends were good and ye have followed them thitherward. Therefore, I pray you, continue as ye have done, and believe as your friends and fathers did, whatsoever these new fellows do say, and do for yourself while ye be here.[3]

The Henrician regime took on the major task of disseminating ideas which many would find anathema, and which would be vigorously opposed by a section of the priesthood. Whatever decisions the king's council might take, its members were faced by the

---

[1] This account is based on the Act of Supremacy and the royal injunctions of 1536 and 1538.

[2] See especially G. R. Elton, *Policy and Police*, 1–170. For a Lancashire example, see Ellis, *Original Letters*, 1st series, II, 45.

[3] PRO, SP 1/92, fo. 128 (*L & P*, VIII, 626).

massive problem of enforcing them, of persuading as many as possible to accept the new forms, of forcing those not amenable to persuasion, and of disposing of those who would not be forced. From 1533 onwards, therefore, Cromwell organised a two-tier campaign: of propaganda to make the new ideas acceptable, and of police-work to enforce acceptance.[1] In Lancashire, however, official efforts met with little success.

Evidence on the operation of the propaganda policy in the county is scarce, but it is apparent that it followed the same lines as in the rest of the country. In both Lichfield and York, the two dioceses of which Lancashire formed part, the bishops supplemented the royal injunctions with diocesan instructions of their own. Although Rowland Lee of Lichfield merely repeated the royal provisions with a few minor additions, Edward Lee of York, despite his reputation for obscurantism, went further than his master and ordered that the Epistle and Gospel were to be read in English at services, that extra sermons were to be provided, and that the clergy were to instruct their flocks that salvation could only be obtained through the merits of Christ.[2] It is difficult to say how much preaching in support of official policies was actually done. Archbishop Lee circulated tracts among his clergy, which the non-preachers could read to their congregations and the others could use as a basis for their sermons. But the booklets were not printed, and it is doubtful whether the team of clerks he set copying out the tracts could produce enough. A second problem was that of enforcement, for as Lee pointed out 'I cannot be in all places, nor shall I peradventure hear of all defaults that may be made, nor I can put in their heads learning and cunning to preach that have it not already.' The archdeacons and rural deans were instructed to report on those who failed in their duty, but Lee knew his diocese was desperately short of preachers and the administrative machine could not have detected those who were lax. Propaganda on the royal supremacy was not always well received; four curates from the Gisburn area were threatened with violence if they publicised the contents of Lee's books.[3] In Lancashire, too, preaching against the pope aroused discontent. Robert Legate, a friar 'put into that monastery of Furness to read and preach to the brethren', declared the supremacy to the monks but they objected to the reformist content of his sermons and refused to listen. William Rede, a priest at Dalton, tried to preach a sermon 'showing the usurped power of the bishop of Rome', but his sermon notes were

[1] Elton, *Policy and Police*, 171–262; J. K. McConica, *English Humanists and Reformation Politics*, 112–49, 167–99.
[2] G. Burnet, *History of the Reformation*, 6 vols. VI, 184–91, 191–5.
[3] BM, Cotton MS, Cleopatra E. VI, fos. 240v–242v, 243v–244v.

taken away and he was 'mishandled' by a local official. John Dakyn, vicar-general of Richmond, alleged that to preach the royal supremacy early in 1537 was to risk his life.[1]

A number of attempts were made to supplement the national propaganda system with local provisions in the north-west. The prayers in the churches which the vicar-general of Richmond was instructed to arrange during the Pilgrimage of Grace were designed to remind men of their duty to the king, and after the failure of the rising the government renewed its efforts to secure acceptance of its policies. Plans were laid in December 1536 for the dispatch of 'virtuous and learned' preachers into Lancashire to teach the word of God, ignorance of which was said to have been a major cause of the rebellion. It is not certain that preachers were, in fact, sent, but the normally absentee rector of Middleton accompanied the royal commissioners who worked in the county, presumably as a preacher.[2] The instructions issued to the earl of Sussex for his mission into the county in 1537 stipulated that the people were to be turned against the monks, and one of Cromwell's clerks drew up a detailed list of arguments which could be used against the religious.[3] The two deputies sent by Cromwell to represent him in Lonsdale and Furness were ordered to ensure that all the parish clergy preached in favour of the royal supremacy, and they were to proceed against those who did not.[4] It must be assumed, therefore, that there were occasional sermons in support of the royal policies in at least parts of Lancashire.

Cromwell realised that it was not enough to put forward reasons for acceptance of the break with Rome and the attack on aspects of traditional religion; such acceptance would, in some quarters, have to be enforced, while the government needed information on the extent of the opposition which had been aroused. There seems to have been a spy in the earl of Derby's household during the Pilgrimage of Grace, and though this seems to have been an unusual precaution the government had ample reason to mistrust the earl. The spy found Derby's servants to be violent critics of Cromwell and his policies; 'Or your Lordship should be there as they would have you to be', he reported to the minister, 'I had liefer to be in Jerusalem to come home upon my bare feet.'[5] The earl himself worked as part of Cromwell's detection system; someone, probably

[1] PRO, SP 1/118, fo. 9; *L & P*, XII(1), 788, 841–2.
[2] BIY, Reg. Lee, R/I/28, fo. 107v; *L & P*, XI, 1410, No. 3, XII(1), 716, 832.
[3] *Ibid.* 302 and App. 1. For a discussion of this propaganda see Haigh, *Lancs. Monasteries*, 87–8.
[4] *L & P*, XII(1), 881, XII(2), 1216.
[5] *L & P*, XI, 859.

Derby, reported to the chancellor of the Duchy that a priest had been speaking out against Henry's second marriage, and the earl was ordered to investigate. The priest was arrested, witnesses were rounded up and examined before the earl's council, and a full report was dispatched to the king.[1] At Furness the friar who had been placed there to preach to the monks kept Cromwell informed on their highly critical attitude towards the royal supremacy and on the opinions of the priests and people of the surrounding parishes.[2]

Although individual informants at Lathom and Furness abbey might make reports, the detection of offenders depended primarily on the efficiency of secular and ecclesiastical government in each area. Whatever the vigour of the political leadership in the capital, the dissidents had to be arrested and the royal programme had to be justified by local officials and clergy over whom the central government had only limited control. The preaching resources of Lancashire were, as we have seen, slender, and though Archbishop Lee of York did what he could to ensure that the royal supremacy was preached there was no certainty that instructions would be, or even could be, fulfilled at the local level. In the last analysis, whether the supremacy was publicised or not depended on the views and abilities of each parish priest. Again, the authorities might arrange the writing and printing of pamphlets to justify the king's policies, but this did not mean that they were read in Lancashire. The distribution difficulties which kept early Lutheran tracts out of the county made it equally unlikely that official literature would penetrate the area. In 1548 a Manchester priest had to send to London for a New Testament,[3] and few were likely to go to such trouble to buy books in support of a policy they may have disliked. Books of any kind were uncommon in Lancashire, and those clergy who owned them had nothing more than works of medieval piety and practical handbooks for pastoral work.[4] The first definite evidence of a book in lay hands does not come until 1543, when William Trafford mentioned a 'new book' in his will, but the volume was richly bound and was clearly a treasured possession. There are one or two casual references to oaths being taken on books, and in 1556 Richard Towneley owned a copy of Erasmus' *Paraphrases*, but there is no evidence of any collection of non-religious books in Lancashire until the will of John Braddyll in 1575.[5] The sparse educational

---

[1] *L & P*, VI, 964; *Derby Correspondence*, 7–13.

[2] *L & P*, XII(1), 841, No. 3, 842.

[3] *Writings of John Bradford*, II, ed. A. Townsend, 2 vols. 15.

[4] Haigh, 'Reformation in Lancashire', 147–51.

[5] *L & C Wills*, II, 63, 108; CRO, EDC 2/2, pp. 85, 220–1; 'Rent Roll of Sir John Towneley, 1535–6', ed. F. R. Raines, *Chetham Miscellanies*, OS, VI, xxi.

provisions have already been discussed, and while most families must have had at least one member with the rudiments of reading, it is doubtful if many could have coped with the sometimes complex political and theological arguments of official tracts.

The policing system was no more likely to be effective in Lancashire than was the propaganda campaign. It has been shown in some detail that the Church's administrative structure in the north-west was peculiarly weak, and diocesan officers could neither impose their will nor know what was happening in most of the parishes. The contribution which the ecclesiastical machine could make towards the enforcement of the Reformation was therefore slight, even after the foundation of the diocese of Chester. In November 1541, only a few months after his appointment as bishop, John Bird warned the king that the people of his diocese were dangerously sympathetic towards 'popish idolatry', and thought that his own episcopal powers were inadequate to enforce reform. Almost a century later, Bishop Bridgeman of Chester was complaining that his authority was insufficient to control the Puritans of his diocese.[1] From the government's point of view, the situation was made even more serious in the 1530s and 1540s by the obvious weaknesses in secular administration.

Conservative in its social structure and violent in its habits, Lancashire posed problems of government and public order which could only be solved by radical initiatives. In the first half of the sixteenth century most areas of England, and even Wales, were taught the virtues of peace, obedience and legality by new or revitalised institutions. In the south-east, obviously, the authority of the Privy Council in London was an immediate sanction, while for Cornwall, Devon, Somerset and Dorset there was a short-lived Council in the West. Wales and the west Midlands were made orderly by the Council in Wales and the Marches, which also controlled Cheshire, a county of equal violence, until 1569. The Henrician Reformation in Wales coincided with a period of intense activity in the pacification of the principality by a provincial council under Bishop Rowland Lee.[2] But the government of the northern counties of England raised greater difficulties: royal authority was dependent on the goodwill of local magnates and impeded by the many franchises, the influence of the border led to widespread theft and violence, and the capital was too far away for all but the rich to take their suits to the royal courts. Special provision was as necessary for the north as it was for Wales and the west, but for much of

[1] PRO, SP 1/75, fos. 7–8; R. C. Richardson, 'Puritanism in the diocese of Chester to 1642', University of Manchester Ph.D. thesis, 1969, 438–9.
[2] P. Williams, *The Council in the Marches of Wales under Elizabeth*, 15–17, 34, 47.

the 1530s the powers of the Council in the North were restricted to Yorkshire and its president, Cuthbert Tunstall, was distrusted by the king. After the Pilgrimage of Grace had exposed the flaws of the Tunstall council, a new body under Bishop Robert Holgate was created in 1537–8. The reformed council acted as a link between central government and the justices of the peace, whose work it supervised; it checked enclosure and other causes of distress, it recovered feudal franchises and it attacked religious conservatism. In the north, and especially in Yorkshire, the council provided the strong local authority which at last began the stabilisation of a difficult area, and there is even evidence of an improvement in public order in the border region.[1]

But the influence of the Council in the North was largely restricted to Yorkshire, Durham and Northumberland; the four annual general sessions were held at Hull, York, Durham and Newcastle, though later a few sessions were held at Carlisle. Lancashire was never placed under the jurisdiction of the Council, partly because it was both a county palatine and a major part of the Duchy of Lancaster. The palatinates of Chester and Durham were subjected to conciliar authority, and the Duchy's lands in Yorkshire and Northumberland were not excluded from the sphere of the northern council, but in Lancashire the vested interests of Duchy and palatinate officers triumphed. The Duchy and the palatinate were not, however, adequate substitutes for a powerful provincial council. The Duchy Court heard equity cases and the Duchy Council acted as an executive body, but the Duchy was primarily a department for the administration of ducal lands and the collection of their revenues; that it provided the model for Cromwell's revenue courts is sufficient evidence of this.[2] The Duchy was a London-based body whose only local officers were stewards, bailiffs, receivers and auditors, and though the Council sometimes dealt with such matters as enclosure and retaining in Lancashire, there is no trace in its records of any initiatives in religious reform. Such was the department's preoccupation with finance that in 1568 it was necessary to point out that 'far more requisite it is to be careful to govern well the subjects than to husband well the revenue of that county'.[3]

The palatine status of Lancashire might once have ensured effective local administration and justice, but it was clear in the reign of Henry VIII that the structure only made the area more difficult to

[1] R. Reid, *The King's Council in the North*, 93–7, 153–8; *L & P*, XIII(1), 1269; A. G. Dickens, *Robert Holgate*, 11; T. I. Rae, *The Administration of the Scottish Frontier, 1513–1603*, 170–4.

[2] G. R. Elton, *The Tudor Revolution in Government*, 164–6, 185, 205.

[3] Quoted in Somerville, *Duchy of Lancaster*, 326.

control. The palatinate organisation at Lancaster was above all a fiscal and judicial machine, staffed by lawyers who were normally non-Lancastrians and had no local power, prestige or knowledge. Revenue collection was unsatisfactory, for the barons of the Lancaster exchequer could not control their subordinates, and taxes, fines and dues were uncollected as sheriffs and other officers were negligent and 'favourable'. The Duchy Council argued in 1547 that the exemption Lancashiremen enjoyed from attendance at the king's courts in Westminster weakened the government of the county, for legal officers at Lancaster were easily intimidated and important statutes were not enforced.[1] Though the evidence should be treated with caution, there are indications that the Lancaster courts did not provide impartial justice; in 1517 and 1523 there were complaints that the sheriff had packed juries, and in 1527 alone there were two petitions against the undue influence wielded in the courts by powerful defendants.[2] The assize justices frequently experienced difficulties in their proceedings; until 1547 there was no proper means of serving writs and ensuring the appearance of those indicted, while the assizes had sometimes to be delayed while the palatinate seal was sent down from London.[3]

In the absence of an effective local body for the execution of policies in an area too far from London to be ruled directly, local government fell into the hands of the earl of Derby. Indeed, the power of the Stanleys was an important reason for the omission of Lancashire from the jurisdiction of the Council in the North in 1537–8. The earl had played a crucial role in the failure of the Pilgrimage of Grace; he almost joined the rebels, but Cromwell bought his loyalty with a commission granting him full powers in Lancashire.[4] After the collapse of the rebellion it was politically unwise to subject the earl to the authority of a provincial council. Moreover, it is significant that the only northern county not subordinated to the Council in the North was the power-base of one of the few north-country magnates whose influence had not been sapped in the 1530s. The Percy inheritance passed to the Crown, the earl of Cumberland's authority had declined until he was not able to control his own men, Lord Dacre never recovered from his disgrace in 1534 and Lord Darcy was executed after the Pilgrimage. But the third earl of Derby remained a powerful feudal magnate. He had his own council, consisting of a group of the most important and able men in Lancashire, which met to deal with the affairs of the county and

---

[1] PRO, DL 42/96, fos. 9–10.
[2] *Duchy Pleadings*, I, 69, 126, 147, 157–8.
[3] PRO, DL 42/96, fos. 9v–10; BM, Lansdowne MS 79, fo. 29.
[4] Haigh, *Lancs. Monasteries*, 63; *Derby Correspondence*, 27–8.

implement royal policies.[1] His household, with a treasurer, a receiver-general, a comptroller, secretaries, chaplains, two almoners and gentlemen-in-waiting, provided posts for members of gentry families and formed a school in which the sons of the influential learned the courtly and military arts. By the 1560s the earl had a household staff of 120, and it cost £1,500 a year to feed this vast concourse and the family and its guests. The Stanley household formed the core of the earl's local power, and the patronage he provided gave him considerable influence over the county gentry.[2]

The earl of Derby and his council, rather than a Lord President and a royal council, formed the link between central and local government. The earl was too important to be bypassed, and the Crown ruled Lancashire through him; orders for the county went first to him, and he decided how instructions were to be implemented and made the necessary arrangements with justices of the peace.[3] The dominance of the Stanley family was recognised institutionally, and though the usual Tudor practice was to change county lieutenancies frequently, the lieutenancy of Lancashire was hereditary in the Stanley family, with only one short break, from 1551 until 1641. The Crown, to a certain degree, abdicated from its responsibilities towards Lancashire and left government in the hands of the earl of Derby, backed by a clique of less than a dozen of the Stanleys' county allies.[4]

The government's enforced reliance on an unsupervised local noble raised obvious problems, and it was almost impossible for the Crown to control its representative in Lancashire, much less the county itself. The second earl of Derby had himself been the major threat to good order in the shire. His substantial military following enabled him to impose his own wishes despite the express commands of the king or the will of local interests, he issued proclamations in his own name and ordered royal officers not to interfere, and his retainers were favoured by the justices at Lancaster. Complaints had been made to the chancellor of the Duchy, but not surprisingly these produced 'as yet but little punishment or remedy'.[5] When rule was left to one man, death became a real threat to government. The deaths of Thomas, the second earl, in 1521 and Lord Mounteagle in 1523, each leaving a minor as heir, created a power vacuum in the

[1] *Ibid.* 10; Foxe, *Acts and Monuments*, VII, 41–2.
[2] *Stanley Papers*, ed. F. R. Raines, II, *passim*; L. Stone, *The Crisis of the Aristocracy, 1558–1641*, App. 24; Peck, *Desiderata Curiosa*, 437; Watson, 'Lancashire gentry and the public service', 49.
[3] *VCH*, II, 219, 222; *Farington Papers*, 123–4.
[4] Coward, 'Lieutenancy of Lancashire and Cheshire', 39, 43, 45, 48–9.
[5] *L & P*, III(2), 1923.

county, and there were even greater disorders among Lanca-shiremen than was usual. The earl of Surrey noted in 1523 that 'there is some little displeasure amongst them, and no man by whom they will be led', and in 1532 the Duchy had to intervene to deal with the instability of the area.[1] Edward, third earl of Derby, was granted livery of his lands in 1531, but even after he had reached manhood he was 'young and a child in wisdom, and half a fool', unable to provide the strong leadership the county required.[2] In the mid 1530s, when the Cromwellian religious changes had to be enforced, the county was ruled by a vacillating young man who could not preserve good order. In 1535 there were riotous assemblies involving the retainers of leading Lancastrians, during the Pilgri-mage the earl lost control of his lands in the north of the county, and he could not even prevent his kinsman Lord Mounteagle from harassing his tenants.[3] Though as he grew older the earl's authority increased, he was too incompetent to use his influence to any effect and he was not always assiduous in the execution of policies he disliked.

Even if he had tried to do so, Derby could not have enforced reform in Lancashire alone, and the bulk of the work fell, as elsewhere, on the justices of the peace. But the commission was totally unsuited to the new tasks which devolved upon it; in 1505 there were only 17 J.P.s in Lancashire, and though this had risen to 24 by 1564 it remained a small commission for so large a county. Essex, a county of similar size, had 37 working justices in 1540, the West Riding had about 60 and Cheshire 32.[4] In some hundreds there were only one or two justices, and these areas were inadequately supervised, but there could be no improvement as, it was noted in 1568, there were not enough gentry of the status necessary for appointment to the bench.[5] To make matters worse, the most powerful men took little part in the routine work of the commission, and administration was left to lesser figures anxious to make their mark. Few attended the quarter sessions with any frequency, and in mid century only about a dozen justices were assiduous attenders. There is a good deal of evidence of laxity and petty corruption among justices, and there was a pronounced tendency to put private interests before public duty.[6] Finally, until the reforms of

---

[1] *Ibid.* 3482; PRO, DL 42/95, fo. 128v.
[2] *L & P*, V, 119, g. 22; XIII(2), 732.
[3] *L & P*, VIII, 984, 1008, 1029, 1030, 1046, 1108; Haigh, *Lancs. Monasteries*, 69; BM, Cotton MS, Vespasian F. XIII, fo. 219.
[4] *Report of the Deputy Keeper of the Public Records*, XL, 544; *Camden Miscellany*, ed. M. Bateson, IX, 77–8; *L & P*, XV, 282, g. 20, 21, 34.
[5] PRO, SP 12/120/21; Somerville, *Duchy of Lancaster*, 325–6.
[6] Watson, 'Lancashire gentry and the public service', 16, 18, 26–7, 29, 30, 31, 53.

1546–7 the quarter sessions were not properly organised; only thereafter was there a fixed rota of regular sessions for each hundred, with juries of constables to make presentments, a procedure for binding over offenders to appear, and liaison with the assize justices.[1]

Where the commission of the peace was as small and ill-organised as in Lancashire, the justices could not be expected to keep watch on the whole of the county and the gentry as a whole had to share in the task. Public order, popular opinion, social stability and reports on the disaffected depended, in any county, on co-operation between local gentlemen and the government. But in Lancashire the gentry formed a much smaller proportion of the total population than in most other areas. In 1563 the population of the county was roughly 95,000 people, but the heralds' visitations recorded only 57 gentry families in 1533, 112 in 1567 and 124 in 1613.[2] In the 1560s there was 1 gentleman for every 800 people, and the position must have been worse thirty years earlier as population cannot have increased as rapidly as the number of recognised gentry families. In Yorkshire, by comparison, at the end of the century there were about 600 gentry families in a population of perhaps 300,000, or 1 gentleman for every 500 others. In the south there were many more gentry, 336 in Essex in 1634, and between 800 and 1,000 in Kent by the Civil War.[3] The Lancashire gentry were also unevenly distributed, and only 20 of the county families returned at the visitation of 1567, one-sixth of the total, had their seats to the north of the Ribble. In 1567 the herald found no gentry in the whole of the deanery of Furness, which was described later in Elizabeth's reign as 'rude, waste and unprovided of gentlemen in those quarters'.[4] A shortage of gentry was crucial in the revolutionary situation of the 1530s and after, when the authorities in the capital needed information that only local gentlemen could provide, to keep in touch with grass roots' opinion and detect those opposed to new policies.

The imposition of the Henrician Reformation was also complicated by Lancashire's inbuilt resistance to authority, and we have seen that the history of royal efforts to control retaining shows that when local and national interests conflicted the former usually prevailed. Failure to obey royal writs and commissions was com-

---

[1] PRO, DL 41/12/22, DL 42/95, fos. 167v–168v, DL 42/96, fos. 9v–10.
[2] Watson, 'Lancashire gentry, 1529–1558', 8. The 1533 survey seems not to have covered the whole county.
[3] J. T. Cliffe, *The Yorkshire Gentry from the Reformation to the Civil War*, 5; Dickens, *English Reformation*, 163–4.
[4] *Visitation of Lancashire, 1567, passim*; BM, Lansdowne MS 56, fo. 174.

mon, and attacks on tax collectors and other officials were dangerously frequent.[1] In the 1540s there were five major cases of refusal to serve in the king's armies, and two more of refusal to contribute towards their cost, while the gentry were anxious to maintain their own retinues rather than allow their men to wear the royal badge.[2] If there are many examples of general disobedience, it is unlikely that instructions which affected the salvation of souls would be accepted with equanimity. Resistance to royal policies was possible because the Crown did not possess the necessary enforcement machinery, and there were too few of the trustworthy local officers who might have exacted conformity.

It is clear that there was considerable opposition in Lancashire to what Cromwell and his master were trying to do. The reaction of the people of the north to the Ten Articles of 1536 was summed up by Hall as 'See, friends, now is taken from us four of the seven sacraments, and shortly we shall lose the other three also, and thus the faith of Holy Church shall be utterly suppressed and abolished.'[3] In 1533 Archdeacon Magnus noted that the clergy of the northern province simply refused to believe news of the parliamentary legislation, and in 1535 the dean of the Arches, who held a Lancashire benefice, thought the royal supremacy would not be understood for three or four years.[4] Other observers found much opposition to official policies in Lancashire; in 1534 Chapuys heard that the people of the county were, like the Welsh, disaffected 'at that which is done against the faith', and in 1536 Latimer reported that in north Lancashire 'pardoning doth prate in the borders of the realm', warning Cromwell that unless he sent in reformist preachers the people would 'perish in their ignorance'.[5] Five years later the new bishop of Chester found the situation in the palatinate of Lancaster unchanged: 'For lack of doctrine and preaching your Grace's subjects be much inferior in the true knowledge of God and their obedience to your Majesty and your laws than your Grace's subjects in the south parts be, namely in observing their accustomed popish idolatry.'[6]

In July 1533 Richard Clerk, vicar of Leigh, was at a house in

[1] *Ducatus Lancastriae*, I, 126, 142, 208, 237, 292, II, 31; *Duchy Pleadings*, II, 43–8; PRO, DL 1/2, B 13, Sta. Cha. 2/5/51; LRO, DDHu/13/3; Watson, 'Lancashire gentry and the public service', 53.
[2] *Ducatus Lancastriae*, I, 171, 175, 245, II, 102; *Duchy Pleadings*, II, 178–9, 185–6, 189–90.
[3] E. Hall, *The Triumphant Reign of King Henry VIII*, ed. C. Whibley, 2 vols. II, 269.
[4] Burnet, *History of the Reformation*, VI, 47; *L & P*, VIII, 955.
[5] *L & P*, VII, 1368, XI, 67.
[6] PRO, SP 1/75, fo. 7 (*L & P*, XVI, 1377).

Croston, where he read aloud the proclamation giving Catherine of Aragon the title of Princess Dowager. A priest named James Harrison called out that 'Queen Catherine was queen, and that Nan Boleyn should be no queen, nor the king no king but in his bearing', and went on to suggest that Henry intended to overturn the priesthood and the sacraments. Another witness deposed that Harrison asked 'Who the devil made Nan Boleyn, that whore, queen, for I will never take her for queen?'.[1] This was the sort of comment which disturbed Henry and Cromwell so much, for those attracted to Catherine's cause might prove willing recruits for a neo-feudal Catholic crusade on behalf of the papacy, especially if Charles V mounted an invasion. Though the news cannot yet have reached Lancashire, only nine days before Harrison's outburst Clement VII had threatened the king with excommunication unless he returned to Catherine, and the proclamation the priest criticised had tried to stifle comment since it declared those who spoke out against Cranmer's Dunstable decision guilty of praemunire.[2] The earl of Derby took depositions of the Harrison case, and the priest was sent up to London by one of the earl's councillors, but what happened to him then is not known. Harrison had spoken what was not yet treason, and in view of similar cases from other parts of England it is unlikely that he was brought to trial. But he seems not to have returned to Lancashire, and he was certainly not working there in 1541.

James Harrison is one of only a small group of Lancashiremen known to have criticised the king's proceedings in public, and it is not surprising that few such cases were reported. Our information is based on delations to the king, but we have seen that the detection machinery was too poor to uncover more than a handful of incidents. There was no necessity to take an open stand against royal policies, since it was unlikely that changes could be enforced with any vigour. The inadequacy of official efforts may be contrasted with the success of conservative leaders in organising resistance. Opposition in the deanery of Furness was encouraged by the archdeacon of Richmond's commissary, who tried to prevent the implementation of reformist legislation. It was reported that the commissary wrote to the curates within his jurisdiction early in Lent 1536, instructing them that despite the abolition of Peter's Pence they were to 'move your subjects both openly and also secretly in hearing of confessions to give penny or halfpenny, the which, as he saith in his letters, shall stand for the remission of their sins'. He also wrote to the parish clergy pardoning them for all payments made to Rome contrary to

---

[1] *Derby Correspondence*, 7–13; Ellis, *Original Letters*, 1st series, II, 41–5.
[2] *State Papers*, VII, 480–1; *Tudor Royal Proclamations*, I, 211–13.

the king's orders, and he protected a priest from Kirkby Ireleth who was reported to him for a breach of the Supremacy Act. A ruridecanal synod was held at Dalton, at which the commissary spoke out against the Act and the clergy present discussed the anti-papal legislation.[1] This evidence is clearly of the greatest importance, for it raises the possibility that the ecclesiastical machine was being used in this part of the country not to impose religious change but to resist it.

The commissary cannot be identified with complete certainty, but he was probably John Dakyn, vicar-general of Richmond and one of the most influential of northern conservatives. The term 'commissary' was often used loosely to describe anyone exercising a delegated jurisdiction, and Dakyn was himself called 'late vicar-general and commissary' of Richmond in 1544.[2] The document from which this account has been taken is unfortunately mutilated, but the writer refers to a Richmond commissary 'called . . . . .'; the next word, the name of the officer, is illegible, but the first letter is almost certainly 'D' and the word is the same length as 'Dakyn'. If Dakyn was the official in question, this fits in well with what we know of his career. In 1533 he proceeded against two Lancashire priests of reformist views, and it was alleged in 1534 that as commissary to the dean and chapter of St Paul's he had appealed to Rome, contrary to the Act in Restraint of Appeals.[3] Although he later tried to minimise his involvement, during the Pilgrimage of Grace he acted as secretary to the rebel 'convocation' at Pontefract, which drew up a wholesale condemnation of royal policies and radical views, and he encouraged the canons of two suppressed Lancashire priories to return to their houses under the auspices of the rebels. The authorities clearly mistrusted Dakyn; he was closely examined after the Pilgrimage, and he was still under suspicion in 1541, though he was dismissed from custody when he agreed to acknowledge the royal supremacy.[4]

Although there are no further examples of the use of the Church's administrative structure to impede reform, opponents of the Crown's policies held other posts of authority in the Lancashire area. Throughout the 1530s the archdeaconries of Chester and Richmond were in the hands of William Knight, who was antipathetic towards change and patronised John Dakyn. On a lesser level, the officer who kept the court books at Lichfield was reluctant to admit alterations;

[1] PRO, SP 1/118, fos. 9–9v (*L & P*, XII(1), 842).
[2] *L & P*, XII(1), 849, No. 26, 878; *Ducatus Lancastriae*, II, 78.
[3] *L & P*, VI, 287, VII, 1605, XII(1), 786, ii, No. 14.
[4] *L & P*, XI, 1279, XII(1), 786–9, 914; *Proceedings and Ordinances of the Privy Council*, VII, ed. H. Nicholas, 7 vols. 248–9.

he continued to date consistory sessions by the regnal years of the pope until six months after the passing of the Act of Supremacy and two months after the bishops renounced their oaths of obedience to the papacy.[1] Although the foundation of the see of Chester in 1541 ought to have increased the regime's ability to enforce its will, this may have been limited by the appointment of reactionaries to posts of power and prestige. By the time he made his will in 1561, the first chancellor of the diocese was determined not to 'swerve from the unity of [the] Catholic and Apostolic Church, which now I do believe in my heart and profess with my mouth', and he asked for prayers for his soul.[2] The first dean of the new cathedral died soon after his nomination, and he was succeeded by Henry Man, who had been a supporter of the Nun of Kent and who left his books to Sheen Charterhouse 'if it should be re-edified'.[3] George Coates, whom Hugh Latimer described as 'wilfully witty, Dunsly learned, Morely affected, bold not a little, zealous more than enough', was appointed to a prebend in the cathedral, and was later in trouble for his 'lewd behaviour' in 'sundry sermons made in those parts'. We may guess the content of the sermons from the 'sinister and seditious sermon' Coates preached at Sheen on Easter Sunday, 1538, when he argued that the laws of God should be obeyed before those of the king, praised the monastic life, and attacked the doctrine of salvation by faith alone.[4]

Despite the Crown's attempts to control preaching, it is clear that conservative sermons could still be heard. Nicholas Wilson, a keen supporter of Catherine of Aragon and a friend of More, was one of a small group of itinerant preachers who tried to keep papal authority alive, and in the early 1530s he preached through Lancashire, Cheshire and Yorkshire.[5] John Ainsworth, a native of Ashton, was patronised by Catherine when she was queen, and eight weeks after the king's marriage to Anne Boleyn he preached in favour of the Aragon marriage near Cambridge. He was in Lancashire between May 1537 and the end of February 1538, but then he went to York where he tried to preach, and when prevented nailed up a copy of his 1533 sermon in which he called the Roman Church 'our Holy Mother Church' and regretted that 'now she is blinded again'. Perhaps he had been silent in Lancashire, but it may be significant

[1] A. G. Dickens, *The Marian Reaction in the Diocese of York*, I, 8; Lich. RO, B/C/2/3, fos. 289v, 295v, 301, 306.
[2] CRO, EDA 2/1, fo. 251.
[3] D. Knowles, *Religious Orders in England*, III, 237, 413n.
[4] Strype, *Ecclesiastical Memorials*, I(1), 470–1; *APC*, II, 483; BM, Cotton MS, Cleopatra E. V, fos. 407–408 (*L & P*, XIII(1), 819).
[5] Foxe, *Acts and Monuments*, VII, 473, 476, 775.

that as soon as he entered the jurisdiction of the Council in the North he was arrested, tried for treason and executed.[1]

How widespread views such as Ainsworth's were among the lower clergy of Lancashire it is difficult to say, but if the monks of Furness were in any way typical there was a considerable body of opposition to official policies. By November 1536 one of the monks, John Green, had had enough of royal interference in the Church, and was determined that 'the king should make no more abbots there, but they would choose them themselves'. Some time after Christmas John Harrington, John Broughton and others were circulating a prophecy that 'the decorate rose should be slain in his mother's belly', whiich they interpreted to mean that the king would be murdered by a priest, for the Church was the king's mother. Soon after this another monk, Henry Salley, was saying that 'there should be no lay knave head of the Church', or, in the version which Abbot Pyle heard, that it was never a good world since 'secular men and knaves rule upon us, and the king made head of the Church'. One of the brothers, it was reported, voiced the dangerous opinion that 'the king was not right heir to the crown, for his father came in by no true line but by the sword', while John Broughton thought that 'the bishop of Rome was unjustly put down, and should be restored again within three years'. The monks translated their words into action, and during the Pilgrimage they gave money to the rebels, commanded the abbey tenants to join the rising, and encouraged both rebels and tenants, saying, 'Now must they stick to it, or else never, for if they sit down both you and Holy Church is undone, and if they lack company we will go with them, and live and die to defend their most godly Pilgrimage.' It is true that a few of the monks did defend the king's proceedings, but in the abbey the loyalists were outnumbered by two to one.[2] The whole Furness area was a hotbed of reaction, and we have seen that one secular priest spoke out against the Act of Supremacy while others continued to make payments which were to go to Rome. But the Lancashire clergy were much less willing to make contributions to the new supreme head; in 1534 a number refused to pay the clerical subsidy, and in February 1537 the vicar-general of Richmond was unable to collect the clerical tenth.[3]

At least some of the clergy of the county were active in encouraging conservative sentiment, and there is evidence that their views

[1] *L & P*, XIII(1), 533, 705.
[2] BM, Cotton MS, Cleopatra E. IV, fo. 134; *L & P*, XII(1), 652, 841, 849. For a full discussion of the relations between Furness and the rebels, see Haigh, *Lancs. Monasteries*, 94–8.
[3] *L & P*, VII, 923, xviii, XII(1), 789, ii.

found ready acceptance among the laity. It is, of course, difficult to analyse the reactions of lay people in the towns and villages of the north-west, especially as so few reports were made to the government, but some cautious statements can be made. There are signs, as among the clergy, of a continuing popular allegiance to the papal primacy; it was said that 300 parishioners of Kendal threatened to drown their curate unless he declared the pope to be head of the Church, the vicar-general of Richmond claimed he could only defend the royal supremacy at the risk of his life, and Aske thought that all the gentry and commons opposed the king's new title.[1] Lancashire sent its own representatives to the rebel councils in Yorkshire, so that the Pontefract articles may also reflect attitudes in the county. One of the proofs offered of the heresy of Henrician bishops was that they had preached against the pope, and it was demanded that 'the supremacy of the Church touching *cura animarum*' should be restored to Rome. Although the senior clergy who met in mock-convocation at Pontefract Priory were far from united, they agreed that by the laws of the Church and the 'consent of Christian people' the pope was 'head of the Church and vicar of Christ'.[2]

It is probable that to many the supremacy itself was only a peripheral issue, and the Pilgrimage followed not the break with Rome but the Ten Articles and royal injunctions of 1536, which altered ceremonies and doctrines. Archbishop Lee of York reported that though few were advancing the authority of Rome, 'at such novelties, specially handled without charity or discretion, the people grudge much'.[3] It is true that the rebel propaganda which circulated in Lancashire in 1536–7 publicised the views of articulate idealists and particularly those of the clergy, but the tracts were designed to stimulate action by appealing to support and so must have reflected more widespread opinions. A rebel manifesto sent to London by the earl of Derby complained that heretic bishops and ministers were 'working most cruelly by spoiling and suppression of holy places' and 'blaspheming also Our Lady and all other saints in heaven, whereby we are ruin in shameful slander throughout all realms Christian'.[4] The clergy meeting at Pontefract demanded the restoration of the abrogated saints' days, new anti-heresy laws, and an end to the official propaganda against traditional practices such as pil-

---

[1] *L & P*, XII(1), 671(2), iii; 786(2), No. 14; 'Aske's examination', ed. M. Bateson, *EHR*, V, 559, 565.
[2] *L & P*, XI, 1155, i–ii; M. H. and R. Dodds, *The Pilgrimage of Grace*, 2 vols. I, 346–73, 383–4.
[3] BM, Cotton MS, Cleopatra E. V, fos. 301–301v (*L & P*, X, 172).
[4] *Derby Correspondence*, 48–9.

grimages and the use of images. The campaign against images must have caused resentment in Lancashire, and it seems to have had a minimal effect. Bishop Bird complained in 1541 that many churches had not removed 'idols and images accustomed to be worshipped', as late as 1548–9 the parish of Prescot was burning forbidden candles before the image of St Mary, and the light to St Nicholas still burned in Lancaster parish church in 1564. Sometimes priests asked to be buried near images, and among the laity, too, they retained their popularity.[1]

The most famous of the 1538 injunctions is that which ordered the provision of a vernacular Bible in each church, to be paid for equally by the incumbent and the parishioners. Not only were Bibles to be placed in the churches, but priests were instructed

that ye discourage no man privily or apertly from reading or hearing of the same Bible, but shall expressly provoke, stir and exhort every person to read the same, as that which is the very lively word of God, that ever Christian man is bound to embrace, believe and follow if he look to be saved.[2]

The great and lasting impact of vernacular Bibles, freely available to be read by those who would, cannot easily be overstressed. Protestantism was a Bible-reading religion in a way that Catholicism had never been, and the wide circulation of the Scriptures contributed, as Cromwell knew it must, to a weakening of the authority of the priesthood and of orthodox theology. That is not to say that the Bible is an obviously Protestant book, but rather that the possibility of each man finding his own version of the truth was not conducive to the maintenance of Catholic unity or the role of the clergy as the interpreters of the laws of God. In 1534 Robert Plumpton sent a copy of Tyndale's New Testament to his mother in Yorkshire with the message 'As for the understanding of it, doubt not, for God will give knowledge to whom he will give knowledge of the Scriptures, as soon to a shepherd as a priest, if he will ask knowledge of God faithfully.'[3] The Bible was a formidable weapon in the enforcement of the English Reformation, and no county in which it had wide currency could remain solid in its conservatism.

We have seen that in Lancashire very few people owned books, and that it is very unlikely that vernacular Bibles reached the county in any number. The provision of Bibles in the Churches, therefore, assumes an even greater importance, for the 1538 injunctions

[1] PRO, SP 1/75, fos. 7–8, *Prescot Accounts*, 27; *Richmond Wills*, ed. J. Raine, 171; A. B. Emden, *Biographical Register of the University of Cambridge*, 86–7; BIY, Reg. Holgate, R/I/29, fo. 78v; *L & C Wills*, I, 6, VI, 30.
[2] H. Gee and W. J. Hardy, *Documents Illustrative of English Church History*, 276.
[3] *Plumpton Correspondence*, ed. T. Stapleton, 232.

ordered Bibles for a society which had not had them before. But it is by no means clear that the order was always obeyed in Lancashire. In the 88 inventories of church goods which survive from 1552, only six English Bibles are listed.[1] This figure is surely far too low to be an accurate estimate, and it is probable that the commissioners of 1552 were concerned mainly with those items which might bring some profit to the Crown. The lists were probably made by church-wardens and then widened on the advice of the commissioners for each hundred,[2] so that one may expect some uniformity among the churches of each hundred. Thus five of the six Lancashire Bibles are listed in the inventories for Leyland hundred, and it is clear that the commissioners there attempted to compile thorough lists. The probability thus arises that in the area in which the commissioners usually listed books, those churches for which no Bibles are given – two chapels and two churches – did not in fact possess any. Unfortunately, Lancashire is particularly poor in Tudor churchwardens' accounts, but in the one set of accounts which survives for the 1530s and after, that of Prescot, there is no sign of the purchase of a Bible and no mention of one until after the royal visitation of 1547 when a lectern was made for the Bible.[3] Failure to provide Bibles was far from being an unusual matter; in 1592 three out of nineteen churches and chapels in Warrington deanery had no Bible, nor any other of the prescribed books for that matter, one other had no Book of Common Prayer, and the only book possessed by another was an old Bible described as 'not sufficient'.[4]

Although it is impossible to make any real estimate of the extent to which clergy and people complied with the Bible order, there are grounds for suspecting that not all churches possessed the required volume. This was certainly true of the diocese of Lincoln, at least initially; in February 1539 it was reported that many Oxfordshire curates had not yet placed Bibles in their churches, and in the same year 40 churches in three deaneries did not have Bibles.[5] In 1541 the government complained in a proclamation that 'divers and many towns and parishes' had failed to provide Bibles for their churches.[6] There are obvious reasons why this should have been so. It has been shown in an earlier chapter that parishioners in Lancashire, as in other areas, were extremely unwilling to make financial contributions to their churches, but Bibles were costly and the Great Bible

---

[1] From *Church Goods*, I–III, *passim*.
[2] Haigh, 'Reformation in Lancashire', 71–2, 74–5.
[3] *Prescot Accounts*, 27.
[4] CRO, EDV 1/10, fos. 115, 117v, 121v, 127v.
[5] *L & P*, XIV(2), 214, App. 6.
[6] *Tudor Royal Proclamations*, I, 297.

bought for a Yorkshire church cost 14s.[1] It is true that the parishioners had to pay only half the cost, but in a parish such as Prescot, where there were perpetual quarrels and lawsuits over who was bound to contribute towards church expenses, even fairly small sums were difficult to collect. A reluctance to contribute may partly have been the product of a mistrust of the Bible, and from many parts of England there was opposition to the 1538 injunctions on the grounds that those who read the Bible were heretics.[2] The attitude of the clergy towards the Bible probably varied from indifference to hostility. When a Manchester priest acquired a New Testament in 1548, having been forced to do so by the king's visitors, he was only interested in discovering how to find the lessons he was supposed to read in church.[3] In 1554 John Standish, a Lancashire-born cleric and former rector of Wigan, published *A Discourse wherein it is debated whether it be expedient that the Scripture should be in English for all men to read that will,* and in the following year be brought out a second edition to which 'the author hath added sundry things'. The first version consisted of over thirty proofs that the Bible ought not to be available in the vernacular, for example that 'the reading of the Scripture in English tended to the people's spiritual destruction. That by this damnable liberty all holy mysteries had been despised, and the people had utterly condemned everything that was not expressed in the letter of their English Bibles.'[4] In 1558 Ralph Parker, chaplain to a highly conservative Lancashire J.P., thought Tyndale's New Testament 'plain heresy and none worse than it', and considered that laymen ought not to read another translation because 'it is not good that they should have such English books to look on, for this and such others may do much harm'.[5] If views such as these were commonplace, then it is unlikely that the vernacular Bible had much influence in Lancashire.

Although it could not be pretended that the Henrician reform campaign had no effect on Lancashire, its impact was much restricted. The weakness of both ecclesiastical and secular government prevented the enforcement of change and the detection of those unwilling to accept it. Conservative clerics fought a strong rearguard action to preserve traditional doctrines and ceremonies in their entirety, and to combat the influence of royal propaganda. The strength of orthodox Catholic piety and the natural conservatism of a backward community made the efforts of the government to change

[1] Dickens, *Lollards and Protestants*, 170.
[2] *L & P*, XIV(1), 525, 897, XIV(2), 301, 796.
[3] *Writings of John Bradford*, II, 17.
[4] Strype, *Ecclesiastical Memorials*, III(1), 269–70.
[5] Foxe, *Acts and Monuments*, VIII, 563. Foxe incorrectly calls him Parkinson.

men's minds on a number of crucial matters much less effective than in other areas. On the three main doctrines attacked by the authorities, the authority of the pope, the cult of the saints and the use of images, the campaign seems to have had little impact, though it is true that the evidence is more likely to record instances of opposition than of acquiescence. Few may have cared much for the pope, but there was a clear feeling that the faith was under attack and a marked resentment against those felt to be responsible. In the conservative propaganda tracts which circulated in Lancashire, Cromwell was called a heretic and his dismissal was said to be one aim of the Pilgrimage.[1] A seditious song called 'Crummock' was popular during the rising and after; Lord Darcy received a copy of the rhyme, which he seems to have found amusing, and in 1538 a minstrel from Cartmel was going round Lancashire singing the song, which was very favourably received.[2] In 1538 the people of Lancashire and other parts of the north were said to be the minister's 'extreme mortal enemies'.[3] In parts of the south the Cromwellian attack on the external ceremonies of religion, and stress on the Bible were welcomed, partly because the Lollards had already preached such ideas and partly because any lessening in the authority of the priesthood was welcomed. But Lancashire had no history of Lollardy and little sign of anticlericalism, and popular religion was flowering into new life rather than decaying; it reacted to the Henrician reformation by rebellion.

[1] *L & P*, XI, 892; see also Haigh, *Lancs. Monasteries*, 69 and refs.
[2] *L & P*, XI, 1086, XIII(1), 1346, 1370.
[3] *L & P*, XIII(1), 119.

9

Militant resistance: the Pilgrimage of Grace[1]

As the ability of the Henrician government to impose its will and detect the recalcitrant was limited, it was possible for dissident Lancastrians to ignore many of the changes of the 1530s. But there was one aspect of the Reformation from which there was no escape, for the suppression of the monasteries was carried through by a succession of local commissions backed by a powerful administrative machine. A rebellion followed hard on its heels, the Pilgrimage of Grace. Only two weeks after the canons of Conishead had been ejected from their priory, the commons of Lancashire were buying arms, and two weeks after that the canons were restored to their house by the rebels.[2] After the rising had collapsed, the government suggested that the outbreak was the result of agrarian grievances. When the earls of Derby and Sussex were sent into Lancashire in 1537 they were told that 'If any commons have been enclosed, or any gentlemen take excessive fines that their tenants cannot live, the Earls shall labour to bring such enclosers and extreme takers of fines to such moderation that they and the poor men may live in harmony.' When Cromwell appointed deputies in Lonsdale and Furness in the same year he instructed them to guard against excessive fees and entry fines.[3] More recently, some historians have also seen the origins of the Pilgrimage in such economic grievances.[4]

There had been unrest in the north-west in 1535, with enclosure riots in Craven and in Cumberland, but in fact these seem to have been exceptional outbreaks caused by the estate policies of the unpopular earl of Cumberland.[5] Furthermore, there were no agrarian riots in Lancashire itself, and though there were disputes over common rights in the early 1530s at eleven townships in the county

---

[1] I have used many of the arguments and examples of this chapter in my *Lancs. Monasteries*, 32–101, which should be consulted for a fuller account. Here I have changed emphasis in some respects, and added new evidence.

[2] PRO, DL 29/158/26; *L & P*, XI, 563, Addenda, 1112.

[3] *L & P*, XII(1), 302, 881, XII(2), 1216.

[4] See especially A. G. Dickens, 'Secular and religious motivation in the Pilgrimage of Grace', *Studies in Church History*, ed. G. J. Cuming, IV.

[5] *L & P*, VIII, 863, 970, 992, 1133; James, 'First earl of Cumberland and the decline of northern feudalism', 53–7.

only one of these later took part in the Pilgrimage.[1] It was obviously in the Crown's interest to suggest that it was the greed of the gentry rather than its own ecclesiastical policy which had caused the revolt, but there is no evidence of general agrarian unrest across Lancashire. We have already noted that common fields and thus enclosures in the county were concentrated in the western lowlands, and the disputes over common land came mainly from this area. The rebellion, however, drew its support from the eastern and northern uplands, where the most important of the Lancashire monasteries were situated. The Pilgrimage in Lancashire was therefore not a general movement of peasants against landlords, but a demonstration against royal policies and in defence of the monasteries.

It is true that many of those who supported the religious houses did so because of the economic insecurity created by the suppression. Among monastic tenants there was a fear that the changes in land ownership entailed at least payment of new entry fines and at worst an alteration in customary tenures. The Pilgrims demanded that lands in Furness, Dent, Sedburgh, Kendal and other areas with extensive monastic estates should continue to be held by tenant right.[2] Sir James Layburne was reported to have said 'If we may enjoy our old ancient customs here, we have no cause to rise.'[3] Robert Southwell, who suppressed Furness Abbey after the rebellion, saw that immediate security would save the commons from fear of an unknown future. He thought that if those who had surveyed the lesser monasteries in 1536 had had 'some small part of the demesnes, upon their suit to the Council, distributed to the poor' the rising might not have taken place. Southwell himself learned from the mistakes of others; at Furness he allowed local people to buy the best of the farm animals, he suggested that plots on the demesne be leased to the unemployed ex-servants of the abbey, and pleaded that 'the poor men be not expelled for no gentlemen's pleasure'.[4]

There is a mass of evidence which seems to show that it was the suppression of the lesser houses and the implied threat to the remainder which drove the commons of Lancashire to revolt. The mobs restored the canons of Cartmel and Conishead, while Lancashire rebels were in close touch with Whalley and Furness and had a hand in the restoration of Sawley Abbey, a little over the border in

[1] *Ducatus Lancastriae*, I, 142, 145, 146.
[2] Article 9 of the rebel demands (Dodds, *Pilgrimage of Grace*, I, 369). On tenant right see Kerridge, *Agrarian Problems in the Sixteenth Century and After*, 44–5 and Lancashire references.
[3] *L & P*, XII(1), 914.
[4] *Ibid.* (2), 205, printed in full in T. A. Beck, *Annales Furnesienses*, 356–60.

Yorkshire. Whenever royal forces moved against one of these houses, the commons rose immediately in its defence.[1] But in the south of the county the priories of Holland and Burscough found no rebels to champion them, though even there the earl of Derby thought pulling down the bells and lead of Burscough too dangerous 'in this busy world'.[2] The Pilgrimage of Grace in Lancashire centred on the north and east of the county, where the earl of Derby and his clients were least influential and where the monasteries – Whalley, Furness, Cockersand, Cartmel and Conishead – were larger and more powerful than the houses in the rest of the county.

The picture which Robert Aske drew of the role of the monasteries in the life of the north[3] may be exaggerated, but in what we know of the houses of north and east Lancashire there is a solid basis of fact for many of his comments. Aske objected to the Act of Suppression firstly 'because the abbeys in the north parts gave great alms to poor men'. Alexander Savine moved from the generalities of monastic apologists to a statistical analysis of charity, and calculated that the almsgiving of the English monasteries amounted to only 2½ % of their gross annual income;[4] Westminster Abbey gave 2.7%, Fountains 1.7%, and St Werburgh's Chester only 1.3% of gross income. But the comparable figure for the seven independent Lancashire houses is three times the national average, a more creditable 7.6%.[5] As Savine knew, but as many of those who have used his work have not noticed, his figures show only a part of the total charitable activities of each house. The fullest available source for an analysis of almsgiving is the 1535 *Valor Ecclesiasticus*, but this includes only the charitable gifts for which tax-exemption could be claimed. These were the 'compulsory' alms, established by foundation, the result of, perhaps, the grant of land to a house on condition that annual gifts were made to the poor. A monastery's standing in the local community reflected not merely its 'compulsory' alms but the total of its charitable gifts, which is much more difficult to calculate. Some Lancashire houses included non-compulsory alms in their 1535 returns, in the vain hope that they, too, might be allowed exemption, and the charity listed in the *Valor* can often be supple-

[1] See below, pp. 130, 132–4.
[2] *L & P*, XI, 118.
[3] *EHR*, V 561–2.
[4] A. Savine, *English Monasteries on the Eve of Dissolution*, 239. The calculations which follow are my own.
[5] The wide discrepancies between the net income of the houses as given in the *Valor* and by the suppressors tend to exaggerate the proportion of income which went to charity (see J. Youings in *Northern History*, VI, 163), but even if it is assumed that the *Valor* gross figures are too low by a quarter, the Lancashire houses still gave over 6% of their income in 'compulsory' alms.

mented from monastic and suppression accounts. If all the known charitable activities of the Lancashire houses for which costs are available are included, the result is a commendable 11% of gross annual income. Whalley Abbey claimed tax-relief on £116 18s 10d given in regular doles to the poor, and the support of 24 almsmen in the house, an amazing 21% of its gross income.[1] The performance of Cockersand, a large but poor house, was only a little less impressive; in 1535 the abbey was allowed £18 13s 4d for alms distributions, but in addition 15 'poor, aged and impotent men found daily at bread and board' cost £22 7s 4d so that 18% of income went to charity.[2] Furness was allowed only £11 10s for 'compulsory' alms, a meagre 1.2% of gross income, but the abbey also kept 13 paupers at a cost of £21 14s and gave weekly sums totalling £12 each year to 8 poor widows, so that the house's charity amounted to a more respectable 5% of income.[3] Cartmel's 'compulsory' alms cost only 6s 8d, but it spent another £12 on daily gifts to 7 poor men, thus giving 11% of its income in alms.[4] Conishead gave £10 10s or 8% of total income, in 'compulsory' alms, but a further £1 was devoted to charity.[5] These north and east Lancashire houses spent 11½% of their gross income on charity, and between them they provided livings for almost 90 poor men and women. But the two independent houses in the south of the county were much less generous, and devoted only 5% of their income to charity; Burscough priory gave £7 each year for the distribution of grain to the poor, while Holland merely kept 2 old men in the house at an annual cost of about £3.[6]

Aske also objected to the suppression on more strictly religious grounds; the dissolution meant a sacrilegious attack on relics, some houses provided services in desolate areas, and by 1537 'the divine service of Almighty God is much minished, great numbers of masses unsaid, and the blessed consecration of the sacrament now not used and showed in those places'. The cessation of the stream of masses which the monasteries had provided was clearly an important loss in a county which still founded chantries and took great care to provide prayers for the dead. We have also seen that relics remained popular and, at the suppression, the parishioners of Cartmel petitioned to keep the priory's relic of the Cross.[7] Only the monasteries had the equipment and manpower to celebrate the great liturgical festivals with due solemnity, and monastic inventories suggest some-

[1] *Valor*, V, 229–30.   [2] *Valor*, V, 261; PRO, DL 43/5/4.
[3] *Valor*, V, 270; PRO, SC 12/9/73.   [4] *Valor*, V, 272.
[5] *Ibid.* 271; PRO, DL 43/5/2, fo. 10.
[6] *Valor*, V, 221; PRO, DL 43/5/7, fo. 4.
[7] PRO, DL 41/12/11, No. 21.

thing of the splendour of the high masses lost to local people.[1] The confiscation of liturgical items caused some difficulty at Cartmel, where it was claimed that a 'suit of copes', a chalice, mass books and vestments, belonged to the parish rather than the priory.[2] Churches used regularly by the laity were threatened for a time; at Cartmel the priory church served also for the parish, while the people of Holland normally attended the priory church as their parish church was some distance away.[3] Even greater uncertainty was caused by the threat to the supply of parochial priests, for the religious houses filled, directly or indirectly, at least 33 clerical posts. Of the county's 57 parish churches, 13 were actually served by monks (9 of them in areas which gave support to the Pilgrimage), while another parish which straddled the Lancashire–Yorkshire border and three Cumbrian benefices were staffed by the county's regulars.[4] It is true that monks were not always conscientious vicars, and that the suppression made little or no difference to endowed vicarages, but the dissolution must have raised fears for the future of parochial cures. When religious houses were being pulled down and the king was thought to be about to suppress some parish churches,[5] any disaster seemed possible. Less important posts were also at risk, for monks staffed three Lancashire chantries.[6] Finally, some secular priests, and therefore the people they served, were threatened, for the stipends of 2 vicars and 13 other clergy came from the religious. Cartmel paid 10 marks to the priest who served the parish altar in the priory church, Furness Abbey paid the curate of Hawkshead and two other priests,[7] Burscough paid 10 marks each to two Huyton chantrists,[8] and Whalley paid stipends to the vicars of Rochdale and Eccles and the chaplain at Clitheroe Castle, two chantrists in Whalley parish church, and the curates of Haslingden, Burnley, Colne and Downham.[9] It would not be surprising if some of these men feared for their livelihood in the autumn of 1536.

[1] e.g. PRO, DL 43/5/4; T. D. Whitaker, *History of the Parish Whalley*, ed. J. G. Nichols and P. Lyons, 2 vols. I, 185–8.
[2] PRO, DL 41/12/11, Nos. 12, 13.
[3] *Ibid.* Nos. 10, 11; W. Dugdale, *Monasticon Anglicanum*, ed. J. Caley *et al.* 6 vols. IV, 412.
[4] Burscough served Huyton and Ormskirk; Cartmel, Cartmel and Pennington; Cockersand, Garstang and Mitton; Conishead, Kendal Hospital and Orton; Croxton, Melling and Tunstall; Furness, Dalton, Millom and Urswick; Lytham, Lytham; Penwortham, Penwortham; Whalley, Blackburn and Whalley (*Valor*, V, *passim*; *VCH*, III–VIII, *passim*; *FOR*, *passim*; PRO, DL 43/5/7, 15; *Duchy Pleadings*, I, 107).
[5] *L & P*, XI, 768, No. 2.   [6] PRO, DL 43/5/4, fo. 1; 43/5/15.
[7] PRO, DL 43/4/12, fo. 1v, SC 11/376, 12/9/73, fo. 12v.
[8] PRO, DL 43/4/6B, 43/5/2, fo. 7; *Valor*, V, 222.
[9] O. Ashmore, 'The Whalley Abbey bursar's account for 1520', *THSLC*, CXIV, 66; West, *Antiquities of Furness*, App. 10, No. 5; *VCH*, VI, 432, 452, 534, 557.

Militant resistance: the Pilgrimage of Grace

Robert Aske argued that there was 'none hospitality now in those places kept', and thought that the houses had served 'strangers and baggers of corn as betwixt Yorkshire, Lancashire, Kendal, Westmorland and the Bishopric'. This claim is difficult to document and perhaps of no more than marginal importance, but the Lancashire monasteries did provide some services for travellers. The abbey of Cockersand, 'standing very bleakly and object to all winds',[1] may have provided a welcome roof, and the house certainly had a guest-master in 1494.[2] During storms, the coastal houses of Cartmel, Conishead and Cockersand rang their bells and lit fires to guide travellers, while Cartmel and Conishead were responsible for the appointment and payment of guides across the sands of Morecambe Bay.[3] Aske regarded the monasteries as something of a tourist attraction, for 'the said abbeys was [sic] one of the beauties of this realm to all men and to strangers passing through the same'. We may suspect that few strangers ever reached Lancashire, but the destruction of long-familiar landmarks must have caused offence locally. Official vandalism towards newly erected buildings must have been particularly galling. In the years immediately before the suppression a new west tower of magnificent proportions was added to Furness, and the last abbot of Whalley built a Lady Chapel. Abbot Paslew's chapel was so admired that the people of Burnley hired his masons and instructed them to add buttresses to their church, 'every buttress having a funnel upon the top, according to the fashion of the funnels upon the new chapel of Our Lady at Whalley'.[4]

The monasteries of the north of England had, Aske thought, 'all gentlemen much succoured in their needs with money', but we know little of the loans made by Lancashire houses. Cartmel Priory lent £20 and £10 to two local men, and at the suppression was a creditor to the tune of £63 9s.[5] The other banking activities of the houses are more easily documented. After the death of Lord Mounteagle in 1523 the abbot of Furness acted as an executor, and when Sir John Husee bought the wardship of the Mounteagle heir from the king he deposited his first payment with the abbot of Whalley.[6] Abbot Paslew also acted as trustee for Sir Thomas Butler's bequest for the foundation of a grammar school at Warrington.[7] In an unruly and

[1] Leland, *Itinerary in England*, IV, 10.
[2] *Collectanea Anglo-Premonstratensia*, Camden Society, 3rd series, X, 122.
[3] PRO, DL 41/12/11, m. 3, 41/11/59, fo. 9, 43/4/12, fo. 6.
[4] Bouch and Jones, *Economic and Social History of the Lake Counties*, 30; J. E. W. Wallis, *History of the Church in Blackburnshire*, 143.
[5] PRO, DL 43/4/12, fo. 2.
[6] *L & P*, IV(1), 13, 2130.
[7] *Lancs. Chantries*, I, 57.

dishonest society, churchmen might be more trustworthy than most, while as supposedly perpetual corporations the monasteries were useful safe-deposits. The Hesketh family deeds were entrusted to the prior of Holland and the abbot of Whalley, while the Cliftons left documents with the abbot of Chester.[1] The most common financial assistance the religious houses rendered the hard-pressed Lancashire gentry was in the form of fees. Furness paid £20 to Leonard Fawcett, its receiver-general, 10 marks to Thomas Holcroft, £6 to John Lambert for holding the courts, smaller sums to sixteen bailiffs, and £10 to the earl of Derby and £6 to the earl of Cumberland as the abbey's stewards.[2] Whalley's fees to laymen totalled £48 3s 4d, and even hard-pressed Cockersand paid out £27. Of the lesser houses Conishead paid fees to six bailiffs and a steward, and Cartmel paid four bailiffs, £4 to an auditor, £1 13s 4d to John Standish for keeping the court and £2 to the earl of Derby as steward.[3] The king attacked the pockets of the gentry as well as the comforts of the monks.

Aske's argument that nunneries provided education for the daughters of the gentry does not apply to Lancashire, as there were no houses of female religious in the county, but the monasteries were involved to a limited extent in wider educational activities. In 1582 an old man, who had been one of the scholars, remembered that Furness had boarded and educated the children of its tenants, in 1536 Holland Priory had 'two children at school' in the house, and Whalley maintained a school of some sort.[4] The larger houses were among the few centres of learning in a backward area; Whalley and Furness had libraries from which books still survive, and even under-endowed Cockersand had a library with glazed windows and 106 books, besides the psalters and mass books in the choir.[5] Whalley and Furness sent monks to Oxford with some regularity, and just before the suppression the former presented one of its graduates, a bachelor of divinity, to the vicarage of Whalley.[6] The intellectual and cultural impact of the monasteries was probably not extensive, but in a county with so few educational opportunities even small benefits were significant.

The substance of Robert Aske's defence of the northern monasteries can thus be confirmed for Lancashire. The government's

---

[1] LRO, DDN/40, DDCl/889.

[2] PRO, SC 12/9/73; *Valor*, v, 270.

[3] Savine, *English Monasteries on the Eve of Dissolution*, 258; *Valor*, v, 271–2.

[4] Bouch and Jones, *Economic and Social History of the Lake Counties*, 29; PRO, DL 43/5/7, fo. 5; P. J. Wallis, 'A preliminary register of old schools in Lancashire and Cheshire', *THSLC*, CXX, 17.

[5] Haigh, *Lancs. Monasteries*, 57; PRO, DL 43/5/4.

[6] Haigh, *Lancs. Monasteries*, 57, 118.

argument that the monks were too evil to be allowed to remain in their houses carried little conviction in an area of habitually loose morals, and it is likely that the religious were judged by their public acts rather than their private behaviour. Even a den of vice might be defended if it eased the lot of the poor. But if some wished to preserve the monasteries for their public services, others were bound to the houses by more formal ties, and if only a fraction of those who owed service turned out in the Pilgrimage they would still have constituted a formidable military force. When Furness was surveyed in June 1537 it was found to have had over 850 horsemen and foot soldiers on its estates, while the ministers' accounts show about 300 armed men on the lands of Cartmel and an even larger number on those of Conishead.[1] The customs of Furness, as set out in 1509, stipulated that the tenants should be sworn only to the king and the abbey, that they were not to take the part of any other in disputes involving the house, and that they were each to provide a horse and armour when required. Furness certainly had a force of liveried retainers in 1525; it remained in being until the suppression and at least one of its members took part in the rebellion.[2]

The religious orders in Lancashire exercised a powerful local influence. The monks had not become remote and impersonal collectors of rents, for only a small proportion of their estates had been leased out and tenancy by custom or at will was much more common.[3] There was less occasion for conflict between monks and tenants in Lancashire than in other areas, for the religious of the county appeared less often in the guise of landlords. Savine calculated that English monasteries received on average about three-quarters of their income from land and other 'temporal' sources, but in Lancashire the proportion was only 58%; four houses received more from tithe than from rent, and in 1520 Whalley Abbey had only 35% of its income in the form of rents.[4] The land which the houses did hold gave them considerable local authority, and the tenants were accustomed to obey the heads of monasteries. Furness Abbey administered the whole Furness area directly, and enjoyed almost total jurisdictional independence; Cartmel Priory held the lordship of Cartmel, and all its manorial courts were held at the priory, while most of Cockersand's courts were held in the abbey.[5]

[1] PRO, SC 11/376, DL 29/2228, DL 29/2273.
[2] Beck, *Annales Furnesienses*, 303–5, 309; *L & P*, XII(1), 632.
[3] R. J. Mason, 'The income, administration and disposal of monastic lands in Lancashire', University of London M.A. thesis, 1962, 85–6.
[4] *Ibid.* 70; Ashmore, 'Whalley Abbey bursar's account for 1520', 50.
[5] *VCH*, II, 120, 141; Mason, 'Income, administration and disposal of monastic lands', 91.

Whalley Abbey's authority was largely spiritual, and as well as nominating and paying eleven priests in its appropriated parishes it wielded ordinary ecclesiastical jurisdiction in the exempt areas of the five royal forests.[1] Heads of houses were thus powerful local figures. In 1516 the abbot of Furness was cited before the Duchy Court, but care had to be taken that no gentlemen of the abbot's 'fee, kin or allied shall be put upon the jury, neither shall any of them be of the retinue of Lord Mounteagle', who was steward of the house.[2] In 1535–6 a plaintiff claimed that he had to take his case outside Lancashire because his adversary, the prior of Cartmel, was 'greatly friended and favoured there'.[3] When Abbot Paslew of Whalley was tried for treason the earl of Sussex was much relieved when the abbot pleaded guilty, 'else otherwise considering my Lord of Derby is steward of that house, so many gentlemen in these quarters the abbot's fee'd men, and others his friends... it would have been hard to find anything against him in these parts'.[4] If the personal influence of an abbot was dangerous even at a treason trial, the potential authority of the monasteries was considerable. Nor was it merely heads of houses who were influential, for most of the monks of the county seem to have been local men. Only about one-tenth of the monks in the seven independent houses did not have fairly common local names, and about half the monks of Furness, Whalley and Cockersand apparently had relatives among the tenants of their house and were probably born on monastic estates.[5] The ejection of a monk in 1536 was an affront to his family, especially when relations faced the possibility of supporting an unemployed and unpensioned cleric. Thus though the monastic population of Lancashire was small, with only seven independent houses, four cells, and about 132 monks and canons, the political, religious and social influence the monks wielded was out of all proportion to their numbers.

The services the monasteries provided and the influence they exerted, help to explain why the suppression was followed by a rebellion, and a final reason may be found in the manner in which the Lancashire houses were dissolved. There are several important distinctions between the suppression process in Lancashire and elsewhere, arising from the fact that the houses of the county were dealt with by the Duchy of Lancaster rather than the Court of Augmentations.[6] The officers of the Duchy were eager to arrest the

[1] *Whalley Act Book*, introduction, *passim*.
[2] *Duchy Pleadings*, I, 68–9.
[3] *Ibid*. II, 70.
[4] *L & P*, XII(1), 630, printed in Beck, *Annales Furnesienses*, 343–4.
[5] Haigh, *Lancs. Monasteries*, 59, 143–7.
[6] *Ibid*. 32–3, 38–41.

decline in the department's land revenues, and so were concerned to carry through the dissolution as cheaply as possible and secure the maximum increase in revenue.[1] The financial motive behind the suppression was made explicit from the start: Lancashire was apparently the only county in which the monks were invited to purchase exemption from the Act of Suppression, and the offers made by the houses were entered in the 'Breviate of the Brief Certificate'.[2] Initially, four of the five houses liable to suppression offered 1,000 marks each, well over four times the net revenue of even the largest of them, and Holland, a very poor house, offered 250 marks. Only Conishead's formal offer is extant, and the Duchy was clearly tempted, as Prior Lord was invited to make a second bid, but he felt unable to go beyond 1,100 marks and this was rejected.[3] Cockersand, however, doubled its original bid and was able to secure exemption; £400 was paid to the Duchy and the rest of the sum was guaranteed by local gentry and friends of the abbey.[4]

The Act of Suppression gave the inmates of the lesser monasteries a choice over their future; they could either be transferred to larger houses not covered by the act, or granted a dispensation from their strictly monastic vows to enable them to serve as secular priests. When the monks of the five Lancashire houses to be suppressed were questioned, four-fifths of them elected to remain in the service of religion, and almost two-thirds were prepared to transfer to other houses if necessary.[5] All the canons of Cockersand asked to remain in religion but there were no vacancies in larger Premonstratensian houses for them, so this and the abbey's offer of 2,000 marks led to its exemption from suppression. But the other monks were denied the choice the law allowed and, though half had expressed a determination to continue as monks, all were ejected. The reasons for this are clear; the Duchy was unable to find places for them in other monasteries, and after Cockersand the Duchy was unwilling to exempt other houses from its meagre haul to accommodate them.[6] The government argued that as the monks had been given a choice over their future, those who left religion did so voluntarily and did not deserve compensation, and only heads of houses, who were not allowed to transfer, received pensions. But most of the Lancashire monks were removed from their homes against their will

[1] See the Act: 32 Henry VIII, c. 57.
[2] *L & P*, X, 1191, XII(1), 1.
[3] PRO, DL 41/11/59, fos. 8–9.
[4] PRO, DL 29/2313, DL 41/11/49.
[5] PRO, DL 43/5/7, fos. 1–5, DL 43/4/11–12, DL 43/5/4, fo. 1.
[6] Haigh, *Lancs. Monasteries*, 42–6; PRO, DL 41/12/11, Nos. 3 and 4.

and without recompense. Dispensations were issued for the monks whether they had requested them or not, and the return of the canons of Cartmel and Conishead to their priories during the Pilgrimage suggests that they at least were angry at their treatment. At Cartmel eight of the nine canons had elected to move to other houses but all were forced to become secular priests and it is not surprising that the eight were later indicted for taking part in the rebellion.[1]

Not only did the land-hungry Duchy ignore the wishes of the monks, but they were also far less generous to the religious than were the Augmentations officers who dealt with other areas. The attorney of the Court of Augmentations advised the Duchy to follow the practice of his department and give the ejected monks money, bedding and their personal effects 'somewhat liberally by the discretion of the commissioners'.[2] But the suppressors chose to exercise little 'discretion'; the monks were given between £1 10s and £2 10s each, and though the value of the goods allowed to each monk averaged £9 at Burscough, it was only £3 11s 7d at Holland, £3 19s 4½d at Cartmel and £1 5s 1d at Conishead.[3] Not surprisingly, the canons of Conishead were soon to ask the northern rebels for assistance in regaining and retaining their priory. But monastic servants, of whom there were almost 200 in the five lesser houses, were treated even more harshly. The Augmentations attorney had suggested that servants should be given 'their full wages and some honest reward beside', and at Conishead each servant submitted a slip bearing his name, occupation, wages owing, and the endorsement of the prior; but they were given no reward and most were paid less than a mark.[4] At Waltham in Essex the Augmentations men had given the servants their full wages and rewards ranging from 10s to £1 13s 4d.[5] The monastic almsmen also fared badly in Lancashire, for though Augmentations gave almsmen about £1 each, the Lancashire suppressors allotted only 16s 8d between seven men at Conishead.[6] Robert Southwell, the Augmentations solicitor, who was in Lancashire early in 1537, thought the suppression commissioners also treated monastic tenants harshly, and the goods of each house and leases of lands went not to the ex-tenants but to the commissioners themselves and important local gentry.[7] After the Pilgrimage, Southwell was to suggest that the rising might not have

[1] PRO, DL 43/4/12, fo. 1, PL 26/13/6.
[2] PRO, DL 41/12/12, No. 5.
[3] Figures from PRO, DL 29/2313.
[4] PRO, DL 41/12/12, No. 19, DL 29/158/27–8, DL 29/2313, mm. 6–11.
[5] Oxley, *Reformation in Essex*, 132.
[6] PRO, DL 41/12/12, No. 17, DL 29/2313.
[7] *L & P*, XII(2), 205; Haigh, *Lancs. Monasteries*, 48–9.

taken place if the commissioners had acted more circumspectly, and it is difficult to disagree with his view.

The last of the Lancashire houses to fall in 1536, Conishead, was suppressed in mid September, and preparations for rebellion began soon after. On 10 October, ten days after the beginning of the Lincolnshire rising, it was reported that the people of Lancashire were buying up arms, and six days later one of Lord Darcy's servants informed him that the county was very restless and arms were still being purchased.[1] On 12 October the ex-monks of Sawley, a Cistercian house just over the Yorkshire border from Whalley, were restored to their monastery by local rebels,[2] and thereafter the idea of restoration spread. By 16 October the canons of Conishead were back in their priory and were writing to the rebel leaders for assistance.[3] The canons of the neighbouring priory of Cartmel were restored soon after, with the aid of William Collins, bailiff of Kendal and a leader of the commons in the north-west.[4] Within a few days of the restoration of Cartmel by north-Lancashire rebels, the east of the county also became heavily involved in the rising. On 23 October a force of Yorkshire rebels marched into Lancashire and swore the men of the Burnley area to their cause, while another Yorkshire group, three or four hundred strong, marched to Whalley. Abbot Paslew and his monks presumably had some sympathy for the Pilgrims, but at this stage they were concerned to avoid the wrath of the king and they refused to admit the rebels. After two hours of waiting the commons threatened to burn the abbey's corn and the house capitulated; the abbot and some of the monks took the Pilgrim oath.[5]

The earl of Derby's preparations to resist the rebels were dilatory in the extreme. He had sent to York for arms in the first week of October, but by the 23rd, when he received the king's third set of orders, the earl had done little but complain to the royal commanders that he had 'little power' and his forces were 'very poor and of small ability'.[6] This delay gave the rebels a chance to recruit, and while the earl and Lord Mounteagle were making their cautious preparations the commons were rising in response to the summons of the rebel leaders.[7] The loyalty of the earl, whom Lord Darcy thought strongly opposed royal policies, was at this stage uncertain, and there is a good deal of evidence that the earl considered declaring

[1] *L & P*, XI, 563, 678.
[2] *Ibid.* 784.   [3] *Ibid.* Addenda, 1112, XII(1), 1089.
[4] *Ibid.* XI, 947, No. 2, ii, XII(1), 965, No. 2.
[5] A. C. Tempest, 'Nicholas Tempest, a sufferer in the Pilgrimage of Grace', *YAJ*, XI, 252–3.
[6] *L & P*, XI, 634, 678, 703, 719, 806, 856.   [7] *Ibid.* 807.

for the rebels.[1] But with the orders Derby received on 23 October came a royal commission granting full powers in Lancashire, which delighted the earl and persuaded him to support the king.[2] Derby, however, was still not anxious to turn openly against the Pilgrims, and though Henry had ordered an immediate attack on Sawley Abbey the earl did not set out from Lathom until 28 October and the rendezvous of loyalist forces at Whalley was not to be until the 31st.[3] Though he may not have intended to do so, the earl ensured that Sawley would be well defended. On 25 October he wrote to the abbot of Whalley and revealed his intention to attack Sawley, but Paslew had already taken the rebel oath and he seems to have passed on the information to his colleague at Sawley. The abbot of Sawley soon knew of Derby's project and asked the west-Yorkshire rebels for aid, as it was feared that the earl would burn down both Whalley and Sawley.[4] The west-Yorkshire leaders met at Manubent to plan their countermeasures, and wrote for assistance to the captains of north Lancashire. The northern leaders instructed their followers to muster near Hawkshead church on 28 October, when they could decide how best to help the Yorkshiremen, who 'goeth forward openly for the aid and assistance of your faith and Holy Church, and for the reformation of such abbeys and monasteries now dissolved and suppressed without just cause'.[5] The rising had begun in an attempt to restore the suppressed houses, and now the rebels were preparing to defend the monasteries again.

The Manubent council also resulted in the publication of a summons to all adult males in the area to gather on Clitheroe Moor, near Whalley, on 30 October, where the two Yorkshire groups, which were to march down opposite sides of the Ribble raising the people as they went, were to join with Lancashire volunteers. When the rebels had assembled they were to wait until Derby arrived and attack him.[6] But by this time Aske and the leaders of the main Yorkshire Pilgrimage had made a preliminary truce with the duke of Norfolk, the king's lieutenant. The threat of a pitched battle between Derby and the rebels of the Lancashire–Yorkshire border caused great consternation, as the captains hoped to secure their aims by peaceful negotiation with Norfolk. When Aske, at Pontefract, heard of the danger he wrote at once to the commons of the Whalley–Sawley region, informed them of the truce, and instructed them

---

[1] *Ibid.* VII, 1206, XII(1), 393, 518, 578, 678, 849, No. 8, 853, 1022, discussed in Haigh, *Lancs. Monasteries*, 72–4.
[2] *L & P*, XI, 806–7; *Derby Correspondence*, 27–31.
[3] *L & P*, XI, 856; *Derby Correspondence*, 32–3, 35–6.
[4] *L & P*, XI, 872, iii; *YAJ*, XI, 255–6.
[5] *L & P*, XI, 892, ii; *Derby Correspondence*, 49.
[6] *Ibid.* 51–2; *YAJ*, XI, 255–6.

'how they should meddle in no condition with the said Earl, although he invaded them, but to withdraw them to the mountains and straits, except he raised fire'.[1] Prompted by Aske, Lord Darcy persuaded the earl of Shrewsbury, one of the royal commanders, to instruct Derby not to break the truce and to disband his forces.[2] The order from Shrewsbury reached the earl of Derby at Preston on 30 October on his way to Whalley; he accordingly dismissed his men and returned to Lathom.[3] Aske's order arrived too late to prevent the rebels mustering on Clitheroe Moor, but when they heard that Derby had retreated they too disbanded, leaving a small garrison at Whalley Abbey in case of further trouble.[4] Only Aske's intervention had prevented a major confrontation between loyalists and rebels in Lancashire.

When the earl of Derby reported these events to the king, he sent in certain 'false and feigned letters and devices' which the rebels had spread 'abroad amongst your subjects by setting them on church doors and otherwise'. These tracts give some indication of the motives of the rebels for, though they were the work of articulate local leaders and probably the clergy, they depended for their effectiveness on the expression of popular grievances. It was asserted that the Pilgrims intended to 'expulse and suppress all heretics and their opinions', especially the 'heretics' and men of 'villein blood' who surrounded the king. The leaders wished to protect 'our faith so sore decayed', and the commons were expected to muster for 'the love ye bear to God, His faith and Church militant'. But the central theme of the rebel tracts was the restoration and protection of the religious houses which had been so cruelly and blasphemously attacked. To this end the order which the Yorkshire leaders had pinned to the door of the minster in York was circulated in Lancashire: the dispossessed monks were to 'enter into their houses again', and the commons were to go to their aid.[5]

In his report to the government Derby also sent the first news of the risings in Lonsdale. A force of between three and six thousand rebels had marched from the Lake District and had occupied Lancaster, where the citizens had taken the Pilgrim oath and the commons had tried to force the mayor to declare for the rebel cause. The earl of Derby had sent two servants to order the commons to disperse, but Atkinson, their leader, had replied 'that they had a Pilgrimage to do for the commonwealth, which they would accom-

---

[1] *L & P*, XII(1), 6; 'Aske's Narrative', ed. M. Bateson, *EHR*, V, 338.
[2] *L & P*, XI, 900, 901, 1046, 1096, XII(1), 1089.
[3] *L & P*, XI, 922, 947; *Derby Correspondence*, 37–43.
[4] *L & P*, XI, 912, 947, XII(1), 1034; *YAJ*, XI, 259; *EHR*, V, 338.
[5] *Derby Correspondence*, 38–43, 47–52; *L & P*, XI, 784, ii; *EHR*, V, 335.

plish or jeopard their lives to die in that quarrel'. The Pilgrims, who
had been able to occupy the administrative capital of the palatinate
without resistance, scorned the earl, and they refused to risk their
position by agreeing to Derby's challenge to a formal battle.[1] Further
north, too, the rebels had met no resistance; they had chased Lord
Mounteagle and Sir Marmaduke Tunstall, both powerful men, from
their homes, and the earl of Derby's deputy at Furness and other
servants had fled south.[2] The extent of rebel support in north
Lancashire must in part be attributed to the influence of the monks
of Furness Abbey. At the end of October a group of monks, with the
approval of the rest, went out to meet a rebel force at Swartmoor and
gave a £20 donation to the Pilgrim cause. The monks marched with
the rebels to Dalton, where the prior called out the abbey's armed
tenants to join the rising, on pain of the destruction of their houses.[3]
The earl of Derby also reported the restoration of the canons of
Cartmel, and noted that the commons of the other trouble spot, the
eastern border with Yorkshire, were also untrustworthy, 'for the
most part of them show themselves to be rebels'.[4] For all Derby's
protestations of strength, he had to admit that these defections
meant his own power was 'minished, and the traitors' strength
thereby the more increased'. Though the earl had been able to hold
down south Lancashire, where there were no popular monasteries,
north of the Ribble his authority had collapsed.

Throughout the rebellion the restored canons of Cartmel and
Conishead remained unmolested in their houses. There is no evidence that the authorities knew the canons of Conishead had returned until after the revolt had collapsed and depositions were
taken, and the king only knew of the restoration of Cartmel because
the prior had fled to the earl of Derby.[5] This lack of information is a
measure of the extent to which north Lancashire had gone over to
the Pilgrims, for there were no loyalists to send in reports. Thus
evidence on the re-established priories is scant, and comes only from
confessions made after the rising. The indeterminate position of the
priories caused some concern, and the canons were anxious to obtain
formal authorisation for their return. This they secured through the
bailiff of Kendal from the vicar-general of Richmond, after the duke of
Norfolk had promised that the religious could return until Parliament made a new settlement.[6] The ownership of the priories'
property caused some dispute, especially after a royal herald had
forbidden the monks to usurp lands and tithes leased out by the

[1] *L & P*, XI, 947, No. 2, i; *Derby Correspondence*, 43–7.
[2] *L & P*, XI, 947, No. 2, iii, iv, vi.
[3] *Ibid.* XII(1), 652, 841, Nos. 2, 3, 3ii, 4. [4] *Ibid.* XI, 947, No. 2, v.
[5] *Ibid.* No. 2, ii. [6] *Ibid.* 1279, XII(1), 787, 914.

king. In the middle of February the king's lessee at Cartmel tried to seize the priory's corn and was forcibly resisted by the canons and the tenants, while the same sort of thing seems to have happened at Conishead. Nothing more is known of the religious until all the canons of Cartmel, except the prior, together with sixteen local men, were indicted for treason at Lancaster in March, apparently for violating the royal pardon by resisting the king's lessee.[1] The government also intended to try the canons of Conishead, who were thought to have initiated the rebellion in north Lancashire, but it was presumably found that there was insufficient evidence to convict them of offences committed after the pardon, and they were deleted from a list of those to be tried.[2]

Despite the truce made between the Yorkshire leaders and the duke of Norfolk, the negotiations between the two sides, and the issue of a royal pardon in December, the Lancashire rebels remained sporadically active until the arrival of a royal commission in the county late in February 1537. On 22 November the rebel council at York led by Aske even debated whether, in view of the militance of Lancashire, they ought to break off the discussions with Norfolk and join the county in a major rising.[3] Early in November the rebels in Lancashire were still recruiting and administering the Pilgrim oath, and in the middle of the month an armed confrontation between the county forces and the earl of Derby was again only averted by the intervention of Aske and Darcy.[4] New areas were still being brought into the rising, and on 28 November armed men with blackened faces went around the township of Chorley swearing men to the cause.[5] Even the earl of Derby's hold on south Lancashire was becoming less secure, and the forces he had mustered were mutinous for lack of pay.[6] The earl spent Christmas repairing his artillery and the fortifications of Lathom, while Lord Mounteagle warned him that the commons were ready to resist any attempt to remove the monks from their houses.[7] In the middle of January the commons of Heysham were still swearing recruits to the rebel cause, and those who refused the oath found larger bands returning to force it upon them.[8] Early in February the parishioners of Melling and Warton were summoned to the aid of the Kendal rebels; parish meetings were held to discuss the call and, though nothing is known to have resulted, at least some were resolved to obey.[9] Later in the same

---

[1] *Ibid.* 914; PRO, PL 26/13/6. [2] *L & P*, XII(1), 849, No. 29, 1088.
[3] *Ibid.* XI, 901, 1135, XII(1), 392; *EHR*, V, 339.
[4] *L & P*, XI, 804, 993, 1009, 1134, 1140, 1153, 1154, 1178; *YAJ*, XI, 261.
[5] *L & P*, XI, 1230; *Derby Correspondence*, 70–5.
[6] *L & P*, XI, 1066, 1097, 1118, 1253. [7] *Ibid.* XII(1), 7.
[8] *Ibid.* 671, No. 2, ii. [9] *Ibid.* 411, 671.

month the people of Cartmel and Conishead were active in the defence of the priories.[1]

The king's pardon for those who had taken part in the Pilgrimage was proclaimed at Kendal on 22 December and at Lancaster on the 31st.[2] In view of the promises of concessions the duke of Norfolk was thought to have made,[3] the issue of the pardon meant the end of the Pilgrimage as a concerted rising. The two priests who tried to raise Lancashire again had no success, and the bill nailed to the door of Shap Abbey asking for aid for Lancashire led to no new rising.[4] Only in north Lancashire, where Cartmel and Conishead had to be defended, and in the east, where Whalley and Sawley were threatened, did the rebels remain active. The king could not defeat the rebels militarily, but he simply waited until the pressures of a northern winter and the hopes raised by Norfolk of a favourable settlement led to the disintegration of the Pilgrimage. The Lancashire rebels ceased operations, but they had not been defeated, and intermittent disorder continued. At the manor of Ightenhill in Burnley there were eleven cases of hedgebreaking in the first half of 1537, and another seven cases of supporting the culprits, though these offences had occurred only four times in the preceding twenty years.[5] In February 1537 Sir Thomas Butler found even the south of the county disaffected, and he thought that if the rising broke out again the whole county might join.[6] The Lancashire rebels were not faced, like those in Yorkshire, by a substantial royal army, nor were they punished, like those in Cumbria, under martial law; they merely returned home undefeated.

The commission appointed by the king for the pacification of Lancashire, led by the earls of Derby and Sussex, began to assemble at Warrington on 26 February, and they remained in the county until 18 April.[7] But during this period only a dilatory effort was made to reassert the king's authority and punish those who had been involved in the rebellion. Though the commission was in Lancashire for more than sixty days, only fourteen were devoted to the lay rebels and six of these were spent on the commons and gentry of south Lancashire, who had taken no part in the rising. The commission laboured under severe difficulties. The loyalty of one of its members, the earl of Derby, was suspect; some time was spent investigating his conduct during the Pilgrimage, and it was clearly with some relief that Sir

[1] *Ibid.* 914.   [2] *Ibid.* XI, 1276, 1392, XII(1), 914.
[3] Dodds, *Pilgrimage of Grace*, II, 15–22; *L & P*, XII(1), 302.
[4] *Ibid.* 849, XII(2), 206.
[5] *CCR*, II, 123–4; Bennett, *History of Burnley*, II, 118–19.
[6] *L & P*, XII(1), 348.
[7] *Ibid.* 520, 970.

Militant resistance: the Pilgrimage of Grace

Anthony Fitzherbert reported on his fidelity.[1] Though the king's representatives took what depositions they could, they suffered from a dearth of information, and it was not until 14 March that they even heard of the treasons of the monks of Furness.[2] Perhaps most important of all, they had no military force at their disposal. The earl of Sussex did not bring an army into the county, while the earl of Derby could not raise recruits because the men who had served under him against the rebels had not yet been paid.[3] The commissioners held their first public session, for West Derby hundred, at Warrington on 28 February, when most of the neighbouring gentry and 900–1,000 of the commons took the oath of allegiance, but those who refused to do so went unpunished.[4] On March 1st, 2nd and 3rd the oath was administered to the gentry and commons of Salford hundred at Manchester, and on 4 March the commission moved on to Preston; the men of Amounderness hundred were expected to take the oath at Preston, and those of Lonsdale at Lancaster.[5] The weakness of these proceedings was that the oath of loyalty could only be put to those who came forward voluntarily to take it, and there were no sanctions for the recalcitrant. Though Lonsdale hundred had been the area most heavily involved in the Pilgrimage, the commission did not go north of Lancaster until 9 April, and then only to take the surrender of Furness Abbey; the treasons of the Furness area were investigated from Lancaster and Whalley.[6]

The king was convinced, and with due cause, that the rising in Lancashire was the work of the monks, so that the object of the Sussex–Derby mission was as much destruction of the influence of the religious as punishment of the rebels.[7] The two earls were armed with detailed instructions on the propaganda they were to spread against the monks, who were to be branded as lazy, disobedient and covetous.[8] The commissioners devoted most of their time to the monks of Furness and Whalley; between 6 March and 18 April Sussex was largely concerned with the accumulation of evidence against them, and the suppression of the two houses which were felt to be too dangerous to be allowed to stand.[9] The authorities' concern

[1] *Ibid.* 518, 578, 630, 970. [2] *Ibid.* 652.
[3] *Ibid.* XI, 1066, 1097, 1118, 1253. [4] *Ibid.* XII(1), 520.
[5] *Ibid.* 520, 632.
[6] *Ibid.* 652, 840, 879, 880. Sussex spent most of his time as far south as Whalley; a household was established there for him on 6 March, and except for his brief visit to Furness he was there permanently from 24 March.
[7] *L & P*, XII(1), 302.
[8] *Ibid.* XI, 1410, No. 3, XII(1), 302 and App. 1, discussed in Haigh, *Lancs. Monasteries*, 86–8.
[9] *L & P*, XII(1), 621, 630, 632, 652, 668, 695, 706, 840, 841, 853, 878, 880, 970; PRO, SC 6/1797, mm. 17–18.

with the religious is also indicated by the trials which took place; 14 of the 32 men indicted were monks, and 3 more were temporarily imprisoned but not brought to trial. Of the 19 men executed, 7 were religious.[1] The earls of Derby and Sussex did not bring Lancashire back to obedience and conformity, they merely suppressed two monasteries.[2]

It is perhaps an unusual criticism to make of representatives of a Tudor government, but if their object was to bring the county into line, then the commission was too lenient and Lancashire escaped lightly. The earl of Derby may have exercised a moderating influence in his own county, the eagerness of the earl of Sussex to return south may have led to laxity,[3] and lack of information may have made greater vigour impossible. Seventeen monks and 18 laymen were marked down for arrest, but only 7 monks and 12 laymen were executed. Apparently 3 monks were released without trial, 3 were acquitted, and 4 escaped; of the laymen, 3 were acquitted and 3 escaped. Of the laymen executed, 2 were not Lancashiremen at all, but outsiders who had spread rebel propaganda in the county, and one of the monks hanged was from Sawley in Yorkshire.[4] After extensive involvement in the Pilgrimage only 16 Lancastrians were executed, a small fraction of the 132 who suffered for their part in the rising, and far fewer than the 74 hanged by the duke of Norfolk in the Carlisle area.[5] The failure of the Pilgrimage presented the Crown with an opportunity to break Lancashire's resistance to the Reformation, but the occasion was allowed to pass. The report made by one of the commissioners as he left the county, that the people were now faithful and true, with their complaints satisfied, and likely to be obedient for many years to come,[6] was a total misunderstanding, born of a lack of reliable information.

The Pilgrimage of Grace made necessary a complete reorganisation of the government of the north, though again Lancashire was not given the extra consideration it required. Most of the members of the Council in the North had been forced to join the rising, and the Council undertook the leadership of the rebellion.[7] The collapse of the Pilgrimage and the mission of the duke of Norfolk made it

[1] PRO, PL 26/13/6; *L & P*, XII(1), 632, 840, 842, 878.
[2] The suppression is described in detail in Haigh, *Lancs. Monasteries*, 91–108.
[3] *L & P*, XII(1), 695, 706, 840.
[4] PRO, PL 26/13/6; *L & P*, XII(1), 632, 840, 842, 878. There is no evidence that the three monks imprisoned were ever brought to trial, and one of them, Ralph Lynney of Whalley, continued as vicar of Blackburn until 1555 (*VCH*, VI, 240–1).
[5] Elton, *Policy and Police*, 387, 389.
[6] *L & P*, XII(1), 970.
[7] Reid, *King's Council in the North*, 137–41.

possible to remodel the administration of the northern counties. The Council's area of jurisdiction was extended to include not only Yorkshire but Durham, Northumberland, Cumberland and Westmorland, and the Council was given wide powers to proceed in cases of treason, murder and felony, and to deal with civil disputes.[1] The membership of the new Council, composed partly of gentlemen who had taken part in the Pilgrimage,[2] ensured that vigorous action would be taken against the disaffected; the gentry had to prove their loyalty by attacking the king's enemies. The Council therefore undertook a sustained campaign against opponents of royal policy, and between the middle of 1537 and the fall of Thomas Cromwell no less than 41 alleged traitors were denounced from the five counties, most of them from Yorkshire; 23 were executed.[3] Overt conservatism was crushed, and the Council had considerable success in enforcing obedience to the Crown's religious policy.[4]

There was no such determined assault in Lancashire. The uncertainty of the powerful earl of Derby's loyalty during the rising may have made the government reluctant to offend him by subjecting him to a provincial council, and Lancashire remained outside the sphere of the Council in the North. The Pilgrimage was followed by no administrative improvements. Only a small number of county gentry had been involved in the rebellion, and the most substantial men turned out to serve the king,[5] so that there was not the same pressure as in Yorkshire for the gentlemen to prove their fidelity by prosecuting opponents of the Crown. The three years after the Pilgrimage saw the denunciation of only two possible traitors, and both seem to have been proceeded against belatedly for their part in the northern rebellion.[6] There was no real attempt in the 1530s to prosecute dissidents; we have seen that few suffered after the

---

[1] *L & P*, XII(1), 98, XII(2), 913, 914, 915, XIII(1), 1269; Reid, *King's Council in the North*, 148–56.

[2] Dodds, *Pilgrimage of Grace*, II, 271–2.

[3] Elton, *Policy and Police*, 392.

[4] Reid, *King's Council in the North*, 161–3; Dickens, *Robert Holgate*, 11; Dickens, *Lollards and Protestants*, 169–73.

[5] Haigh, *Lancs. Monasteries*, 80–1; *L & P*, XI, 1251, ii.

[6] The two were John Standish of Lancaster and one Dickonson of Cartmel (*L & P*, XIV(2), 417). Standish had been court steward of Cartmel Priory and was one of the men who guaranteed the unpaid portion of Cockersand's fine for exemption from suppression, for which he was rewarded with a long lease from the abbey (*Valor*, V, 272; PRO, DL 41/11/49; *Cockersand Chartulary*, ed. W. Farrer, 1195). He was mayor of Lancaster when it was occupied by the rebels; they tried to force him to take the oath, and he seems to have done so (*Derby Correspondence*, 43–7; *L & P*, XII(1), 914). Dickonson was probably either Miles or John Dickonson, both of Cartmel, who were to have been tried for treason for aiding the canons of Cartmel against the king's lessee but evaded capture (PRO, PL 26/13/6).

Pilgrimage, and besides those punished in 1537 only 3 men were denounced to the authorities, as against 52 from Yorkshire.[1] In view of Lancashire's consistent opposition to reform, which still by the reign of Elizabeth was to mark out the county from all others in England,[2] it cannot be assumed that the small number of prosecutions in the 1530s reflected an absence of outspoken conservatism. Few were being hounded, not because the county was compliant, but because the machinery which existed to detect the disaffected was still inadequate.[3] The Pilgrimage of Grace and its aftermath represent not merely the failure of the conservatives to mount effective resistance to religious change, but the failure of the government to defeat opposition.[4]

[1] Elton, *Policy and Police*, 396. The Lancashire trio were James Harrison in 1533, and Standish and Dickonson in 1539.

[2] In 1574 the Privy Council described the county as 'the very sink of Popery, where more unlawful acts have been committed and more unlawful persons holden secret than in any other part of the realm'. (*APC*, VIII, 276–7).

[3] See above, pp. 102–7.

[4] Though studies of the 1536 risings by Margaret Bowker, C. S. L. Davies, M. E. James and R. B. Smith have stressed the role of gentry and secular clergy, the emphasis here has been on monks and their supporters. There *was* discontent among seculars (see above pp. 108–11), and no doubt Lancashire gentry shared the concern of others over uses, but the surviving evidence does not suggest that such issues were important in the Lancashire rising. Rebel propaganda in the county was almost exclusively concerned with the threat to the monasteries, while only a handful of gentry were known rebels and the one incumbent we know was involved was in any case a monk (Haigh, *Lancs. Monasteries*, 80–1). The inability of the Sussex commission to acquire information has left us with only a dozen Lancashire depositions taken after the rising; half of these concern the role of the monks, and the rest are on the loyalty of Derby and the events elsewhere. Though the evidence *may* reflect the interests of the authorities, it does suggest a revolt which was largely monastic in orientation.

10

The official Reformation under Edward VI

The regime nominally headed by the young King Edward denied, one by one, the major points of Catholic doctrine and practice: purgatory and prayers for the dead, the use of images, clerical celibacy and Catholic priesthood; meanwhile affirming characteristically Protestant views on justification by faith, predestination and the correct form of church service. The second wave of the Reformation was thus much more obviously Protestant than the changes which had been imposed under Henry VIII, and even more difficult to enforce, therefore, on a still unalterably conservative area. The task of the new government was nothing less than the destruction of Catholic observance and belief in a county which had already shown its sympathy towards both, and the persuasion of a population almost untouched by reformist trends to become Protestant or, at least, to comply with the outward signs of the new religion.

Edward's ministers appear to have realised that it would require more forceful initiatives than those of the 1530s to achieve their aims. They began with a royal visitation in 1547, when England and Wales were divided into six groups of dioceses and dealt with by commissions of visitors. The province of York was placed under William Benson, the dean of Westminster, Sir John Heresly, Nicholas Ridley as preacher and Edward Plankney (formerly of the episcopal establishment at Chester), as registrar. Although the visitation began in September 1547, a small commission covering the four northern dioceses had a massive task, and progress must have been slow. The court of the commissary of Richmond was inhibited for the visitation until February 1548, and the churchwardens of Prescot were not called before the commission until later in that year.[1] We know nothing of the work of the visitors in Lancashire, nor of the visitation by Bishop Bird which followed hard on its heels,[2] but later events suggest that their success was limited. Certainly, the achievements of the next royal visitation, in 1559, were to be minimal.

[1] J. Strype, *Memorials of Archbishop Cranmer*, 2 vols. I, 209; LCL, RD/A/1A, fos. 112v–116; *Prescot Accounts*, 27.
[2] PRO, SP 10/3/4; CRO, EDC 2/3, *passim*.

By 1550 it had clearly been decided that conventional methods of controlling the religious life of Lancashire were inadequate, and a return was made to the experiment of 1543. In July 1550 the Duchy appointed an impressive commission, which included the earl of Derby, Lord Mounteagle, the bishop of Chester and his chancellor, Duchy and palatinate officers and leading members of the county hierarchy. The new body was to proceed against those 'as by the ecclesiastical correction yet could not be brought to forsake their detestable crimes and offences of adultery, incest, fornication and bawdry, much used in those parts'. The royal visitors of 1547–8 had attempted to combat such misconduct, but 'although heretofore being otherwise by our visitors admonished' some offenders continued 'so wilfully and openly as it were thought of them no crime'. The commissioners were also to organise collections for the repair of churches, and ensure that the gentry paid their share. Mandates were issued for the local clergy to report 'all such enormities, fornications and adulteries' and 'all churches and chapels ruinous and in decay, for the due re-edification of the same', and the commission held sessions at Wigan and Lathom.[1] It is unlikely that the sexual morals of the county were reformed overnight, but these efforts produced at least a temporary improvement in the condition of church fabric, for about this time bells and chalices were sold to pay for repairs at Childwall, Walton, Halsall, Ormskirk and Aughton.[2]

The religious changes of the 1530s may have impinged little on parochial life, so that Thomas Cromwell was able to rely on the normal social and administrative structures of county and diocese for their enforcement. But the Edwardian authorities had to resort to more radical expedients, and it became necessary to supplement the strictly ecclesiastical machinery with bodies in which laymen could play a leading role. Under both Edward and Elizabeth, the Council in the North was expected to assist in the imposition of the royal injunctions and the Prayer Book.[3] The authority of the Council did not, however, extend into Lancashire, and there the duty of enforcing reform was entrusted to special commissions or to lords lieutenant. In 1547 the earl of Shrewsbury was made lieutenant of a group of counties which included Lancashire, and a further commission may have been granted in 1550. Shrewsbury's jurisdiction over Lancashire was transferred to the earl of Derby in the following year, and Derby received commissions in 1551, 1552 and 1553. Copies of the Lancashire commissions have not survived, but we

[1] PRO, DL 42/96, fos. 33v–34; CRO, EDC 5, 1550; *Prescot Accounts*, 29.
[2] *Church Goods*, II, 91, 94, 107, 111, 114.
[3] Reid, *King's Council in the North*, 171–2, 187–8.

may assume that, like those granted for other areas, they instructed the lieutenant to do all he could for the advancement of the new religion.[1]

Shrewsbury and Derby, however, were singularly inappropriate magistrates of the new religion, and in the House of Lords the latter voted against all the major reformist legislation in the reign of Edward.[2] In 1551 the two men were apparently involved in a plot with the deposed Protector Somerset that they would raise the north against the earl of Warwick's radical religious policies while the duke seized London. The agreement was sealed by a marriage between Derby's heir, Lord Strange, and one of Somerset's daughters, and Strange, a confidant of the young king, was to persuade Edward to marry another of the Seymour girls. Early in the year the Spanish ambassador heard that Warwick intended to strike against conservative peers such as Derby and Shrewsbury, and the two may have heard what was afoot since they asked for permission to be absent from the St George's Day feast. At the beginning of April a group of nobles loyal to Warwick went north – it was said to watch the two earls – and the Privy Council heard rumours that Princess Mary intended to flee to Shrewsbury. Warwick was now afraid that the earls were intriguing with Somerset, and when he summoned them to Court they seem to have refused to go. Shrewsbury was then threatened with dismissal from his offices and Derby was apparently ordered to give up his title of king of Man, but he declined to do so and prepared to resist by force. In May the frightened Privy Council ordered the arrest of those spreading rumours of discord between the Council and the two earls, but some sort of accommodation must have been reached since Derby was appointed lieutenant of Lancashire and he and Shrewsbury agreed to go to Court. On their arrival in London they were feted by the government and Derby was admitted to the Privy Council, but this was merely an honorific post as he was specifically instructed not to attend meetings unless explicitly summoned.

Part of the agreement between the earls and Warwick may have been that they would assist in the attack on Somerset, for when the duke was arrested in October 1551, Derby and Shrewsbury were asked to return to London to help with the prosecution and Lord Strange was a leading government witness at the ensuing trial. When Somerset's trial came, however, Derby arrived an hour late and Shrewsbury failed to appear at all; perhaps there were limits even to Stanley and Talbot duplicity. The import of these events is not

[1] G. S. Thomson, *Lords Lieutenant in the Sixteenth Century*, 23, 31–3; Strype, *Ecclesiastical Memorials*, II(1), 262–3, 278; *APC*, III, 259, IV, 50, 257.
[2] *Journals of the House of Lords*, I, 331, 384, 401, 421.

altogether clear. Most of our information comes from the Court gossip reported by foreign ambassadors, but the story remained consistent for nine months and there is a good deal of circumstantial evidence to support it, besides the possibly manufactured testimonies at Somerset's trial.[1] Even if we conclude that there really was a plot, the motives of the two earls are far from clear. They were probably as incensed by Warwick's attempts to weaken the authority of northern magnates and build a power-base for himself in the north[2] as they were by his religious programme. For our purposes, however, the distinction is insignificant, for Derby and Shrewsbury clearly resented governmental interference in their spheres of influence and were far from willing tools of official policy.

The county gentry, too, were more anxious to preserve their own power and interest than to obey orders from London, and when royal policy came into conflict with the habits and social relationships of the county it was the latter which prevailed. In the early 1540s there was vigorous opposition in Lancashire to the Crown's attempts to raise forces against the Scots, for the enrolment of tenants as royal soldiers seemed to weaken gentry authority. Richard Towneley, Edward Radcliffe, Robert Holt and others would not allow their tenants, or royal tenants of lands the gentlemen had leased from the Crown, to muster for the king or obey the king's officers. Peter Farington and Richard Bannester assembled their tenants in armour, retained them as their followers and forbade them to wear the king's badge or serve under the royal banner, and they enlisted the powerful baron of Walton to protect them against the royal stewards.[3] The particularist interests of the gentry could be equally important in ecclesiastical affairs, after about one-third of English advowsons passed into the hands of laymen following the suppression of the monasteries. In Lancashire local gentlemen presented to almost 40 % of parochial livings in 1550, and by 1560 this had risen to 47 % while, as we have seen, many of the assistant clergy owed their posts and salaries to the gentry. Churchwardens, too, were often appointed and supervised by local notables: in 1523, 1527, 1528 and 1543 the wardens of Prescot were chosen by John Eccleston and Henry Halsall, and the churchwardens' accounts were

[1] PRO, SP 10/13/67; *Chronicles and Political Papers of Edward VI*, ed. W. K. Jordan, 93, 99; *CSPS* (1550–2), 215, 263, 279–81, 283, 291, 300, 323, 347, 386, 393, 406, 408; *CSPF*, I, 119–20; R. Steele, *Tudor and Stuart Proclamations*, 2 vols. I, 42, No. 398; *APC*, III, 240–1, 259, 264, 328–9.
[2] R. Reid, 'The political influence of the "North Parts" under the later Tudors', *Tudor Studies*, ed. R. W. Seton Watson, 215–16.
[3] *Duchy Pleadings*, II, 178–9, 185–6, 189–90.

subject to regular audit by gentry of the parish.[1] Religious change could only be imposed with the cooperation of the squirearchy.

We know little of the processes by which the Reformation was enforced under Edward, and this in itself is significant. The bishop was inactive, Cromwell's system of reports from the localities was allowed to lapse, and the relaxation of the Henrician additions to the treason laws indicates that the regime was not greatly worried about conservative opposition. It is therefore difficult to assess the extent to which the Edwardian legislation was obeyed. There was no sign of widespread resistance to the new Prayer Books in Lancashire, and perhaps the penalties imposed by the acts of uniformity were sufficient to deter all but the most indomitable. There were difficulties, it is true. The first Prayer Book was to come into use on Whit Sunday 1549, but the Prescot churchwardens were unable to purchase a copy immediately and two men were paid 2 shillings to write out the important parts for use in the church. But two Prayer Books were bought in 1550, and in 1552 the parish found these were redundant and the new version had to be acquired.[2] However, we need not be surprised that, except for an abortive rising in Yorkshire, the abolition of the mass did not provoke rebellion in the north as it did in the west. The Edwardian wars against the Scots saved the regime from militant opposition in the north, for even the most discontented conservative could not turn his attentions towards London and leave the border undefended against the traditional enemy.

This does not mean that the Edwardian changes were accepted without demur. The statute of 1550 which ordered that the old service books were to be delivered to the civil authorities and thence to the bishop for destruction seems to have been widely ignored. The Prescot accounts give no indication that the books were handed over, and there was certainly no need to purchase replacements in the reign of Mary. Although possession of Catholic service books was punishable by fine and imprisonment, three Lancashire churches listed missals when the inventories of 1552 were taken and mass books are mentioned in the only two known inventories of private chapels between 1550 and 1553.[3] These examples presumably suggest ignorance of the law rather than flagrant disobedience confessed before officials, but where the law is not known it cannot be obeyed. There must have been a similar lack of information following the order of November 1551 for the replacement of altars by communion tables, and as there was no visitation of Lancashire for the rest of Edward's reign enforcement was difficult. The wardens of Prescot

[1] Hill, *Economic Problems of the Church*, 54–5; *VCH*, III–VIII, *passim*; Bailey, 'Churchwardens' accounts of Prescot', I, 138–9, II, 15.
[2] *Prescot Accounts*, 29.   [3] *L & C Wills*, I, 109, 112.

paid 5s to have their altar taken down and a table erected, and the two altars removed from Eccleston church had not been replaced by 1554. But in 1552 four Lancashire churches openly admitted that they had altars, and under Mary altars were 'restored' so rapidly that one suspects they had never been removed. In the diocese of Canterbury in 1557 at least 47 of the 243 churches visited did not yet have a high altar and a further 90 had no side altar, but of the 49 Lancashire churches and chapels visited between 1554 and 1557 only 1 did not have the required altars.[1] Either the Lancashire altars had not been removed, or parishioners had kept them hidden and they were ready to be replaced.

Although we have some evidence that official decrees were not always obeyed at the local level, the orthodox were acutely aware that their faith was under attack. In the case of Ellis Hall this feeling provoked a reaction which amounted to temporary insanity. Hall, the son of a Manchester carpenter, was in his youth 'given to solitariness, abstinence and prayer', but about 1530 he married and 'began to have a covetous mind in setting all my whole mind in worldly things'. In the reign of Edward he was able to take advantage of the unusual economic circumstances, 'when the great fall of money was', to make £500 in one year as a draper. But one night in 1551, while he was studying his accounts, he heard a voice say, 'Eli, thou carpenter's son, arise, and make thine account quickly, fast and pray, for the day draweth near.' Hall then saw a vision of the Five Wounds, but he dismissed it all as a dream, until in March 1552 a severe illness kept him in bed. Then he saw the same vision, and a voice told him 'Thou art elect and chosen of God to declare and pronounce unto his people his Word, for thy virtuous living in thy youth time, and art at this time so plagued because thou didst utterly forsake God's will and commandment and wholly gave thyself into the world.' The voice instructed him to 'write of the revelation that thou hast seen of baptism, repentance and amendment of life, and show it to the magistrates and rulers, and that which thou shalt write shall be put into thy head by the Holy Ghost'. Ellis Hall later reported that between 9 April and 11 April 1552 he was taken into heaven, where he saw Christ enthroned and was instructed to fast and pray and then write after seven years. Accordingly, Hall began to wear strange clothes and gave himself to 'virtuous living in fasting and praying', though with the return of Catholicism under Mary he again lived a normal life and became junior constable of Manchester in 1557.[2] Early in the reign of Elizabeth, when his

---

[1] *Prescot Accounts*, 29; Hughes, *Reformation in England*, II, 237; CRO, EDV 1/1, fos. 120–155, 169–174v, 1/2, fos. 33–42v, 65–85.
[2] *Manchester Court Leet Records*, ed. J. Harland, 170.

religion was again under attack, Hall was again driven to fanaticism; he wrote a treatise on obedience and a 'great book', and then went off to the capital where he demanded to see the queen. Needless to say, he was not taken seriously by the Privy Council or the bishop of London, and he was pilloried 'for seducing the people by publishing false revelations'.[1] Although Hall was clearly a madman, it is interesting that his mind was apparently unhinged under Protestant governments only, and he may have been an extreme case of an anguished Catholic whose faith was threatened.

The Edwardian regime attempted to destroy Catholicism, but made little effort to substitute a new religion. Martin Bucer noted in 1550 that reforms in England were carried out in too negative a spirit, 'by means of ordinances which the majority obey very grudgingly, and by the removal of the instruments of the ancient superstition'.[2] The government relied too much on coercion, for which Lancashire had neither adequate machinery nor reliable personnel, and made no more than a token effort to ensure that the new religion was preached with evangelical fervour. The two much-praised official attempts to bring Edwardian Protestantism to Lancashire[3] in fact came to nothing. The 1551 project for six itinerant chaplains to the king, who would in turn tour the conservative areas beginning with Lancashire, Derbyshire and Wales, was soon all but abandoned. The six preachers were first reduced to five, then to four, and there is no evidence that any of the remainder ever reached Lancashire. George Marsh, the Dean martyr, left a list of those who tried to evangelise the county under Edward VI, but the four royal chaplains were not included.[4] It has also been suggested that when the earl of Derby bought the site and lands of Manchester College from the king, one of the conditions of the purchase was that he was to nominate three or four preachers and provide stipends of £40 a year for each one. But the original grant to the earl makes no mention of preachers, and specifically excludes advowsons connected with the College. In 1546 it was estimated that the site and

[1] This account is a conflation of Hall's statement to the Council (Bodleian Library, Tanner MS 50, fo. 16) and his examination before Grindal in 1562 (PRO, SP 12/23/39). There is a short account, apparently based on the latter, in Strype, *Annals of the Reformation*, I(1), 433–5. Hall said consistently that his troubles began in 1551, and he was clearly a Catholic: he had a vision of the Five Wounds, he abstained from flesh, he refused to answer questions on the mass, transubstantiation and purgatory, and he refused to receive the sacraments under Elizabeth.
[2] Quoted by D. M. Loades, *The Oxford Martyrs*, 97.
[3] See, for example, C. Hill, 'Puritans and the "Dark Corners of the Land"', *TRHS*, 5th series, XIII, 79.
[4] *Chronicles and Political Papers of Edward VI*, 101; Strype, *Ecclesiastical Memorials*, II(1), 521–2; Foxe, *Acts and Monuments*, VII, 65.

lands would yield only £1 6s 8d each year in rent, and in 1549 the earl paid only £268 6s 8d for these lands and some chantry property in Manchester and Huyton, which in all were expected to yield £12 13s 2d in rents. Clearly Derby's interest in the property would not support stipends of £120 or £160, and only if he had been granted the tithes of Manchester, which were in fact leased to other men, could the earl have endowed preacherships. The 'Derby preachers' never existed; although Hollingworth, the seventeenth-century Manchester historian, suggested that the earl nominated 'ministers officiating in the church', his only authority was what 'our forefathers have told us', and when the college was refounded by Mary its only endowed posts were two curacies.[1]

The government and its leading representative in Lancashire totally failed to develop the dynamic approach to religious change which conditions in the county demanded. This is, perhaps, surprising, since Archbishop Cranmer was certainly aware of the need for a positive preaching of reform, and the Homilies of 1547 provided a short course for parishioners, Sunday by Sunday, in the essentials of Protestant theology. The universities, especially Cambridge, were now producing a stream of young reformers, and though several Lancashire graduates were given preaching licences there was no consistent attempt to direct resources towards the conservative areas. The regime was bedevilled by financial difficulties, and with an economic crisis and the war against Scotland there could be no heavy investment in the conversion of England. Bishop Bird of Chester had tried to secure the provision of preachers for Lancashire from the revenues of Manchester College,[2] but the Crown could not afford so large an exception from the act dissolving colleges and chantries. Thus the official Reformation under Edward VI was confined to the destruction of Catholic institutions and belief, and such an approach could only provoke the strongest resentment.

Even more obviously than the attack on the monasteries, the suppression of the chantries was an assault on Catholic doctrine. The statute of 1547 argued that the chantries were to be dissolved because 'superstition and errors' had resulted from 'vain opinions of purgatory and masses satisfactory'. Professor Dickens has drawn attention to the offence confiscation would cause to those who held these 'vain opinions', while suggesting that few still accepted the orthodox doctrine.[3] But we have seen that in Lancashire chantries

---

[1] *CPR*, Edward VI, III, 138–9, Philip and Mary, III, 513; *Lancs. Chantries*, I, 12; PRO, DL 14/5/24–9; Hollingworth, *Mancuniensis*, 63, 66.
[2] BM, Harleian MS 604, fo. 82 (*L & P*, XXI(1), 967).
[3] *Statutes of the Realm*, IV, 24–5; Dickens, *English Reformation*, 207, 211.

were founded until just before the act, and other methods of providing prayers for the dead remained popular, so that the implications of the legislation were horrifying; the government was restricting the ability of Lancashiremen to attain salvation. To make matters worse, the chantry and stipendiary priests formed almost a quarter of the total clerical staff of the shire, and in an area already short of priests the suppression was a serious blow. It is therefore not surprising that patrons, priests and local sympathisers took evasive action.

The attack on the monasteries seems to have provoked fears for the future of similar institutions, and between 1536 and 1544 at least three conservative families closed down their chantries. The Henrician Chantries Act of 1545 naturally gave impetus to the process of resumption, and by 1547 three more foundations had been revoked.[1] With care, even surviving chantries could be protected from the Crown and, when the royal commissioners conducted their survey in 1546, sixteen chantries, more than one-fifth of those remaining, were successfully concealed from them.[2] Although a second, and more thorough, survey in 1548 uncovered all but one of the chantries, concealment of endowments was still possible. Between the survey of 1548 and the death of Mary, Duchy officials found it necessary to organise no fewer than seventeen local searches for chantry property, one in 1550, four in 1552, two in 1553, five in 1554, four in 1555 and one in 1557.[3] Once property had been detected it was leased out by the Duchy, but several lessees encountered difficulties. In 1549 Thomas Fleetwood, lessee of the chantry at Eccleston, complained that the former incumbent, Laurence Halliwell, refused to leave the chantry and the tenants of its lands continued to pay their rents to the priest. There were similar cases at Blackrod and Eccles, while at five other chantries the tenants staged rent-strikes and others tried to prevent confiscation by disputing the Crown's claim to chantry property.[4] The motives of those involved were presumably economic more often than religious, but the Duchy's successive enquiries reveal an impressive record of obstruction in Lancashire.

Particular ingenuity was expended on preventing the confiscation of liturgical items belonging to chantries and free chapels. Three commissions had tried to track down plate and other metal valuables by 1554, but the bells of seventeen chapels were still outstanding. The officers who conducted a fourth search managed to unearth the

[1] *Lancs. Chantries*, II, 176–7, 186, 199–200, 231, 238.
[2] *Ibid.* I, 164, II, 193, 201, 204, 216, 220, 228, 229, 239–41, 246–52.
[3] PRO, DL 42/96, *passim*.
[4] *Duchy Pleadings*, III, 30–1, 69–70, 103–6, 115, 116–17, 123–4, 126, 235–40; *Ducatus Lancastriae*, I, 238, 287.

bells of fourteen of the chapels, and a fifth enquiry found the bells of Oldham. But at Bispham the chapel wardens claimed that their bells had already been confiscated and sold, while at Haslingden it was said that two local men had stolen the bells before officials could remove them.[1] Churchwardens themselves were not above this sort of peculation, and at Farnworth the wardens had persuaded a local smith to cut up a metal candelabra so that they could sell the pieces for their own profit. But more often churchwardens acted in the interests of the local community, and fought to protect chapel property. The Farnworth wardens managed to persuade the Duchy to return confiscated vestments and other things on the grounds that theirs was such an important chapel, and the same argument was tried at Goodshaw without success. At Burnley the wardens claimed that the chapel's vestments and ornaments should never have been removed, as it was a parish church and not a chapel of ease, but this deceit produced no results. The parishioners of Lancaster were the most successful of all; they managed to conceal the almshouse chantry from each commission, and the priest continued to pray for the founders until 1560.[2]

Much of the opposition to confiscation came from free chapels, for the provision in the Chantries Act that chapels as well as chantries and colleges were to be suppressed was potentially ruinous for the Church in Lancashire. Almost two-thirds of the county's churches were in fact only chapels, and about a third of the inhabitants of the shire attended a chapel rather than a parish church. The legal status of the chapels is difficult to determine, but a widespread attack on them would have been disastrous; a massive parish such as Whalley, covering 180 square miles, with 30 townships and a population of roughly 10,000, could not possibly have operated without its fifteen chapels.[3] The chantry commissioners paid no attention to the chapels, apparently relying on the clause in the suppression act that chapels of ease in hamlets far from parish churches were not to be molested. But the later commissions for concealed property looked closely at the chapels. The accounts of Edward Parker, receiver to these commissions, show that a comprehensive attack was made on ornaments and silverware, and when the 1552 commissioners for the seizure of church goods came to do their work they found little left for them in the chapels. Parker and his colleagues removed chalices from 22 chapels, bells from 24 and

[1] PRO, DL 42/96, fos. 36–37, 57–58, 59–60; *Lancs. Chantries*, II, 258–78, 281–2; *Ducatus Lancastriae*, II, 163; CRO, EDC 1/13, fo. 165.
[2] *Duchy Pleadings*, III, 158–9, 199–204, 260–1; PRO, DL 42/96, fos. 122, 152, DL 44/29.
[3] BM, Harleian MS 594, fos. 101–105, 108; PRO, SP 12/31, fo. 86.

ornaments from 29, with a total profit of £180 and 230 ounces of silver.[1]

The drive against the chapel buildings themselves was much more dangerous, and commissioners appointed in November 1552 took as their target 25 chapels judged not to be exempt from the act. Of these, 23 are recorded in the commission's returns as seized for the king and then sold, though the total realised by the sales was only £19 12s 4d.[2] We know that most of the chapels sold were still in use over the next twenty or thirty years, so it is probable that many were purchased by the local inhabitants and services were not interrupted. Certainly Littleborough chapel and one of its bells were bought back by the parishioners for £2, expressly so that divine service could continue in a chapel so far distant from its parish church, and at Accrington the people had to pay £2 6s 8d for their chapel and its contents. Rivington chapel was bought by Richard Pilkington, a local gentleman, and services continued there. At Rossendale the chapel was not sold but rented out by the Crown to John Nuttall, but after the inhabitants had petitioned for the restoration of their chapel Nuttall eventually surrendered his tenancy to a group of feoffees for the use of the people.[3] But although many of the chapels were maintained in this way, it is simply not true to say that, of the 90 or so Lancashire chapels built by the reign of Edward, none were disturbed.[4] Tarleton chapel, despite its local importance, was sold to Sir Thomas Hesketh for 12s 4d; he had the building pulled down and there was no church there for another century. The chapel at Billinge in Wigan was bought by an unpopular local landlord and turned into a barn; it was certainly not used for services early in the reign of Elizabeth. The same sort of thing happened at Westhoughton in Dean parish, where the chapel was sold to the lord of the manor, who refused to allow services there. Garston chapel, with its bell, glass, timber and benches, was purchased by Sir William Norris, and though the building remained standing it fell into ruin and was not used for services.[5] The example of Garston chapel raises problems, for though, by chance, the deed of sale survives, the transaction was not recorded in the commissioners' accounts.

At least four Lancashire chapels were withdrawn from religious use, and the fate of others is not known. In all, the commissioners

[1] *Church Goods*, II, 81, III, 5; *Lancs. Chantries*, II, 273–8.
[2] *Lancs. Chantries*, II, 277–8.
[3] Gastrell, *Notitia Cestriensis*, II, 133, 341; Whitaker, *History of Whalley*, II, 288; *VCH*, V, 289, 293; BM, Harleian MS 594, fo. 102; *CCR*, III, 214–15, 220.
[4] Thus *VCH*, II, 46; followed by Dickens, *English Reformation*, 212.
[5] *Lancs. Chantries*, II, 174, 277–8; *Duchy Pleadings*, III, 235–40, 257–8; *VCH*, III, 257–8; BM, Harleian MS 594, fo. 102; *Ducatus Lancastriae*, I, 296; *Norris Deeds*, ed. J. H. Lumby, No. 230; *Commonwealth Church Survey*, 69.

seized the bells, chalices, ornaments or the buildings themselves of at least 52 chapels, and 27 chapels were certainly sold. The chapel commissioners worked in a haphazard fashion, their accounts were inaccurately and perhaps fraudulently kept, and there is often no rational explanation for their treatment of individual chapels. Some of the most important chapels in the county, such as Liverpool and Didsbury, were seized and sold, though it is probable that the terms of the Chantries Act exempted them. The case of Garston suggests that chapels not listed in the commission's accounts were sold, and others may have been confiscated without record. But fortunately for the supply of churches many local communities were able to buy back their chapels, and Mary came to the throne before more than a handful could be withdrawn from use.

Although the impact of the Chantries Act on the chapels was potentially disastrous, its effect on the chantry priests has been much exaggerated. The Duchy of Lancaster allotted pensions totalling almost £300 to 64 chantrists, two fellows of Manchester and the warden of the suppressed college. In terms of income the dissolution made no difference at all to half of the 64 chantry priests, those whose incomes had been £5 or less, since each received a pension equal to his former salary, and even for the rest only small reductions took place. Other chantrists had the copyhold properties which had supported their foundations assigned to them for life, and the lands were sublet to the former tenants. The future of those priests who had been schoolmasters was also assured; one recent foundation which may never have been effective was confiscated, but continuation warrants were issued for all the other chantry schools and the Duchy now paid the masters' stipends.[1] The average chantry pension was only a mark less than the average chantry income, and if ex-chantrists suffered hardship it was not because the government treated them harshly but because Lancashire chantry stipends, to which pensions were related, had been so low.

We have noted the crucial role played by chantrists in the understaffed parishes of Lancashire, and the suppression of the chantries seemed likely to mean a damaging reduction in the supply of clergy. But most priests used their government pensions in place of chantry stipends and continued to serve in their old parishes. In parishes for which we have visitation call-book lists for 1554, there had been 86 chantrists and stipendiaries at work; of these, 46 were still serving as assistant clergy six years after the fall of the chantries, and only 6 of them had changed parishes. Another 12 ex-chantrists had died in the

[1] PRO, DL 28/27/18, mm. 1–2d, DL 42/96, fo. 25; *Statutes of the Realm*, IV, 32; *CCR*, I, 161–6, 385–7, II, 217–24, 228–9, III, 159–62; A. F. Leach, *English Schools at the Reformation*, 125; *VCH*, II, 563, 602.

meantime, so that only 28 at the most did not continue to serve.[1] Two elderly ex-chantrists went into retirement and two more became private chaplains, but these were exceptional cases. After 1548 the priests were no longer tied to foundations and were free to serve the community as parochial clergy, so that in a strictly practical sense the dissolution of the chantries may have been beneficial. In the long term, of course, the value of fixed pensions was eroded by inflation, and as each priest died the income which had financed his service lapsed. But before such influences could operate on a wide scale, the Elizabethan settlement had reduced the number of clergy needed by abolishing many of the time-consuming aspects of Catholic liturgy. However, though the immediate practical impact of the fall of the chantries was not severe, it remained a massive affront to those who believed in the efficacy of prayers for the dead.

The confiscation of chalices, vestments and other church goods in 1553 was equally offensive, for either they had been hallowed by use in the mass or they had been purchased only recently. It has been suggested that clergy and parishioners conspired on a grand scale to conceal church goods, and certainly at Bolton the churchwardens stripped lead from the steeple and sold it, together with candlesticks and other valuables from the church.[2] But by the time the confiscation took place, three surveys of church goods had been conducted, in 1547–8, in 1549 and in 1552, and it would therefore have required ingenuity and consistency to deceive the commissioners.[3] The argument for evasion rests entirely on the brevity of the inventories, but in Lancashire at least the lists were short because there was little property to record. The detailed investigation of 1552 was conducted by a group of county gentry and mayors under the earl of Derby, and the returns were sent to London late in the year. It was found that there had been some embezzlement, sales or losses from almost a quarter of the churches in the few years before the survey, but they were not attempts at evasion since with one or two exceptions the churches were taken by surprise and several had only recently purchased new plate or bells.[4] But there was no enthusiasm for hasty compliance with the Council's instructions, and though plate and valuables should have been dispatched to London at the very beginning of 1553 they had not left Lancashire by Edward's death in July.[5]

[1] Cf. *Lancs. Chantries*, *passim*, and CRO, EDV 1/1, fos. 31–49, 65–66v.
[2] Somerville, *Duchy of Lancaster*, 298; CRO, EDC 2/9, pp. 30–1.
[3] PRO, SP 10/3/4, 10/6/25, DL 42/96, fo. 56; *APC*, III, 467; *Church Goods*, *passim*, especially II, 58, 63, 66, 75, 111, 113. The confiscation of the goods of all churches should not be confused with the removal of property from chapels under the Chantries Act.
[4] *Church Goods*, *passim*, especially I, 27, 32, II, 63, 75, 87, III, 20, 21.
[5] *CPR*, Edward VI, IV, 392–3; *APC*, IV, 219, 360.

The Reformation under Edward VI saw a wholesale attack on the beliefs, liturgy, popular institutions and property of the Catholic Church. There was, moreover, a drastic contraction in the supply of clergy in Lancashire, and some disruption of relations between the Church and the laity. Religious change coincided with debasement of the coinage and serious inflation between 1547 and 1551, and a crisis of over-production in the cloth industry from 1552. In Lancashire a hitherto peaceful agrarian scene was disturbed in 1548 by disputes over common lands at Penwortham, Hindley, Stalmine, Aspull, Westhoughton, Burnley, Colne, Longton Moss, Ightenhill, Claydon, Cuerden, Turton and Dean Moor. In 1549 the tenants of the earl of Derby claimed new rights over commons at Ashworth and Bury, there were lawsuits over trespass on common lands at Prestwich and Tonge Moor, and conflicts over pasture at Brockhurst manor, Lowton Waste, Newton, Ainsworth, Middleton and Cockey Moor. The following year saw disturbances over commons at Chatburn, in 1551 a similar conflict arose at Westhoughton, and in the latter year there were troubles over the use of the waste at Coppull Moor and Worthington. Thereafter there seems to have been less discontent, and though there were a few legal conflicts under Mary these were mainly the result not of popular demands but of disputes between landowners for control of the profitable peat beds.[1]

Economic difficulties soured relations between laymen and clergy, as those who found it difficult to make ends meet found tithe increasingly irksome. Only 14 Lancashire tithe disputes had gone to the bishop of Chester's consistory in the four years 1544–7, but in the five years 1547–51 there were 38. This increase was not only due to the activities of rapacious lay lessees; in the first four years there were 7 cases in which an incumbent had to sue his parishioners for refusal of tithe, but in the five-year period there were 15. After this peak there was a marked decline in tithe litigation, and there were only 23 cases in the five years 1551–5, only 6 of them involving priests.[2] It is interesting that the number of tithe causes began to fall at the same time as the number of conflicts in the secular courts over common lands. The reign of Edward also saw a disruption in the finances of Prescot church, for the wardens' receipts from parish dues and other sources fell from £3 10s in 1546–7 to £2 12s 7d in 1547–8, and in 1548–9, when the income was only £2 9s 4d, £1 10s 8d of this was profit from the sale of some 'iron' belonging to the church. In 1549–50 the wardens' revenue for the running expenses of the church was only 15s 9d, and thereafter they had no

---

[1] *Ducatus Lancastriae*, I, 222, 223, 224, 226, 228, 229, 230, 240, 249, 261, 262, II, 94, 101; *VCH*, II, 289–90.
[2] CRO, EDC 1/11–13, *passim*.

receipts until 1554. The parishioners had simply stopped making contributions, and the churchwardens had to meet urgent expenses out of their own pockets.[1] Although the refusal of tithe and church dues was more probably the result of economic pressures on the laity, it is possible that there was some reluctance on the part of conservatives to contribute towards a heretical Church.

Some of the clergy, too, must have been in serious economic difficulties. Rectors who received all the tithes, and vicars who had the small tithes had few problems, but salaried vicars and the mass of the assistant clergy who received stipends from local gentlemen or from levies on householders found their real incomes eroded. As assistants' incomes in Lancashire were already much lower than elsewhere, pressure on priests to emigrate to more prosperous areas increased with inflation, and the dramatic decline which took place in the number of serving clergy may have been, in the first place, the result of emigration. Stipends became even more inadequate for those priests who, after changes in the law, contemplated marriage, and the unusually large proportion of clergy in Lancashire who remained single may have done so as much for reasons of poverty as of conservative social pressures.[2]

A second explanation for the decline in the number of clergy may have been the practical implications of a Protestant liturgy. In 1548· Lancashire was staffed by something over 400 priests, but thereafter the fall of the chantries and the abolition of the mass and other ceremonies reduced the number required to man a parish, and some may have become redundant. Parishioners were unlikely to continue paying for priests whose usefulness was no longer obvious. If we may assume that the reformed Church needed 2 priests to serve a parish church and 1 to serve a chapel, then after 1549 Lancashire had places for only about 220 clergy; this may explain why the number of serving priests in the county fell to a little over 250 by 1554.[3] We know of several priests who simply retired into private life after 1548. George Parker, for example, appeared at the visitation of 1548, but though he did not die until 1560 he did not serve in the Church thereafter, and the same is true of William Bimson of Standish, who died in 1563.[4] The evidence of parish registers and the high average age of chantry-priests both suggest that clergy had normally continued in service until death, but with the contraction in demand for clerical labour some were leaving ten or more years earlier.

[1] Bailey, 'Churchwardens' accounts of Prescot', I, 167–9, 171.
[2] See below, pp. 181–2.
[3] CRO, EDV 2/3–4, *passim*, EDV 1/1, fos. 31v–49, 65–66v.
[4] CRO, EDV 2/3, fos. 19, 20, *Ormskirk Reg.* 135, *Standish Reg.* 136.

A third possibility, which may account for the withdrawal of some priests, is that there was a reluctance to serve in a Protestant Church. As elsewhere, some Lancashire clergy remained at their posts whatever the religious complexion of the regime they served. Roger Mason, ordained as early as 1510, was vicar of Huyton from 1517 until his death in 1558, Richard Halsall held the family rectory of Halsall between 1513 and 1563, and Roger Bradshaw was rector of Heysham at least from 1535 to 1568. Examples could easily be multiplied, and no Lancashire rector or vicar resigned his benefice for religious reasons in the reign of Edward. That incumbents should have been pliable vicars of Bray is, however, not surprising, for all the worldly pressures of status, home, comfort and income were on the side of conformity. But these considerations did not apply to all, and for a principled stand we should look to those with less to lose, men such as the priest John Janson, a mere chapel clerk at Liverpool, who fled to Spain in 1551.[1]

Whether it was for economic, practical or religious reasons, there was a mass withdrawal of labour by the unbeneficed clergy of Lancashire from the Church as reformed by Cranmer and his colleagues. The number of priests serving in the four deaneries of south Lancashire fell from 277 early in 1548 to 166 in 1554, and in Warrington deanery the decline was catastrophic, from 107 to 56. The trend was similar in the eleven parishes of north Lancashire for which we have figures, falling from 54 to 34. In 1548 369 priests served in parishes for which there are visitation call-book lists for both 1548 and 1554, but by 1554 183 of them, a fraction under half, had disappeared, and only 32 are known to have died. No fewer than 151 priests, 41% of those serving in 1548, disappeared for reasons other than known death during the reign of Edward. In the years between 1548 and 1554, 49.6% of the clergy disappeared for all reasons including death, as against only 26% in the relatively calm years 1541–8.[2] The decline cannot be attributed to the suppression of the chantries, for only 32% of ex-chantrists vanished inexplicably between 1548 and 1554, as against 44% of the non-chantry priests.

In normal circumstances ordinations to the priesthood would produce enough new recruits to maintain a fairly constant labour force, and we have seen that in the first half of the sixteenth century the number of priests in Lancashire remained fairly stable. But in the reign of Edward the supply of ordinands from the county almost

[1] *Liverpool Town Books*, ed. J. Twemlow, I, 32; *THSLC*, NS, XVIII, 100 and n.
[2] Cf. *Clergy List*; CRO, EDV 2/3–4, EDV 1/1. The dead are those marked 'mortuus' in the 1554 lists, or those whose deaths are recorded in the fairly wide selection of parish registers for these years, but of course the figure given for deaths is likely to be an underestimate.

dried up and vacancies were not filled; in 1554 there were only 49 priests serving in the parishes who had not been there in 1548, to replace 183 who had left or died. In the years 1542–6 an average of about 40 priests were ordained each year at Chester, about half of them from Lancashire. There was a fall in 1545, perhaps as a result of the Henrician Chantries Act, but ordinations returned to their former level in 1546. In 1547, however, the number of priests ordained fell by two-thirds, and the lesser orders reflected the pattern. In 1547 3 ordinations were held, but none came forward to be ordained acolyte or subdeacon, and though 11 priests and 19 deacons were ordained in March 1547 the rest of the year produced only 3 priests and 11 deacons. The first ordination register of the bishops of Chester covers the years 1542–58, but there is no record of any ordinations between the end of 1547 and the beginning of 1555. Unless ordinations for the intervening years were recorded in a separate volume (and as the entries in the extant register begin again with the arrival at Chester of the first Marian bishop there is no reason to suppose this) there can have been no Edwardian ordinations in the diocese after 1547.[1] William Herdman, ordained deacon in 1547, was not priested at Chester until the first available opportunity in 1555, while John Millington, made deacon in 1546, had to go to London to become a priest in 1554. There is also a gap in the ordination lists of the diocese of Durham between 1547 and 1555, and in these years there were very few ordinations at York. In the case of Chester, it is apparent that so few of the young men of the diocese wished to be ordained that no ceremonies were held locally, and the small number who aspired to Edwardian orders were ordained in London on letters dimissory.[2]

It would be interesting to isolate any differences between those priests who remained in service in Lancashire and those who withdrew but, as we know little beyond the names of most unbeneficed men, only one line of enquiry has proved possible. In general, the younger men were more likely to disappear and the older tended to remain at their posts. As we have noted, 49.6% of the priests listed

[1] Ordinations declined before the missing years, whereas a change of volume would have meant a sudden halt. The original register, CRO, EDA 1/2, has now been repaired, so that it is impossible to say with certainty that Edwardian folios have not been removed. But the editor of *Ordination Reg.* in 1895 saw no sign of this. There was no reason to remove folios under Mary, since the orders granted between 1547 and the introduction of the Edwardian Ordinal in 1550 were just as valid as Henrician orders, which were accepted. There can be little doubt that the lacuna results from a lack of ordinations, which presumably resulted from a lack of candidates.
[2] *Ordination Reg.* 70, 80, 82; W. H. Frere, *The Marian Reaction*, 101, 266, App. 12; *Registers of Cuthbert Tunstall and James Pilkington*, ed. G. Hinde, xvii; BIY, Reg. Holgate, R/I/29, *passim*.

in 1548 did not appear in 1554 but, despite the fact that one would expect more of them to have died, only 36% of the men who had been in service in 1541 as well as in 1548 disappeared under Edward VI. This explains why ex-chantrists were more likely to remain in their posts than others, for they were usually older men.[1] A much higher proportion of the younger clergy resigned Lancashire posts; 26 of those serving in 1548 had been ordained at Chester since 1542, most of whom must have been aged under thirty early in Edward's reign, and exactly half of them had gone by 1554. To sum up, half of the newly ordained men resigned, 41% of all priests disappeared for reasons other than known death, and of the older men 36% went, including those who died.

For those who were already priests and for those who might have considered ordination, service in the Lancashire Church became markedly less attractive in the reign of Edward VI, but the reasons for this are far from plain. We have already seen that there had been a high level of clerical emigration in the preceding reign, almost certainly because of a lack of opportunity for advancement. In the Edwardian period rapid inflation made the inadequacy of assistants' incomes even more pronounced in Lancashire, and it would presumably have been the younger men, especially those who wished to marry, who went in search of more lucrative offices elsewhere. The introduction of a reformed liturgy reduced the demand for clerical labour, while after the suppression of the chantries there were almost 100 fewer beneficed posts in the county, and the clerical profession became less inviting. But the impact of the 1545 Chantries Act on recruitment had not been severe, and while the Henrician chantry commissioners were conducting their survey in 1546, ordinations at Chester had returned to their former high level. Inflation and debasement were not new phenomena, and one may doubt whether the economic climate worsened so suddenly in the early years of Edward's reign that a mass withdrawal from the Church resulted from this. Most of the Lancashire clergy were paid by individuals and groups of laymen, and there may have been some willingness to increase stipends as the drift from the priesthood became obvious.

A religious motivation, that in a strongly conservative area there was some unwillingness to serve in a Protestant Church, seems more convincing than an economic explanation. Ordinations at Chester followed the pattern of religious change, falling from mid 1547 when the trend of Edwardine policy became clear, and then after the restoration of Catholicism rising to an even higher level than under

---

[1] In 1548, 63% of Lancashire chantrists were aged over 50, significantly more than in most of the areas studied in Wood-Legh, *Perpetual Chantries*, 232; cf. *Lancs. Chantries, passim.*

Henry VIII.[1] It is difficult to see why the Marian Church was so much more attractive than the Edwardian, unless it was because it was Catholic, for career opportunities did not improve. But some men, such as James Buckley of Middleton and Ralph Birch of Manchester, withdrew from service under Edward and returned under Mary.[2] One possible explanation of the age differential between those who withdrew and those who did not is that the conformists, the older men, were set in their ways and already resigned to vacillating religious policies, while the younger and newly ordained were more confident of finding less compromising employment.

This hypothesis raises two major difficulties. First, if priests left the Church because it became Protestant, it is curious that the decline in serving clergy continued under Mary. A fragment of a 1557 visitation list, found in a consistory act book for 1596–8, shows that the number of priests in sixteen parishes of the deaneries of Manchester and Warrington fell from 84 in 1554 to 60 in 1557, though vacancies in the see of Chester had reduced the number of ordinations and hampered recruitment. Second, if we regard those who disappeared between 1548 and 1554 as conservatives protesting against the Reformation, there must have remained a considerable body of conformist and even reformist opinion. But of 172 priests named in 1554 in parishes for which there are call-book lists for 1563, all but 51 had disappeared by the latter date.[3] If religion was the main motive for withdrawal, then over two-thirds of the 'Protestants' of 1554 refused to serve the Elizabethan Church! It is possible to escape from this inconsistency, for conformists may have found the piecemeal ecclesiastical legislation of Edward VI easier to accept than the integral settlement of 1559, and it is dangerous to compare lists almost a decade apart for an area of high emigration. However, the argument for religious motivation cannot be proved, and it is wisest to avoid the temptation of monocausal explanations. Whatever the reason, the Church in Lancashire was obviously seriously weakened in the reign of Edward VI.

The Edwardine Reformation was almost entirely destructive; the old Church was damaged but Protestantism was not enforced. The government failed to develop a programme of mass evangelism, and the only measures it took in this direction would have their effect in decades rather than a few years. The new Prayer Books and the Homilies would in time have moulded a new religious consciousness, but time, as it happened, was one commodity the regime did not have. In the absence of a trustworthy and effective detection system,

---

[1] See below, p. 200.
[2] *Clergy List*, 12, 13; CRO, EDV 2/3, fo. 14v, EDV 1/1, fo. 32, *Middleton Reg.* 121.
[3] Cf. CRO, EDV 1/1, *passim*, EDC 1/29, fo. 123/1; EDV 1/3, fos. 21–34.

we do not know how much local resistance there was to the changes in religion, and we cannot assess the impact of the new legislation satisfactorily. We shall see that the few lasting conversions made to Protestantism under Edward were not the product of official efforts, but the achievement of a handful of free-lance preachers working in Lancashire. Without these men, the Reformation in Lancashire would have made no positive progress in the reign of Edward VI.

11

The unofficial Reformation: the beginnings of Protestantism

In the early sixteenth century Lancashire had been isolated from the main currents of social, intellectual and political change. No more than the merest trace of Lollard and early Protestant heresy appeared in the county, because there were few means by which new ideas could be carried into the area and because conventional Catholicism was still robust. But by the middle of the century Lancashire was being drawn into the economic and cultural world of London, the universities and the south. Most of the county remained untouched, but those parts which were geographically closest to the capital and which developed trading links with the towns of the south were opened to wider influences. Cloth manufacture in early Tudor Lancashire had been on a small scale and predominantly for a local market, but the unusual economic circumstances of the reign of Edward VI, in which Ellis Hall, the draper, made a fortune in a few years, gave a great stimulus to the textile industry.

Though it is impossible to be precise, the early sixteenth century saw a significant increase in the population of Lancashire, especially in the south-east of the county. In the hundreds of Salford and Blackburn nineteen new chapels had to be built between 1500 and 1550, and probably eight of these were established in the 1540s.[1] The population of the parish of Middleton in 1548 was perhaps 1,200 people, but by 1563 it was thought to be 1,500; over the same period the population of Bolton may have risen from 1,500 to 2,000, that of Ashton from 900 to 1,400, and that of Blackburn from 3,000 to 5,000.[2] Growth in population led to the creation of new farms from the waste, and to the sub-division of existing holdings, so that in some places farmsteads became too small to support families and an additional domestic industry was necessary. There are many indications that the number of clothworkers increased considerably in the 1540s. Bolton and Middleton acquired their first fulling mills about this time, and in 1542 Manchester was deprived of its status as a sanctuary-town, since the undesirable characters thus attracted were prejudicial to the expanding textile industry.[3] Towards the

---

[1] Tupling, 'Pre-Reformation parishes and chapelries', App. 2.
[2] *Lancs. Chantries*, I, 124, 128, 153, II, 253; BM, Harleian MS 594, fo. 102.
[3] Wadsworth and Mann, *Cotton Trade and Industrial Lancashire*, 26–7; *VCH*, II, 296.

middle of the century we find the first known examples of Lancashire clothiers selling outside the county, beginning with John
Webster of Manchester, who sold woollens to a Herefordshire priory
in 1535. One of the first Lancastrians to sell on the London market
was Edmund Sorocold in 1543, Adam Byrom followed him in 1544,
and thereafter there were many more.[1] The passing in 1551 of the
first legislation on the size of 'all cottons called Manchester, Lancashire and Cheshire cottons' suggests that the county's cloth was now
being exported and that fixed standards were necessary; in the year
1565–6 Chester and Liverpool exported 30,000 'cottons' to ports in
France, Spain, Portugal and Ireland. It is clear that the industry was
expanding rapidly, and the years of greatest progress may have been
the 1540s. Wool and linen yarn were imported through Chester for
Lancashire and some of the county's cloth was exported from the
port, so that the trade of Chester partly reflects the scale of the
textile industry. In 1542–3, 86 ships used the port, about the same
number as in earlier years, but in the following year the number rose
to 163 and between 1548 and 1552 an annual average of 117 ships
traded with Chester.[2]

The growth of the textile trade had far-reaching influences on
south-east Lancashire. The booming cloth industry lifted some of
those involved in it out of the poverty which had made the purchase
of books, travel and higher education impossible. The farmer–
weaver may have been more independent of his landlord than the
tenant whose only source of income was his land. As the overwhelming influence of the conservative squire was weakened, so that of
the woollen merchant, with his wider interests and contacts, was
strengthened. The cloth trade created the first real ties between
Lancashire and London. In 1553 two merchants met at Bartholomew Fair in the capital, one from Ashton and one from Manchester,
and eight years later sixteen local merchants took cloth to Blackwell
Hall.[3] Commercial links led to the apprenticeship of Lancashire
boys to London clothiers, and soon youths were being sent to learn
other trades. A steady stream of Lancashiremen went to London
in search of a fortune, and the successful ones remembered their
county of origin in a tangible fashion; between 1480 and 1660 28%
of the donations made to Lancashire charitable causes came from
Londoners, almost all the donors having been born in the county.[4]
The potential importance of such connections is shown by the case

[1] Lowe, *Lancashire Textile Industry*, 59; PRO, C 1/1099/62–4.
[2] Hewart, 'Cloth trade in the north of England', 22; *Chester Customs Accounts*, 74–6,
82–6, 96–9, 151–2.
[3] *Duchy Pleadings*, III, 166; Ramsay, 'Distribution of the cloth industry', 364–8.
[4] *Calendar of Moore MSS*, No. 251; *Lancashire and Cheshire Antiquarian Notes*, ed.
W. D. Pink, I, 4; Jordan, *Social Institutions of Lancashire*, 98.

of Roger Holland, who went up to London as an apprentice, was converted to Protestantism, and tried to pass on his new faith to his family in Lancashire.[1] The failure of Holland's proselytising underlines the conservatism of the county gentry from whom he came, but it does not weaken the example. Trading links presumably did not take sophisticated theology into Lancashire, but they did carry an awareness of new ideas.

As parts of Lancashire grew more prosperous, so their transactions became more complex, and as southern influences civilised the people so they became more likely to settle their disputes in the courts rather than by violence.[2] There was thus an increasing demand for trained lawyers, while the rising wealth of those gentry involved in wool-growing or coal-mining made possible a legal education for their sons. Though there must have been working lawyers in the area before, it was towards the middle of the century that attorneys became more common in Lancashire; a local man was legal adviser to royal commissioners in the county in 1537, about 1540 a young lawyer was active in various local property settlements, and in the 1550s Arthur Ashton, attorney, worked in Rochdale. A growing number of young Lancastrians spent some time at one of the Inns of Court and, though the records of admissions to the Middle Temple for the years 1525 to 1551 are lost, there were many more Lancashire students there after 1551 than there had been before 1525.[3] The Inns did not merely provide additional communications between capital and county, for they contained influential Protestant cells and at least two early reformers of Lancashire extraction acquired their radicalism there. Hugh Latimer first interested John Bradford in the reformed faith, but his actual conversion was the work of Thomas Sampson, a fellow-student at the Inner Temple. William Fleetwood's main contact with Protestantism was through his friendship with Bartlet Green, the Marian martyr, with whom he studied at the Middle Temple.[4]

If the Inns of Court could provide Lancashire with informed Protestants, the universities were even more likely to do so, for strong bonds were forged between the county and a number of

[1] Foxe, *Acts and Monuments*, VIII, 472–8.
[2] I have developed this point in relation to ecclesiastical courts in 'Slander and the Church courts in the sixteenth century', *TLCAS*, LXXVIII.
[3] *L & P*, XII(1), 781, XV, 1028; Raines, *Vicars of Rochdale*, 39; H. A. C. Sturgess, *Register of Admissions to the Middle Temple*, 3 vols. I, 17, 22, 23, 24. For the general expansion in recruitment to the inns of court in the middle of the century, see W. R. Prest, *The Inns of Court under Elizabeth I and the Early Stuarts*, 5–7.
[4] *Writings of John Bradford*, I, 30, II, xiii and n; P. F. Johnston, 'The life of John Bradford, the Manchester martyr', University of Oxford B. Litt. thesis, 1963, 21–4, 32–5; Foxe, *Acts and Monuments*, VII, 742.

colleges. At St John's, Cambridge, Lady Margaret's original statutes and Bishop Fisher's revision of 1530 stipulated that at least half the fellows were to be from northern counties, while Roger Ascham noted that almost all the early gifts to the institution came from northerners. Lancashire influence was particularly extensive: when Hugh Ashton founded four fellowships and four scholarships in 1522 he reserved two of each for natives of his own shire; in the middle of the century even 'utensils for college use' were from the county, and the college was ruled by a succession of Lancastrian masters.[1] At Peterhouse, too, there was an important Lancashire presence, since Warkworth's statutes had provided that half the fellows were to be from the northern dioceses.[2] Later in the century the shire acquired links with other colleges: Rochdale Grammar School was under the protection of Corpus Christi College, from 1569 scholars from Blackrod School had an exhibition at Pembroke, and in 1580 William Marshall founded scholarships at Pembroke, Clare and Jesus for natives of Lancashire and three other counties.[3]

There were similar connections between Lancashire and Oxford, where at Brasenose College natives of the shire occupied an even more privileged position than at St John's in Cambridge. The founder, Bishop Smith of Lincoln, was born near Widnes, and his original statutes insisted that the principal and twelve fellows should all be from the diocese of Coventry and Lichfield, with preference for natives of Lancashire and Cheshire and especially of the parishes of Prescot and Prestbury. In 1543 Humphrey Ogle, a Prescot man, founded two Brasenose scholarships with preference for candidates first from Prescot and then the diocese of Chester, and in the 1570s the queen and Alexander Nowell established no fewer than thirteen scholarships to take boys from Middleton School to Brasenose, while boys of Whalley and Burnley were similarly provided for.[4] Other colleges, too, had Lancashire connections; Corpus Christi, to which the Lancastrian Bishop Hugh Oldham had given a major endowment at its foundation, had one fellowship and two scholarships restricted to natives of his county, while the president of the college appointed the master and usher of Manchester Grammar School. Gilbert Lathom endowed three scholarships from Lancashire to Oxford colleges in 1544.[5] Thus within a few decades two new

[1] J. B. Mullinger, *St John's College*, 22, 54–5; R. Ascham, *Works*, III, 233; J. E. B. Mayor, *College of St John the Evangelist*, I, 352–3.
[2] J. B. Mullinger, *The University of Cambridge*, II, 633.
[3] *VCH*, II, 606–7; Jordan, *Social Institutions of Lancashire*, 47.
[4] Churton, *Lives of Smith and Sutton*, 316; A. Wood, *History of the Colleges of Oxford*, ed. J. Gutch, 359; *VCH*, II, 577, 604, 608.
[5] J. G. Milne, *The Early History of Corpus Christi College*, 3; Wood, *History of the Colleges of Oxford*, 392; *VCH*, II, 583; Jordan, *Social Institutions of Lancashire*, 41.

colleges, St John's at Cambridge and Brasenose at Oxford, were founded with firm links with Lancashire, a third, Corpus at Oxford, had only slightly less strong links, and scholarships to several other colleges were established.

It has often been suggested that Protestantism was carried into new areas along trade routes, by the merchants and artisans who picked up heretical ideas in London and the south-coast ports and took them back to their own towns. This may indeed have happened in some counties, but evangelisation by the laity was very uncertain; counties without important trading contacts, which Lancashire lacked until the 1540s, were excluded, and when a faith was disseminated by the uneducated, as Lollardy was, it often developed eccentricities or was debased into a materialistic anticlericalism. Protestantism was taken to Lancashire not by anonymous traders but by Lancashire-born, university-trained theologians, who worked on their own initiative to convert their friends and relations, for the provision of new university places for Lancashiremen coincided with the development of heretical groups at the universities, and at Cambridge the most reformist college of all, St John's, had the strongest Lancastrian links.

Some of the young men who took up the new university places joined the growing band of academic heretics, and Alexander Nowell, of Read Hall in Whalley, was the most notable of Lancashire's Oxford Protestants. While studying at Brasenose, Nowell shared a room with John Foxe, the martyrologist, and he was tutored by Hawarden, to whom Foxe dedicated a treatise on the Eucharist. Nowell was of a distinctly humanistic turn of mind; at Oxford he lectured on logic from Rudolph Agricola, as master of Westminster School he introduced the reading of parts of the New Testament in Greek, and he wrote prologues to the plays of Terence and Seneca for his pupils.[1] By the middle of the century Nowell was certainly a Protestant; Edward VI gave him a preaching licence and a prebend at Westminster, and in the reign of Mary he felt sufficiently compromised to flee abroad. In 1557 Alexander was joined in Germany by his brother Laurence, whose career had followed a similar pattern, from an early training at Brasenose to the mastership of an influential school and then escape from Mary's government.[2] Although the two Nowells were to achieve prominence in the reign of

---

[1] *Brasenose College Register 1509–1909*, Oxford Historical Society, LV, 7; R. Churton, *Life of Alexander Nowell*, 6–7; J. F. Mozley, *John Foxe and his Book*, 16–17; Bodleian Library, Brasenose College MS 31 (I am grateful to Dr A. B. Emden for drawing my attention to this document).

[2] *CPR*, Edward VI, IV, 111; C. H. Garrett, *The Marian Exiles*, 237, 239; *Brasenose College Reg.* 8; Churton, *Life of Alexander Nowell*, 12.

Elizabeth, a third Brasenose Lancastrian was more famous in the Edwardian years and notorious later. Henry Pendleton took his B.A. in 1542, was ordained priest at Chester two years later, and then studied for a doctorate in divinity. Before the end of Edward's reign he was preaching Protestantism in Manchester, but he conformed under Mary despite his earlier determination that 'I will see the uttermost drop of this grease of mine molten away, and the last gobbet of this flesh consumed to ashes, before I will forsake God and his truth.'[1]

At Cambridge the careers of many young Lancashiremen were subject to the reforming but eirenic influence of John Redman of Urswick in Furness, a seminal figure whose studies took him to Corpus Christi, Oxford, to Paris and then to the radical St John's College, Cambridge. By 1537 he was a doctor of divinity, chaplain to the king and public orator of Cambridge, and he later held the Lady Margaret chair of divinity. Redman was master of King's Hall between 1542 and 1546, and as he seems to have been the major influence behind Henry VIII's foundation of Trinity College it was fitting that he should have become the first master. But Redman was no mere university administrator; he was a major classical scholar, and a defender of Cheke in his conflict with Bishop Gardiner over Greek pronunciation.[2] As he did not always agree with the Protestants, his approval could carry great weight, and according to Burnet he was 'esteemed the most learned and judicious divine of that time'. His views on justification and the Eucharist remained conservative to the end, but he admitted that on other matters he had been extensively influenced by his friend Martin Bucer.[3] Redman's last years in Cambridge were marred by illness and he died of consumption in 1551, but in the three eventful decades he spent in the university he was friend and mentor of many fellow-Lancastrians. His open-minded and conciliatory approach to doctrinal problems must have attracted scores of students, and his wide circle of reformist friends at St John's formed the core of Cambridge humanism and Protestantism.

Among those in contact with Redman was Thomas Lever, first student and later fellow of St John's, who argued in the college chapel against the scriptural basis of the mass soon after the accession of Edward. By 1550 the Bolton man was one of the most radical preachers in London and Cambridge, combining exhortations to 'embrace sincere Christianity' with fury at the cruelty of merchants

---

[1] *Brasenose College Reg.* 10; *Writings of John Bradford*, I, 449–50; Foxe, *Acts and Monuments*, VI, 629.
[2] A. B. Cobban, *King's Hall, Cambridge*, 290; Ascham, *Works*, I, 294–5, III, 232, 237; Burnet, *History of the Reformation*, IV, 250.
[3] *Ibid.* I, 550, 572, 575, II, 314–69, 488, IV, 338.

who profited from the needs of the poor, and disgust at the cynical materialism of the lay Protestant leaders. In 1551 Lever became master of St John's, but the succession of Mary made his position untenable and he fled from the college, taking over twenty of the fellows with him. Ascham noted that in 1553 'more perfect scholars were dispersed from thence in one month than many years can rear up again'.[1] Those who left with the master included four other Lancashiremen, Lever's own two brothers and the two Pilkingtons, and the master and nine fellows escaped to the continent. James Pilkington, a native of Rivington, was a fellow of St John's, and in 1549 he was one of the leaders of the Protestant side in a disputation on transubstantiation and the sacrificial nature of the mass. Of his brothers, Leonard was also a fellow of St John's and John was a fellow of Pembroke, and at least one of them went into exile with James in Mary's reign.[2] Another member of the group led to the continent by Lever was William Birch, of Birch Hall in Manchester, who had been an undergraduate of St John's but later became a fellow of Corpus and an official preacher.[3]

The most eminent of the Cambridge Lancastrians was Edwin Sandys, who as a student at St John's had been tutored by John Bland, burned for heresy in 1555. By 1553 Sandys was master of St Catharine's and vice-chancellor, and on the death of Edward VI he openly declared his allegiance to the duke of Northumberland. He preached before the university a clarion call for loyalty to a Protestant regime, and Thomas Lever and one of his brothers were booted and spurred, ready to carry the sermon to printers in London, when news arrived that Mary had been proclaimed queen. The vice-chancellor was soon in the Tower, but after he had been transferred to the Marshalsea he was able to escape with the assistance of the Lancastrian knight marshal, Sir Thomas Holcroft. At Cambridge Sandys had influenced young Lancashiremen towards his own Protestant views and James Taylor, one of his students at St Catharine's, also fled to the continent.[4]

The Mancunian John Bradford spent a shorter time at Cambridge than most of the other Lancashiremen, but for our purposes he was

[1] Mullinger, *St John's College*, 39–40; H. C. Porter, *Reformation and Reaction in Tudor Cambridge*, 67, 76; *Sermons of Thomas Lever, 1550*, ed. E. Arber, *passim*; Ascham, *Works*, III, 236.
[2] Burnet, *History of the Reformation*, VI, 676; J. Pilkington, *Works*, ed. J. Scholefield, 523; Garrett, *Marian Exiles*, 250–2.
[3] F. Raines, *Wardens of the Collegiate Church of Manchester*, I, 70–1; Garrett, *Marian Exiles*, 91.
[4] *VCH*, VIII, 352, 371; Foxe, *Acts and Monuments*, VII, 287, VIII, 590–1, 594–5; Porter, *Reformation and Reaction in Tudor Cambridge*, 75; Strype, *Ecclesiastical Memorials*, III(1), 156; Garrett, *Marian Exiles*, 302.

the most important of all. He worked in the army commissariat during the French wars and was involved in some sort of peculation, but in 1547 he entered the Inner Temple as a student to begin a new career.[1] In London he came under the influence of Hugh Latimer and Thomas Sampson, and was soon studying theological topics with some enthusiasm; he sent a New Testament and books by Melanchthon, Bucer and others home to Lancashire, and he began to translate works himself. His studies led him to Cambridge, where he joined the Lancashire coterie; he was admitted to Edwin Sandys' college in the early summer of 1548, and he was examined for his M.A. by James Pilkington.[2] It had been Bradford's ambition to secure a fellowship, and after some competition between Sandys and Bishop Ridley he accepted a post at the latter's college, Pembroke. He was then much influenced by Ridley himself, and especially by the new Regius Professor of Divinity, Martin Bucer, who became Bradford's great friend and guide and whom Bradford comforted in his last illness.[3] After ordination by Ridley, Bradford became one of the most effective preachers in London, and the twin influences of Cambridge and the Inns of Court turnèd a rascally public servant from a conservative family background into a forceful Edwardian radical.

Another Lancashireman who took to Protestantism and preaching late in life was George Marsh, a farmer from the parish of Dean. After the death of his wife Marsh was, as Foxe says, 'most desirous of godly studies', and he entered Christ's College in 1551. He did not study for long, but in the following year he was ordained and became curate and schoolmaster under Laurence Saunders, first at All Hallows in Bread Street, one of the focal points of London radicalism, and then at Langton in Leicestershire. It is unfortunate that we know so little of Marsh's earlier career for he was, as we shall see, an influential figure among Lancashire Protestants. But it is unlikely that he was a convinced reformer before he went to Cambridge, for it was he who introduced Protestantism into the Dean–Eccles area, and he can presumably be numbered among those converted at the universities.[4]

From the 1520s onwards Lutheranism, and later home-grown and other foreign variants of Protestantism, provided the radical ortho-

---

[1] *Writings of John Bradford*, I, 493, II, 6, 10–13, 17; Foxe, *Acts and Monuments*, VII, 791; W. H. Cooke, *Students Admitted to the Inner Temple*, 2.

[2] *Writings of John Bradford*, I, 1–15, 30–2, II, 6–7, 10–11, 16–17, 19, 20–1, 22–4; *C.U. Grace Book* Δ, 57–8.

[3] *Writings of John Bradford*, II, 26–7; Johnston, 'Life of John Bradford, the Manchester martyr', 109; Porter, *Reformation and Reaction in Tudor Cambridge*, 51–2, 71.

[4] J. and J. A. Venn, *Alumni Cantabrigiensis*, Part 1, 4 vols. III, 144; Foxe, *Acts and Monuments*, VII, 39, 41, 54.

doxy of young students, and many followed the fashion. The Marian Bishop Day remarked to a Lancashire reformer 'Oh, Master Bradford, you were but a child when this matter began. I was a young man then coming from the university, I went with the world.' Even Stephen Gardiner was almost attracted into the reformers' circle: 'Because there was not in them malice and they maintained communication having some savour of learning, I was familiar with such sort of men.' John Bradford recognised the impact of his years at Cambridge; in his 'farewell' he wrote of 'thou, my mother, the university', and gave thanks to God that He 'hath vouchsafed our mother to bring up any child in whom it would please Him thus [i.e. by martyrdom] to magnify His holy name'.[1] The effect of the universities was particularly important for men from a conservative area, for at home they had little opportunity to taste the new ideas, and only the support of other students could help them to withstand the cold douche of reactionary scorn they must have suffered from their families. The experience of Laurence Chadderton was perhaps typical. In 1562 he went up to Christ's College, where he contracted the disease of Protestantism, not to mention Puritanism, from Edward Dering. The orthodox Catholic Chadderton senior wrote to his erring son in 1565 that 'If you renounce the new sect you have joined, you may expect all the happiness which the care of an indulgent father can secure you; otherwise, I enclose in this letter a shilling to buy a wallet. Go and beg for your living.'[2]

As far as we know John Bradford's conversion did not provoke such disgust from his family, but though he was able to influence his sister and brother-in-law the rest of the family remained conservative and gave him little encouragement. When first attracted by reformist views Bradford expected hostility from his mother and Thomas Hall, an unimaginative Manchester priest who was her spiritual mentor. In the spring of 1548 Bradford's confidant John Traves thought Hall and Mrs Bradford were tampering with his correspondence, and eighteen months later Bradford remarked that his mother needed instruction in the new religion. In the reign of Mary the Bradfords were loyally Catholic, and a relation was dispatched to London to persuade John to recant rather than inflict on the family the shame of death as a heretic.[3] Young men from a conservative background found the universities provided one of the few avenues of escape from the pervading presence of traditional Catholicism, and a chance to sample the heady wine of the new religion.

---

[1] *Writings of John Bradford*, I, 442, 523; *Letters of Stephen Gardiner*, 176.
[2] W. Dillingham, *Life of Laurence Chadderton*, 2–4; P. Collinson, *The Elizabethan Puritan Movement*, 127.
[3] *Writings of John Bradford*, II, 16, 18–19, 29; Foxe, *Acts and Monuments*, VII, 167.

Lancastrians were converted to Protestantism not by the intrusion of alien ideas into the county by traders, but through the use by students of the benefactions of the Lady Margaret, Bishop Smith and other pious Catholics.

In the reign of Henry VIII, when academic Protestants were still liable to be prosecuted as heretics, there could be no sustained missionary effort into the conservative areas of England. In a county such as Lancashire, reformers would find few kindred spirits, and where heresy was hated the risk of detection was immeasurably higher. Henrician Protestants could hope only to extend their influence into the old Lollard areas, where they might find some sympathy and where delation to the authorities was less likely. Thus men such as Barnes, Garret, Bilney, Coverdale and, from Lancashire, Robert Singleton and Edmund Scambler, tried to modify Lollardy rather than create new areas of support.[1] But in the reign of Edward VI, when more young Lancastrians were going up to the universities, Protestantism was encouraged and only the most extreme were at risk. The most effective reformist preachers, including a number from Lancashire, were licensed to preach the new religion throughout England, and official approval enabled the academics to switch their attention from the established Lollard centres to the more difficult regions.[2]

The Lancastrian who devoted most effort to his native county was John Bradford, who was issued with a preaching licence in December 1550. He usually wrote regularly to his family and local friends and, though most of his work was in London, the absence of letters to Lancashire between early in 1550 and October 1553 may indicate frequent visits to the county. We know that Bradford preached in Lancashire in the summer of 1552, and his Christmas sermon in Manchester the same year became famous in local lore for its threat that if the town did not 'readily embrace the word of God, the mass would be said again in that church and the play of Robin Hood acted there, which accordingly came to pass in Queen Mary's reign'.[3] Bradford's proselytising was concentrated especially on the Manchester area, and he later wrote a 'farewell' directed to 'thou Manchester, thou Ashton-under-line, thou Bolton, Bury, Wigan, Liverpool, Mottram, Stockport, Wilmslow, Eccles, Preston, Middleton, Rad-

---

[1] See, for example, Rupp, *Studies in the Making of the English Protestant Tradition*, 6–14; M. Aston, 'Lollardy and the Reformation: survival or revival?', *History*, XLIX, 149–70.
[2] R. W. Dixon, *History of the Church of England*, 6 vols. II, 485–6; Dickens, *English Reformation*, 235; Hill, 'Puritans and the "Dark Corners of the Land"', *TRHS*, 5th series, XIII, 79.
[3] Strype, *Ecclesiastical Memorials*, II(2), 258; *Writings of John Bradford*, I, 31, 41–2, 454; Hollingworth, *Mancuniensis*, 75–6.

cliffe and thou city of Westchester, where I have truly taught and preached the word of God'. This represents a missionary effort of some intensity, and he had some impact on his audiences. Those who heard his sermon on repentance in 1552 asked that it should be printed, and one of his converts remembered him 'teaching the Gospel to the comfort of our souls'. Alice Seddon told him 'For truly you are my greatest comfort, next unto Christ and his word, not for your person bodily but for the holy word's sake which you have purely and godly preached unto me and others.'[1]

Though none tried as hard as Bradford, several other university men preached in Lancashire. George Marsh noted that James Pilkington and Thomas Lever had preached in the county, probably in their native Bolton, and Bishop Ridley considered that Lever and Bradford, together with Latimer and Knox, had been the most effective preachers of Protestantism and moral reform under Edward.[2] Marsh, writing in the reign of Mary, was careful to omit the renegade Henry Pendleton from his list of 'faithful ministers of Christ' who had worked in Lancashire, but there can be no doubt that Pendleton had spread the new gospel with vigour. According to Bradford, Pendleton preached Protestantism in Lancashire even before he did himself, and Pendleton delivered so many sermons in Manchester that a seventeenth-century antiquarian thought he had been an endowed preacher.[3] The activities of Marsh himself are more difficult to evaluate. At his heresy trial in April 1555 Marsh was said to have

preached and openly published most heretically and blasphemously within the parish of Dean, Eccles, Bolton, Bury and many other parishes within the bishop's diocese, in the months of January, February, or some other time of the year last preceding, directly against the pope's authority and Catholic Church of Rome, the blessed mass, the sacrament of the altar and many other articles.

Marsh had, in fact, been arrested in the middle of March 1554, but it is most unlikely that he had been so rash as to preach in such open violation of official policy when, as he himself said, he was merely visiting the county to see his relations and friends before fleeing abroad. Marsh had, however, preached in Lancashire with his London colleague the saintly Laurence Saunders in 1552 or early in 1553.[4]

There is ample evidence, then, of Edwardian Protestants preaching in Lancashire; none was beneficed in the county, none was on an official mission, and all, with the exception of Saunders, in any case a friend of one of the others, were local men converted at one of

---

[1] *Writings of John Bradford*, I, 31, 41, 454, II, 226.
[2] Foxe, *Acts and Monuments*, VII, 65; N. Ridley, *Works*, ed. H. Christmas, 59.
[3] *Writings of John Bradford*, I, 449–50; Hollingworth, *Mancuniensis*, 75–6.
[4] Foxe, *Acts and Monuments*, VII, 39–41, 45, 49, 65.

the universities. The impact of their sermons is not easy to assess; the county Protestants savoured them, but the reaction of the population at large was probably much less favourable. Radical young graduates, whether Protestants or Maoists, returning home with their new-fangled university ideas, have never been successful in influencing the wider community. More important, one may doubt the effectiveness of the sermon as a means of evangelism where the bulk of the audience is hostile and the local clergy unsympathetic. Conversion from traditional Catholicism to the new gospel was too momentous a change to have been the result of mere attendance at occasional sermons by visiting academics, no matter how able the preachers. Lasting conversions require weeks of encouragement and pastoral care by the local clergy, but this the conservative priests of Lancashire would not provide. Sermons were, in any case, generally resented as prolonging services, and it was not until the reign of James I that preaching became a common and popular element in local worship. Lancashire parishioners chatted through sermons or walked about in the churchyard, others preferred ale to the discourses of their clergy, and in 1522 two men from Tottington regularly whiled away a tedious service by playing card games in church.[1] Antipathy towards sermons was likely when churches did not always have seating for the whole congregation; it was not until late in the reign of Elizabeth that full ranges of pews were erected in the chapel at Church and the parish churches of Eccles and Ormskirk, while Chester cathedral did not have seating for the congregation until the 1620s.[2]

The new faith was planted in Lancashire not by mass propaganda, but by personal links between the academic reformers and their families and friends. The survival of many of the letters of John Bradford enables us to trace his influence in the county, and especially his relationship with John Traves, an elderly Manchester trader.[3] In 1548 Bradford was at the beginning of his theological development, and advice from an old and intelligent friend whose religion was following a similar course was invaluable. Later, the effect of Cambridge, the influence of Ridley and Bucer and his own experience as a preacher strengthened Bradford's self-confidence, and he created the nucleus of a Protestant group in Lancashire. Thereafter, Traves was less the personal confidant and more the

[1] See below, p. 244 and n; *Whalley Act Book*, 54, 55, 59, 60, 139; CRO, EDA 12/1, p. 17, EDV 1/1, fos. 141, 142; *CCR*, III, 289. Cf. the complaint of Roger Edgeworth in 1557, quoted by G. Williams, *The Welsh Church from Conquest to Reformation*, 509.
[2] CRO, EDA 2/2, fos. 18v, 189, 227, EDA 3/1, fo. 130v.
[3] I have tried to dispose of misconceptions concerning Traves' identity and his relationship with Bradford in 'Reformation in Lancashire', 537–8.

leader of Bradford's reformist friends in the county, while Bradford
was less the anguished convert and more the group's link with the
London Protestant intelligentsia and the book market. Bradford
kept the Manchester radicals well-supplied with recently published
volumes, including Melanchthon's *Commonplaces*, Bucer's book on
celibacy, Urbanus Regius' *Declaration of the Faith* and his own
translations. A Manchester priest was sent an English and Latin
New Testament, and even in prison in 1555 Bradford wrote *The
Hurt of Hearing Mass* for his friends, and sent it into Lancashire.[1]

John Bradford's proselytising in the palatinate was centred on his
family and its friends. In December 1549 he planned a visit to
Manchester to give his mother Protestant instruction, and he arranged for the lessons to be continued by Traves and Roger Beswick.
The latter, who had married Bradford's sister Margaret, became an
enthusiastic reformer, and his ministrations to his brother-in-law
while the preacher was in prison and on his way to the stake
presumably indicate the source of his conversion.[2] Bradford also
tried, again with the help of Traves, to influence his sisters, and the
two men had some success. The other members of the circle were
Protestants because they were friends rather than friends because
they were Protestants, and they were probably converted by the
scholar. Bradford chose Thomas Scorocold and his wife, Laurence
and James Bradshaw and their wives and families, Roger Shalcross
and his wife, R. Bolton, John Wild and Thomas Riddleston, from
among 'all that love and I trust live in the Gospel' for particular
mention in his correspondence, and many of them occur in more
than one letter. They are sometimes referred to as if Bradford's
mother, who was by no means sympathetic to Protestantism, knew
them well, and this suggests that they were old family friends.[3]

Bradford and Traves also tried hard to influence their friends
among the local clergy, who would be ideally placed to assist in
future conversions. The main target was Thomas Hall, who was
spiritual mentor to Bradford's mother; Bradford sent him a New
Testament and other books, which he exhorted him to read, and
asked Traves to 'water Sir Thomas Hall'. The priest allowed
Bradford to believe that the new religion was finding another
adherent, but the future martyr had later to admit that 'Sir Thomas
Hall hath deceived me, but himself most', though Bradford still
hoped for greater success on his next visit to the county. Despite
these efforts Hall remained unmoved, and in the middle of Mary's
reign Bradford was praying 'God turn Sir Thomas's heart'.[4] Traves

[1] *Writings of John Bradford*, II, 7–10, 15, 16, 19, 236.
[2] *Ibid.* 31, 45, 76, 250; Foxe, *Acts and Monuments*, VII, 148.
[3] *Writings of John Bradford*, II, 28, 41, 76–7, 232, 236.
[4] *Ibid.* 7–10, 15, 16, 20, 77.

and Bradford had rather more success with Thomas Hall's brother Laurence, who was among Bradford's friends in 1548 and was included in the reformer's list of Protestants in 1554, but even Laurence conformed to the Marian restoration and was serving in Manchester in 1557.[1] Attempts were made to convert another Manchester priest, an elderly ex-chantrist named Nicholas Wolsencroft, and William Carlton, a chaplain at Stockport, seems to have gone over to the reformers temporarily. In addition, Bradford implied in his 'farewell' to his mother that 'Master Vicar', probably the vicar of Bolton, and the parson of Mottram were among the local radicals.[2] By the end of Edward's reign there were perhaps five or six fair-weather Protestant clergy in the Manchester area and, as none were university men, it is likely that they were converted in Lancashire by John Bradford and his circle.

Much less is known of the local contacts of the other academics, but we can trace something of the influence of George Marsh. His first successes were among his own family, and his mother, sisters, brothers and mother-in-law were at least attracted by his views. One of his sisters married Geoffrey Hurst, a nail-maker from the neighbouring village of Shakerley, and Protestantism was introduced into a new family; by the reign of Mary, Geoffrey's brother and their mother were sympathetic, and Geoffrey and his sister Alice were committed Protestants. It was perhaps through Marsh that the Hursts were able to obtain their small library of radical religious books. George Marsh also had strong links with some of the members of John Bradford's group, and he corresponded with them while he was in prison in 1554–5.[3]

Those who became Protestants in Lancashire formed a small, tightly knit circle, the members of which were in close touch with each other and their leaders outside the county. It is possible that this picture results from the nature of the evidence at our disposal – for letters between the university men and their converts naturally emphasised personal influences – but the accusations of heresy made at Marian visitations tend to confirm our impression. We know of about 40 laymen and women who were definitely Protestants by the reign of Mary, and of these only 3 had no obvious connections with the groups formed by Bradford and Marsh. At the visitation of 1554 14 Lancastrians were accused of heresy and, though only 3 of them occur in the correspondence of the two Cambridge reformers, all but one bore the same surname or lived in the same township as correspondents did. The exception, Adam Poulton of Liverpool,

[1] *Ibid.* 10, 77; CRO, EDC 1/29, fo. 123/1.
[2] *Writings of John Bradford*, II, 10, 15, 16, 76–7, 236–7; CRO, EDV 1/1, fos. 30v, 31.
[3] Foxe, *Acts and Monuments*, VII, 40–1, 63, 66, VIII, 562–4.

was probably not a Protestant at all; alone of those accused of heresy he appeared before the correction court when summoned, denied the charges and was dismissed by the chancellor.[1]

With the possible exception of Poulton, the Protestants were drawn from only five parishes in the Manchester area and were heavily concentrated in two: Prestwich, with 10 of the group, and Bolton, with at least 15. Many of the reformers were relations as well as neighbours, and besides the Bradford, Marsh and Hurst families there were 4 married couples, 4 Langleys of Prestwich and 7 Bradshaws of Bolton among the 40. While imprisoned at Lancaster in 1554, George Marsh wrote to Robert Langley and others that they would soon receive his account of his arrest from 'my brother or some one of the Bradshaws of Bolton'. An analysis of the membership of the Protestant community strengthens the view that it was created by the academic radicals. As many as 22 of the known Protestants were relations or correspondents of Bradford and Marsh, and most of the others had the same surnames as these or lived in the same towns. Between a third and a half of the known reformers lived in Bolton, and as both the Levers and the Pilkingtons were natives of the parish it is possible that their influence had supplemented the efforts of Bradford and Marsh. Certainly one of the Bolton Protestants was named James Lever, and Thomas Lever visited the area from Cambridge.[2]

Many of the Protestants were lesser men, such as the three weavers who fled in the reign of Mary to the exile community at Aarau led by Thomas Lever, but they did not come from among the poor. George Marsh sprang from a family of small farmers, and his brother-in-law Geoffrey Hurst was a fairly prosperous nail-maker. Ellis Crompton, a correspondent of Marsh, farmed land in Bolton which he leased from the powerful Tildesley family, and he was sufficiently affluent for his house to be burgled while he was away in the Scots' war. John Crompton, who was accused of heresy in 1554, was also a Bolton farmer, though he seems to have been a little richer than the others and was owed £40 by the time of his death. John Traves, a small Manchester merchant, came from a family wealthy enough to secure for him a good education, for his letters reveal a knowledge of Latin based on more than a mere acquaintance with the Vulgate text of the Bible.[3] The Prestwich Langleys and the Bradshaws of Bolton may have been yeoman branches of substantial

---

[1] CRO, EDV 1/1, fos. 126v, 128, 133–133v, 134v, 141v.
[2] Foxe, *Acts and Monuments*, VII, 63, 65, 66.
[3] Garrett, *Marian Exiles*, 303, 316, 321; Foxe, *Acts and Monuments*, VII, 39, 63, VIII, 562; *Ducatus Lancastriae*, I, 148, 289, II, 165; CRO, EDV 1/1, fo. 133, EDC 2/7, fos. 64–70; *Writings of John Bradford*, II, 16–17.

local families, but there is no evidence of gentry support, and George Marsh denied he had said there were 'many good gentlemen of my opinion'. Foxe says that while Marsh was in prison he was visited by a number of local gentry, both for and against his views, but the three he names, Westby, Ashton of the Hill and Ashton of Chadderton, do not appear to have been Protestant in the Edwardian period.[1] Late in the reign of Elizabeth the branches of the ubiquitous Ashton family were evenly divided between Catholics and Puritans, and the Westbys produced a long line of dogged recusants.

The available evidence points to the likelihood that the Lancashire Protestants were predominantly small farmers, traders and artisans. But whatever their origins, there can be no doubt that some of them were surprisingly well educated. The case of John Traves may have been exceptional, but we have enough correspondence to and from a number of the others to indicate a high standard of comprehension and composition. James Bradshaw, who was a correspondent of both Bradford and Marsh, and who was in trouble for heresy in 1554, seems to have been one of the leaders of the Bolton group, and he had certainly studied the Bible and Protestant confessional literature in some detail. A letter from Bradshaw to George Marsh in 1554 included Biblical references to Abraham and the Chaldeans, Lot and the Sodomites, Isaac and Ishmael, David and Saul, Jacob and Esau, Moses, the prophet Job and John the Baptist. Bradshaw concluded his layman's sermon exhorting Marsh to have courage with the words: 'Therefore, now, whosoever is ashamed of the cross of Christ and aggrieved therewith, the same is ashamed to have Christ for his fellow and companion, and therefore shall the Lord Christ be ashamed of him again on the latter day.'[2] The letter written to John Bradford in 1554–5 by Elizabeth Longshaw, an Eccles woman who was facing a heresy charge, is almost equally impressive.[3] Though her scriptural references are fewer and less precise than those of James Bradshaw, she had a thorough grounding in the Bible and the controversies between Catholics and Protestants. She had refused to attend the Marian Church services because the liturgy and doctrine of the mass were unscriptural, and she would not accept that they could be justified by tradition, 'unwritten verities or rather vanities of Pharisees'. Elizabeth Longshaw had a clear grasp of the orthodox position on the Eucharist, and could argue forcibly against it: God 'is not eaten with the teeth, neither dieth he any more. But our vicar

[1] Foxe, *Acts and Monuments*, VII, 46.
[2] *Ibid.* 67–8; CRO, EDV 1/1, fo. 133. In 1555 he had a copy of Bradford's *The Hurt of Hearing Mass* (*Writings of John Bradford*, I, 236).
[3] *Ibid.* 227–8; CRO, EDV 1/1, fo. 134v. Bradford had sent her a copy of his book to encourage her to stand firm.

will have it to be the same body that hanged on the cross, flesh, blood and bone. To this belief of theirs say I "Nay".' This passage is significant, for some historians have doubted the adequacy of the doctrinal instruction given to the laity. Transubstantiation and the unity of the Eucharistic sacrifice with the sacrifice at Calvary had been taught by the non-graduate vicar of an unimportant parish, with an intelligent response from at least one member of his congregation.

The letters which Marsh and Bradford wrote to their Lancashire followers were packed with Biblical allusions, they included complex arguments on controversial issues, and the Protestants were frequently encouraged to read the Bible. The adherents of the new religion in Bolton, Prestwich, Eccles, Dean and Manchester were well taught; they knew what the Roman Church demanded and they knew the reformers' objections to traditional views. This is a further indication of the importance of the university men in the establishment of Lancashire Protestantism, for there is no trace of the simple and unschooled assertions of heretics with predominantly lay connections. The early Protestants of Yorkshire were 'unliterary and sceptical' neo-Lollards, but those of Lancashire shared an Edwardian religion, grounded on the Bible, the Book of Common Prayer and the teachings of the reformist preachers.[1] The efforts of a small group of local men, whose university studies had introduced them to new currents of thought, had brought into Lancashire what can only be seen as an early form of Anglicanism, though the influence of John Bradford had given it a pronounced Puritan strain.

The known Lancashire Protestants were drawn entirely from the south-east of the county. As this was the area of growing prosperity and strongest links with the south, it is possible that the universities had attracted more young men from Manchester deanery than from other parts of the shire. Thus the preachers who took Edwardian Protestantism into Lancashire were all natives of the Manchester region, and the friends and relations they influenced naturally lived there. John Bradford's preaching had no noticeable impact on Wigan, Liverpool and Preston, and this underlines the ineffectiveness of evangelism by sermons alone, especially in areas lacking good communications with more radical regions. The old corporate boroughs of Wigan, Liverpool, Preston and Lancaster, with their guild restrictions, controlled markets and unfavourable geographical positions, did not share in the transformation which affected Bolton and Manchester in mid century. At Wigan the influence of the traditionalist Langtons made the town almost a pocket borough, and

[1] Dickens, *Lollards and Protestants*, 248–50; see below, pp. 187–8.

The unofficial Reformation: the beginnings of Protestantism

Protestantism was still weak there in the 1580s when the fiery Puritan Edward Fleetwood led an official assault on the old religion.[1] Although seaports were notoriously radical, Liverpool's trading links were with Catholic countries, the port was small and the conservative Stanleys and Mollineux controlled the town, so that reform made little progress until Liverpool rose to prominence as a military port.[2] The Catholic Houghtons wielded considerable authority in Preston, the town's trading contacts were mainly localised, and even in the 1580s the government of the borough was in reactionary hands.[3] Lancaster had links with London as it was the administrative capital of the palatinate, and it may have been the exception among the ancient boroughs. The mayor and schoolmaster seem to have been sympathetic towards George Marsh in 1554–5, and some of the townspeople used to listen to Marsh reading the Prayer Book and the Bible from the window of his cell.[4] However, the mere fact of a heretic reading forbidden books aloud was quite enough to attract an inquisitive crowd, and Foxe says that some of those who heard Marsh complained.

Protestantism was first established in that part of Lancashire which was to be notoriously Puritan in the early seventeenth century. There is some evidence of continuity between the first reformers and the later Puritans, and Bolton, home of the strongest of the Edwardian Protestant circles, later became known as the 'Geneva of the North'. In the reign of James I, Bradshaws and Cromptons led the Bolton Puritans as their ancestors had led the Bolton Protestants. In 1620 John Bradshaw, Ellis Crompton and James Lever were among almost thirty parishioners who refused to receive the Eucharist kneeling;[5] seventy years earlier there had been seven Bradshaws, an Ellis Crompton and a James Lever among the local reformers. The emergence of a Puritan community of any size in south-east Lancashire was to be a long process, which cannot be separated from the threat presented by large numbers of recusants and church-papists, and in the middle of the sixteenth century the radical groups were very small. But the vigorous proselytising of Bradford, Marsh, Lever and the others, all on the left wing of Edwardian Anglicanism, established a brand of Protestantism which was notably Puritan in its emphasis.

[1] *VCH*, IV, 59, 63, 72, 82, 103, 117.
[2] Muir, *History of Liverpool*, 84; Walker, *Historical Geography of South-West Lancashire*, 65; G. Chandler and E. B. Saxton, *Liverpool under James I*, 26, 93.
[3] *VCH*, II, 570, VII, 75; H. W. Clemensha, *History of Preston in Amounderness*, 109–11.
[4] Foxe, *Acts and Monuments*, VI, 564–5, VII, 46–7.
[5] Richardson, 'Puritanism in the diocese of Chester', 81, 250–1; *State Civil and Ecclesiastical*, 38.

The unofficial Reformation: the beginnings of Protestantism

The converts recruited by the Edwardine academics were militant reformers rather than passive men of piety, and we shall see that they were determined not to conform to the Marian Church. At Bolton in 1557 the Protestants took the lead in resisting the payment of tithes, and of the nine men sued by the farmers of the rectory four were Cromptons, including the John Crompton who had already been in trouble for heresy, and one was a Bradshaw.[1] In the following year three J.P.s took a number of Bolton men before the Duchy court and charged them with disturbing the collection of tithes; one was a Lever and another was Robert Bolton, perhaps the 'R. Bolton' who had been a friend of Bradford.[2] One Protestant sympathiser turned to violence, and in the reign of Mary, Rider of Smedley was imprisoned at Manchester, 'for that he, in King Edward's days, was one that pulled a popish priest out of the pulpit, that a preacher might go up'.[3] The work of the university preachers had not attracted large numbers to the new faith, but what the Protestant group lacked in size it compensated for in understanding and determination.

[1] CRO, EDC 1/15, fos. 256, 267–267v.
[2] *Ducatus Lancastriae*, I, 305; *Writings of John Bradford*, II, 76.
[3] Hollingworth, *Mancuniensis*, 75.

12

The reign of Mary: counter-reform

Popular Protestantism had made minimal progress in Lancashire by the death of King Edward. There had been very few conversions to the new faith, and these had been drawn from only one corner of the county and from the lower end of the social scale. There is very little evidence of support for reformist ideas among either the gentry or the clergy, so that radicals lacked influential local leadership and protection. With only a handful of Protestants to be attacked, therefore, the 'Marian reaction' in the palatinate was an undramatic event, overshadowed by the positive achievements of the reign. Lancashire saw none of the persecuting zeal of the Counter-Reformation, and there were few clerical deprivations and no burnings within the county itself. But in the north-west of England a surprisingly well-organised attempt was made to eradicate all traces of heresy and to undo those changes which the rule of a Protestant regime had allowed. The machinery available to the Marian authorities was little better than that which had existed under Henry VIII and Edward VI, but the new queen's policies had a much greater chance of success than those of her predecessors. For it is clear that there remained a strong foundation of sympathy for the old religion and its forms, so that Mary was able to obtain the local cooperation which her father and brother had failed to secure.

Among the clergy the most easily traceable failing, because it had caused a good deal of offence in the parishes, was marriage. The royal injunctions of March 1554 ordered all bishops and other ecclesiastical officers to proceed against the priests who had broken the rule of celibacy, but this could hardly be done in Lancashire until the bishop of Chester, himself a married man, had been removed. Bishop Bird was determined to retain his see if this was possible; he obtained a royal pardon for all offences committed before Mary's coronation and he attempted to repudiate his wife voluntarily. But after six conservative bishops had been commissioned by the Crown to deal with episcopal marriages, Bird was tried and deprived of his post on 16 March 1554.[1] George Wilmesley, the chancellor of the diocese, had also married but he was able to escape

[1] *CPR*, Philip and Mary, I, 175, 446; Strype, *Ecclesiastical Memorials*, III(1), 218; *Diary of Henry Machyn*, 58.

his bishop's fate. The chancellor had powerful family connections in Cheshire and Bishop Bonner was his half-brother so he was able to retain his place, though shorn of some of his powers by the first Marian bishop.[1]

The administration of the diocese ground to a halt at the death of Edward VI, probably because of uncertainties over the future of Bird and Wilmesley and over the policies to be followed. The consistory did not sit from June 1553 until June 1554, from just before the young king's decease until the effective beginning of the episcopate of Bird's successor. It is just possible that a section of the consistory act book has been lost, but the method of binding, the coincidence of dates and a similar gap in the depositions-book series make this improbable.[2] The first Marian bishop was George Coates who, as a proven opponent of religious change and a resident prebendary of Chester, was well fitted for his new office. He was consecrated in London a fortnight after Bird's deprivation, but he did not enter his diocese as bishop until early in 1555, when his first official acts took place. Coates was content to leave the early stages of the reconstruction of Catholicism to the experienced and conservative Chancellor Wilmesley, and the work began in June 1554 with the first Marian sessions of the consistory and a visitation of the parishes. The visitation, conducted by Wilmesley, covered the whole diocese, for, though the presentments for the archdeaconry of Richmond do not survive, the itinerary and the call lists include the parishes to the north of the Ribble, and Coates joined his chancellor at Lancaster for the last part of the survey.[3] Although it had got off to a dilatory start, the campaign against Edwardine Anglicanism was under way.

It was intended that married clergy were to be proceeded against in the consistory rather than the correction court, and only two Lancashire priests were formally presented at the visitation for having taken wives. The churchwardens of North Meols reported that their rector, Laurence Waterward, had married, and it was found that he had fled from the county; Peter Prescot was instituted to the rectory in August. The change of incumbent led to some difficulties, for John Fleetwood, who had obtained a lease of the rectory from Waterward, refused to allow the new rector use of the parsonage and glebe. Prescot argued that the lease was invalid, since it had been granted after Waterward had incurred automatic deprivation by his marriage.[4] The second Lancashire case, that of William

---

[1] Haigh, 'A mid-Tudor ecclesiastical official', 17–19.
[2] CRO, EDC 1/13, fos. 151v–152, EDC 2/5–6.
[3] *Diary of Henry Machyn*, 79; *Ordination Reg.* 81; Foxe, *Acts and Monuments*, VII, 47; CRO, EDV 1/1, fos. 1–1v, 44, 65.
[4] CRO, EDV 1/1, fo. 142v, EDA 1/1, fo. 44v; *Duchy Pleadings*, III, 163–4.

Sawrey, the Edwardian vicar of Urswick, was also a troublesome one. Sawrey, a graduate, pluralist and former chaplain to the earl of Essex, had been deprived of two benefices in the diocese before the visitation, presumably by the commissary of Richmond. When the chancellor reached Kirkby Ireleth, Sawrey (called 'late vicar of Urswick') appeared before him and was ordered not to consort with his wife on pain of excommunication, and to appear at Chester in September 1554. We do not know what happened in the autumn, but when his successor at Urswick died in 1557 Sawrey tried to secure a new presentation for himself. A further enquiry into his case was held, at which Sawrey argued that he had made a marriage contract and ratified it by consummation in 1540, six months before he 'received any holy orders or had thought to be a priest'. The marriage had incensed his father, who had packed him off to Cambridge with some sort of letter from the local curate which ensured that he 'might lawfully be a priest and yet retain his wife'. Though he obviously regarded himself as a special case, the authorities were not disposed to take notice of Sawrey's pleas and Thomas Dobson was instituted to Urswick instead.[1]

The visitation saw no further proceedings against married clergy, but immediately after its completion in March 1555 a special session of the consistory, presided over by the bishop, was held at Chester. On this occasion three Warrington priests, Richard Taylor, who had been schoolmaster there for thirty years, Robert Wright, a former chantrist, and Robert Houghton, were ordered to repudiate their wives on pain of excommunication. In addition, Thomas Clayton submitted to correction and was forbidden to live with Margaret Rainford, but although Roger Mason, vicar of Huyton, was cited before the court by one of his curates he was found to be innocent of marriage. These were the only Lancashire clergy prosecuted for marriage before the consistory, while in the diocese as a whole only eight clerks were charged and two of them were cleared.[2] The priests were treated with leniency and merely instructed to separate from their putative wives, because those convicted in the consistory were all assistant clergy. The injunctions had provided for the deprivation of beneficed men, with the bait of another benefice for those who abstained from the company of their women, but there was no effective sanction for the assistants. Robert Wright was separated from Janet Cartwright in March 1555, but four months later he was again before the court for continuing to 'frequent' her and was warned that his property would be sequestrated if he persisted. Two years later he was reported at visitation as still seeing Janet, and was

[1] CRO, EDA 1/1, fos. 42, 50, EDV 1/1, fo. 130/1, EDC 2/6, fos, 152–153.
[2] CRO, EDC 1/14, fos. 12v–13, 32–32v, 39v.

excommunicated and suspended from his priestly functions. The loss of his livelihood forced Wright into temporary conformity and he was absolved, but within five months he was found to be actually living with his wife, and on this occasion the court ran out of patience. He was ordered not to live within twenty miles of Janet, to eat bread and water as penance, and to confess his faults publicly in three local churches. One of his Warrington colleagues, Richard Taylor, also caused the authorities trouble, and he too was called before the consistory again for 'frequenting' the woman he had married.[1]

Discussions of the proceedings against married clergy have usually been based on the most convenient source, diocesan institution records, on the assumption that institutions 'per deprivationem' early in Mary's reign indicate that the previous incumbents had been removed because of their marriages. This is an unsatisfactory approach, since deprivations took place for other reasons, the non-beneficed clergy are omitted, and, at Chester at least, the institution books do not always record the reasons for vacancies and not all institutions are listed. But, used with care, apparent deprivations can give some guide to clerical marriages. Edward Keble, an absentee pluralist, had probably married, since he lost his prebends at Salisbury and Westminster at the same time as the rectory of Warrington. The removal of Edward Morecroft from Aughton was presumably because of marriage, for he was restored in 1559 with the other married men and had a wife under Elizabeth.[2] Gabriel Rayne's deprivation from the vicarage of Cockerham is not recorded, but he was replaced by the middle of 1554 and was proceeded against for marriage by the archbishop of York. It is also possible that William Rothwell, vicar of Dean, was deprived, for though the reason for the vacancy of his benefice is not known he was replaced at about the same time as the other married men.[3]

There were only seven definite priestly marriages in Lancashire, with two more probabilities and another possibility, and as 257 clergy served in the county in 1554 this represents no more than 4% of the total clerical body. In contrast, it has been suggested that one-fifth of all the English clergy took wives under Edward, and the figure in some areas was certainly higher. About a quarter of the clergy of Norfolk and Suffolk married, while more than a quarter of Essex incumbents were deprived. In the north, however, men were

[1] CRO, EDC 1/14, fos. 12v, 51, EDC 1/15, fo. 60, EDV 1/2, fos. 65, 68v.
[2] CRO, EDA 1/1, fo. 45; Venn, *Alumni*, III, 1; J. le Neve, *Fasti Ecclesiae Anglicanae*, ed. T. D. Hardy, 3 vols. III, 351; *VCH*, III, 289–90.
[3] CRO, EDV 1/1, fos. 33, 44; Dickens, *Marian Reaction*, I, 26; *CPR*, Philip and Mary, I, 41.

less willing to change their ways or less able to support a wife: only about 10% of the York diocesan clergy married.[1] The married priests in Lancashire seem to have been concentrated in the south of the county, although some north-Lancashire assistants may have been proceeded against by the commissary of Richmond. Only two priests north of the Ribble are known to have married, both university-educated pluralists who perhaps had reformist sympathies, and 40% of the maximum number of married clergy in the whole county were graduates. It was geographical position and outside contacts which made men more likely to marry, rather than the ability to support a family, for the incidence of marriage was only slightly higher among the incumbents than among the assistants.

The clergy of Lancashire might take mistresses, but an open breach of the age-old prohibition of marriage commended itself to few; priests at Blackburn, Prescot and Eccles certainly had children but did not take the opportunity to legitimise them.[2] It is noticeable that four of the nine or ten married priests served in the parish of Warrington, and there may have been safety, or at least respectability, in numbers. There was popular hostility towards clerical marriage, and few braved public opinion. In July 1549 a prebendary of Chester testified that Hugh Bunbury, priest, made a marriage contract with Anne Andrew, but 'the said Anne did desire the said Hugh that the said Hugh would tarry, and not to marry her until there were some other priests married, the which the said Hugh granted that he would tarry until Midsummer or Michaelmas'. Anne was presumably worried about local reactions to her marriage, and she must have found the prospect daunting, for the wedding never took place. The marriage of Robert Wright of Warrington may have caused comment, for he had to sue a local woman for slander in March 1549. Married priests in Yorkshire suffered when Mary came to the throne, for, as Robert Parkyn put it, 'the common people would point them with fingers in places when they saw them', and in both Yorkshire and Lancashire married ministers provoked a good deal of scorn under Elizabeth.[3]

If clerical marriage had made very little headway in Lancashire, the same is true of clerical Protestantism. The Marian authorities were prepared to allow those who could conform their consciences to

---

[1] Dixon, *History of the Church of England*, IV, 143–4; G. Baskerville, 'Married clergy and pensioned religious in Norwich diocese', *EHR*, XLVIII, 44–5; H. E. P. Grieve, 'Married clergy in Essex', *TRHS*, 4th series, XXII, 141–3; Dickens, *Marian Reaction*, I, 14–15.

[2] CRO, EDC 2/8, fos. 40, 60v, *Farnworth Reg.* 34; *VCH*, IV, 359.

[3] CRO, EDC 2/4, p. 119, EDC 1/12, fos. 118v, 121v; Dickens, *Lollards and Protestants*, 190; P. Tyler, 'The Church courts at York and witchcraft prosecutions, 1567–1640', *Northern History*, IV, 94–5; see below, p. 221.

retain their posts, and there was no purge of Protestants. The handful of reformist sympathisers caused no trouble, and the few priestly friends of John Bradford served on. It is true that though there had been only one vacancy of a Lancashire benefice in 1544 and one in 1549 there were nine vacancies in 1554, but three resulted from the deaths of incumbents, three from deprivation for marriage and the other three were probably for the same reason. None of the 67 priests who fled abroad under Mary had served in Lancashire.[1] There was, in fact, a considerable degree of continuity between the clergy of Edward's reign and those of Mary's, much more than there was to be between the reigns of Mary and Elizabeth. This was one result of the limited impact of the Edwardian Reformation.

If officials found little to complain of among the serving clergy of the county, they were to encounter more trouble from the local laity and Lancashire-born clergy working elsewhere. But the threat posed by reformers was not serious, and the regime could afford to move cautiously. It is significant that when the first move was made against a Lancashire Protestant in March 1554, the victim was not sought for offences committed in the county; the earl of Derby told George Marsh that he had heard of him in London and had resolved to arrest him there or in Lancashire.[2] Marsh's arrest in the northwest, rather than in the areas in which he worked (London and the Midlands), shows how much more dangerous life was for a heretic where there was no popular sympathy for his stand. George Marsh was apprehended on a visit to Lancashire by the servants of a local justice, taken to the earl of Derby for examination, and then imprisoned in Lancaster gaol. After an appearance at the quarter sessions he was kept in a secular prison for almost a year until in March 1555 he was handed over to the diocesan authorities and taken to Chester for trial. He was burned outside the city on 12 April 1555.[3] Whatever the charges laid against him, Marsh did not preach heresy in Lancashire in the reign of Mary. He was arrested not because of his activities but because of his known opinions, and the intention was not to punish him but to reclaim him for Catholicism. Despite his complaint that he was given no blankets when detained at Lathom and Bishop Coates' original refusal to have anything to do with

---

[1] CRO, EDA 1/1, *passim*, supplemented by *VCH*, III–VIII, *passim*; Garrett, *Marian Exiles, passim*.

[2] Foxe, *Acts and Monuments*, VII, 45.

[3] *Ibid*. 39–53. No records have been discovered which might supplement Foxe's account, but there is no doubt that the martyrologist's version is substantially accurate. He used Marsh's own report of his arrest, and his letters to friends, and Foxe was able to name officials in Lancashire and Cheshire, areas with which he cannot have been familiar. He must have had a reliable informant.

him, he was treated with leniency and consideration until his condemnation.

The earl of Derby and his council had no desire to burn a heretic, and wished merely to weaken local Protestantism by inducing one of its founders to recant. Marsh was examined by Robert Brassey, vicar of Prescot and a gentle Catholic of the old school, unwilling to force Tridentine definitions upon the theologically unsophisticated; Foxe described him as 'a worthy old man, both for his wisdom and his hoar hairs'.[1] At their first meeting Brassey and Marsh discussed the mass, and the former professed himself content with the answers he received, which were adequate for a beginner. But this remark produced an unfortunate effect, for Marsh would not agree that his replies could be interpreted in a Catholic sense, even if an abler scholar than he were satisfied. When he was again examined by Brassey, together with the well-born rector of Wigan, Richard Gerard, he stated bluntly that 'the whole mass did offend me'. Though Marsh argued that the mass was full of abuses, Brassey and Gerard still pressed him to conform and tried to interpret the text of the service in a sense he would find acceptable. The interrogators were doing their best to accommodate him, but he was determined to go on record as a heretic. When his courage failed he pleaded with the earl of Derby to save him from burning, but there remains a suspicion that he courted martyrdom; he had given himself up as soon as he heard a J.P. was searching for him.[2]

Despite their lack of success, Derby's council and the two clerics continued to work on Marsh, and two attempts were made to persuade him to sign four articles which Edward Crome had accepted in one of his many recantations. The articles were far from extreme, but they covered the issues which would divide unlearned Protestants from orthodoxy. Marsh gave his answer after half an hour, denying that the mass was 'according to Christ's institution', affirming the necessity of communion in both kinds, and denying the need for confession, though he admitted it was useful for 'rude people'. But on the crucial question, transubstantiation, Marsh said he was unable to answer and, despite his short time at Cambridge and his work with Laurence Saunders, he had more zeal than learning. He was determined not to agree with his examiners, and when he read Alphonso y Castro's book on the punishment of heretics he refused to accept any of it.[3]

During his imprisonment at Lancaster further efforts were made to convince Marsh that he was in error, or merely that his views were

---

[1] *Ibid.* VIII, 266.
[2] *Ibid.* VII, 40, 42, 45.
[3] *Ibid.* 44.

not incompatible with the Catholic position. Many local priests and gentry discussed the Eucharist with him, in a concerted attempt to reclaim him for orthodoxy. His confinement was lax and he received visits from his friends, although when Bishop Coates discovered what was going on conditions were made more severe. At his trial in Chester, Marsh was given every opportunity to recant, and George Wilmesley, vicar-general and the last person to be a persecuting rigorist, twice stopped Coates passing sentence, as once that had been done a recantation could not save Marsh.[1] The case exemplifies the Marian persecution in Lancashire; Marsh was given more chances than the letter of the law allowed, to escape the fire and even to escape trial, and it was almost a year before he was handed over to the ecclesiastical arm. While there is every indication that heresy was hated, there was no bitterness towards the Protestants themselves, and clergy and laity could afford the luxury of distinguishing between the criminal and his crime, because heresy was not a threat. Other heretics were detected, but only Marsh was burned.

In the 1554–5 visitation it soon became obvious that the diocese had hardly been touched by heretical currents of thought and in the seven Cheshire deaneries only one case of heresy was uncovered. Wilmesley, the visitor, first reached south Lancashire in July 1554, and though the numbers involved were small the situation there was not quite so good. The first case to be unearthed was that of Adam Robinson of Prestwich, and the registrar recorded 'notatur quia sit sacramentarius et absentat se a divinis et contempsit'. At Prestwich five others were reported as 'sacramentarii et spernunt eucharistiam', and there were isolated heretics at Eccles and Liverpool.[2] It is interesting that the fourteen were noted as 'sacramentaries' rather than mere heretics, though the significance of this is not clear. 'Sacramentary' was the term used, mainly in the 1530s, to describe those with Zwinglian views on the Eucharist, and John Bradford's radicalism may lie behind this aspect of the Lancashire Protestants' theology. But the word has a dated ring by 1554, and it probably records what it was about the heretics that orthodox parishioners found most objectionable.

Detection in the visitation raised difficult problems for the radicals, and Elizabeth Longshaw of Eccles wrote to tell John Bradford of her predicament. She reported that 'the cause why I must suffer is for not going to church and committing spiritual fornication with their strange gods', and justified her stand by a series of arguments against transubstantiation and the mass. She was faced, she thought, with three alternatives, 'either to flee, or abide and deny my God

---

[1] *Ibid.* 47, 50–2.
[2] CRO, EDV 1/1, fos. 126v, 128, 133-134, 141v.

(which the Lord forbid), or else to be cast in prison to suffer death', and she asked for Bradford's prayers 'that I may never shrink from the truth you have taught and preached, either by word, deed or writing, but that I may stand to it even to the fire'. Finally, Elizabeth mentioned for 'remembrance in your prayers a maid of the parish of Prestwich whose name is Alice Seddon, which doth not cease praying for you night and day'.[1] Alice, too, had been presented at the visitation, and she, with the others, was summoned to appear before the visitation correction court in March 1555. Of the fourteen summoned only Adam Poulton of Liverpool appeared, and he was able to prove his innocence; the remainder must have been excommunicated for contumacy, but thereafter there are at least two possibilities. Excommunication rarely forced the obstinate to submit and, rather than signify large numbers each year for arrest by the secular authorities, officials at Chester usually allowed excommunicates to go free. If the Protestants were felt to pose no serious threat, it is possible that this course was adopted in 1555. The significations for the Lancashire portion of the diocese are lost, and it may be that the thirteen were signified, arrested by the sheriff and imprisoned. George Marsh certainly saw some of his friends in prison at Lancaster, and they may have been those reported at the visitation.[2] But what is clear is that the heretics were not brought to trial.

Thomas Warberton was among those imprisoned at Lancaster, but either he was released or he made a false recantation for by 1557 he was an exile at Aarau. Some heretics, including Thomas Riddleston and Wharmby, were detained in Manchester College; the former had been a member of Bradford's group, but in 1555 Bradford thought he had compromised by attending 'this false service', the mass.[3] But although almost twenty local Protestants were presented on visitation or arrested later, only George Marsh, who seemed determined to be burned, suffered at the stake. We do not know what happened to the others, though by 1557 John Crompton and Thomas Warberton were certainly free. In Yorkshire, where Marian heresy was primarily Lollard, a simple rejection of parts of Catholic doctrine rather than a positive faith, the heretics prosecuted normally recanted. But Lancashire heresy was backed by a new theology, and its leaders, Bradford and Marsh, constantly encouraged their followers not to give way. It is possible that the Protestants escaped burning not because they recanted, but because they were not forced to choose between the fire and recantation; certainly

---

[1] *Writings of John Bradford*, II, 227–8.
[2] Foxe, *Acts and Monuments*, VII, 46.
[3] *Ibid.* 46–7; Garrett, *Marian Exiles*, 321; Hollingworth, *Mancuniensis*, 79; *Writings of John Bradford*, II, 236.

Marsh insisted that his friends had remained steadfast.[1] Officials in Lancashire were apparently unwilling to proceed to extremities, and heretics were allowed to remain in prison or even to go free. Those arrested by secular officers could only be tried for heresy if they were first handed over to the Church, but except in the case of the obstreperous George Marsh this seems not to have been done.

Official lenience is also shown in the case of Geoffrey Hurst, the last of the county Protestants to be harassed under Mary. He was a member of the reformist group centred on the Marsh family, and when he refused to attend church in 1553 he was called 'heretic and Lollard' by his neighbours.[2] To escape arrest he fled into Yorkshire, a far safer area for heretics, and he returned only occasionally to visit his family. When his father died in 1558 Hurst spent eight weeks hiding in his mother's house, but he must eventually have been denounced because Thomas Leyland, a local J.P., planned to search the house for books and Geoffrey himself. The family heard of Leyland's intention, and Hurst was hidden away with a collection of heretical books. While the justice berated Mrs Hurst for allowing her son to fall into heresy, his chaplain unearthed a Tyndale New Testament and pointed out that 'then are all their goods lost to the queen and their bodies to prison'. But whatever the letter of the law, the Hursts did not suffer for their books, and when in 1557 a Manchester man was found with a 'biblia anglicana' he was merely ordered to surrender it and fined half a mark. The searchers did not find Geoffrey, and his mother and brother were bound on a surety of £100 to produce him and his sister within a fortnight. The two appeared before Leyland as instructed, but refused either to attend the mass the justice had arranged for them or to relinquish their views. They were therefore bound over to appear again before Leyland three weeks later, to be sent to Lancaster gaol, but Mary died in the meantime and no further action was taken.[3] The Hursts had been given time and encouragement to recant or escape, and Leyland had tried to sort out matters for himself without calling on the full weight of the heresy laws.

Our discussion of the correspondence of the Lancashire heretics suggested that they were recently converted Edwardian Anglicans rather than late Lollards, and it is clear from their conduct under

[1] CRO, EDC 2/6, fos. 171–171v; Dickens, *Lollards and Protestants*, 230–1, 235, 244, 250; Foxe, *Acts and Monuments*, VII, 46.
[2] Professor Dickens has suggested that the Yorkshire heretics were called 'Lollards' because that was what they were. But Hurst's link with Marsh, the family's Prayer Book, the secret services with visiting Protestant preachers and Hurst's refusal to attend church, show that 'Lollard' was an inadequate description and resulted from local ignorance of the brands of heresy rather than the nature of his beliefs.
[3] Foxe, *Acts and Monuments*, VIII, 562–4; CRO, EDV 1/2, fo. 36.

Mary that this was so. Though Lollards occasionally held their own conventicles, it was rare for them to refuse to attend church; they were a persecuted minority too adept at self-concealment to draw attention to themselves by unnecessary gestures. But the new Protestants of Lancashire were rigid in their refusal to attend, and his unwillingness to compromise lay at the root of Geoffrey Hurst's troubles. At the visitation of 1554 several of the heretics were said to 'absent themselves from services', and Elizabeth Longshaw told Bradford this was why she had been presented. Bradford did his best to keep his followers from the mass, and while in prison in London he composed *The Hurt of Hearing Mass* for his Lancashire friends. The mass, he argued, was not merely an impure service, it was an idolatrous perversion expressly forbidden by God, and Marsh shared his views.[1] Early Lancashire Protestantism was solidly based on a rejection of the mass and an acceptance of the Edwardian Prayer Book which, although 'the most devilish thing that ever was devised' to one local rector, was to the reformers a godly liturgy and the norm of their faith. The Hurst family had only a handful of books, but a Prayer Book was among them; when Marsh and Warberton were in prison they recited morning and evening prayer and the litany from their Prayer Book. The Protestants of the Bolton area held secret services, and Geoffrey Hurst led preachers over from Yorkshire to serve a congregation which varied in size between sixteen and twenty-four.[2] The Edwardian Reformation had been short, but it had given the radicals strength by providing a positive (and once official) theology and liturgy.

The Protestant circles were, however, small; they were soon left almost leaderless, and once many of the members had been detected at the visitation of 1554 there were no further reports of heretics at the visitations of 1556 and 1557. The Levers and the Pilkingtons fled abroad from Cambridge, Bradford was imprisoned in London a month after Mary's accession, and though Marsh spent a month or two in the Bolton area he was soon arrested. John Traves' close links with Bradford gave him a position of some authority, and Hurst's Yorkshire contacts made him something of a leader, but there were no reformist clergy active in Lancashire and ministers from Yorkshire had to make fleeting visits across the Pennines. The leaderless state of the Protestants explains the role which the letters of Bradford and Marsh came to play, for the rank and file were dependent for advice and instruction on those in prison. Bradford instructed the recipients of his letters to burn them, lest they should fall into

[1] *Writings of John Bradford*, II, 227, 228, 236, 312–18; Foxe, *Acts and Monuments*, VII, 47.
[2] *Ibid.* 41, 47, VIII, 562, 563.

official hands and lead to arrests,[1] but the letters to Lancashire were carefully preserved and are still extant. The earl of Derby thought Bradford's letters made an important contribution to the survival of Protestantism in the palatinate. Secretary Bourne reported at Bradford's first examination that it had been said

this parliament time by the Earl of Derby that he [Bradford] hath done more hurt by letters and exhorting those that have come to him in religion than ever he did when he was abroad by preaching. In his letters he curseth all that teacheth false doctrine (for so he calleth that which is not according to that he taught), and most heartily exhorteth them to whom he writeth to continue still in that they have received by him and such like as he is.

At the next examination Stephen Gardiner also mentioned Derby's account of 'letters to no little hurt to the queen's people', and the correspondence was raised again at the last interrogation.[2]

Bradford's role in the maintenance of Lancashire Protestantism led to an unusual plan to send him into the county to be burned. Heretics were usually executed where they had been arrested but, though most of Bradford's work and his arrest had been in London, it was widely thought early in February 1555 that he would be sent north for his burning. By 19 February, however, the writ for the execution had been cancelled and by the end of the month Bishop Ridley was remarking that 'they have changed their purpose and prolonged your death'.[3] The reason for this may be gauged from the events of the next two months, when Bradford was subjected to a barrage of conferences with some of the most eminent Catholic theologians: Harding, Harpsfield, Weston, Bonner, Heath, Day and two Spanish friars, and some of the conservatives among Bradford's friends, Percival Cresswell, Stephen Beck, George Collier and Henry Pendleton. It was presumably hoped that a recantation might be obtained from Bradford, who could then be used as Henry Pendleton had been, to teach Catholicism to those he had previously taught Protestantism.[4] John Coppage, a Manchester priest who had served at the college there, certainly knew what was afoot; 'I doubt not', he told Bradford, 'but if you will come unto us you should be able to help many, and your friends also, than ever you were.'[5] A preacher who recanted was more useful than a martyr who was burned, and the earl of Derby instructed one of Bradford's relations

[1] *Writings of John Bradford*, II, 76.
[2] *Ibid.* I, 469, 474, 487.
[3] *Ibid.* 434, 448, 517, II, 187, 191, 193, 199.
[4] *Ibid.* I, 449, 492, 496, 497, 499, 500, 502, 518, 530, 538, 541, 550, 552; Foxe, *Acts and Monuments*, VI, 630. It is interesting that Pendleton was among those used to try to reconvert Bradford.
[5] *Writings of John Bradford*, I, 517.

to offer him exile in return for a recantation.[1] These efforts were a unique testimony to Bradford's influence in Lancashire and the need to destroy it.

Until the middle of 1555, Lancashire Protestantism was centred on two prisoners, who were visited, written to and prayed for, and thereafter it was centred on the letters of two dead men. The dependence of the reformed religion on the academic evangelists made it particularly vulnerable, and this weakness was exploited by the authorities. The efforts to reconvert Bradford and Marsh were prompted by a hope that they might be used to break the faith of their followers, as Henry Pendleton and John Standish were. The defection of Pendleton was a severe blow to the Lancashire Protestants, for he had been one of the first preachers of reform in the county. Soon after the accession of Mary he began to preach Catholicism from his London pulpit, 'becoming', as Foxe put it, 'of a faithful pastor a false runagate, and of a true preacher a sworn enemy to God's everlasting testament'. The utility of such a man was soon realised; he was used on several occasions as a preacher at St Paul's Cross, he contributed to Bonner's book of homilies and, as an interrogator who might persuade others to follow his course, he examined at least half a dozen heretics including Philpot and Bradford. In 1555 Pendleton was sent into Lancashire to preach against Protestantism, and John Bradford had to warn his friends against the apostate.[2] John Standish was a less dangerous defector, but he was a useful Catholic propagandist; he wrote tracts on the papal supremacy and vernacular scripture, and was used in the heresy prosecution of the Lancastrian Roger Holland in London.[3] Although the Marian campaign against Lancashire Protestants was not vindictive it did have some success, and by the second half of the reign they were a small group of leaderless, and perhaps dispirited, artisans, traders and small farmers, living in an area in which heresy was unpopular.

It was the laity rather than the clergy who enforced the Marian reaction. The first statute in the campaign against heresy placed the onus for action on the justices of the peace, and in 1555 the king and queen sent a circular letter to J.P.s which ordered them to detect and arrest the heterodox. In England as a whole perhaps a third of the Marian martyrs were first arrested by local justices, and another fifth

[1] *Ibid.* 499–500.
[2] Foxe, *Acts and Monuments*, VI, 629–30, 718, VII, 620, 740–1, VIII, 111; Strype, *Ecclesiastical Memorials*, III(1), 155, 213, 321, (2), 2–3; *Writings of John Bradford*, I, 449–50, 541–4.
[3] *Short Title Catalogue, 1475–1660*, ed. A. W. Pollard and G. R. Redgrave, Nos. 23207–8, 23211; Foxe, *Acts and Monuments*, VIII, 474.

by constables.[1] Dr Loades suggests that the persecution was weakened because anticlericalism and a fear of Spanish domination often
made justices sympathetic towards heretics, while opposition to
burning meant laxity in the conduct of searches and prosecutions.[2]
This may be a reasonable analysis of events in the south, but as a
picture of what happened in the north-west it is less convincing.
There anticlericalism was not the potent force in local life that it had
become in some areas, and the diocesan administration was so
incapable of imposing the episcopal will that fear of a clericalist
dominion was unlikely. There were no burnings in Lancashire itself,
and the whole diocese saw only two. We have already discussed lay
attitudes towards heresy and, though these would not lead us to
expect vigorous persecution, few laymen can have been sympathetic
towards the reformers.

The detection of heresy in Lancashire was usually the result of lay
initiatives. The earl of Derby instructed local justices to search for
the Protestant George Marsh, Marsh surrendered to a J.P. who was
looking for him, and his early examinations were conducted by the
earl's council. Much of the detailed questioning at Lathom was done
by two priests, but they were acting as theological advisers to Derby
rather than as ecclesiastical officials, and on two occasions Marsh
appeared before an almost exclusively lay council. Marsh was then
sent to Lancaster where, as the law prescribed, he appeared before
the justices at quarter sessions and was again examined by the earl.
Although the justices found there was a case to answer, Marsh
was not handed over to the bishop's officers until a year after his
arrest.[3] The earl of Derby also played a part in the prosecution
of John Bradford, though the arrest took place in London. It was
he who reported the letters Bradford had sent into Lancashire,
and he sent one of his servants to persuade the preacher to recant.
The earl was said to have pleaded for Bradford's life on two occasions between the decision to have him burned in Lancashire and the
postponement of the execution, so it is possible that the plan to
delay the burning, while attempts were made to secure a recantation,
was his.[4]

Though Derby had overall responsibility for the enforcement of
the reaction in Lancashire, and was consulted on the implications for

---

[1] D. M. Loades, 'The enforcement of reaction, 1553–1558', *J Eccl. Hist.* XVI, 56;
Burnet, *History of the Reformation*, III, 398–9; Hughes, *Reformation in England*, II,
274.
[2] Loades, *The Oxford Martyrs*, 157–8, 164, 166, 242; Loades, 'Enforcement of
reaction', 60–1.
[3] Foxe, *Acts and Monuments*, VII, 39–45, 47–8.
[4] *Writings of John Bradford*, I, 469, 474, 499, 517, 538, 541, 552.

the county of the trial and condemnation of Bradford, he was far from being a pro-Spanish clericalist. His career under Mary was chequered, for although he was one of the powerful nobles to whom the queen owed her throne he was soon complaining that those who had served her well were treated with disdain. He received a substantial pension from Philip of Spain, but the earl was no favourer of the Spanish match and he seems to have threatened to leave Mary's service if she persisted in her plans. Derby's position must have been common knowledge, for he was one of the conservative lords asked to desert Spain in an open letter from an accomplice of the rebel Thomas Stafford. Thereafter, his standing in the eyes of the government and his attitude towards the regime can be traced in his attendance at Council meetings. His presence was recorded fairly regularly in the first year of the reign, but after the middle of 1554 he attended only infrequently, and between February 1555 and January 1558 he was present on only three occasions.[1] The earl's withdrawal from Court was not a result of opposition to the Crown's religious policy; it took place nine months before the first burnings, and Derby himself was active in heresy prosecutions. The earl was an ideal figure to direct an attack on Lancashire Protestants, for he had great power and prestige in his own county and his reputation was untarnished by subservience to the interests of Spain. But his hatred of heresy was more intense than his dislike of Spaniards, and he organised a visit to John Bradford by two Spanish friars.[2]

Processes against other Lancashire heretics resulted from lay efforts. Thomas Leyland, a J.P. with strong conservative principles, organised a search for Geoffrey Hurst, and if Mary's death had not intervened he would have placed Hurst and his sister safely in Lancaster gaol. The arrests made by justices were only possible because of popular antipathy towards heresy, and as Marsh and Hurst were taken on rare visits to the county they must have been reported by neighbours; Foxe thought Marsh was arrested 'by detection of certain adversaries'.[3] It is even likely that the fourteen suspects detected at the visitation of 1554 were presented by laymen. Unless the Protestants had been rash enough to make their views known to conservative local priests, they must have been named to the visitor by the churchwardens and sworn men of their parishes. This indicates either a common dislike of heresy or a fear of the censures of the Church which the weakness of the diocesan machine

---

[1] *CSPS* (1553), 166–73; J. Froude, *History of England from the Fall of Wolsey*, V, 219–20, 234, 311–12, 366, 398; Strype, *Ecclesiastical Memorials*, III(2), 340–54; *APC*, IV–VI, *passim*.

[2] *Writings of John Bradford*, I, 518, 530.

[3] Foxe, *Acts and Monuments*, VII, 39, VIII, 562–4.

did not warrant. Lancashire did not witness the large numbers of burnings which might have turned the laity against persecution, and it is not surprising that local Catholics assisted in the defence of their Church against organised heresy.

There was sufficient lay opposition to Protestantism to ensure that the heterodox were usually reported, and at least half of the known county radicals were brought to the attention of the officers of Church or state. But though there is no sign of the partiality towards heretics which might have helped reformers to escape detection, there was no strong desire for their punishment. The secular authorities were slow to hand men over to the Church for trial, several heretics were imprisoned but, as far as we know, never tried, and it is clear that the processes against Marsh and Hurst would have been dropped had they shown a willingness to compromise. The orthodox went to some length to help their misguided friends and relations. While John Bradford was imprisoned in London, attempts to recovert him were made by a Manchester merchant who was a distant kinsman, the ex-warden and one of the priests of the suppressed Manchester College, and Henry Pendleton, who had been one of Bradford's colleagues on the unofficial Protestant mission into Lancashire. When Roger Holland was tried in London before Bishop Bonner, a party of his conservative relatives and friends travelled from Lancashire to appear on his behalf. Lord Strange, Sir Thomas Gerard, Mr Eccleston and 'divers other of worship both of Cheshire and Lancashire' were present at his last examination. Eccleston, a close kinsman of Holland, hoped for his conversion: 'I thank your good Lordship', he said to Bonner, 'your honour meaneth good to my cousin; I beseech God he have the grace to follow your counsel.'[1]

Protestantism was not sufficiently widespread, even in the southeast of the county, to have constituted a threat, and there were no social divisions between Catholics and reformers. In 1548 Thomas Hall, a conservative-minded priest, was a frequent visitor to the house of John Bradford's mother, and when Bradford sent him a New Testament he asked the advice of the Protestant John Traves on how to find the Epistle and Gospel of the day.[2] Normal social intercourse between the orthodox and the heretics continued even in Marian Bolton. Richard Rothwell, a conservative friend of the reformist John Crompton, stayed at the latter's home during his last illness in 1557, and the new vicar of Bolton was called to the house to give Rothwell the Catholic sacraments before his death.[3] It is in the nature of our sources that we should have few such intimate glimpses

[1] *Ibid.* 474, 477.
[2] *Writings of John Bradford*, II, 16–17.
[3] CRO, EDC 2/6, fos. 171–171v, 177.

into the private lives of conservatives and radicals, but our impression must be that the orthodox reserved their repugnance for heresy in the abstract, rather than the heretics they knew.

However, although their numerical supremacy was so overwhelming that they could afford to be tolerant, Lancashire Catholics were vulnerable at one important point. The first generation of Protestants had been taught by university-trained scholars, and they were able to argue their case in a way that local conservatives could not. The Catholics, in contrast, were not well informed, and the wills which survive from the middle of the century show a good deal of theological confusion. Two prominent gentlemen hoped to be saved by the merits of Christ but asked for prayers for their souls, as did the rector of Ashton, who ought to have known better. A Manchester merchant left his soul to God, the Virgin and the saints, but trusted to find salvation through Christ's merits.[1] In the diocese of York the proportion of wills which were radical in temper declined under Mary, but in Lancashire the traditional formulae actually became less common in these years. All 7 of the 43 wills from the 1550s which mentioned the merits of Christ date from Mary's reign, and in that decade the number of wills which asked for prayers for the soul fell below 60% of the total for the first time. To laymen the Protestants were merely those who, in the words of one Lancashireman, 'pulled down crosses in the church and pulled down the rood-cellar and all the saints'. Some priests were no better schooled in the contested issues, and Ralph Parker, chaplain to Thomas Leyland, knew only that Protestantism had something to do with vernacular books; 'It is not good that they should have such English books to look on', he said of a Latin grammar he found in a search, 'for this and such others may do much harm.'[2] If the heretics were not to gain further ground at the expense of the orthodox, then reform of the Church was needed, and in particular the education of clergy and laity had to be improved. To a limited extent, the reign of Mary saw such reform.

[1] *L & C Wills*, I, 90, 131, 157, IV, 6.
[2] Foxe, *Acts and Monuments*, VIII, 563, 565.

13

The reconstruction of the Church

The Marian reaction in Lancashire saw not merely an attack by the officers of Church and state on Protestant sympathy, but an attempt to reinstate and improve traditional Catholicism and its institutions. It is true that Mary, Pole and Gardiner mounted no propaganda campaign to counter twenty years of anti-papal and, latterly, anti-Catholic preaching and writing,[1] and that continuing financial problems prevented the refoundation of more than a handful of religious houses and chantries. But within the limits set by time, money and manpower the achievements of the Marian period were not inconsiderable. It should be remembered that in 1553 the new regime faced a Protestant episcopate, an heretical liturgy, neglected churches and a depleted priesthood, while in theory the vestments and ornaments needed for the celebration of masses had been destroyed. By 1558 some of the damage the Church in Lancashire had sustained had been repaired; progress had been made in the fields of diocesan organisation and finance, the quality and supply of the clergy, the condition of church fabric and even the education of the Catholic laity. The success of these measures should not be exaggerated, there were no radical new initiatives and there is little evidence of popular religious enthusiasm, but there are many indications that, by the accession of Elizabeth, the Church in Lancashire was better able to withstand attack than it had ever been before.

A prerequisite for reform at the parochial level was an improvement in the administrative structure of the diocese, so that the bishop could exercise greater control over his clergy and people. We have seen that effective rule had been impossible under Bishop Bird, when there were no archdeacons and administration was in the hands of only two men, the diocesan chancellor and the commissary of Richmond. There was no proper contact between episcopal officers and the parishes of a large and unwieldy diocese, while the central administration was understaffed and overworked. The consistory court had to be suspended while the chancellor was conducting a visitation as vicar-general, for he could not be at Chester to

[1] Loades, *The Oxford Martyrs*, 148, 258–9.

adjudicate as official principal. George Wilmesley's monopolisation of office made reform of the chancellorship essential under Mary, especially as he had married in the reign of Edward, had two mistresses as well, and had used his position to obtain lucrative leases of episcopal and other Church property. Bishop Coates, who must have been aware of Wilmesley's failings since he himself had lived in Chester for some time as a prebendary, seems to have been reluctant to offend the chancellor's powerful relations, for he did not dismiss him. But Coates began to ease his chancellor out of office by forcing him to share his power with others, and in 1556 Bishop Scott completed the process by removing Wilmesley from the chancellorship.[1]

Reform of the office of chancellor was, however, more important than the mere deprivation of an unsatisfactory incumbent, and this too was tackled by the Marian bishops. Coates may have resented his complete dependence on Wilmesley, for late in 1554 he appointed two new diocesan officers. John Hampson, who had been a scholar of Balliol while Coates was master, was made archdeacon of Richmond and Robert Percival, a Cambridge bachelor of divinity, became archdeacon of Chester.[2] The authority of the old archdeacons had been vested in the bishop at the foundation of the see, and in 1554 Coates chose not to delegate any of his powers. But the new posts were not mere sinecures, as they were to become under Elizabeth, and the two salaries of £50 each year paid officials who could assist in the general administration of the diocese. Initially, Percival played little part in the work of the see, but government of the diocese was now shared between Wilmesley and Hampson. The interval between the death of Bishop Coates in December 1556 and the arrival of Bishop Scott in the following November saw the final eclipse of George Wilmesley. Early in March 1557 Hampson was appointed custodian of the spiritualities and commissary to the archbishop of York during the vacancy at Chester, and thereafter the office of chancellor was not resurrected until 1562. In October 1557 Scott made Percival his commissary-general and official principal, and Hampson and William Collingwood were nominated to assist him.[3] Until the royal visitation of 1559, the consistory at Chester was invariably presided over by Hampson as Percival's substitute, so that the commisary-general himself was left free for less routine matters. Percival was never able to monopolise effective power in the diocese as Wilmesley had been, and from the beginning of Scott's episcopate both he and Hampson were special commissaries of the bishop;

---

[1] Haigh, 'Mid-Tudor ecclesiastical official', 7–10, 15–21.
[2] Le Neve, *Fasti*, III, 266–7.
[3] CRO, EDC 1/14, fos. 96v, 113, 145v–146.

later, they may even have been appointed joint commissaries-general and officials principal.[1]

The diocesan appointments made under Mary were particularly suitable ones. George Coates, we have seen, had been a determined opponent of the Reformation in the reigns of Henry VIII and Edward, and the officers he named to assist him were apparently of a similar cast of mind. Both Percival and Hampson refused to conform to the Elizabethan settlement, were deprived of their positions and persisted in their resistance.[2] The second Marian bishop, Cuthbert Scott, a local man like his predecessor, was something of a Catholic rigorist. He was responsible for the vigorous attempts to root out heresy in Cambridge which culminated in the burning of the bones of Martin Bucer, and in 1559 he made an uncompromising speech in the House of Lords against the royal supremacy.[3] But the efforts of these men to revitalise the Church in Lancashire were hampered by long episcopal vacancies. We have seen that the administration of the diocese was effectively suspended for the whole of Mary's first year, and the reimposition of the mass may have been delayed. In March 1554 two justices of the peace reported on the problems the people of Burneston in Yorkshire were experiencing in the restoration of Catholic worship, and pointed out that their task was complicated by the fact that 'the town aforesaid is in the diocese of Chester, whereof there is no ordinary to make complaint unto'.[4] Further difficulties arose after 28 November 1555, when the last session of the Chester consistory held in the name of Bishop Coates took place; no commissary was nominated until 27 March 1556 so that the consistory could not sit, and the new bishop did not assume effective rule in his diocese until the following November.[5] Despite the quality of the Marian officials, they were unable to proceed with the catholicisation of the diocese for two of the five and a half years of Mary's reign.

The efficient conduct of diocesan government was also impeded by the poor finances of the see. In August 1553 Bishop Bird had still not been able to pay to the Crown £1,088 in tenths and subsidies collected from the clergy of his diocese since 1550, but Mary's officials saw that this was a crippling burden and Coates was released from his predecessor's debt.[6] This brought no lasting improvement, and from 1554 the net revenues were cut by more than a quarter as

[1] CRO, EDC 1/14, fo. 145v, 1/15, fo. 165v, EDA 2/1, fos. 99, 103v.
[2] G. Ormerod, *History of the County Palatine and City of Chester*, 3 vols. I, 115, 117; PRO, SP 12/10, fos. 74–74v, SP 15/11/45.
[3] Foxe, *Acts and Monuments*, VIII, 266–8; Porter, *Reformation and Reaction in Tudor Cambridge*, 55–7; Strype, *Annals*, I(2), 408–23.
[4] Strype, *Ecclesiastical Memorials*, III(1), 154. See above, p. 179.
[5] CRO, EDC 1/14, fos. 96–96v, 145v–146, EDC 2/6, fos. 41–41v.
[6] PRO, DL 42/96, fos. 83–83v; *CPR*, Philip and Mary, I, 389.

£100 a year was paid in archdeacons' salaries. By 1558 the see's financial problems were so acute that Bishop Scott must have appealed to the Crown for assistance, and in February the queen made a substantial grant to the bishop.[1] In 1547, as part of the property exchange between Henry VIII and Bird, the see had been granted the rectory of Workington but, though it was soon found that the rectory had already been given to someone else, no adjustment had been made. In compensation, Mary granted the bishop the reserved rent of £143 16s 2½d which Sir Thomas Challoner paid her for the estate of St Bee's, though the rent of £63 8s 4½d the bishop had to pay to the queen reduced his annual profit to £80 7s 10d. Scott had done well, nevertheless, for though the valuation had certainly been too low, Workington was said in 1535 to be worth only £23 10s, and from it the bishop would have had to pay fees and stipends totalling over £8.[2] In addition, Scott was given help towards the salaries of his archdeacons, for the rectories of Cartmel and Childwall were transferred to him, together with a licence to annexe them to the archdeaconries of Richmond and Chester. In 1535 the rectories were thought to be worth about £62 a year, but this was far too low and they were soon yielding £112 in rents. Scott saw that Cartmel and Childwall were profitable acquisitions, and he chose to keep them in his own hands while continuing to pay fixed stipends to the archdeacons.[3] Together, these grants added almost £200 to the episcopal revenues, nearly half the previous gross income. The gains made in 1558 were not merely financial, for Mary also gave Scott the patronage of the six prebends of his cathedral. The Henrician exchanges and the Marian assignment considerably extended episcopal influence in the diocese, for the bishop now presented to 2 archdeaconries, 6 prebends, 20 rural deaneries and 33 parochial benefices; in the early 1540s the patronage had been confined to the deaneries and 6 parochial benefices.[4]

The connected administrative and financial improvements which took place and the appointment of vigorous diocesan officers made it possible for the bishop of Chester to impose his authority on the parishes. The Marian period saw three episcopal visitations within four years: in 1554–5, in 1556 and in 1557. It is true that these varied in thoroughness and that the less accessible parts of the diocese were sometimes ignored, but the populous areas of Lancashire were visited with a much greater frequency than they were in the reigns of Edward or Elizabeth. The disciplinary authority of the consistory

---

[1] *Ibid.* IV, 260–1; CRO, EDA 3/1, fos. 64–65v.
[2] *Valor*, V, 265; CRO, EDA 3/1, fos. 53–58v.
[3] *Valor*, V, 222, 272; CRO, EDA 3/1, fos. 131v–133; *CSPD* (1603–10), 497.
[4] CRO, EDA 3/1, fos. 35v, 50.

was also extended; the court had dealt with only 46 office prosecutions in the four years 1547–50, but in the years 1555–8 it instituted 133 of these cases.[1] The increasing burden of office work forced the consistory to sit more often, and where there had been 26 sessions in 1542 and 30 in 1550, there were 40 in 1558.[2] The Marian bishops tackled local problems in a way that Archdeacon Knight and Bishop Bird had never done. In 1555 Bishop Coates imposed a settlement of the conflict which had embittered relations between the parish church of Prescot and its dependent chapel at Farnworth for thirty years, and thereafter there was very little trouble in the parish.[3] A decree from Bishop Scott in 1558 concluded the century-old dispute between the parish church of Prestwich and the chapel at Oldham, and a little outside Lancashire Scott imposed a similar composition on the parishioners of Stockport and the chapelry of Disley.[4]

After the apparent laxity of the Edwardian years, Coates and Scott seem to have paid particular attention to the conduct of their clergy. In the century before Mary's accession only one Lancashire incumbent was deprived, in 1493, but even excluding married clergy two priests were forced out under Mary. In 1557 Richard Gorstilowe, vicar of Rochdale, was deprived for negligence, and the vicar of Eccles, Thomas Crane, was apparently forced to resign for immorality.[5] There were less serious proceedings against other incumbents as a result of the visitation of 1554. The rector of Eccleston was in trouble for his failure to provide a curate, and the rector of Aldingham was called before the Privy Council to account for his behaviour; the latter's offence was presumably neglect of his duties, for which he was to be rebuked again in 1559 and 1562.[6] Discipline seems to have been tightened, too, among the lower clergy and, besides the four chaplains proceeded against for marriage, eight assistants were prosecuted 'ex officio' in the consistory between 1554 and 1558, though there had been only three such cases between 1547 and 1551.[7]

Largely through the efforts of Bishop Scott and one of his

[1] CRO, EDV 1/1–2, *passim*, EDC 1/12, 1/14–15, *passim*. The cases which would not have led to prosecution under Edward, heresy and clerical marriage, accounted for only a handful of the cases in 1555–8.
[2] CRO, EDC 1/10, 1/12, 1/15, *passim*.
[3] CRO, EDC 1/3, fo. 28; Bailey, 'Churchwardens' accounts of Prescot', I, 142–3; CRO, EDA 2/1, fos. 406v–407v.
[4] Booker, *Memorials of the Church in Prestwich*, 252–5, 257–9; CRO, EDC 1/14, fo. 255, EDA 2/1, fos. 92–93.
[5] Raines, *Vicars of Rochdale*, 39–40; CRO, EDC 1/14, fo. 261; *VCH*, IV, 359, V, 198.
[6] CRO, EDV 1/1, fo. 147; *APC*, IV, 426; PRO, SP 12/10, fo. 122; CRO, EDC 1/16, fo. 239.
[7] CRO, EDC 1/12, EDC 1/14–15, *passim*.

commissaries, John Hampson, by 1558 the Church in Lancashire was showing signs of health which had been absent for more than a generation. The numbers of Lancashire-born ordinands entering the priesthood had been falling since about 1525, but by late in Mary's reign the Church was attracting recruits on a scale equal to the peak years of the early 1520s. Bishop Coates held a series of ordinations in 1555 at which a total of 12 priests, 19 deacons, 30 subdeacons and 34 acolytes received their orders.[1] There was, naturally, a build-up of candidates beginning with the lesser orders, after the cessation of ordinations under Edward VI. Progress was halted by the death of Coates and the work of his successor in London and Cambridge, so that in 1556 there were no ordinations, but in the following year Scott ordained 17 priests, 19 deacons, 37 subdeacons and 54 acolytes. The year 1558 turned out to be the 'annus mirabilis' of the Lancashire priesthood; pressure for ordination was so great that for the first time in the diocese five ceremonies were held in one year, and 70 priests, 57 deacons, 76 subdeacons and 63 acolytes received their orders, far higher numbers than the diocese had ever produced before in a single year.

A high proportion of the new ordinands were from Lancashire. Those ordained to the rank of subdeacon and above had to produce a title to orders from a benefice or a gentleman, and the titles make it possible to establish a candidate's area of origin. Under Mary at least half the men ordained each year were Lancastrians, though in the last three pre-Marian years in which ordinations were held the county produced only a third of the diocesan total. In 1558 pressure from Lancashiremen for ordination made it necessary for the sacrament to be performed at Preston parish church, the first occasion on which an ordination had been held outside Chester, and as Bishop Scott was not available Thomas Stanley, bishop of Sodor and Man and a Lancashire pluralist, had to be called in to officiate. Well over three times the number of Lancashiremen were ordained subdeacon and above in 1558 as had proceeded to these orders in 1547. The reasons for this dramatic increase in recruitment must have been religious rather than economic, for very few new clerical posts were created under Mary and there were presumably still enough priests among those who had withdrawn in Edward's reign to provide the larger numbers needed for a Catholic liturgy. It was probably the opportunity to serve in the traditional Church which attracted men to the priesthood again, as a contrast between recruitment in 1547 and 1558 may indicate. The order of sub-deacon is perhaps the most significant, for in 1547 a man ordained to that rank entered a clerical career in the knowledge that Protestantism was likely to be estab-

---

[1] These and the following figures are calculated from *Ordination Reg.*

lished, while in 1558 new subdeacons could expect to serve in a Catholic Church. In 1547 6 Lancashire subdeacons were ordained, but in 1558 there were 37.

The cooperation between an energetic diocesan administration and an enthusiastic laity which increased the supply of clergy also led to the rapid and complete restoration of the mass, despite the difficulties involved. As the vicar and churchwardens of Burneston in Richmondshire found, the immediate obstacle was the havoc created by the Edwardine confiscations, and in March 1554 they complained of 'the lack of things necessary for the setting forth [of] divine service'. In some areas, including Lancashire, the confiscated church goods had not yet been dispatched to London, and the commissioners were instructed to return property to the parishes from which it had come.[1] The vestments and so on which had been sold by the commissioners to local people proved more difficult to reclaim, for men had to return what they had only recently paid for. At Haslingden the curate had to sue a man before the consistory for refusal to give up vestments, and it cost the wardens of Prescot £2 16s 8d in lawyers' fees and other expenses to obtain an order from the bishop for the return of church and chapel goods to their original use. The goods of Burnley chapel had been confiscated by the chantry and chapel commissioners, and in an attempt to regain their property the people sued the officers responsible in the Duchy court.[2] Although there were problems in some parishes, the interiors of Lancashire churches were soon restored to their pre-Reformation state. Collections in Prescot in 1554–5 raised £4 8s to put lights before the images again, and thereafter annual donations kept candles burning before the images of the Virgin, St Nicholas and St Anthony, and once again there were lights before the rood, the sepulchre and the high altar, as well as 'the apostles' light'.[3] At Cockerham the parishioners were anxious to have a new rood as attractive as the one destroyed under Edward by their radical vicar, Gabriel Rayne, and at Middleton the rood light was soon burning.[4] In the parish of Walton a 'church ale' was held to raise money 'for the new adorning of the church', and the 'church ale' at Great Harwood was probably organised with the same object. By 1556 money was again being left to the rood loft at Harwood, incense was used in the church, and in that year and in 1557 rushbearings were held which realised more than five shillings on each occasion.[5]

[1] Strype, *Ecclesiastical Memorials*, III(1), 154; *APC*, IV, 360. Cf. *ibid*. 338, 348, 354, 361, 371.
[2] CRO, EDC 1/13, fo. 165; *Prescot Accounts*, 30; *Duchy Pleadings*, III, 158–9.
[3] *Prescot Accounts*, 32, 36, 40, 41–2, 44.
[4] Foxe, *Acts and Monuments*, VI, 564; *Lancs. Chantries*, I, 124.
[5] *Liverpool Town Books*, I, 51; *Great Harwood Reg.* 438–9.

The diocesan authorities supervised the process of restoration closely, and it is clear from the presentments that the main purpose of the three Marian visitations was to ensure that the mass was properly restored. Of the 31 Lancashire churches and chapels visited in 1554, 7 had no cross or other ornaments, 5 lacked the required books, 1 had no altar and another had no images. But the efforts of officials and churchwardens met with some success, and in 1557 only 3 of the 34 churches visited did not have the full complement of books and ornaments, and only one of the three had been visited three years earlier.[1] This may be contrasted with the situation revealed at a visitation of Kent in 1557, where almost a fifth of the churches still had no high altar, a tenth had no rood and a quarter had no cross.[2] We might fairly assume that the restoration evoked much greater enthusiasm in Lancashire than it did further south.

Part of the legacy of the disruptions of Edward's reign was the deplorable state into which the fabric of many churches had fallen as a result of neglect. At Prescot, for example, the churchwardens' revenues had almost dried up, so that essential repairs were not carried out and the dilapidation of the roof and walls of the church became so serious that the building was in danger of collapse.[3] At the visitation of 1554 half the churches and chapels visited in Lancashire were found to be in need of repair, but the efforts of royal and diocesan authorities thereafter produced considerable improvements. The fabric of Huyton church had been in poor condition for some time, and though in 1543 the Duchy had commissioned a survey and arranged for the provision of materials it is doubtful if much was done. In 1555 a further commission found that the chancel was 'in so sore ruin and decay that it must be repaired because the parishioners cannot have divine service there, but are obliged to have service done in the body of the church, as it rains in many places in the chancel and the roof is ready to fall'; it was estimated that renovation would cost £34, and arrangements were made to have the work done. At another Crown rectory, Urswick, repairs were carried out under the auspices of the Duchy, and the receiver of Furness was ordered to deliver stone from the abbey for the reconstruction of the chancel.[4] At Prescot pressure from the diocesan chancellor and the bishop prompted the churchwardens to organise a double levy on the parishioners, and repairs costing almost £16 were carried out by local

[1] CRO, EDV 1/1, fos. 120–155v, 1/2, fos. 33–42v, 65–85.
[2] Hughes, *Reformation in England*, II, 237.
[3] Bailey, 'Churchwardens' accounts of Prescot', I, 167–9; CRO, EDA 2/1, fos. 406v–407v.
[4] PRO, DL 42/95, fo. 156, 42/96, fos. 111–111v, 121–121v; *Duchy Pleadings*, III, 191–2.

masons and glaziers.[1] The chancellor did his best to ensure that improvements were made; at Winwick, Sefton, Aughton, Walton, Prescot, Halsall, North Meols, Huyton and Warrington, to name only those churches in the deanery of Warrington, wardens were threatened with fines if repairs were not completed within six months, and some of those convicted of sexual laxity were ordered to pay their fines towards the renovations. These efforts were apparently successful, and although two-thirds of the churches criticised in 1554 were visited again three years later, none of them had fabric defects in 1557.[2]

One of the most important contributions made by the Crown towards the revitalisation of the Church in Lancashire was the refoundation of Manchester College. The Edwardian suppression had been a serious blow, and the 22 priests in Manchester in 1548 had fallen to 16 by 1554. Most of those who remained were ex-fellows and chantrists living on government pensions, and when these men died the 6,000 communicants of the parish would have been left in the care of only the two curates appointed at the fall of the college.[3] In July 1556, however, apparently after the earl of Derby had raised the problem of the college, letters patent of re-foundation were issued for an establishment consisting of a warden, eight fellows, four clerks and six choristers. The patent provided for daily masses for the king and queen and for the souls of the faithful departed.[4] The first warden of the Marian foundation was George Collier, a former Oxford scholar who had headed the college before the Edwardine dissolution. Collier was a dogged conservative, described under Edward VI as 'a resolved papist and could not be brought to comply with the present world', and in 1555 he was one of those used to try to persuade John Bradford. The reformer wrote that 'the said warden did discommend King Edward, and went about to set forth the authority of the pope'.[5] Two former fellows of the old foundation, John Coppage and Laurence Vaux, were named with Collier in the 1556 patent, and the other fellows were to be nominated on the advice of these three.

Laurence Vaux was a seminal figure in the development of Lancashire Catholicism, with perhaps a wider influence locally than William Allen. A native of Blackrod, he was an Oxford graduate, a fellow of Manchester College by 1548, chaplain to Bishop Brooks of

[1] *Prescot Accounts*, 33–6.
[2] CRO, EDV 1/1–2, *passim*.
[3] CRO, EDV 2/3, fo. 13, 1/1, fo. 31; PRO, DL 28/27/18, m. 1; *Lancs. Chantries*, I, 10.
[4] PRO, SP 11/11/39; *CPR*, Philip and Mary, III, 513–14.
[5] Raines, *Wardens of Manchester*, 60; *Writings of John Bradford*, I, 538.

Gloucester in 1554 and a bachelor of divinity in 1556. On the death of George Collier in 1558 Vaux was promoted to the office of warden, the first fellow ever to be advanced to that dignity. In Manchester he was a popular and compelling figure; Hollingworth reported that Vaux was 'a man well beloved and highly honoured by the generality', and suggested that his appeal was one of the reasons why 'many thereabouts were lother to be reclaimed from Popery than about Rochdale'. As we shall see, Vaux resisted the Elizabethan settlement, fled to the Continent, and returned to be one of the first to press his co-religionists not to attend Anglican services.[1] John Coppage, also named in the foundation charter, was less eminent but no less determined, and he was to play an important role in the formation of a recusant tradition in Lancashire. A native of the north of the county, he was a fellow of the college by 1533 and was pensioned by the Crown at the suppression in 1548. Under Mary he was among those used in the conferences with John Bradford, in 1559 he was removed from his fellowship, and in the 1560s he was an active recusant priest in Lancashire and Cheshire. From 1571 he spent the rest of his life in various local prisons, but his influence was not lessened and at the New Clink in Salford he formed and directed a college of Catholic priests.[2]

The appointments made in the Marian charter indicate that Manchester College was intended to be a centre of militantly Catholic devotion and scholarship. Collier had opposed change in the reign of Edward, and Coppage and Vaux were to do so under Elizabeth, while Vaux later wrote a catechism which became a standard text for English Catholics. At least two of the fellows nominated on the advice of these three were cast in a similar mould. James Dugdale was presented to a fellowship in 1557, and later he too became a recusant priest and was active in Lancashire until the 1590s.[3] When the royal commissioners visited Manchester in October 1559 Richard Hart appeared as a fellow of the college, but refused to subscribe to the new religious settlement. After his deprivation he was ordered to remain out of harm's way in Kent or Sussex, but by 1561 he was already active among the Catholics of Lancashire.[4] The Marian refoundation was thus notable not only as a rare example of a Tudor foregoing revenue in the cause of popular religion, but also for the calibre of the staff recruited to it. In the

---

[1] Raines, *Wardens of Manchester*, 62–4; Hollingworth, *Mancuniensis*, 80–1; see below, pp. 248–50.
[2] *L & C Wills*, II, 13; PRO, DL 28/27/18, m. 1; *Writings of John Bradford*, I, 517; see below, App. 1 and p. 257.
[3] *CPR*, Philip and Mary, IV, 247; *VCH*, VII, 298; *CRS*, V, 181–2.
[4] See below, App. 1.

time available, the fellows of the college could presumably do little to enliven piety in the Manchester area, but their appointments show what was intended and their contributions came later, in the reign of Elizabeth rather than in that of her sister.

There is some other evidence that official patronage was deliberately used to place well-qualified and committed conservatives in the more important parishes of Lancashire. As well as the impressive presentations to Manchester College, Mary and Cardinal Pole presented thirteen men to Lancashire benefices, of whom five were graduates, one was to go into exile to escape Anglicanism, three were to become recusant priests, one was to get into trouble for intruding Catholic practices into the liturgy of the Book of Common Prayer and another was outlawed by Elizabeth for some unknown reason.[1] James Hargreaves, removed from his benefice in 1562 and active as a recusant priest for much of the reign of Elizabeth, was presented to the vicarage of Blackburn by the queen in 1555. Two years later Pole nominated John Hampson, archdeacon of Richmond, to the vicarage of Rochdale; in 1561 Hampson was deprived of the vicarage and he went into exile.[2] Two presentations made by the queen in 1558, of James Dugdale to Garstang and William Baines to Lancaster, may never have been effective, but both men were working as Catholic priests in the reign of her successor.[3] Another royal appointee, Edward Lowe of Huyton, was called before the Ecclesiastical Commission in 1564 for his offences, and he may have been deprived later.[4] The Marian clergy of the county were certainly well chosen.

Manchester College was the only major refoundation in Lancashire during the reign of Mary, but there were a number of lesser re-endowments. In 1555, for example, Duchy commissions were issued for return of the stock which had been given for prayers and the maintenance of services at Farnworth chapel. Similarly, the provost of King's College, Cambridge, was instructed to ensure that 'certain stocks of kine and other things' given to support priests at the college's appropriated church of Prescot were returned to their proper use. In 1554 and 1556 orders were issued for the restitution of the lands which had belonged to the chantry school at Blackburn.[5] At an unofficial level, too, there were attempts to restore suppressed

---

[1] Presentations from *CPR*, Philip and Mary, and *VCH*. The outlaw was Hugh Griffith, rector of Ashton (*Ducatus Lancastriae*, II, 265).
[2] See below, App. 1.
[3] *CPR*, Philip and Mary, IV, 428, 447; see above, p. 204, and below, pp. 256–7.
[4] See below, p. 217, and App. 1.
[5] PRO, DL 42/96, fos. 122, 152; Bailey, 'Churchwardens' accounts of Prescot', I, 198–200; Stocks, *Records of Blackburn Grammar School*, x–xi; *VCH*, II, 590.

foundations. The curate of Penwortham tried in 1555 to secure the re-establishment of the chantry which had been at Longton in his parish, while at Eccles two of the former chantrists had managed to repossess their chantry property by 1556–7.[1] These moves may have reflected a more widespread desire to return to traditional modes of piety; we have already seen that parishioners again burned candles before their favourite images and the rood, and in addition trentals were once more mentioned in wills and at least one temporary chantry was founded.[2]

Alongside the attempts to recreate the past, there are signs of an awareness that the old religion needed to be revitalised. The theological subtlety of the early Lancashire Protestants has already been noted, and it may be that this prompted Catholics to provide a more solid religious education for their children. In August 1554, in response to a petition from the people of Clitheroe and Whalley, the queen founded a grammar school at Clitheroe. The statutes of the school were to be drawn up by the governors in consultation with the bishop of Chester, and the first governors, named by the queen in the patent of foundation, were of a distinctly conservative cast of mind. Alexander Houghton's father had been a Lancashire delegate to the Pilgrim conferences in 1536, and Alexander himself was a recusant by 1577. Two governors, Richard and Thomas Greenacre, were brothers; the former was married to Houghton's sister and his son was a papist in 1590. Of the remaining three governors, one was Houghton's father-in-law and though another, Giles Parker, was suggested for the commission of the peace in 1564 this was not because he was reliable in religion but because he was 'learned in the law' and there was no-one else available.[3] Those who founded a school at Huyton in 1556 were even more staunchly Catholic. The first schoolmaster, Edward Lowe, was in trouble in 1564 for using holy water and encouraging the parishioners to pray in the old ways. Of the eleven Huyton men who signed the foundation indenture, one died in 1557 and left money for a chantry, five were in trouble for recusancy under Elizabeth, and the wife and children of another were recusants by 1584.[4] At Lancaster the mayor and burgesses petitioned the Duchy for an increase in their schoolmaster's stipend, while at Preston in 1557 a master suspected of reformist sympathies

---

[1] *Duchy Pleadings*, III, 189–91; *Ducatus Lancastriae*, I, 287.
[2] *L & C Wills*, I, 74, II, 148, III, 120.
[3] *CPR*, Philip and Mary, II, 192–3; Stokes, *Queen Mary's Grammar School, Clitheroe*, 7–8, 163–7; *L & P*, XI, 1155; *CRS*, IV, 184, XXII, 70; *Camden Miscellany*, IX, 77.
[4] LRO, DDM/33/1; CRO, EDA 12/2, fo. 80; PRO, SP 12/168, fo. 34, 12/175, fo. 41; BIY, R VI, A 7, fo. 47, A 12, fo. 70v; *CRS*, IV, 200, LVII, 61, 85.

was replaced by Peter Carter, a Cambridge graduate who was himself removed for religion early in the next reign and was in 1571 'supposed to be a papist and to be privy with the roving priests'.[1] These Marian efforts to provide Catholic education foreshadowed the determined attempt by Elizabethan recusants in Lancashire to ensure that their children received an education untainted by heresy.

In the few years available the achievements of the Marian Church in the north-west were considerable. The administrative structure of the diocese was overhauled and staffed with reliable officers, the finances of the see were improved, the great collegiate church of Manchester was refounded and the level of recruitment to the priesthood reached impressive heights. In the parishes of Lancashire the mass was restored with thoroughness and rapidity, altars and images were soon rebuilt, the fabric of the churches received much-needed repairs and where possible traditional forms of piety were restored. The work of priests and laymen was not confined to re-establishment, however, and there may have been some awareness of a need for reform. The disciplinary activities of the ecclesiastical courts were extended, and the provision of Catholic education and the staffing of Manchester College would have led in the long term to real improvements in standards. Although stress on discipline and education was characteristic of the reform movement, it would, of course, be absurd to see the Marian Church in Lancashire as the Counter-Reformation in action. There was no awareness of the need to train men for the priesthood, no hint of the pastoral asceticism of the new orders, and none of the evangelical preaching associated with post-Tridentine spirituality. Even the reformist Bishop Scott was frequently absent from his diocese, and he was an efficient administrator rather than a resident pastor on the Trent model. The Marians of Lancashire were recapturing the past rather than building for the future, and the people of the county provided prayers for their souls, left money to the Church, gave new vestments and ornaments for services, disliked heresy and entered the priesthood in the same ways and in remarkably similar numbers in the late 1550s as they had done in the late 1520s.

Although the achievements of the Marian period have been unduly minimised by some historians, it is true that such advances as took place were hardly the product of central policy and initiative. In education, in recruitment and in the refoundations, the determination came from the localities. After the early honeymoon between the earl of Derby and the queen, the earl was soon disillusioned by the increasing influence of Spaniards, and the queen quickly lost

---

[1] *Ducatus Lancastriae*, I, 294; J. Gillow, *Biographical Dictionary of English Catholics*, 5 vols. I, 412–13; BIY, R VII, HCAB 6, fo. 67v.

interest in Lancashire, simply because it posed no threat. It was one of Mary's tragedies that fear of heresy and rebellion focussed the attention of the regime on the south, away from the areas in which the stability of Catholicism would have allowed a royal policy of creative reform. The county was left to its own devices, and the re-establishment of Catholicism in a more than merely legal sense was left in the hands of the priests and laymen of Lancashire. Local men carried out the task with some success, and in a few short years the Church in the north-west gained the confidence which enabled it to mount a determined resistance to the policies of the next government. Thomas Leyland, the arch-conservative justice, knew by 1558 that Elizabeth would succeed to the throne, but thought that Catholics would never allow another Protestant settlement to survive. 'Thou old fool', he said to Geoffrey Hurst's mother, 'I know myself that this new learning shall come again; but for how long? – even for three months or four months, and no longer.'[1] He was, of course, over-optimistic, but the 'new learning' was to have to fight hard to make an impact.

[1] Foxe, *Acts and Monuments*, VIII, 563.

PART THREE

14

The attempt to impose Anglicanism

It has long been the task of historians of the English Reformation to explain the apparent ease with which the settlement of 1559 was accepted. The old Church had been beaten and bruised under Henry VIII and his son, its confidence had been sapped by failure under Mary, its leaders fled or were imprisoned in 1559 and, so the conventional schema goes, the rank-and-file were too disorganised and demoralised to resist the 'wolves' who were 'coming out of Geneva, and other places of Germany, and have sent their books before them, full of pestilent doctrines, blasphemy, and heresy, to infect the people'.[1] But as an outline of the history of the Church in Lancashire this is woefully inadequate. We have noted the limited impact at the grass-roots level of the changes introduced by Henry and Edward, and we have seen that the episcopates of Coates and Scott saw a vigorous campaign of restoration and renewal, at least at the clerical level. It ought not, then, to be surprising if the later ecclesiastical history of Lancashire does not quite fit into the traditional Elizabethan framework of Protestant triumph and Catholic humiliation.

The Elizabethan Reformation began, as the Edwardian had done, with a royal visitation, and this revealed few hints of any widespread resistance. Only the priests of the reformed Manchester College stood out against change; Laurence Vaux, the warden, was absent from the visitation and sent a prominent conservative merchant as his proctor, John Coppage did not appear, and Richard Hart turned up only to refuse the supremacy oath. The congregation at Manchester may have been equally opposed to recent legislation, for one tactless reformer was 'in danger of losing his house and goods for taking away of a mass book from the curate sithence the Queen's Majesty's proceedings'.[2] Elsewhere there were only isolated signs of

---

[1] The Marian bishop of Winchester, quoted in Strype, *Ecclesiastical Memorials*, III(2), 542.
[2] PRO, SP 12/10, fos. 51–51v, 117v.

209

opposition to the new settlement; the curates of Radcliffe and Bury had failed to read the Epistle, Gospel, Lord's Prayer and Commandments in English, as required by proclamation. Even the absence of clergy from the visitation gave no cause for alarm, for the twenty-three men noted as having failed to appear formed only between one-tenth and one-sixth of the clerical body, and we know that some of them subscribed to the supremacy later.[1] We must assume that the remainder dutifully appeared and took the prescribed oath. The ease with which the subscriptions were acquired probably explains the laxity and leniency with which the absentees were treated. Fifteen of them worked in south Lancashire, which was visited again in 1563, and by that stage three of the fifteen had died and three more had been deprived. Of the remaining nine only two subscribed to the supremacy in 1563; two were excused by the bishop, one appeared at the visitation but was not made to swear, two again evaded by absence, and two had disappeared.[2]

But what had begun so well was soon lost by delay. Matthew Parker was only too well aware of the danger of keeping the northern sees vacant, and warned Cecil that 'Whatsoever is now too husbandly saved will be an occasion of further expense of keeping them down' if (as God forfend) they should be too much Irish and savage.'[3] Chester was one of the last of the English sees to be filled, and until February 1561 the administration of the diocese was in the hands of John Hampson, the deprived archdeacon of Richmond, who acted as commissary. Hampson can have done little in the crucial first months of the reign, and later in 1561 he joined other Catholics in exile on the Continent.[4] In May 1561 William Downham, who had been Elizabeth's Catholic chaplain in Mary's reign, was consecrated bishop of Chester, but he was a weak man, dominated by his sharp-tongued wife, and reluctant to offend the conservative gentry among whom he made his friends.[5] Downham seems to have persuaded the archbishop of York to abandon the metropolitan visitation planned for the autumn of 1561, and, as Bishop Pilkington of Durham complained, 'the bishop of Chester has compounded with my lord of York for his visitation, and gathers up the money by his servant; but never a word spoken of any visitation or reformation; and that, he says, he does of friendship, because he will not trouble the country nor put them to charge in calling them together'.[6]

[1] *Ibid.* fos. 117v, 118v, 157v–159. There had been about 250 priests in the county in 1554; by 1563 there were about 130; the 1559 number is unknown.
[2] PRO, SP 12/10, fos. 157v–159; CRO, EDV 1/3, fos. 27v–34.
[3] *Correspondence of Matthew Parker*, ed. J. Bruce and T. T. Perowne, 123.
[4] CRO, EDC 1/16, fos. 14v, 40, 44–45, 51, 55; *CSPD*, Addenda (1547–65), 524.
[5] CRO, EDA 3/1, fos. 126, 128; BIY, R VII, G 1883; PRO, SP 12/48, fo. 75.
[6] CRO, EDC 1/16, fo. 60v; *Correspondence of Matthew Parker*, 222 (misdated to 1564).

The bishop did not appoint a chancellor for the diocese until March 1562, and the office of commissary of Richmond was not filled until the following year.[1] Only then could the achievement of the royal visitation be followed up, but Downham was to find that the advantage seized in 1559 had already been lost.

By the beginning of 1563 Downham was worried by the attitude of his clergy towards the Elizabethan settlement, and he required them to acknowledge that the queen was head of the Church and that the Book of Common Prayer was 'agreeable to the Scripture's word of God and the order of the primitive Church'. The articles were signed by some of the clergy of the cathedral, Cheshire, and the Lancashire deaneries of Blackburn and Manchester, but in the latter the response was hardly overwhelming; only 24 of the 45 men serving in the deaneries in that year actually subscribed.[2] This may have provoked the bishop to more vigorous action, and at long last he held a visitation of at least part of his diocese. The visitation 'detecta' were extremely thin, reporting little more than poor church fabric and sexual laxity, but the most important aspect of the visitation was yet another attempt to obtain subscriptions to the settlement. In south Lancashire 98 incumbents and curates appeared at the visitation, but only 55 took the oath offered to them; 6 were explicitly 'excused' by the bishop, 14 more were marked 'decrepit' and were not expected to swear, and a further 23 did not take the oath.[3] Downham seems to have respected tender consciences and allowed massive evasion; 4 of the 6 'excused' were later in trouble for flagrant conservatism, and the 'decrepit' category included several who lived for many more years and 4 who later became recusant priests.[4] In all, 43 of those who appeared failed to subscribe, and of these 7 became recusant priests and 8 were proceeded against within the next ten years for papistry. Downham's motives for such leniency can only be guessed; he was far from a radical himself, he may have thought a cautious approach would mean long-term success, and he perhaps realised that a systematic enforcement of the legislation of 1559 was impossible. As the early history of the Elizabethan Church in Lancashire was to demonstrate, such a course would have led to wholesale deprivations, would have left many benefices and especially chapels unserved, and would have revealed the narrow basis of support on which the new Church rested.

[1] CRO, EDA 2/2, fos. 52–53, EDR 6, p. 103.
[2] *Cheshire Sheaf*, 3rd series, I, 33–5.
[3] CRO, EDV 1/3, fos. 27v–34.
[4] The term 'recusant priest' is used hereafter to describe the clergy serving Catholics from outside the Elizabethan Church, excluding seminary priests and Jesuits, that is, those ordained into the official Church who withdrew into recusant service.

The attempt to impose Anglicanism

In August 1564 Downham turned from the clergy to the churches, and the churchwardens of 20 of the 34 parishes visited in the previous year were called before the Ecclesiastical Commission at Chester. The wardens were given instructions, probably on the removal of altars and images from the churches, which were to be put into force by Michaelmas, and the rural deans were ordered to check that all had been done.[1] We shall see that some churches took little notice of this directive, and it is doubtful if the rural deans took care to enforce it, for several of them were of a markedly conservative temperament. Thomas Leeming, dean of Leyland, had absented himself from the royal visitation, and was excused from the oath by Downham in 1563, so that he may never have subscribed to the settlement. At the visitation of 1571 he was presented as 'A papist. A suspect enemy to religion', and he had a copy of Harding's attack on Bishop Jewel and the Church of England in his possession; though he was reported in 1592 to be still sympathetic to the Catholics, he was dean of Leyland at least until 1588.[2] John Fielden, the dean of Blackburn, had been excused by Downham as 'decrepit' in 1563, but by 1565 he had left his post as curate of Colne and in 1570 the High Commission at York ordered his arrest as a recusant priest.[3] Thomas Bland, dean of Lonsdale and Kendal, whose appointment was renewed in 1567, was in trouble for a series of offences in 1571, when he was 'detected for a papist' and accused of harbouring 'runagate priests' and having mass said in his house.[4] Though nothing is known of the religion of other deans, we shall see later that some of them were wanting in other respects. The commissary of Richmond, Robert Hebblethwaite, was no better than some of the deans; in 1564 he was before the High Commission for some unknown offence, but it was presumably conservatism of some sort, as he was warned 'to avoid the danger of the laws hereafter'. Hebblethwaite was dismissed from office soon after, and in 1582 he was thought to be a recusant.[5]

With officers such as these, the 1559 settlement can have been enforced only tardily. The particular problems of ecclesiastical administration in the diocese of Chester seem to have been realised as early as 1562, when the diocese was equipped with an Ecclesiastical Commission of laymen and clergy to enforce the new legislation and reform the Church. All its twenty-one members were still in

[1] CRO, EDA 12/2, fos. 76v, 77, 79v.
[2] PRO, SP 12/10, fo. 157v; CRO, EDV 1/3, fo. 34, EDC 5, 1588; BIY, R VII, HCAB 6, fos. 66, 132; PRO, SP 12/243, fo. 223.
[3] CRO, EDV 1/3, fos. 29v, 68v; BIY, R VII, HCAB 5, fo. 10; HCAB 6, fo. 114v.
[4] *Ibid.* fo. 64; CRO, EDA 3/1, fo. 155v.
[5] BIY, R VII, HCAB 1, fos. 167, 172v, 186; H. Aveling, *Northern Catholics*, 16.

office in 1567–8, when it was found necessary to conduct a purge. Seven of the members were removed from the commission; one, a Chester prebendary, was thought to be over a hundred years old, two Lancashire members were absentees and inactive, a knight of the county was 'of vicious life', and three Lancashire men were 'suspected in religion' – two of these last were actually recusants.[1] The failure of the Ecclesiastical Commission to proceed vigorously against Catholics was thus hardly surprising! But even the purged commission was no engine of reform. It was headed by the earl of Derby, whose household was a nest of conservatives and plotters, while Thomas Carus and William Glaseor had close Catholic relations and were themselves to be suspected.[2]

If the Ecclesiastical Commission was not wholly reliable, the commission of the peace in Lancashire was even less trustworthy. Bishop Downham reported in 1564 that only six of the twenty-five justices were 'favourable' to the new religion, and the loyalty of two of his six was dubious. But the shortage of gentlemen of stature in Lancashire and their distribution over the county made the removal of conservatives difficult. Eight of the 'unfavourable' J.P.s were still alive in 1583, and four of them were active justices.[3] Officers of the Duchy of Lancaster were soon worried by the composition of the Lancashire commission, and it was noted in 1568 that 'there be not at this instant many that are known to be of good religion and sufficient living to supply those places'.[4] Sheriffs, too, were not easy to find, and with one exception the first nine Elizabethan sheriffs of Lancashire were conservative in sympathy.[5] The sheriff in 1562 was Sir John Southworth, a recusant by 1568, and he was notably slack in his execution of warrants from the High Commission at York; he was threatened with a fine of £40 for his failures, and it was only after the receipt of three orders that he made one arrest.[6] But it may have been the power of the office rather than the enthusiasm of the holder which was wanting, for between 1568 and 1571 the three sheriffs who served were unable to find any of the fifty conservative priests they were instructed to arrest.[7]

Though the detection machinery was defective, somehow information was gathered, and the authorities were able to proceed

---

[1] PRO, SP 15/13, fos. 271–271v.

[2] *Salisbury MSS*, I, 575–6, XIII, 100; CRO, EDA 1/3, loose leaf at fo. 24; Strype, *Annals*, II(1), 497; PRO, SP 15/27/94; K. R. Wark, *Elizabethan Recusancy in Cheshire*, 150.

[3] *Camden Miscellany*, IX, 77–8; R. S. France, 'Lancashire Justices of the Peace in 1583', *THSLC*, XCV, 131–3.

[4] Somerville, *Duchy of Lancaster*, 325–6.

[5] *Ibid.* 463–4.

[6] BIY, R VII, HCAB 1, fos. 2, 11v, 13, 14–14v.   [7] *Ibid*, HCAB 4–6, *passim*.

against some of the more obstreperous clergy. Unfortunately, there is a gap in the institutions books at Chester for the crucial years 1561 to 1569, so that it is difficult to be sure how many incumbents were deprived. But it is clear from other sources that the warden and two fellows of Manchester and seven other Lancashire incumbents had been deprived of their places by 1575, and it is possible that three others were removed. Eight of the fifty-seven parishes of the county lost their rector or vicar, and of the ten men definitely deprived one went into exile and six became recusant priests.[1] Probably the first to suffer deprivation was Laurence Vaux of Manchester, but before he went he spirited away the muniments and plate of the college into safe Catholic hands.[2] It took other men several years before they refused to compromise any longer. When William Langley, rector of Prestwich, was called before the Ecclesiastical Commission in June 1569, it was pointed out that he had for some years performed the services of the reformed church, to which he replied, 'that indeed for a time he so said service and administered the sacraments, howbeit he so did against his conscience very sore, and thereof now grievingly repenteth'. The Commissioners offered to allow Langley to retain his benefice if he would perform the required services, but he thought that 'the divine service as it is now used in the Church of England is contrary to the order and institution of the Catholic Church of Christ', and that the sacraments were 'administered and given against the order of the Catholic Church.' Langley was removed from his rectory, and forbidden to persuade men to depart from the established religion.[3] It was not only clergy presented under Mary who had to be deprived; Christopher Thompson did not become rector of Winwick until 1569, but in 1575 he was removed as he had 'divers and sundry times and at divers and sundry places taught unsound doctrine against the laws of God and this realm'.[4] Thompson went to Douai and became a seminary priest.

Other incumbents did not wait to be deprived, but took matters into their own hands and either fled or resigned. Seven men had vacated their benefices by the end of 1571, some of whom are known to have been opposed to the new religion, and two other conservatives resigned thereafter.[5] Anthony Mollineux of Walton was absent from the visitation of 1559, by 1563 he was 'ultra mare' and he was replaced as rector. Gowther Kenyon of Bury was called before the York High Commission in 1571, but proceedings against him were

---

[1] See below, App. 1.
[2] *Vaux's Catechism*, xix–xxi, ci–civ.
[3] CRO, EDA 12/2, fos. 119v–120, 121, EDA 1/1, Part 3, fo. 1.
[4] CRO, EDC 5, 1575.　　　　　　　　　　　[5] See below, App. 2.

dropped when he agreed to resign. The case of William Crosse, vicar of Childwall, presents a problem; he was excused the oath of 1563 and he resigned his post in 1570, but in the following year the curate of Hale in Childwall bore the same name and was presented as a 'naughty papist'.[1] Taking those who seem to have resigned or may have been deprived together, it is possible that as many as 22 benefices in 20 of Lancashire's 57 parishes were vacated as a result of the nature of the 1559 settlement, though the true figure is presumably lower.

But incumbents had a considerable vested interest in at least minimum conformity, and Bishop Downham was tolerant in his approach. Active conservative rectors and vicars, such as George Dobson of Whalley and James Lingard of Ribchester, preferred to remain in service and adapt Anglicanism to their own predilections. Resignation was, as in the reign of Edward, more likely among the unbeneficed assistants, and it is to the clerical body as a whole, rather than to the incumbents alone, that we must look for a full picture. In 1554 172 priests had worked in south Lancashire, but there were only 98 in 1563 and 79 by 1565.[2] These figures conceal a situation which was even more alarming to the authorities. Of the 172 men serving in 1554, 21 were dead by 1563 and 2 had resigned under Mary, leaving 149 priests apparently able to serve in 1563; only 51 of them (34%) were in fact ministering in that year and only 25 subscribed to the settlement, so that over 80% of the Marian clergy did not subscribe. In addition, 9 more ex-Marians were expected to appear in 1563 and failed to do so, so had presumably withdrawn recently; one had gone abroad, one soon became a recusant priest, and another was in trouble in 1564 as 'an hinderer and obstinate against the religion now most godly set forth'.[3] To take a later list of Marian clergy, 57 names survive on a visitation fragment of 1557 for the deaneries of Warrington and Manchester; 4 of the men were dead by 1563, but of the rest only 20 appeared at the visitation and only 13 took the oath; 23% of those serving in 1557 subscribed in 1563.

In 1563 63 new ministers, men ordained late in the reign of Mary or early in that of her sister, with some immigrants from other areas, were expected to appear to replace the dead and withdrawn. But only 31 of the new men appeared at the visitation and subscribed, 18 appeared and avoided subscription, and 14 were absent; 2 of the absentees were soon recusant priests, and another was described as

---

[1] PRO, SP 12/10, fo. 158; CRO, EDV 1/3, fos. 33, 33v; *VCH*, III, 7, 106; BIY, R VII, HCAB 6, fos. 72, 87.
[2] The following calculations are based on visitation call lists for 1554 (CRO, EDV 1/1, fos. 31–42), 1557 (17 parishes only, EDC 1/29, fo. 123/1), 1563 (EDV 1/3, fos. 27v–34) and 1565 (ibid. fos. 65–73).   [3] CRO, EDA 12/2, fo. 85.

'aufugit'. Withdrawal from the Church did not stop in 1563, for only 53 of the 98 serving in 1563 were still there two years later, though 6 others were absentee pluralists; to replace the 39 who had disappeared, there were only 16 new recruits. In all, no fewer than 151 clergy withdrew from service between 1554 and 1565 in south Lancashire alone. As we found in the Edwardine period, the motives of those who withdrew were probably both religious and economic. We shall see that the stipends of assistants became increasingly inadequate, leading to a shortage of clergy throughout the reign of Elizabeth. But Lancashire soon had a large body of recusant clergy, drawn partly from those who had refused to serve the established Church in the county; the incomes of these men were even more precarious than those of the curates, and some chose even greater poverty for the sake of principle. A considerable number of priests took the road of recusancy in response to the settlement of 1559. The extent of this refusal is difficult to assess, when such a large proportion of the clergy were mere assistants and visitation call lists infrequent and inaccurate. It is clear, however, that whereas several historians have thought that only 2–3% of the English clergy withdrew or were removed following the Elizabethan settlement, the proportion in Lancashire was very much higher. All that can be said with certainty is that two-thirds of the 1554 clergy who are not known to have died in the meantime were not serving the official Church in Lancashire in 1563.

But recusancy was only one of the possible responses to the new religion and in the circumstances of the early 1560s it may have been, even from a Catholic point of view, the least constructive. Many other priests continued to provide for their flocks something approaching traditional Catholicism within the parochial framework. Some of the clergy had avoided subscription to the settlement, while many of those who took the oath did so less than enthusiastically. Despite the massive withdrawal of conservatives, there remained a considerable body of traditionalist opinion within the Church, and the cautious, if not lax, approach of local ecclesiastical and lay authorities allowed the public provision in the churches of some semblance of Catholicism. Between 1563 and 1572 as many as 25 serving Lancashire clergy were in trouble before the Ecclesiastical Commissions at York or Chester, the Chester consistory or visitation courts for conservative words or practices; the total clerical body numbered no more than 130 men. Only 10 of the 25 had served in Lancashire before 1559, and many of the practising conservatives were new recruits rather than old men; 4 of the 10 parochial incumbents and 2 fellows of Manchester had been presented to their benefices under Elizabeth.

Their offences covered a wide range of traditional views and practices. In 1564 the curate of Farnworth was proceeded against 'for shriving, and for suffering candles to be burned in the chapel upon Candlemas Day, according to the old superstitious custom'. In the same year the curate of Wigan was found to be 'obstinate against the religion now most godly set forth', and one of his colleagues had spoken out in defence of images. The vicar of Huyton had been using holy water and persuading his people to pray in the old ways, while the curate of Liverpool altered the Prayer Book services to suit his own views.[1] In 1571 the rector of Halsall was said to be a 'simoniacal papist', one of the fellows of Manchester was 'of unsound religion, favoured papistry and heresy privately, and never favoureth the preachers of the Gospel', and another of the fellows elevated the bread and wine at the communion service and bowed before them.[2] John Sherburne, a county pluralist and chaplain to the earl of Derby, was said in 1572 to have denounced the 'nakedness of the Church of England, for want of ceremonies', he had associated with recusants and recusant priests, and had taught salvation by good works.[3]

The conservatives were almost always treated leniently, and most of those called before the Chester Ecclesiastical Commission were merely admonished to reform themselves and instructed to read a declaration to their congregations. Three spent a short time in prison, a fellow of Manchester was given a period of probation, and three of the incumbents were deprived, but this was mildness indeed. Bishop Downham was reluctant to proceed to extremes, and he would have been in difficulties if he had deprived all the unruly incumbents and suspended the curates. Offenders who were prepared to make a token submission were able to continue their work, as the career of George Dobson, vicar of Whalley, shows. Dobson was first denounced in 1561, when Bishop Pilkington reported him 'as evil a vicar as the worst', but Downham was more sympathetic and Dobson was excused the oath of 1563. In 1569–70 he was hauled before the High Commission at York, and at the visitation of 1571 he was 'detected for a naughty papist and that he keepeth and pro-claimeth holy days abrogated and harboureth papists'; his punish-ment was to read a declaration on holy days in his church. In 1573 he was suspected to have buried a recusant priest in the church late at night, but he denied the offence and nothing could be done, and in 1575 he was accused of a whole range of crimes:

---

[1] *Lancs. Chantries*, I, 77; CRO, EDA 12/2, fos. 73, 74, 80, EDC 1/17, fo. 88v.
[2] BIY, R VII, HCAB 6, fo. 86v; F. R. Raines, *Fellows of the Collegiate Church of Manchester*, 61–3.
[3] *VCH*, v, 125.

Item, he doth teach in the church the seven sacraments and persuadeth his parishioners that they shall come and receive, but in any case but to take it but as common bread and wine as they may take it at home or elsewhere, for that it is so, far differing from the word of God; and that this Church of England is a defiled and spotted church, and that no man may come to it lawfully in time of divine service except he at his coming in heart exempt himself from this service and all that is partaker of it, and make his prayer by himself according to the doctrine of the Pope of Rome.

Item, he hath been accustomed at every Easter to give to certain of his parishioners as he termeth them 'consecrated hosts', saying in them was salvation, but in the other there was nothing worthy acceptance.

Dobson denied the charges strenuously, and the case was transferred from the Chester consistory to the High Commission at York, but though the charges have the ring of truth Dobson's lack of cooperation and the distance between York and Whalley defeated the prosecution. Some of those at Whalley were furious that their vicar had escaped retribution yet again, and they complained at the visitation of 1578 that 'their vicar hath been lately suspected of popery, yet convented and dismissed'; once more Dobson was made to read a declaration in his church. This, as far as we know, was his last clash with authority, though his resignation followed suspiciously soon after Bishop Chadderton visited Whalley in 1580; Dobson died in 1583.[1] Though he had served the Church of England for more than twenty years, Dobson's contribution to the survival of traditional religion was probably as great as that of any recusant priest.

When so many of the parish clergy were crypto-Catholics, the letter and spirit of the settlement of 1559 were disregarded and even the celebration of public and private masses could not be prevented. In December 1559 the curate of Lawe said mass in his chapel, assisted by the parish clerk and a congregation of forty, and a local J.P. had to protect the man who reported the incident from the wrath of the parishioners. Ralph Parker, domestic chaplain to Thomas Leyland, provided communion openly for the local people and mass in private for his master.[2] Even when the mass was not celebrated, it was possible to adapt Anglican services to meet Catholic tastes; the Prayer Book services were not performed properly at Liverpool in 1564 and at Prescot in 1573.[3] In 1571 one of the fellows of Manchester was doing his best to make the Church of England communion

---

[1] *Correspondence of Matthew Parker*, 222; CRO, EDV 1/3, fo. 29; BIY, R VII, HCAB 4, fo. 183v; HCAB 5, fo. 10; HCAB 6, fo. 65v; HCAB 8, fos. 116, 132, 137, 165; HCAB 9, fos. 4, 15v, 22, 30; *VCH*, VI, 359; BIY, R VI, A 7, fos. 55, 74; *Whalley Reg.* 153.
[2] *Stanley Papers*, II, xxvii–xxviii; Foxe, *Acts and Monuments*, VIII, 564.
[3] CRO, EDC 1/17, fo. 88v; *Prescot Accounts*, 73.

as much like the mass as he could, and at Preston three years later the people received the sacrament in their mouths not in their hands.[1] Most churches continued to use wafers rather than bread in the communion, and the ministers who baulked at this concession to tradition were unpopular with their congregations even in the 1580s and 1590s.[2]

Other aspects of popular Catholicism were intruded into the churches. Holy water was used at Huyton in 1564, at St Helen's in 1578, and in a private house in Wigan as late as 1604. Church bells were tolled for the dead at Preston in 1574 and at Manchester, Walton and Whalley in 1578. Abrogated saints' days were still observed at Whalley in 1571, and at Goosnargh seven years later the bells were still rung on All Saints' Day.[3] At least until 1573 it was usual for the congregation to make offerings at a minister's first communion, which was clearly as significant as a priest's first mass. In many respects the community life of the unreformed parish remained unchanged; rushbearings were common, and even in 1604 there was music and dancing at a rushbearing in Whalley church.[4] Those who did not appreciate the new services could stuff their ears with wool and concentrate on their rosaries, and the use of 'beads' in church was the most common of conservative survivals; eight people were using rosaries at Eccleston as late as 1604.[5] Among both clergy and laity the reformed liturgy was regarded as a poor imitation of the real thing; William Langley, John Sherburne and George Dobson have already been quoted, and in 1604 the curate of Wigan 'said he would rather go to see mass than to the communion, and said the mass was more sufficient'. The earl of Derby would not allow the Prayer Book services to be said in his house, at Preston the people refused to sing Genevan psalms, and at Winwick one member of the congregation signified his disapproval by singing Latin psalms at the top of his voice.[6]

The church buildings changed as slowly as the behaviour of the parishioners who used them. In 1563 a Manchester man tried to forestall the destruction of the church images by hiding them in his

[1] Raines, *Fellows of Manchester College*, 62–3; *Lancs. Chantries*, II, 206.
[2] Peck, *Desiderata Curiosa*, 91–2; CRO, EDV 1/7, fo. 18; *VCH*, VI, 31.
[3] CRO, EDA 12/2, fo. 80, EDV 1/13, fo. 102v; *Lancs. Chantries*, II, 206; BIY, R VI, A 7, fos. 37, 46v, 47, 55, 61v; R VII, HCAB 6, fo. 65v.
[4] *Ibid.* HCAB 7, fo. 147v, R VI, A 7, fo. 60v, R VI, A 8, fo. 60v; CRO, EDV 1/13, fo. 175.
[5] PRO, SP 12/240, fo. 295; *State Civil and Ecclesiastical*, 4; CRO, EDA 12/2, fo. 82, 12/3, fos. 4–4v, EDV 1/4, fo. 13v, 1/10, fos. 122v, 155, 1/12a, fo. 117, 1/13, fos. 163v–164; BIY, R VI, A 7, fo. 38v.
[6] CRO, EDV 1/13, fo. 100v; *Salisbury MSS*, I, 575; *Lancs. Chantries*, II, 206; H. Foley, ed. *Records of the English Province of the Society of Jesus*, II, 26.

house, and when in 1564 Bishop Downham ordered the pulling down of images, altars and rood lofts there was an outcry from those who had been less far-sighted. At Wigan a priest led the opposition to the removal of images, and the parishioners of Prescot sent a deputation to ask the bishop to exempt their rood loft. The wardens who removed the rood and images at Leigh were roundly abused and told 'you were best now to go paint a black devil, and set him up and worship him, for that will serve well for your religion'. There was some relief in 1565 when a rumour went round that altars were to be restored, but this was soon quashed by Downham.[1] At some churches defacement was prevented; the Preston images were buried in the vicarage garden, and in 1572 another Mancunian had 'monuments of superstition' hidden in his house. Sometimes the offending objects were not removed at all; there were still undefaced 'shrines' in Manchester church in 1571, at Preston the altar was still standing in 1574, and the rood loft at Stalmine did not come down until 1590. In 1578 there were forbidden crosses in the churchyards at Winwick, Ormskirk and Brindle, and the ancient banner of Cockerham church was safe from destruction until the curate rashly used it in a Rogation procession.[2]

If the bishop could not control such public matters as the interiors of churches, nor could he restrict the private prayers of individuals. Several men and women were caught praying on Latin primers, and this was not surprising when vicars such as Lowe of Huyton and Dobson of Whalley encouraged their people to pray in the old ways. Even in 1601 a group from Leigh were in trouble because they 'desired the people to pray for a dead corpse', and there were presumably prayers for the dead at the burials conducted in the 1590s by the parish clerk of Winwick 'to the great offence of the zealous in religion and encouragement of the recusants'.[3] In view of the great importance attached to prayers for souls in the first half of the century, it cannot be believed that praying for the dead stopped sharply in 1559. There remained the few optimists who hoped the established Church might provide prayers for their souls; Sir John Byron did not alter the will he had made in 1558 leaving £100 for masses, in 1572 George Trafford left money to the poor to pray for his soul and to a priest to say mass 'if God's law be consonant that it so may be', and in 1581 John Orrell left, without comment,

[1] CRO, EDV 1/4, fo. 13, EDA 12/2, fos. 73v–75, 93v; *Prescot Accounts*, 53; Foxe, *Acts and Monuments*, VIII, 565–6.
[2] *Lancs. Chantries*, II, 206; BIY, R VII, HCAB 7, fo. 6v, HCAB 6, fo. 90v; R VI, A 7, fos. 48, 48v, 58v, 72, A 11, fo. 70v; Raines, *Fellows of Manchester College*, 63.
[3] CRO, EDA 12/2, fos. 80, 81v, 132v, 12/3, fos. 28–28v, EDV 1/12b, fo. 158v; EDC 5, 1596.

'unto the curate of Bolton ten shillings to pray for my ancestors' souls, my soul and all Christian souls'.[1]

It was widely felt that there was not much to commend a religion which did not provide the full sacraments for the solace of the living and prayers for the souls of the dead. The new offence of 'railing against religion' was frequently presented on visitation, and in 1585 two Rochdale men abused their vicar and said 'that the old religion which he belied was better than that used in these unquiet times'.[2] Inevitably, the clergy bore the brunt of criticism of the new services, and it was alleged in 1561 that the farmer of the tithes at Rochdale refused to pay the curates' stipends because he objected to the new religion they administered. 'Railing on God's preachers' was a common reaction, and in 1573 the curate of Padiham was told by a man who 'would fall to argument in defence of the Romish doctrine' that 'he would neither hear him nor such as he was'.[3] The new ministers did not have the aura of the old clergy; in 1595 the vicar of Leyland was 'no priest but only a minister made in the Queen's Majesty's time that now is', and in 1603 it was thought that 'the King's Majesty could not be crowned until he were annointed by an old priest'.[4] With public opinion behind them it was easy for the conservatives to make the ministers apppear ridiculous; the parish clerk of Winwick was 'generally noted to gibe and mock the ministers of the Word', and his most popular trick was to give the names of men and women who disliked each other to the curate to read out as marriage banns, to the confusion of the curate and the amusement of the congregation. Married ministers were the most scorned of all; in 1574 the vicar of Ribchester reported that one of his parishioners 'cannot suffer or abide a married minister, and hath said that he had rather receive the holy communion at the devil or at a dog than at the hands of this excipient, being a married minister', and four years later Jane Scarisbrick was licensed as a midwife only on condition that she did not refuse to attend the wives of ministers.[5]

Conservatives sentiments and practices survived widely within the framework of the Church of England, not merely in the deaneries notable for their recusancy but even in the deanery of Manchester, which became a stronghold of radical Protestantism and returned hardly any recusants. Rochdale was served by the fervent Puritan

---

[1] *L & C Wills*, II, 158, IV, 85–6, V, 133–6.
[2] BIY, R VII, HCAB 6, fos. 66v, 86, 93, 114v; HCAB 9, fo. 171v, R VI, A 7, fos. 49, 49v, 62v; *State Civil and Ecclesiastical*, 46.
[3] Raines, *Vicars of Rochdale*, 40–1; CRO, EDV 1/4, fo. 12, EDC 5, 1573; *Salisbury MSS*, I, 575–6.
[4] *VCH*, VI, 31; *Lancashire Quarter Sessions*, 167–8.
[5] CRO, EDC 5, 1574, 1596; *Stanley Papers*, II, 154.

Richard Midgeley from 1561 and it was closely linked to the radical cloth towns of the West Riding, but in the 1580s it was no Genevan paradise. 'Papists and other vain gentlemen' played bowls on Saturday evenings when they ought to have been preparing for the sabbath, a prominent local man was described as 'a Romish fellow and in my judgement a secret papist', during church services minstrels played and there was dancing in the streets, and Midgeley's preaching was heartily resented by inn-keepers and their customers.[1] Those who are tempted to believe that the English Church was made Protestant in the 1560s would do well to read the despairing comments of a group of Lancashire ministers in 1590. Recusancy was only a part of the problem they faced, for those who attended church would say private prayers 'with crossing and knocking of their breast, and sometimes with beads closely handled', crowds stood outside the churches throwing stones to disturb the services, popish practices were intruded into the communion, weddings, christenings and burials, and ministers who dared to protest were 'oft abused with reproachful terms', even in their own churches. In 1604 Lancashire was still notorious as an area in which the people were used to 'signing themselves with the sign of the cross on the forehead at all prayers and blessings, and therefore they call it a blessing therewith to bless themselves when they first enter into the church, and in all their actions, even when they gape'.[2]

Within ten years of the accession of Elizabeth, Lancashire had acquired the reputation for a more vigorous resistance to official attempts to impose the new religion than any other county in England. In 1568 the Spanish ambassador thought that the whole county was Catholic in sympathy, and in the same year the queen complained of Catholic opposition in Lancashire 'as we hear not of the like in any other parts'. The danger presented by the palatinate intruded into the choice of an officer of state, and it was regarded as 'very necessary that the chancellor of the Duchy of Lancaster be very well affected in religion, because that county is so showed with notorious papists as if those of good religion be not favoured and their proceedings well approved from the chancellor there will be neither good peace kept nor justice well administered'.[3] In 1567–8 there were fears of a Catholic rising in the shire, and in 1570 there were rumours of an approaching Spanish invasion linked with a rebellion in Lancashire. The Privy Council, in its reply to the earl of

[1] *Ibid.* 178; BM, Harleian MS 286, fo. 133v (I am grateful to Fr J. F. Fox for drawing this document to my attention); *Kenyon MSS*, 582; *Chetham Miscellanies*, V(1), 46.
[2] *State Civil and Ecclesiastical*, 4–9; *Montagu MSS*, 40.
[3] *CSPS* (1568–79), 12; Strype, *Annals*, I(2), 254–5; Somerville, *Duchy of Lancaster*, 325.

The attempt to impose Anglicanism

Derby's report in 1574 'touching certain popish disorders', summed up the position: the county was 'the very sink of popery, where more unlawful acts have been committed and more unlawful persons holden secret than in any other part of the realm'.[1]

Bishop Downham, however, remained unperturbed and inactive, except for two cursory visitations and the occasional use of the Ecclesiastical Commission against those who made their opposition too obvious. He was warned by his officers of the serious situation in Lancashire, but in 1567–8 he agreed to proceed against a few conservative gentlemen only when a member of the Commission threatened to report him to the Privy Council if he did not. The fault was not entirely Downham's, for the members of the Commission were at loggerheads over policy and the conservatives had tried to prevent any proceedings.[2] But the bishop was the 'principal minister in these causes', and when the queen's anger at the news she received from Lancashire boiled into a stinging reprimand it was to Downham that the missive went. 'We find great lack in you', the cleric was told, especially as the Ecclesiastical Commission gave him adequate powers to control disorders, and he was ordered to hold an immediate visitation. In the summer of 1568 Downham visited his diocese, and though he complained of the heat he was well satisfied with the result, for he 'found the people very tractable and obedient'. The Ecclesiastical Commission proceeded against eight conservative Lancashire gentry, and in the autumn Downham sent in a grossly exaggerated report on the success of his campaign: 'the punishment of these men hath done so much good in the country that I trust I shall never be troubled again with the like'.[3]

Others were less easily convinced than the bishop, and in the autumn of 1568 the York High Commission began a massive interference in the affairs of the diocese of Chester which was to continue until the more energetic William Chadderton became bishop in 1579. The High Commission found it necessary to deal with several conservative clergy whom Downham had left unmolested, and it was probably as a result of this that in November 1570 the bishop was again blamed for 'sundry disorders committed within his diocese, specially in the county of Lancaster', and summoned to London to account for his stewardship.[4] A full-scale episcopal enquiry into Downham's conduct was held and, despite his protests to Archbishop Grindal, his authority was inhibited from April 1571 until the

[1] PRO, SP 12/44, fos. 116–116v, 12/48, fos. 73–74; *CSPD*, Addenda, (1566–79), 321–2; *APC*, VIII, 276–7.
[2] PRO, SP 12/48, fos. 73–74; CRO, EDA 12/2, fos. 109–110, 114v–115.
[3] Strype, *Annals*, I(2), 254–5; PRO, SP 12/48, fo. 75.
[4] BIY, R VII, HCAB 4–5, *passim*; *APC*, VII, 399.

summer of 1572. During this period the bishop of Carlisle was commissioned to hold a visitation of the diocese of Chester, and his work, as we shall see in chapter 16, revealed the extent to which the situation in Lancashire had been allowed to get out of hand.[1] But although it is true that Downham's laxity had delayed the imposition of the Elizabethan settlement on Lancashire and had allowed the conservatives time to organise themselves, it is doubtful whether the failure of the Anglican Church throughout the whole of Elizabeth's reign can be blamed on him. There were more fundamental flaws in the Church in Lancashire than the mere character of its bishop.

[1] *APC*, VIII, 5, 26; *CSPD*, Addenda (1566–79), 340–1; CRO, EDC 1/19, fos. 38ff; BIY, R VII, G 1673.

15

The Elizabethan Church in Lancashire

The Anglican Church in Lancashire could not expect an easy victory in its fight against traditional religious allegiances. The history of the reform movements under Henry VIII and Edward VI had demonstrated that the old ways of thought and practice died hard in an area which had experienced a flowering of conventional piety. The fairly intensive efforts at conversion made in the reign of Edward had reaped only a meagre harvest, and Protestantism had gained very little support by 1559. Though habits of regular church attendance might give the Elizabethan Church a period of grace in which Catholic opinion could be attacked and a reformed theology promulgated, success would only be achieved by a sustained campaign of propaganda and coercion. There would be no automatic obedience to new regulations. The regime needed to work through institutions and men which could command the respect and enforce the obedience of the majority; but in Lancashire the institutions were weak and among the officers of Church and state there were few with sympathy for the new liturgy and new doctrine of the established Church.

The effective administration of the diocese of Chester depended partly on sound finances, but the see was one of the least well endowed in England. Some improvements had been made under Mary, and in 1559 Matthew Parker was able to ensure that because of Chester's 'exility' the Marian augmentations would remain.[1] The income of the bishopric was still inadequate, however, and in 1568 William Downham claimed to have 'the least revenue that any man of my calling have in this realm'. In 1603 Bishop Vaughan asserted that it was common knowledge 'how little able the small revenues of this see is to defray the charge thereof', and two years later his successor was complaining of his poverty. Bishop Bird had exchanged the lands of the see for appropriated rectories, which he then rented out on long leases, and Downham was right when he alleged 'I have of the bishopric nothing but bare rent, and much of it evil paid.' The see had no proper financial records until 1619, but Downham estimated that for himself and a household of 40 he had a

---

[1] *Correspondence of Matthew Parker*, 100.

net annual revenue of only 500 marks.[1] Bishop Chadderton's position may have been even worse, for after payment to the queen of a tenth, half a subsidy and other expenses, his income for the first half of 1595 was only £73 7s 4d, and the net total for the whole year was no more than £300. Bishop Bridgeman was later able to increase the revenues of the see, but in the 1620s his average net annual income was £673, less than most English bishops had had fifty years earlier. In 1632 Chester was described by the king as one of the sees where the revenues 'have been so diminished that they suffice not to maintain the bishops which are to live upon them according to their place and dignity'.[2]

In such a precarious situation, the payment of taxes to the Crown was a serious worry for any bishop. In 1561 Bishop Downham was excused the payment of one-seventh of his first-fruits and allowed to pay the balance over three years, and in 1572 he persuaded the queen to discharge him from the tenths of some of the see's appropriations.[3] But by 1580 the plight of William Chadderton was even more difficult, and when anguished letters to Burghley and Walsingham prompted no reduction in first-fruits (though he was permitted to make his payments over five years) the new bishop had to go cap in hand to his clergy, to plead for help with the 'divers extraordinary charges laid and happened upon the said Reverend Father'. The clergy agreed to give a benevolence of 5% of their income for 1580, but only on condition that they were never again asked for a similar levy.[4] With inadequate revenues from the see, bishops of Chester had to supplement their income from other sources; Downham, Chadderton, Bellot, Vaughan and Lloyd were each licensed to hold two other livings in plurality to augment, as Vaughan put it, a 'poor bishopric'. Bishop Downham leased a rectory from the dean and chapter of Chester, and Chadderton was forced to adopt some doubtful expedient which earned the disapproval of his successor.[5]

Both Chadderton and Vaughan thought that insufficient revenues made it impossible to perform their duties properly, and this was probably true in a diocese 'full of moors and mountains and stretching out all along from Orton in Wales by the sea side to the Scottish borders' – though, after six years as bishop, Chadderton should have known that his diocese reached no further north than Workington![6]

---

[1] PRO, SP 12/48, fo. 75v; *Salisbury MSS*, XII, 669, XVI, 320–1; CRO, EDA 3/1, fo. 130v.

[2] PRO, SP 12/252, fos. 177–177v; CRO, EDA 3/1, fos. 131v–145, 251v–252.

[3] *CSPD* (1595–7), 404; PRO, E 334/7, fo. 121v; CRO, EDA 3/1, fos. 73–74v.

[4] PRO, SP 12/143, fos. 19, 32–32v; LCL, RD/A/2, fos. 1v–2v, 33v.

[5] PRO, SP 12/48, fo. 75v, 12/252, fos. 177–177v; *Salisbury MSS*, V, 210, XII, 669, XVI, 320–1; CRO, EDC 1/30, fo. 80.

[6] PRO, SP 12/143, fo. 19; *Salisbury MSS*, XII, 669; PRO, SP 12/189, fos. 33–33v.

The Elizabethan Church in Lancashire

In an unwieldy diocese, Chester was not the most convenient of administrative centres, and this became the more obvious when Lancashire recusancy made that county the focus of any bishop's attentions. In 1581 Chadderton was able to use his position as warden of Manchester College to make the town his headquarters, but in 1605 Bishop Lloyd was equally conscientious and less fortunate, so that he had to hire a house there as his centre of operations.[1] Here, as in several aspects of administration, economy and efficiency were in conflict.

A bishop of Chester ruled his difficult diocese through four instruments: the consistory, the visitation court, the rural deans and the Ecclesiastical Commission, but, despite the array of officials and sanctions at his disposal, the ability of any bishop to control his flock may be questioned. Throughout the reign of Elizabeth the consistory court held 19 or 20 major sessions each year, with between 20 and 40 minor sessions to deal with difficult cases. But there was a considerable expansion in the business of the court, from 154 cases in 1564 to 221 in 1573, 222 in 1584 and 278 in 1595, and the extra business was crammed into the same number of sessions. Office prosecutions remained a minor element in the court's work, and the vast majority of cases, as much as 97% in 1584, were instituted by individual litigants. The expansion of business was in the field of testamentary causes and defamation suits; the increase in the former was probably a result of growing prosperity, while the latter, which mainly resulted from slanders of sexual laxity, may have increased from a fear of prosecution before the new Ecclesiastical Commission.[2] Though litigants were resorting to the consistory in large numbers, the heavy costs which might be incurred were a serious deterrent; in 1569 an Eccleston man said 'he hath paid to the parson the like tithe now in demand because he would, being a poor man, avoid the suit of law'. In 1568–9 a not unduly complex tithe suit had cost the rector of Halsall £1 15s in court fees, 15s in fees to his proctors, and £2 1s 7d in travelling expenses for himself and his witnesses. In 1595–6 an attempt by the churchwardens of Eccleston to force a parishioner to pay his dues involved 23 court sessions and a cost of £7 19s 6d, while in 1596 the churchwardens of Flixton had to spend only 19s 5d on the ordinary affairs of the parish but £23 2s 0½d in suing parishioners for their dues. Even a brief and straightforward testamentary case in 1597 cost 14s 11d at a time when a

[1] Peck, *Desiderata Curiosa*, 110; *Salisbury MSS*, XVI, 321.
[2] Figures from CRO, EDC 1/17, 1/20, 1/25, 1/28. The increase in testamentary cases was from 17 in 1564, 38 in 1573 and 32 in 1584 to 65 in 1595; in the same years there were 20, 40, 48 and 53 defamation suits respectively. See Haigh, 'Slander and the Church courts', *passim*.

farm-bailiff's wage was only £2 8s a year in Lancashire, and farm labourers had £1 5s.[1] It is perhaps not surprising that some tried to reduce their costs by not paying their proctors, and in 1593–4 five proctors had to sue their erstwhile clients for fees.[2]

It must have been especially galling for litigants when the law for which they paid so much was not even dignified, and the calm of the consistory was occasionally disrupted by scandal and farce. In 1564 Robert Leche, the chancellor of the diocese, had to appear in his own court with Bishop Downham sitting as judge, to sue Maria Bostock for breach of matrimonial contract. In 1597 his successor, David Yale, was involved in an unseemly row with one of the proctors, which ended with a humiliating public apology by the proctor.[3] But it was normally the lower officials of the consistory who brought the court into disrepute. Christopher Cooke, the court apparitor, was described as 'a corrupt person, a common briber and extortioner', and he was removed from office in 1570–1 for taking bribes to conceal offences. His successor, George Holme, was certainly no improvement, and at the metropolitan visitation of 1571 he was presented as 'a bribing knave, disobedient to all good order'; he too was dismissed.[4] The cost of the consistory and the low quality of some of its officers made the judges and the court unpopular. In 1579 one of the Chester clergy, who regularly deputised for the chancellor, was accused of fornication by a parishioner and forced to produce compurgators; and in 1597 another deputy had to proceed to compurgation when he was framed by a beggar and his wife and blackmailed.[5] There seems to have been some resentment of the procedures of the court, and in 1576 one defendant declared that 'being compelled to make answer to these articles, I make this protestation that whatsoever I confess of the same articles not to be prejudicial against me, and this being registered I answer'; there was a similar protest in 1581. It is probable that many others shared the resentment of Church discipline which prompted a man from Aysgarth in Richmondshire to boast that

he would make my lord archbishop spend £100 and call him up to London, and that if his friends knew that he were here in trouble by means of the vicar some of them would meet him in a water and turn him off his horse, and hang his foot in the stirrup and see how he could swim.[6]

---

[1] CRO, EDC 2/8, fo. 259; EDC 5 1568, 1596, 1596; EDC 1/29, fo. 203v; *Tudor Royal Proclamations*, III, 149–50.
[2] CRO, EDC 1/28, fos. 19, 53v, 73, 111, 158v.
[3] *Ibid.* 1/17, fos. 128v, 134, 1/30, fo. 60.
[4] CRO, EDC 5, 1574; BIY, R VII, HCAB 6, fo. 88.
[5] CRO, EDC 1/22, fo. 20, 1/29, fo. 470.
[6] CRO, EDC 1/21, fo. 60/1, 1/23, fo. 307; BIY, R VII, HCAB 7, fo. 203.

The consistory was expensive and unpopular, so many simply disregarded it and the court had a major problem in getting defendants to appear. Persistent absence from the court was an effective way of ensuring that a case would be dropped, and between a fifth and a third of suits were disrupted in this way.[1] Sir John Holcroft had been before the Ecclesiastical Commission in 1563–4 for keeping a concubine, but he was not deterred by his punishment and in 1569 the consistory proceeded against him. Between 4 August and 29 October Holcroft failed to appear on six occasions despite threats of excommunication; he sent servants with a variety of excuses – that he was raising forces for Ireland, that he was holding musters, and that he had been ordered to make a collection for the poor – until at last his object was achieved and the case was dropped.[2] In November 1595 Ralph Ashton was ordered to pay tithe to the farmer of Prescot, but he neither obeyed the mandate nor appeared before the consistory to defend himself. He was excommunicated for contumacy early in December, and the case came up on eight further occasions until, in June 1596, the farmer gave up and the suit lapsed.[3] Absentees were excommunicated for contumacy, but if excommunicated persons did not submit there was little that could be done; 24 contumacious defendants were excommunicated at three sessions near Easter 1594, but only one ever submitted and all the other suits were abandoned. It may have been a realisation of the benefits of non-cooperation which led a barrack-room lawyer at Winwick to persuade his friends to ignore mandates.[4]

The bishop of Chester had a double difficulty because, contrary to the usual practice, he had two consistory courts; the whole diocese was subject to the consistory at Chester, while the commissary of Richmond had concurrent jurisdiction in the archdeaconry and a consistory court. This naturally led to conflict, and in 1601 the joint commissaries of Richmond tried to assert their independence and they had to be excommunicated before, after sixteen months, they submitted. There were similar crises in 1690 and in 1757.[5] For most of the reign of Elizabeth the office of commissary was shared by two brothers, Robert and Edmund Parkinson, who were unreliable and difficult to control. In 1570 one was called before the York High Commission for an unspecified offence, and in the following year they were in trouble for commuting penances without permission.

[1] Cases held up: 20 of 99 on 23/10/95; 28 of 103 on 23/4/96; 35 of 110 on 1/3/99 (CRO, EDC 1/28, fos. 300–310v; *ibid*. fos. 402–412v; 1/30, fos. 243–256v).
[2] CRO, EDA 12/2, fos. 16v, 46v, EDC 1/18, fos. 325, 326v, 328, 343v, 351v.
[3] *Ibid*. 1/28, fos. 330, 334/1, 339, 348v, 358, 379v, 397, 407v, 419, 433, 444.
[4] CRO, EDC 1/28, fo. 3 and *passim*, EDC 5, 1596.
[5] CRO, EDC 1/32, fos. 55v, 66, 80, 174v, 382; Bodleian Library, Tanner MS 152, fos. 43ff; CRO, EDR 6, *passim*.

There were complaints in 1578 that they failed to punish offenders presented to them, and in 1601 the bishop had great difficulty in bringing them to heel.[1] If the bishop could not control his commissaries, he certainly could not control Richmond. The northern deaneries of Lancashire were in a limbo between Chester in the south and Richmond to the east, and cases from the north of the county rarely went to either court. On the infrequent occasions the commissary did turn his attention to Lancashire, he had little success; early in 1588 he cited 62 men and women from Amounderness deanery to appear in his court, but only 3 did so.[2] Consistory courts were too far removed from events in the parishes to be a real force in diocesan government.

The visitation mechanism was much more likely to keep the bishop in touch with the grass roots, especially if it was used regularly. Between 1563 and 1605 Lancashire was visited with impressive frequency, and there were four metropolitan and sixteen diocesan visitations. But frequency did not necessarily mean that discipline was any more effective, for local control depended on the thoroughness of the visitor, the cooperation of parish officers, and the willingness of the people to accept Church discipline. The earliest Elizabethan visitations with surviving returns were cursory affairs and, as Bishop Pilkington complained, the object was profit rather than reform. In 1594–5 Bishop Chadderton was prevented from holding his triennial visitation, but his major worry was that 'I lost two hundred marks and more'. Chadderton's concern was understandable, for even in the 1620s when they were said to be 'almost lost', over one-sixth of the bishop's average net income came from synodals and procurations.[3]

Even if the visitor was enthusiastic, the effectiveness of the exercise depended almost entirely on the cooperation of churchwardens. The office of warden was an unpopular one and sometimes, especially at chapels, no-one could be found who was willing to serve.[4] Reluctance to act as a warden stemmed largely from the abuse the conscientious officers received from parishioners. There were cases of abuse of wardens at Eccles in 1578 and 1588, at Childwall and Huyton in 1589, at Leigh, Ormskirk, Bury and Flixton in 1592, at Birch and Ormskirk in 1598 and at Leigh, Prescot

---

[1] CRO, EDA 3/1, fos. 126v–127; LCL, RD/RP/8, fos. 146–146v; BIY, R VII, HCAB 4, fo. 209; HCAB 6, fo. 128v, R VI, A 7, fo. 65.
[2] LCL, RD/A/4, fos. 105–108v. All the office prosecutions at Richmond in 1579–81 were from the eastern deaneries (RD/A/1–3b, *passim*).
[3] *Correspondence of Matthew Parker*, 222; PRO, SP 12/252, fo. 177v; CRO, EDA 3/1, fos. 130v, 144v–145.
[4] CRO, EDV 1/12b, fo. 115, 1/13, fos. 209, 224v, EDC 5, 1582; BIY, R VI, A 8, Roll F.

and Whalley in 1604. Sometimes men went beyond verbal tirades, as at Ormskirk in 1598 when John Ireland was presented 'for abusing the churchwardens, saying he would strike them when he met them', or at Leigh in 1604 when a man was in trouble for brawling with the wardens.[1] Intimidation of wardens was easier when, as was claimed in 1587, they were 'in many places (as we hear) men of meanest quality', or, as a group of disgruntled ministers put it in 1590, they were 'of the meanest and lewdest sort of the people, and therefore most fit to serve the humours of the gentry and multitude'.[2] Churchwardens who could not be coerced might be bribed, and this was alleged at Manchester in 1590 and at Winwick in 1596.[3] For fear or favour, churchwardens were often negligent in their present-ments; at Eccleston and Leigh in 1601 and at Eccleston, Burnley, Clitheroe and Samlesbury in 1604, the wardens were cited because they 'have not made a full presentment'.[4] It was far from unusual for some parishes to make no returns at all, and this happened at four churches in 1590, ten in 1592, five in 1595 and five in 1604.

Professor Dickens has argued that the character of Elizabethan parish life, with small and closely integrated communities, made the detection of offenders almost certain, but in the large and frag-mented parishes of Lancashire the churchwardens' task was ex-tremely difficult. Supervision by wardens was easy in small southern parishes with 40 or 50 households, but in 1563 the average Lanca-shire parish contained 350 households; a survey of 1603 suggests that there were on average 243 communicants to each parish in England as a whole, but 696 in the diocese of Chester.[5] It is true that about one-third of the people of Lancashire attended chapels rather than parish churches, but chapels sometimes had no wardens, were often unrepresented at visitation, and not infrequently had no resident minister to watch over them; 30 of the 85 chapels in use in 1610 had no minister, though 6 of these had lay readers.[6] Nine parishes were especially difficult to supervise, for parts of them were physically separate from the main body of the parish; seventeen sections, some of them large, were thus severed, and Lancaster and Middleton each had four subsidiary areas within the geographical limits of other parishes.[7] We can therefore be sure that the detection-

[1] BIY, R VI, A 7, fo. 38v; CRO, EDV 1/7, fo. 26v, 1/8a, fos. 53, 58, 1/10, fos. 120, 122–122v, 141v, 166v, 178, 1/12a, fos. 90v, 130v, 1/13, fos. 92v, 144v, 177.
[2] *Kenyon MSS*, 594; *State Civil and Ecclesiastical*, 9–10.
[3] BIY, R VI, A 11, fo. 87v; CRO, EDC 5, 1596.
[4] CRO, EDV 1/12b, fos. 123, 158v, 1/13, fos. 162, 168v, 169, 171.
[5] A. G. Dickens, 'The first stages of Romanist recusancy in Yorkshire, 1560–90', *YAJ*, XXXV, 159; BM, Harleian MS 594, fos. 101–108; Magee, *English Recusants*, 83.
[6] *Kenyon MSS*, 6–13. For the date of the survey, see Jordan, *Social Institutions of Lancashire*, 79n.   [7] *VCH*, III–VIII, *passim*. See map p. xiii above.

rate for offenders was low, particularly if the local community was sympathetic, and some offences went unpresented for years. In 1571 the visitor found two men who had kept mistresses for twenty and fourteen years without prosecution, and in 1596 a Clitheroe man was detected for getting his wife pregnant before marriage seven years and three visitations earlier.[1]

Presentment merely brought offenders to the attention of the authorities, and trial and punishment depended on the accused's attendance at the correction court. But in many dioceses less than half of those cited appeared before the court, and at metropolitan visitations of the diocese of Chester the attendance-rate was only one-third. Diocesan visitations were even less effective, and at the visitation of Lancashire in 1592 only 27% of the charges were answered by defendants. The Church's sanctions had lost some of their impact, for at the visitation of 1554–5 84% of charges had been answered in the deaneries of Manchester and Warrington.[2] The appearance-rate was low under Elizabeth partly because some of those cited were recusants, who rarely attended for correction, but even in 1592, when few recusants were presented, only a small minority of all those accused actually appeared before the court.[3] When men did not attend for correction, visitation was an ineffective disciplinary exercise. It was pointed out in 1590 that a group of Whalley parishioners had not received communion for nineteen years, and had been 'divers times complained upon since that time but no reformation'. In 1595 the rector of Wigan was 'presented for not building up his chancel; often presented, not reformed'; he was in trouble for the same failure at seven visitations between 1578 and 1604.[4]

We have noted that the early bishops of Chester tried to impose discipline at the local level by extending the authority of their rural deans, but in the later sixteenth century the deans' effectiveness was much reduced and the office and its sanctions fell into disrepute. The bishop had lost a considerable revenue by devolving the probate of wills to the deans, and to recoup his losses he rented out the deaneries for life. A potential dean's tender became more important than his suitability, and the deans themselves sometimes sub-let to men of even less worth.[5] A dean's primary aim was thus a return on his investment, which led to the widespread commutation of penances, despite the hierarchy's efforts to prevent this. In 1571 five of

[1] BIY, R VII, HCAB 6, fo. 81v; CRO, EDV 1/9, fo. 48.
[2] R. A. Marchant, *The Church under the Law*, 121, 205–6, 210–11; CRO, EDV 1/10, *passim*, 1/1, fos. 120–144v.
[3] 41 out of 224 Lancashire recusants cited appeared in 1578, 81 out of 481 in 1595, and 37 out of 754 in 1601.   [4] BIY, R VI, A 12, fo. 55, A 15, fo. 5.
[5] CRO, EDA 3/1, fos. 35v, 131, 170v; BIY, R VII, HCAB 6, fos. 66, 82.

the eight Lancashire deans were presented for commuting penances against official instructions, and two of them were accused of taking bribes to commute. A former deputy-dean who had been dismissed for accepting bribes was commuting penances over which he no longer had authority. These prosecutions led to no obvious improvement, and commutation was still taking place in the deanery of Amounderness in 1578 and in Manchester in 1595. In 1591 a meeting of the bishops of the northern province issued a series of orders which included a total prohibition of the commutation of penances without the licence of the ordinary, and a later instruction insisted that only bishops could commute.[1]

To prevent this and other abuses the bishops of Chester tried to discipline their deans. In 1594 Bishop Chadderton ordered his deans to submit annual reports on their proceedings, and those who failed to do so were suspended from office. Richard Vaughan called the deans before him in 1599, examined their records, and organised annual deanery courts on fixed days, but his major contribution was the imposition of a common registrar on the deans of the diocese. The new registrar was clearly regarded as an episcopal spy, and the deans appealed to the archbishop of York against the intrusion, but they had to submit to Vaughan's demands when he threatened them with suspension. The victory was, however, short-lived, and as Bishop Lloyd had to proceed against six Lancashire deans for contempt of his authority seven years later it is probable that Vaughan's instructions had not been obeyed.[2] It thus became clear that the difficulty of controlling the deans outweighed the benefit of their local influence, while the bishop was finding it difficult to pay the salaries of his other officers. In 1615, therefore, Bishop Lloyd annexed all the Richmond deaneries, except Amounderness, to the office of commissary, and in 1635 Bishop Bridgeman divided the remainder between the archdeacons of Chester and Richmond and his own chaplains.[3]

The issue of ecclesiastical commissions by the Crown was an admission of the inadequacy of the Church's existing disciplinary machine; Elizabeth expected bishops who had a commission to be particularly successful, while bishops who could not control their dioceses by conventional methods applied for commissions.[4] An

---

[1] C. Hill, *Society and Puritanism*, 300–2; BIY, R VII, HCAB 6, fos. 64, 66, 75v, 82, 119, R VI, A 7, fo. 63, A 14, fo. 19; CRO, EDA 2/2, fos. 30, 377.

[2] *Ibid.* fo. 198, EDA 3/1, fo. 170, EDC 1/30, fos. 359, 361; BIY, PN2, 1599 (I wish to thank Mr J. Addy for drawing this document to my attention); Raines, *Fellows of Manchester*, 72.

[3] CRO, EDR 6, pp. 71–5, EDA 3/1, fos. 131, 135, 162v–163, 258–259.

[4] Strype, *Annals*, I(2), 254–5; BM, Lansdowne MS 33, fo. 14; *CSPD*, Addenda (1580–1625), 7.

Ecclesiastical Commission was a mixed body of laymen and clerics with powers to imprison, to impose bonds, and to order a sheriff to arrest the contumacious. Lancashire was subject to the concurrent jurisdiction of the provincial Commission at York and a diocesan Commission, but the High Commission at York intervened only occasionally between 1562 and 1569, very extensively between 1569 and 1580, and infrequently thereafter. Though the commissions seem to have been powerful bodies, their effectiveness was exaggerated by contemporaries and some historians have accepted Puritan propaganda at face value. An Ecclesiastical Commission faced the same problems as the traditional Church courts, an inability to force defendants to appear and to extort its penalties, and it was no more successful in overcoming them.

The Commissions at both York and Chester were able to try only a minority of those cited before them, for the accused simply failed to attend court sessions. On 12 October 1571 33 Lancashiremen were due to appear before the York High Commission, but only 6 did so, and during a drive against Lancashire recusants in 1578 only 6 of 139 cited ever turned up.[1] The Chester Commission did no better; it imposed 222 fines from mid 1580 to mid 1583, but 207 of them were for contempt of the court in failing to appear before it.[2] As the Privy Council saw in 1581, the Ecclesiastical Commission depended on secular officers to force offenders to appear. The process of attachment by sheriffs seems to have failed more often than it succeeded, and we have already noticed the failure of Sir John Southworth to execute the orders of the High Commission in 1562. Nine years later the same court ordered the attachment of 77 Lancashire priests and laymen, but only 2 of them could be found by the sheriff. Even if attachment was successful, it might only be after a long delay, and in 1586 William Sagar of Colne was produced before the High Commission two years after an attachment had first been ordered.[3]

If the process of attachment was ineffective, the Commission then relied on fines for contumacy to force offenders to appear. There was a furore in 1583 when the Privy Council was told by enemies of the Chester Commission that it had collected £3,000 in fines; an Exchequer enquiry found that in three years fines totalling £757 3s 4d had been imposed, but only £40 13s of this had been paid in to the Commission's receiver. The fines which had been collected were

[1] BIY, R VII, HCAB 6, fos. 81–88v; HCAB 9, fos. 168v–175.
[2] PRO, E 134/25 Elizabeth, Trinity No. 5, mm. 1–8; *CSPD*, Addenda, (1580–1625), 11–12.
[3] Peck, *Desiderata Curiosa*, 106–7; BIY, R VII, HCAB 6, fos. 82–115; HCAB 11, fo. 62v.

those imposed on convicted offenders, and for the collection of outstanding fines for contumacy the Commission relied on the cooperation of the sheriff. In 1580–1 fines totalling £547 5s had been imposed, almost all for contempt, and the sheriff had to resort to the cumbersome process of distraint on lands and goods. He obtained writs of 'distringas' against only seven Lancashire offenders and collected only £91 6s, one-sixth of the sums owed. The High Commission at York faced similar difficulties, and in the 1590s only paltry sums were collected in fines.[1] It is true that the powers of the Commission made it a formidable weapon against those who appeared before it, but as only a minority of those cited ever attended and procedures for dealing with the recalcitrant were unreliable, the court's real impact was limited.

The Church's main sanction to force men to attend its courts and obey their decrees was excommunication, and the whole disciplinary system depended on men's fear of excommunication. But almost all the evidence available suggests that excommunication was widely disregarded.[2] Between 1580 and 1586 the Chester consistory excommunicated 781 contumacious defendants, an average of 112 each year, but only 85 of them, an average of 12 each year, ever submitted to the court. By the 1590s as many as 1,000 Lancastrians were being excommunicated at each visitation for failure to attend the correction courts, and only a handful of them are known to have submitted. A group of Puritan ministers complained in 1590 that the penalty of excommunication held no terror, and 'many like to continue in that state'.[3] Excommunication could only be a successful weapon if, as happened in theory but nowhere else, the offender was ostracised by society, but with such large numbers involved this was clearly impossible. In 1595 Bolton was said to have a large excommunicate population, and when in May 1597 a further 137 were added there must have been an excommunicate person in most households of the parish. The Church courts were caught in a vicious circle: large numbers were excommunicated because men did not attend the courts, but the penalty was of no consequence because so many incurred it, and there was no sanction to combat contumacy. Excommunication presented a problem only to those who had to deal with official bodies, so that in 1587 a Cheshire gentleman was forced to

---

[1] Peck, *Desiderata Curiosa*, 139; PRO, E 134/25 Elizabeth, No. 5, mm. 1–10, 13–14; *APC*, XII, 103–4; PRO, SP 12/138/18; P. Tyler, 'The Ecclesiastical Commission for the province of York, 1561–1641', University of Oxford D. Phil. thesis, 1965, 132–8.
[2] Hill, *Society and Puritanism*, 344–69; Marchant, *Church under the Law*, 210–11; F. D. Price, 'The abuses of excommunication and the decline of ecclesiastical discipline', *EHR*, LVII, 107, 109.
[3] CRO, EDC 1/23, fos. i–iv, 1/24, fos. 1–3, 1/25, fos. 1–3v; *State Civil and Ecclesiastical*, 12–13.

submit because he had a suit before the mayor's court at Chester, and in 1600 a Manchester man submitted only because he wished to initiate a testamentary case.[1]

If an excommunicate person had not submitted within forty days, the ordinary could request Chancery to issue a write of 'significavit' to the sheriff of the county, who was then responsible for the arrest of the offender. This process was often used by the commissary of Richmond, but the Chester records show that, as in the diocese of Gloucester, the bishop and chancellor rarely 'signified' obstinate offenders.[2] Requests for the signification of those living in Cheshire went to the palatinate of Chester, those for excommunicates in the rest of the diocese except Lancashire went to Chancery and, though they seem to be lost, Lancashire 'significations' must have gone to the palatinate; the involvement of so many jurisdictions suggests an easy method of evasion for those living near county boundaries. It is not possible to trace the process in action in Lancashire, but the rarity of its use and the fact that excommunication was no deterrent imply that it was found to be inadequate. We know that the less cumbersome process of attachment did not work, and 'signification' was even less likely to succeed.

The elaborate system of ecclesiastical administration for Lancashire, while not totally ineffective, was able to discipline only those who willingly accepted its authority. In the large and unwieldy parishes of the county, over-looked by a weak detection and coercion machine, men were safe from the attentions of the Church courts, and only those offences which might provoke popular hostility and reports to the authorities had to be avoided. Even after an offender had been detected, it was not difficult to avoid punishment and, except for the few unlucky enough to be caught by sheriffs, apparitors and pursuivants, punishments were almost voluntarily incurred. Those who, like the indifferent and the Catholic recusants, were not worried by the spiritual sanctions of the established Church,[3] could go free, and the disciplinary machine could cope only with the frightened and the conscientious Anglican.

If the Elizabethan Church in Lancashire did not possess the institutions which could force men to conform to the letter of the settlement of 1559, neither did it have the energetic and well-qualified resident clergy who might attract them to its spirit. The rich Lancashire rectories still attracted the attentions of the influen-

---

[1] BIY, R VI, A 14, fo. 22v; CRO, EDC 1/29, fo. 231/2, 1/26, loose leaf at fo. 312, 1/31, fos. 64v–65.
[2] The commissary signified 99 in 1587 and 90 in 1588 (LCL, RD/A/4, fos. 74v, 91, 129). For Gloucester, see Price, 'Abuses of excommunication', 112–13.
[3] See the bishop of Lichfield's comment in 1582, Strype, *Annals*, III(2), 217.

tial, and a third of the incumbencies of rectories between 1558 and 1642 were filled by pluralists. William Chadderton noted in 1586 that the best benefices were held by non-residents, and in 1590 about a third of all Lancashire benefices were held by absentees.[1] When assistant clergy were in short supply and reform demanded close supervision by an experienced cleric, non-residence led often to neglect. William Whitlock of Prescot, who had a dispensation for pluralism, was absent almost continuously between 1559 and 1583.[2] The farmer of the vicarage failed to provide preachers for this large parish of almost 600 households, the services had not been properly reformed by 1573, and one of the chapel curates was still using holy water in 1578. The churchwardens failed to collect the 12d absence fine, and as early as 1578 there were 42 known recusants in the parish; recusant priests and a Catholic schoolmaster were able to work freely.[3] At Eccleston the rector, who was chaplain to the earl of Derby, was non-resident throughout the reign of Elizabeth, and in 1578 he was said never to have performed services since his institution in 1563. Sermons were not provided, the children were not catechised, the church rarely had the prescribed books and the fabric was allowed to decay. The wardens were negligent and the Elizabethan presentments of recusants were totally inadequate, though 169 recusants were recorded in 1619.[4] The position at Winwick, where the pluralist rector was non-resident from 1576, was if possible even worse. The fabric was in disrepair, the proper books were often not provided, the children were not catechised, the 12d absence fine was not levied and recusants, 'which are very many in that parish', numbered 127 by 1604. Between 1593 and 1596 the parish was dominated by a rascally parish clerk of marked conservative sympathy, who conducted burials himself, had an illegitimate child by his cousin and lived with another woman, disturbed the services by piping and dancing, and made fun of the curate as he tried to perform the liturgy.[5]

If the wealth of some benefices could lead to disorder, poverty could create equally serious problems. Bishop Chadderton thought

[1] Lambert, 'Lower clergy', 161; PRO, SP 12/189, fo. 33v; *VCH*, III–VIII, *passim*; BIY, R VI, A 11, fos. 36–102, A 12, fos. 51–76v, A 14, fos. 19–75v; PRO, SP 12/31, fos. 85–86.
[2] PRO, SP 12/10, fo. 123v, 12/76, fo. 6; CRO, EDA 12/3, fo. 26, EDV 1/3, fos. 33, 70v; BIY, R VII, HCAB 6, fo. 48v, R VI, A 7, fo. 47.
[3] BIY, R VII, HCAB 9, fo. 174, R VI, A 7, fo. 47; *Prescot Accounts*, 73.
[4] *Stanley Papers*, II, 23; PRO, SP 12/31, fo. 85; CRO, EDV 1/6d, fo. 12, 1/8b, fo. 2v, 1/10, fo. 154v, 1/12a, fo. 95, 1/12b, fo. 123, 1/13, fos. 160–164, 1/21, fos. 47–50; BIY, R VI, A 7, fos. 58, 72.
[5] PRO, SP 12/235, fo. 8; CRO, EDV 1/12a, fo. 126, 1/12b, fo. 142, EDC 5, 1596; BIY, R VI, A 7, fo. 48, A 14, fo. 26v.

that half the benefices in his diocese had 'no other incumbents than very beggarly vicars and curates', and a survey of *c*. 1590 estimated that south-Lancashire vicars had an average income of £23 9s 3d, when twice that amount would have brought no luxury and the rectors had eight times as much.[1] In addition there was a large body of unbeneficed clergy, and the 1578 visitation call list for five Lancashire deaneries gives 35 incumbents and 74 assistants; the latter really were 'beggarly'. In *c*. 1590 17 chapel curates in the survey were said to receive an average of only £3 18s per year, in 1610 the 7 chapel curates of Whalley parish had only £4 each, and 17 other ministers were dependent on the voluntary offerings of their people. As late as 1650, 44 of Lancashire's 101 chapels had no settled endowment, and another 36 yielded £4 each or less. These meagre sums went to men who served chapels which were, as Bishop Vaughan pointed out, 'as populous as mother churches'.[2] It was impossible for curates to survive on such stipends, and many of them had to undertake additional employment. Schoolteaching was probably the most common source of a supplementary income, and we know that the curates of Gorton, West Derby and Newton had schools in 1578. The curate of Blackley also opened a school for local children, but as his clerical stipend was only £2 3s 4d he could not afford a licence from the bishop.[3] Other underpaid ministers opened alehouses, including a fellow of Manchester in 1571, the vicar of Huyton and the curate of Singleton in 1578, the curate of Stretford in 1581, the curate of Ormskirk in 1601 and the vicar of Ribchester three years later.[4] Richard Hall of Manchester tried his hand at surgery, which was an unfortunate choice as several of his patients died, and his colleague Oliver Carter turned to the law, becoming 'a common solicitor in temporal causes, by reason whereof he is often absent'.[5] Apart from the inevitable farmers, ministers also became coal-miners and sellers, wool-traders, spinners and weavers.[6] The more enterprising found ways of making profits from their positions, and in 1571 a fellow of Manchester was conducting secret illegal marriages for money. It was probably a flourishing business of this kind which got Roger Blakey, the curate of Colne, into trouble so often for conducting clandestine marriages, and it was presumably

[1] PRO, SP 12/189, fos. 33–33v, SP 12/31, fos. 85–86.
[2] BIY, R VI, A 8, Rolls A, B, F, I, K; PRO, SP 12/31, fo. 86; *Kenyon MSS*, 9–12; Lambert, 'Lower clergy', 12–13; *CRS*, LIII, 147.
[3] BIY, R VI, A 8, Rolls I, K, A 11, fo. 95; CRO, EDV 1/6d, fo. 42.
[4] Raines, *Fellows of Manchester College*, 62–3; H. Fishwick, *History of Kirkham*, 45–6; H. T. Crofton, *History of the Ancient Chapel of Stretford*, I, 60; BIY, R VI, A 7, fo. 47; *Lancashire Quarter Sessions Records*, ed. J. Tait, 101; CRO, EDV 1/13, fo. 205v.
[5] Raines, *Fellows of Manchester College*, 61–2; BIY, R VI, A 11, fo. 79v.
[6] Lambert, 'Lower clergy', 61–3.

his stipend of only £4 which forced him into the trade, because his successor kept it up.[1]

For all but the privileged few who could secure presentation to rich rectories, the clerical profession in Lancashire held few attractions, and this, combined with a widespread reluctance in a conservative area to serve a Protestant Church, led to serious problems in staffing the churches. Bishop Downham's conservative temperament led him to adopt the same sort of ordination policy as his Catholic predecessors, and he was clearly concerned to fill the clerical posts in his diocese irrespective of the quality of the ordinands. Between 1562 and 1569 he ordained no fewer than 176 priests from his own diocese; there was not one graduate among them, and 56 of them were marked, in the ordination book, 'tolerantia domini episcopi', which presumably means that they were ordained despite their failure to come up to the prescribed standards. In his seventeen-year episcopate Downham ordained an average of 22 Chester men each year, and among them all there were only 4 graduates. There was an abrupt change in 1580, when William Chadderton held his first ordination, and from then until 1603 an average of fewer than 4 priests a year were ordained from the diocese, and of the total of 80 as many as 29 were graduates.[2] Downham and his successors clearly had different solutions to the dilemma of quality or quantity.

But despite the large numbers ordained by Downham, there remained an acute shortage of clergy in Lancashire. The number of serving clergy in the four south-Lancashire deaneries had fallen to 79 by 1565, well under one-third of the 1548 level, and in 1578 the number was still almost static at 81. This was clearly insufficient, chapels went unserved and the Church had to recruit lay readers to fill some of the gaps. In 1563 a cursory visitation of four deaneries found 1 parish church and 6 chapels without curates, in 1575–6 eight lay readers had to be licensed for Lancashire chapels and in 1578 11 out of 60 chapels in five deaneries were served only by a deacon or a lay reader and 3 more were not served at all. By 1610 a quarter of the chapels which had been founded by the middle of the sixteenth century were no longer in use, and 24 of the 85 chapels nominally in use were unserved, while 6 more had only lay readers.[3]

The quality of the clergy who did serve seems not to have been high for, partly as a result of Downham's ordination policy and

---

[1] Raines, *Fellows of Manchester College*, 63; CRO, EDC 2/7, fos. 249–250v; BIY, R VII, HCAB 1, fos. 103v, 111v; HCAB 13, fo. 211v, R VI, A 7, fo. 53v, A 12, fo. 51.
[2] CRO, EDA 1/3, fos. 2v–34v.
[3] CRO, EDV 1/3, fos. 1–34, EDR 1, fos. 4–69; BIY, R VI, A 8, Call Rolls A, B, F, I, K; Tupling, 'Pre-Reformation parishes and chapelries', 12–16; *Kenyon MSS*, 7–13. For the effect of this shortage on recusancy, see below, p. 272.

partly, as the Duchy chancellor put it, 'on account of the smallness of the church livings', there were 'few or no incumbents of learning or credit amongst them'. Even Chadderton was twice accused of admitting unworthy incumbents, and the curates were twice described as 'utterly unlearned'.[1] In 1562 a Manchester curate was ordered to 'come daily to the grammar school to hear the lessons' and to learn a chapter of the New Testament each month for examination. In 1565 the rector of Ashton was reported to be insufficiently learned to serve his cure, and was dispatched to Oxford University for three years by the Ecclesiastical Commission; whether failing eyesight or the inadequacies of an Oxford education were to blame is not clear, but in 1604 he was unable to read the service.[2] Chadderton's overthrow of his predecessor's ordination policy and his establishment of 'exercises' to improve the education of his clergy show what he thought of their quality when he entered into his charge. It is probable that his restrictions on ordinations led to improvements; by 1592 there were 103 graduate clergy in the diocese, as against 273 men 'poorly learned', and in 1604 there were 131 graduates.[3]

Lack of education was not the only fault of the Lancashire clergy, and clerical marriage did not mean the end of sexual laxity among the clergy; between 1571 and 1601 eight ministers were presented on visitation for adultery or fornication.[4] George Hesketh, though never presented at visitations, acquired a formidable reputation for lechery among his parishioners at Halsall; the manorial court at Ormskirk had forbidden the people to allow his putative mistress into their homes, and one man had said, 'This is he (meaning the said George Hesketh, clerk, and pointing at him with his finger) that corrupteth all the women in the county.'[5] Drunkenness was probably even more common, and ten Lancashire clerics were in trouble for this offence in the reign of Elizabeth.[6] George Dobson, the vicar of Whalley, acquired a reputation as enviable as Hesketh's; it was alleged in 1575 that he was

a common drunkard, and such an ale-knight as the like is not in our parish, and in the night when most men be in bed at their rest then is he in the ale-house with a company like to himself, but not one of them can match

[1] E. Axon, 'The King's Preachers in Lancashire', *TLCAS*, LVI, 69; PRO, SP 15/27/94, SP 12/240, fo. 292.
[2] CRO, EDA 12/2, fos. 81v, 100v, EDV 1/13, fo. 70.
[3] Usher, *Reconstruction of the English Church*, I, 242; *CRS*, LIII, 147.
[4] BIY, R VII, HCAB 6, fos. 84v, 87, 90v, R VI, A 7, fo. 37, A 11, fo. 57, A 14, fos. 23v, 74v; CRO, EDV 1/12b, fo. 108v.   [5] CRO, EDC 5, 1584.
[6] PRO, SP 12/10, fo. 51; CRO, EDA 12/2, fos. 42v, 81v, EDV 1/9, fo. 54, 1/12b, fo. 108v, 1/13, fo. 83; BIY, R VI, A 7, fo. 55, A 11, fo. 62v; Raines, *Fellows of Manchester College*, 61–2; *VCH*, IV, 136.

him in ale-house tricks, for he will, when he cannot discern black from blue, dance with a full cup on his head, far passing all the rest.[1]

Richard Senhouse, rector of Claughton, set his flock an equally bad example; he was 'a dicer and carder at such times as he should edify the flock, and draweth men's servants to play with him'.[2] The faults of other ministers were perhaps more dangerous, for in 1571 the curate of Harwood was bound not to 'use any predictions, divinations, sorcerings, charmings or enchantments', and the curate of Kirkby was described as 'a sorcerer, a hawker and a hunter'.[3]

The offence which most limited the prospects of the reform movement in Lancashire was negligence, though this is not an easy fault to discuss as the parishes with neglectful incumbents were frequently those which made the thinnest presentments on visitation. But two particularly bad examples can be quoted. The vicar of Croston in the deanery of Leyland was in trouble for the same failings at almost every late-Elizabethan visitation. He allowed the church fabric, his section of the churchyard and the vicarage to fall into decay, and the vicarage was used as an ale-house. The children were not catechised, the vicar did not administer the communion properly, and he appointed no curate so that the parish 'is not so well served as they ought to be'. The surplice was not worn – from laxity rather than Puritanism – he churched an adulteress, and there were no perambulations. The vicar was thought to be sympathetic to the Catholics, the 12d absence fine was not collected, and though few recusants were presented while he was in office there were 150 in the parish by 1630.[4] In the last decade of Elizabeth's reign, the character of the vicar of Dean led to a serious state of affairs in his parish. The vicar was apparently a drunkard who had fathered an illegitimate child, and he held secret marriage ceremonies without calling banns. He provided no sermons and did not catechise the children; he seems to have had an aversion to preaching for he was once described as 'a lewd minister, neither preacher himself nor will suffer any other to preach'. During his incumbency the church fabric was in almost permanent disrepair, and in 1598 no services could be performed for six months because of the condition of the building. In 1601 he did not conduct services for five weeks and, to make matters worse, he was 'suspected not to be of sound religion'. It is not altogether surprising that his parish seems to have been the only one in the deanery of Manchester with a significant recusancy problem.[5]

[1] *VCH*, VI, 359.   [2] BIY, R VI, A 14, fo. 61v.
[3] BIY, R VII, HCAB 6, fos. 64v, 87v.
[4] CRO, EDV 1/8b, fo. 2v, 1/12a, fos. 96–96v, 1/12b, fos. 124–125, 1/13, fo. 152; PRO, SP 12/243, fo. 223; BIY, R VI, A 7, fo. 58v, A 22, fos. 70v–71v.
[5] CRO, EDV 1/10, fos. 164v–165, 1/12a, fo. 86, 1/12b, fos. 108v–109; *Kenyon MSS*, 12.

It is not suggested that such men as these were typical of Lancashire clergy, but they were sufficiently common to colour the attitude of the laity towards their pastors. The bishops had to be careful of the reputation of their clergy, and when a Cheshire rector was ordered to pay £20 towards the marriage of a girl with whom he had committed fornication, Bishop Downham kept the affair quiet 'forasmuch Mr Elcocke was an honest gentleman and a preacher, lest it should redound to the reproach of the ministry'.[1] Most of the details of individual failings given here come from the presentments of churchwardens on visitation, and the mere fact that such accusations were made suggests that the ministers concerned were unpopular. At Halsall the character of George Hesketh, the rector, was the object of considerable speculation and criticism; in 1584 the rector had to sue ten parishioners, including a certain 'William of the shop', for defamation, and the earl of Derby intervened to prevent relations between pastor and people being soured completely.[2] Sometimes antipathy towards a minister took a more concrete form, as when people refused to contribute towards curates' stipends at Cartmel and Stretford in 1595 and at Milnrow and Littleborough in 1602.[3] Parishioners' dislike of clergy could also lead to violence and the disruption of services, as happened at Warton, Bury and Culcheth in 1590 and at Bolton-le-Sands and Woodplumpton in 1595.[4] The disturbance of services at Ribchester in 1592 was part of a running battle between the negligent pluralist Henry Norcrosse and a section of his congregation; the malcontents were always ready to make accusations against their vicar, going as far as a charge of simony in 1574, and he certainly did sell ale and victuals and was eventually deprived for drunkenness and violence.[5]

The Church in Lancashire did not possess the disciplinary machine which could coerce its people into the paths of salvation, nor did it have the pastors who might entice them. In neither organisation nor personnel was the Church geared persuading men from Rome in the 1560s and 1570s, nor to withstanding the competition of the seminary priests in the 1580s and 1590s. A comment made by Edmund Spenser on the clergy of Ireland might be applied equally to their fellows in Lancashire:

It is great wonder to see the odds which is between the zeal of popish priests and ministers of the Gospel, for they spare not to come out of Spain, from Rome, from Rheims, by long toil and dangerous travel hither, where they

---

[1] CRO, EDC 1/26, fo. 25v.   [2] *Ibid.* 1/25, fos. 110, 117, 122, 125v.
[3] BIY, R VI, A 14, fos. 19, 65; CRO, EDC 1/32, fos. 259v, 304.
[4] BIY, R VI, A 11, fos. 36, 94, A 14, fos. 57v, 72v; *Lancashire Quarter Sessions,* 6.
[5] *Ibid.* 41; CRO, EDV 1/12a, fo. 121, 1/13, fo. 205v, EDC 1/20, fo. 319v, EDC 5, 1574; *VCH,* VII, 42.

know peril of death awaiteth them, and no reward nor riches is to be found, only to draw the people to the Church of Rome; whereas our idle ministers, having a way for credit and estimation thereby opened unto them, and having the livings of the country offered them without pains, without peril, will neither for the same, nor any love of God nor zeal of religion, nor for all the good which they might do by winning of so many souls to God, be drawn forth from their warm nests and their sweet love's side to look into God's harvest.[1]

The clergy of Lancashire were not equipped for 'winning of so many souls to God', and the prospects for widespread conversions to Anglicanism were poor.

Francis Walsingham pointed out to Bishop Chadderton in 1580 that coercion could lead only 'to an outward obedience', and hearts could only be changed by 'a competent number of good, learned preachers'. But there was general agreement among bishops, administrators, local gentlemen and people that the county lacked 'a competent number'.[2] A Puritan survey of *c.* 1590 found only 23 preachers, a mere 7 of them considered adequate, to serve 39 parish churches and their chapels. A more optimistic official assessment of 1592 suggested that 45% of the clergy of the diocese were preachers but, as the earl of Huntingdon remarked, 'the want of diligent and faithful preaching doth wonderfully hinder the building of our Church'. In 1599 the government was forced to improve the provision for Lancashire by appointing four Queen's Preachers to serve in the county, at a total cost of £200 per annum.[3] These appointments, and the ordination policy which was adopted in the second half of Elizabeth's reign, had created a much better situation by 1610, when 49 of the 114 ministers in Lancashire were said to be preachers. But two major difficulties remained, one being the uneven distribution of preachers, for in the deaneries of Blackburn, Amounderness, Lonsdale, Kendal and Furness only 17 out of 60 ministers could preach in 1610. A second problem was non-residence for, as Chadderton saw, preachers were often sufficiently influential to become pluralists, and in about 1590 it was estimated that there were only 16 resident preachers to serve 102,000 communicants in the county.[4]

The preponderance of non-preachers and the laxity of those who could preach left many parishes without sermons; there were complaints that there had been no sermons at Eccleston at the visitations

[1] E. Spenser, *A View of the Present State of Ireland*, ed. W. L. Renwick, 162.
[2] Peck, *Desiderata Curiosa*, 92, 130, 137–8; *Kenyon MSS*, 601; *CSPD* (1598–1601), 7, 15; *APC*, XXXI, 44–5; PRO, SP 12/240, fo. 292.
[3] PRO, SP 12/31, fos. 85–86; Usher, *Reconstruction of the English Church*, I, 242; Axon, 'King's Preachers', 69–70.
[4] *Kenyon MSS*, 6–13; R. Simpson, *Edmund Campion*, 268; PRO, SP 12/31, fos. 85–86, 12/189, fo. 33v, 12/240, fo. 292.

of 1578, 1580, 1592 and 1598, and in 1578 it was reported that there had been no sermons at the parish churches of Huyton, Eccleston, Lancaster, Pennington, Ulverston, Kirkby Ireleth and Tatham. Chapels were even less likely to have sermons, and the incumbents of Manchester, Whalley and Blackburn were lax in the provision of sermons for their dependent chapelries.[1] Even when sermons were provided, they were not always appreciated by the congregation. Many in Lancashire must have shared the view of a Richmondshire man that 'the preaching of the Gospel is but bibble-bubble, and I care not a fart of my tail for any black coat in Wensleydale, and I had rather hear a cuckoo sing'. In 1585 two Rochdale men were in trouble because

> both of these speak evil and contemptuous words against Mr Midgeley, a godly and approved learned preacher and our vicar, and said that the old religion which he belied was better than that used in these unquiet times, and that he was a Yorkshire plague, and moreover said that he had travailed to bring Mr. Greaves and other strange prattling preachers of no good report, who clog with their tongues and only for much wages.[2]

These were not the only cases of the expressed unpopularity of sermons and preachers.[3]

In the absence of sermons at some churches, regular readings from the royal injunctions and the books of homilies played an essential role in breaking down conservative sentiment. But visitors found that the injunctions were not read at Rossendale and Denton in 1592, at Rossendale and Wigan in 1598, or at Aughton, Poulton, Bispham and Ribchester in 1604.[4] Even more serious for the prospects of the conversion of Lancashire was the lack of one or both volumes of the official homilies, and in visitations of varying completeness the homilies were found to be wanting at four churches in 1578, three in 1581, seven in 1601, and no less than eighteen in 1604.[5] It is thus unlikely that in many parishes the formal services of the Church of England can have contributed much to the growth of Protestant opinion.

One must have grave doubts on the efficacy of the established Church as an instrument of reformation in theology and morals, in

---

[1] BIY, R VI, A 7, fos. 47, 58, 62v, 64v, 65v, 70, 90v.

[2] Tyler, 'Church courts at York and witchcraft prosecutions', 102; *State Civil and Ecclesiastical*, 46.

[3] CRO, EDV 1/4, fo. 13; *Salisbury MSS*, I, 575–6; *Lancashire Quarter Sessions*, 224. It is noticeable that all Dr Richardson's examples of enthusiasm for sermons are from the 17th century (R. C. Richardson, *Puritanism in North-West England*, 83f).

[4] CRO, EDV 1/10, fos. 147v, 165, 1/12a, fos. 85v, 139v, 1/13, fos. 83, 198v, 205–205v.

[5] BIY, R VI, A 7, fos. 37, 39, 48, 49; CRO, EDV 1/6d, fos. 40v, 42v, 47, EDV 1/12b, *passim*, 1/13, *passim*.

part because the clergy found it difficult to get their people into the churches. Quite apart from deliberate Catholic recusancy, there is a good deal of indirect evidence that the church services were poorly attended, and two separate reports alleged that preachers had to give up their sermons for want of 'a competent congregation in any church to preach unto'.[1] The other attractions which were available on Sundays to distract men from their religious duty proved more enticing than preaching, and services had to compete with piping and dancing, even in the church and churchyard,[2] markets, bear-baiting and cock-fighting,[3] and bowling, horse-racing and gaming.[4] At every visitation there were large numbers of presentments for selling and drinking ale during services; even those who did not succumb to such temptations found other things more interesting than the reformed liturgy, and 54 offenders at Prescot were presented in 1604 'for standing gazing in the street in time of divine service on sabbath days and holy days'.[5] The Privy Council thought that Sunday 'side-shows' were especially organised 'by such as are evil affected in religion' to draw people from 'the service of God', and it was this feeling that the sabbath was being deliberately sabotaged, as much as Puritan sympathy, which led to the long series of restrictions on Sunday games.[6]

At least one prominent Lancashire incumbent realised that many adults were past redemption, and that the Church needed to concentrate its resources on the next generation. Thomas Meade, the vicar of Prescot, wrote in 1586 that 'The only reformation that we can hope for in this corrupt country is that children be truly and diligently catechised, for I think that superstition is so grounded in the aged that without the rare mercy of God death must part it.'[7] But the catechising of children and servants was one of the most widely neglected duties of the Lancashire clergy, and in 1592 both Meade and his curate were themselves in trouble for failure to catechise. The clergy of Manchester College, who ought to have been a great reforming force in south-east Lancashire, were proceeded against for neglect of this duty in 1578, 1592, 1598 and 1601. Visitation returns

[1] PRO, SP 12/235, fo. 146, 12/240, fo. 292v; *State Civil and Ecclesiastical*, 2.
[2] CRO, EDV 1/7, fo. 18v, 1/9, fo. 79v, 1/10, fos. 115v, 166v, 1/12b, fo. 167, 1/13, fo. 175, EDC 5, 1596.
[3] PRO, SP 12/240, fos. 292v–293; *Kenyon MSS*, 582–3; CRO, EDV 1/12a, fo. 128.
[4] *Kenyon MSS*, 572; CRO, EDV 1/10, fo. 124v; BIY, R VI, A 11, fo. 81v, A 14, fo. 24.
[5] CRO, EDV 1/13, fos. 143v–144v.
[6] *APC*, XXII, 549; *Kenyon MSS*, 587, 590; *Farington Papers*, 128–9; E. Baines, *History of the County Palatine and Duchy of Lancaster*, 5 vols. I, 549–50; *Manchester Sessions, 1616–1623*, xxiv.
[7] F. A. Bailey, 'Prescot grammar school in Elizabethan times,' *THSLC*, LXXXVI, 3.

reveal that there was no catechising at five churches in 1578, seven in 1592, four in 1595, six in 1598, seven in 1601 and nine in 1604. Even if the clergy were willing to catechise, only half the problem was solved, for they had great difficulty in persuading their parishioners to send their children and servants; there was widespread absence from catechetical classes at Sefton and Croston in 1578, Childwall and Rossendale in 1592, Bury, Didsbury and Winwick in 1598, Halsall and Winwick in 1601 and Eccleston and Lancaster in 1604.[1] At most of the visitations no more than half of the county is covered by the surviving returns, and the real extent of the neglect of catechising was very much greater. If the children were not taught the principles of the reformed religion, Catholicism was not likely, as the government hoped, simply to die out with the pre-1559 generation.

Elizabethan bishops of Chester faced an impossible task. They were expected to create a Protestant Church when they had only an inadequate administrative machine, and when the parish clergy on whom they had to rely were in short supply and often conservative or negligent. Where the disciplinary institutions were ineffective, conservative 'Anglicans', recusant priests, and Catholic laymen could practise the old religion undetected or, at least, unpunished. Where chapels were unserved through a shortage of ministers, recusant priests and, later, seminarians were available to fill the gaps. Where churches were served by men of low ability and less vocation the Church was brought into disrepute, and where ministers were unable or unwilling to propagandise the new faith the Catholic clergy found an audience which did not have to be reconverted but merely reconciled. The task of recusant priests and seminarians was relatively simple, for the established Church offered little serious competition.

---

[1] CRO, EDV 1/10, 1/12a, 1/12b, 1/13, *passim*; BIY, R VI, A 7, A 14, A 15, *passim*.

16

The emergence of recusancy

Refusal to attend services at the parish church was not a natural reaction to the theological revolution of 1559. We have already seen that the parish church or chapelry was the centre of community life, not merely of the community's religious life. The curate of Rossendale told the Chester consistory court in 1603 that

> the congregation of people, men and women, which do daily assemble and come to the church of Rossendale, do use after evening prayers on Sundays and holy days is ended to stay in the church conferring or talking one with another by the space of an hour at the least, except it be in the cold of winter.[1]

Churches were the objects of intense communal loyalties, and in 1578 the people of Rossendale were refusing those of Wolfenden Booth permission to attend their chapel.[2] Recusancy could thus entail not merely withdrawal from the Church of England, but withdrawal from the village community and its decision-making process. As Dr Bossy has noted, a recusant of the first generation was not merely a man who did not attend parish services, but a man who had once attended and had taken a deliberate decision to cease.[3] Before 1559 absence from church in Lancashire seems to have been uncommon, and between 1510 and 1529 there were only nineteen detected cases of absence from the chapels of the exempt forest areas of Blackburnshire.[4] In 1559 an Eccles woman was said not to have been to church for twenty years, but the fact that she was almost the only Lancashire lay person presented before the royal visitors underlines the peculiarity of her case.[5] It is thus not surprising that historians have argued that there was very little recusancy in England in the first fifteen or twenty years of the reign of Elizabeth. The emergence of a separate Catholic religious community has been dated from the arrival of the seminary priests, armed with instructions from Rome and steeled by the ardour of post-Tridentine

---

[1] CRO, EDC 5, 1603.
[2] BIY, R VI, A 7, fo. 54.
[3] J. A. Bossy, *The English Catholic Community, 1570–1850*, ch. 6. Dr Bossy was kind enough to allow me to read his work in typescript before publication, so that I am able to give only chapter references.
[4] *Whalley Act Book, passim.*
[5] PRO, SP 12/10, fo. 118.

missioners, so that a discontinuity between the pre-Reformation Church and later recusancy has been stressed.[1]

Recusancy at an early date might be expected even less in Lancashire than elsewhere. By the early years of Elizabeth's reign Protestantism had made only the most insignificant impact on the county and, as we have seen, the laxity of Bishop Downham and the difficulties of ruling his diocese allowed the practice of something approaching traditional Catholicism to continue in many churches and chapels. There was, it seems, no *need* for recusancy. In a church-attending society, absence from church was almost unthinkable, and even Lancashire Anglicanism's pale imitation of the pre-Reformation Church was preferable to nothing. But the one inescapable necessity before recusancy could exist was provided on a considerable scale in Lancashire: a body of priests who had withdrawn from the established Church and could provide alternative forms of worship. The withdrawn clergy could revert to secular occupations and so lose their status in the community, or they could become private chaplains to the conservative gentry, as did Henry Crane, the curate of Padiham, who entered the household of John Towneley.[2] But not all priests could or would adopt these courses, and for them their one source of livelihood was to ply their trade, to become recusant priests.

It is thus not surprising that there were active recusant priests in Lancashire before there were lay recusants. Among the gentry the occasional doughty individual like Thomas Brereton of Dean might cease attending church as soon as the Elizabethan settlement was imposed, and Thomas Leyland of Leigh claimed to be too old and infirm to go to church and had mass provided at home by his chaplain.[3] But these are the only known examples; recusant clergy were much more common, and the number of those active in the county grew rapidly. In 1561 Laurence Vaux and Richard Hart, late of Manchester College, Nicholas Bannester, former schoolmaster at Preston, and John Murren, who had been chaplain to Bishop Bonner, were 'lurking' in Lancashire and were thought to be maintained by gentlemen there.[4] In February 1568 the sheriff of the county was ordered to arrest six recusant priests who 'do seditiously pervert and abuse our good subjects to our no small grief' and were 'secretly maintained in private places'; they included Vaux, Murren, Dr Marshall, the former dean of Christchurch, Oxford, and James

---

[1] A. G. Dickens, 'The first years of Romanist recusancy', *YAJ*, XXXV, 169–70, 177–8, 180–1; Bossy, *English Catholic Community*, chs. 6, 8; P. McGrath, *Papists and Puritans under Elizabeth I*, 100–21.　　　　　　　　　　　　[2] PRO, SP 12/48, fo. 85.
[3] BIY, R VII, HCAB 6, fo. 83v; Foxe, *Acts and Monuments*, VIII, 564.
[4] *CSPD*, Addenda (1547–65), 522–4.

Hargreaves, the deprived vicar of Blackburn.[1] By May of that year the Ecclesiastical Commission at Chester had the names of no fewer than 17 priests working in Lancashire, and at the visitation of 1571 38 Catholic priests were returned as active in the county.[2] Even this considerable figure was an understatement, and the available sources, taken together, suggest that at least 56 recusant clergy were working in Lancashire between 1568 and 1571, 29 of whom are known to have served the official Church in the county under Mary or in the early 1560s. After the first decade of Elizabethan Anglicanism, there were 40 recusant priests active in the four deaneries of south Lancashire; the established Church itself could muster only 79 clergy in 1565, and many of these were, as we have seen, conservatives preaching Rome rather than Canterbury.

The early existence of such a large body of recusant clergy could not help but lead to the creation of lay recusancy. In 1561 John Murren was circulating a broadsheet locally which poured scorn on the liturgy of the new Church and argued that 'The religion now used in the Church was not heard of before Luther's time, about forty years ago.'[3] By 1563 both the Inquisition at Rome and a committee of the Council of Trent had ruled that in no circumstances was it lawful for English Catholics to be present at the services and sermons of heretics.[4] In 1566 Laurence Vaux was in Rome, where he had an audience with the pope and was commissioned by Dr Sander and Dr Harding, the papal commissaries for the enforcement of the decrees in England, to act as their deputy. Vaux then carried into Lancashire a set of instructions from Sander, which he circulated among the gentry of south-west Lancashire, including Sir Richard Mollineux and Sir William Norris, and among the recusant clergy of the area. There was apparently some doubt among priests and laymen on the interpretation of these instructions, and Vaux was asked for a written elucidation. This he provided, in November 1566, in the most unambiguous terms:

I am charged to make a definitive sentence, that all such as offer children to the baptism now used or be present at the communion or service now used in churches in England, as well the laity as the clergy, do not walk in the state of salvation; neither we may not communicate nor sociate ourselves in company with schismatic or heretic in divine things; there is no exception nor dispensation can be had for any of the laity, if they will stand in the state of salvation.[5]

[1] W. Allen, *Letters and Memorials*, 21.
[2] CRO, EDA 12/2, fos. 118–118v; BIY, R VII, HCAB 6, fos. 82, 84, 88v, 89v, 93, 114v.
[3] *CSPD*, Addenda (1547–65), 524; Pilkington, *Works*, 480–6.
[4] C. G. Bayne, *Anglo-Roman Relations, 1558–1565*, 163–71, 177–80.
[5] Printed in *Vaux's Catechism*, xxxiii–iv.

Vaux's letter, probably addressed to the recusant clergy, was to be circulated among the gentry, and it produced an immediate effect. John Murren, together with John Peele, another non-Lancashire priest attracted into the county by the prospect of a harvest of lay recusants, began to administer an oath of loyalty to the pope as head of the Church, which committed the swearer to follow the instructions from Rome on abstention from Anglican services. Two priests who had served at Sefton until 1563 took the oath, as did Sir Richard Mollineux and his whole family, Sir William Norris, John Mollineux of Melling in Halsall, and Robert and Richard Blundell of Sefton. Two other priests had already been saying mass in the Blundell household, and outright recusancy was now added to mere conservative opposition.[1]

When these events came to the ears of members of the Ecclesiastical Commission they caused a furore; it was thought that 'this confederacy is so great that it will grow to a commotion or rebellion', and that all but one of the gentry along the south-west Lancashire coast had joined the recusant faction.[2] In the early summer of 1567 John Mollineux was called before the Ecclesiastical Commission, and when he refused to divulge any information he was temporarily committed to Chester Castle.[3] In October 1567 Mollineux and eleven others were interviewed several times by members of the commission and the earl of Derby's council, but no action seems to have been taken, though John Rigmaiden of Garstang was arrested and sent to the Fleet prison in London for hearing mass.[4] By December 1567 some of the commissioners were seriously worried, and warned Bishop Downham that if he and the earl did not take action against the recusants they would submit a critical report to the Privy Council. Though mandates were issued for some of the priests and gentlemen to appear before the commission, the commissioners were unable to agree on a policy towards the recusant gentry and they shelved the issue by sending John Mollineux and John Towneley to the Privy Council and binding Francis Tunstall and John Rigmaiden to appear when ordered.[5]

[1] This account is reconstructed from two long, informative and neglected letters, Vaux's letter to his fellow priests, printed in *Vaux's Catechism*, xxxii-ix, and a report sent to members of the Ecclesiastical Commission (PRO, SP 12/48, fos. 71–72v).
[2] PRO, SP 12/48, fos. 73–74.
[3] CRO, EDA 12/2, fos. 109–109v, 109v–110.
[4] PRO, SP 12/48, fos. 71–72v; *CRS*, I, 49.
[5] PRO, SP 12/48, fos. 73–74, 77; CRO, EDA 12/2, fos. 114v–118v; *CSPS* (1568–79), 12. The state papers used here have been noticed by some historians, but they have usually been dismissed as alarmist nonsense. With the discovery of the Ecclesiastical Commission records at Chester, and the 1571 visitation, discussed below, in the York High Commission Act Books, this is no longer possible.

The Privy Council was clearly dissatisfied by these dilatory proceedings, and resolved on more vigorous action. Sir John Southworth, who had been dismissed from the Ecclesiastical Commission,
was called up to London and examined by Archbishop Parker, but
he refused to sign a submission apologising for his contempt of the
laws and for receiving recusant priests. Southworth was determined,
as he later told Bishop Grindal, to 'follow the faith of his fathers: he
will die in the faith wherein he was baptised'.[1] The Council also sent
John Mollineux and John Towneley back to Chester, and instructed
the commission to proceed against the gentlemen against whom
information had been laid. On 31 July 1568 a special session of the
Ecclesiastical Commission was held in the earl of Derby's dining
chamber at Lathom, attended by the earl, Bishop Downham, and
the leading Lancashire commissioners. Seven prominent Lancashire
gentlemen, Francis Tunstall, John Talbot, John Rigmaiden,
Edward Osbaldeston, John Westby, Towneley and Mollineux, and
one prosperous yeoman, Matthew Travers, were examined by the
commission. Four of the accused admitted that they did not attend
church, though the others claimed to be occasional conformists, and
all admitted that they did not receive communion. Each of the eight
had received into their houses recusant priests from a list of twelve
submitted to them, and within the past three years seven of the
priests, including Vaux, Murren, Dr Marshall and John Peele, had
stayed with Mollineux. The Council had ordered that all those who
promised conformity should be treated leniently, and all but Westby, who had earlier said 'he would willingly lose his blood in these
matters', agreed to attend church and receive communion. All eight
were dismissed on bonds of 300 marks each to appear within twenty
days of any summons. Bishop Downham, who had been pushed so
reluctantly into action, was anxious to prove the success of his
proceedings. Three months later, after a desultory visitation of his
diocese, he reported that 'the punishment of these men hath done so
much good in the country that I trust I shall never be troubled again
with the like', and claimed to 'have found the people very tractable
and obedient'.[2] The absurdity of his judgement was soon to be
proved. The prosecutions were totally ineffective, for all the accused
men were later leading recusants, and only a small number of those
involved in the emergent recusant movement had been dealt with. In
particular, only one of the south-west Lancashire Catholic gentlemen, John Mollineux, had been tackled, and the bigger fish, Sir
Richard Mollineux, Sir William Norris, and the Blundells, remained
undisturbed. It is true that the two knights were soon to die, but

---

[1] *CSPD* (1547–80), 312; *Remains of Archbishop Grindal*, 305.
[2] PRO, SP 12/48, fos. 73–74, 75–86; CRO, EDA 12/2, fos. 123–124.

their families continued to cause difficulties. Most important of all, despite a series of increasingly frantic orders from the Council, neither the Ecclesiastical Commission nor the sheriff had been able to track down any of the recusant clergy. Attempts to discipline even the most influential of the recusant gentry would achieve little while the priests went free.

The year 1569 was a quieter one in Lancashire, as Bishop Downham rested on his laurels and the Catholics became, presumably, more circumspect. In the spring and early summer, Dr Nicholas Morton was in England as a messenger from the pope, and he seems to have stayed in Lancashire with the earl of Derby and Lord Mounteagle.[1] In the late summer the earl was consulted by the duke of Norfolk on the latter's plan to marry Mary, Queen of Scots, but Derby seems to have counselled caution.[2] In the early autumn the earl of Northumberland informed Derby of the projected rising in the north, but Derby neither replied to the letter nor reported it to the queen.[3] Edward Stanley was clearly playing the game at which he had excelled in 1536, waiting to gauge the strength of the opposing forces before throwing in his lot with the stronger. When the rising of the earls of Northumberland and Westmorland began in mid November the earl did nothing, but by the time Elizabeth sent him a commission of lieutenancy and instructions, on 20 November, it was clear that the rising was a futile affair, and Derby wrote immediately to the queen promising to do his best to keep Lancashire in order. Appeals from the rebel earls to Derby and Mounteagle produced no response, and the earl's political judgement had been as sound as ever.[4] The northern rebellion was confined almost entirely to the tenants and allies of the earls of Northumberland and Westmorland, and there was little chance of Lancashire joining a rising whose centre lay so far to the north-east, and which was merely designed to protect the two earls from arrest. There was even less likelihood of Derby leading Lancashire into a Catholic revolt, even if he thought one could have succeeded, for his equivocal posture and his albeit reluctant activities on the Ecclesiastical Commission had divided him from the Catholic body; as Sir Francis Leek put it, it was now clear that 'all the keys of Lancashire do not hang at the Earl of Derby's old girdle'.[5]

But the possibility of revolt in Lancashire must have caused great concern and, soon after the northern rising collapsed, the Chester

[1] *CRS*, LIII, 193, 230; Hughes, *Reformation in England*, III, 273n.
[2] *Salisbury MSS*, I, 433, 526–7.
[3] *CSPD*, Addenda (1566–79), 405.
[4] *Salisbury MSS*, I, 443, 445, 446; *CSPD* (1547–80), 347.
[5] *CSPD*, Addenda (1566–79), 159.

Ecclesiastical Commission moved against more Lancashire recusants and other Catholic offenders. In late March and early April 1570 a procession of seventeen new gentry offenders was called before the commissioners, for recusancy, failure to receive communion, having mass at home and harbouring papist priests; most were released on bonds, but William Singleton spent a short time in Chester gaol before he was released on grounds of 'vehement sickness'.[1] Also in April, the commissioners received their first concrete evidence that the emerging recusant movement was not confined to the gentry, and eight lesser men from the parishes of Blackburn and Ribchester were summoned; three of them had harboured yet more recusant priests, others were irregular attenders and non-communicants, and Robert Seede was a recusant and possessed 'a book called a *Catechism* made by Vaux, late warden of Manchester'.[2] Vaux's *Catechism* had been printed in Louvain in 1567 and this, together with Allen's visit to Lancashire in 1562–5, Vaux's mission to Rome, and the possession in 1571 of a copy of one of Harding's books by a conservative incumbent were early signs of dangerous links between Lancashire and the Continent. Another continental influence soon felt in the county was Pius V's bull 'Regnans in Excelsis', which was nailed to the door of the bishop of London's palace in mid May and apparently carried into Lancashire by John Westby.[3] In October 1570, Bishop Barnes of Carlisle reported that since the bull had been published things had gone from bad to worse in Lancashire; 'on all hands the people fall from religion, revolt to popery, refuse to come at church; the wicked popish priests cause them to abjure this, Christ's religion, and that openly and unchecked'.[4] The bull may have changed the attitude of the earl of Derby, for he stopped Anglican services in his household and was visited by popish priests and messengers from the Continent. In August 1570 the earl of Huntingdon reported that Lancashire Catholics confidently expected Derby to lead a rising, Cecil noted later that the earl had borrowed six or seven years' rent from his tenants, and Bishop Barnes and the Spanish ambassador thought there were widespread preparations for rebellion.[5]

Though Derby's role is uncertain, his sons had been considering revolt for some time. As early as 1566 Sir Thomas Stanley, the earl's second son, was offering to help Mary Stuart, and in the summer of 1570, after the tacit encouragement of the bull of excommunication

---

[1] CRO, EDA 12/2, fos. 126v–130v, 132v–133v.
[2] *Ibid.* fos. 130–132v.
[3] *Salisbury MSS*, I, 575–6.   [4] PRO, SP 12/74/22.
[5] *Salisbury MSS*, I, 575–6, XIII, 100; *CSPD*, Addenda (1566–79), 321–2; *CSPS* (1568–79), 277; PRO, SP 12/74/22.

and with Mary conveniently imprisoned at Chatsworth, a plot to free her was hatched. Sir Thomas, his younger brother Sir Edward, Sir Thomas Gerard and some minor Lancashire figures hoped to release her from Shrewsbury's custody and take her to the Stanley stronghold of the Isle of Man. The Spanish ambassador thought something on a larger scale was planned in Lancashire itself, and he may have been right; Bishop Barnes reported secret musterings and the preparation of arms and horses. There are hints that the Lancashire activists were hoping for the assistance of a Spanish invasion, and when this failed to materialise the Stanleys probably settled for a more limited exercise. But the plans, which could hardly have been concealed while a large-scale rising was being considered, soon leaked out, and the two Stanleys and Sir Thomas Gerard were summoned to Court and consigned to the Tower. It was an indication of the inadequacy of their plans that they timorously obeyed, but their cooperation was rewarded and they were released after little more than a token imprisonment. In view of the potentially dangerous situation in Lancashire and the unpredictability of the earl of Derby, the Council presumably decided not to make a serious issue out of a hare-brained scheme.[1]

These events, though they had come to nothing, merely underlined the failure of Bishop Downham's efforts in 1568, and it was at this point that, as we have seen, he was summoned to London for investigation. After the inhibition of Downham's authority, the diocese was visited by Bishop Barnes of Carlisle, on commission from Archbishop Grindal of York, and the visitation 'detecta' were handed over to the High Commission at York for proceedings to be taken against the more serious offenders. The visitation revealed a truly alarming situation in Lancashire. A total of 54 lay recusants, 40 of them gentry, was presented, over half of them from the deanery of Amounderness of which, as yet, little had been heard. In addition there were 23 known non-communicants and, most serious of all, 38 active recusant priests; a further 8 clergy, nominally within the Anglican Church, were presented for various Catholic practices and beliefs.[2] Only 11 of the 88 conservatives called to appear at York actually did so, and when the High Commission tried to attach the remainder only 2 could be found. Of the laymen presented, 16 were

[1] N. Williams, *Thomas Howard, Fourth Duke of Norfolk*, 99, 209–10, 212–14; *Salisbury MSS*, I, 503–18; *CSPS* (1568–79), 274, 277, 279, 281, 287, 436; *CSPD* (1547–80), 397; *Autobiography of an Elizabethan* (John Gerard), ed. P. Caraman, 1.
[2] BIY, R VII, HCAB 6, fos. 64–119. In the middle of the presentments of Catholics in the deanery of Blackburn, one folio, which had been part of the return, has been torn out, from between fos. 65 and 66; there were probably more detected recusants etc. than those we now know.

said to have been reconciled to Rome, 14 men and women were noted as harbourers of papist clergy, and there were details of Catholic masses, marriages and baptisms. Although the number of lay recusants presented was small compared with those detected in later years, the visitation shows the success with which Catholics had avoided and circumvented the Anglican settlement in the dozen years since its inception.

Though the preponderance of gentlemen in the returns, when we know the recusant clergy were living among and working with lesser men, suggests that only the most prominent recusants were detected, there will remain dispute over whether Bishop Barnes heard of all, or only a fraction, of the lay recusants. But there can be no doubt about the large number of recusant priests. The names of 38 working in the five southern deaneries of the county were given, and we know that there were others stationed further north who were not reported by name.[1] As a number of recent historians have seen English recusancy as the creation of the seminarians, it is worth emphasising the role of the recusant clergy. Henry Garnet, who, like other Jesuits, had difficulties with the old clergy and regarded them as little more than a stop-gap, nevertheless saw their importance; 'there were some bishops and very many priests who not only professed the Catholic faith themselves but also led back to the truth others who had strayed from it'.[2] Though one may wonder how much 'straying' had really taken place, the case of Lancashire suggests that Garnet was right for at least one area: a sizeable corps of Catholic clergy existed and was able to lay the foundations for a vigorous recusant community before the arrival of the seminary priests.

No fewer than 75 named recusant priests are known to have worked in Lancashire; at least 33 of them had once served the official Church in the county, and 22 of them had served briefly under Elizabeth, most of them withdrawing before the visitation of 1565. Others were prominent outsiders attracted to the area, such as John Ashbrooke, an Oxford M.A. and former fellow of Brasenose, and William Smith, a bachelor of divinity, who both worked in the Prescot area between at least 1568 and 1578,[3] and we have already noted the presence of the former dean of Christchurch and one of Bonner's chaplains. The earliest activists were at work by 1561, and the last 'old priest' at work to be named was Peter Jackson, who had been at Kirkby chapel in the early years of the reign but was saying mass at Crosby by 1567 and was chaplain to the Norris household at

[1] BIY, R VII, HCAB 6, fo. 64.
[2] P. Caraman, *Henry Garnet, 1555–1606 and the Gunpowder Plot*, 109.
[3] CRO, EDA 12/2, fos. 118–118v, 124; PRO, SP 12/48, fos. 84, 86; BIY, R VII, HCAB 6, fo. 88v; HCAB 9, fo. 174.

Speke until at least 1599.[1] The last references to an 'old priest', name unknown, were at Chipping and Bleasdale in 1604.[2] There were at least 31 recusant priests still working in Lancashire about 1580, when they outnumbered the newly arrived seminarians by more than two to one, and even about 1590 a quarter of the Catholic clerical staff of about 40 men was composed of 'old priests'.[3] Of the recusant priests, 21 are known to have served in Lancashire for more than ten years. Nicholas Bannester, who had been schoolmaster at Preston and was under surveillance by 1561, was reported active as a priest in 1568, in 1571 and 1578 he was in the Manchester area, and in 1586 he was seen near Warrington.[4] Evan Bannester, also of Preston, was a 'wanted' priest by 1568, and in 1570 he was in Mitton; by 1571 he was in the deanery of Amounderness, in 1580 he was still in the Fylde area, he is known to have said mass near Lancaster in 1586, and a year later he was in Preston.[5] James Darwen had withdrawn from his chaplaincy at Sefton by 1563, he was reconciled to Rome by Murren in 1567, he was working in Sefton and Ormskirk in 1578, and in 1586–7 he was in the household of Richard Blundell of Crosby in Sefton.[6] Examples could be multiplied, with Henry Duckson in central Lancashire between 1571 and 1592, Edward Howard in the Ribble valley between 1568 and 1590, Richard Smith in the Prescot area from 1568 until at least 1593, and Francis Stopford, who worked in the Fylde, Eccleston, Ormskirk and Wigan between 1571 and 1588, and had moved to Yorkshire by 1593.

Sometimes recusant priests lapsed into conformity. William Baines was curate of Caton from 1548, and in 1569 he was summoned before the High Commission, presumably for some conservative malpractice, but he left his post to avoid prosecution. By 1571 Baines was an active recusant priest in Amounderness deanery, but he later moved further north and was arrested in 1580 as 'a seducer of the people'. Dean Hutton of York persuaded him to attend Anglican services, and he eventually took communion; he died six years later, and as his will was proved at Richmond he must have

---

[1] PRO, SP 12/48, fo. 72v; *Salisbury MSS*, IX, 18.

[2] CRO, EDV 1/13, fos. 210v, 211, 224.

[3] N.B. This underestimates the old priests' contribution, because the *Douai Diaries*, giving dates of departure for England, and the official anxiety to catch them, make our information on the seminarians much more extensive.

[4] *CSPD*, Addenda (1547–65), 523; CRO, EDA 12/2, fos. 118–118v; BIY, R VII, HCAB 6, fo. 84, HCAB 7, fo. 52, R VI, A 7, fo. 37; BM, Harleian MS 360, fo. 32.

[5] CRO, EDA 12/2, fos. 118–118v; BIY, R VII, HCAB 5, fos. 7, 19, 81, HCAB 6, fo. 93; PRO, SP 12/175, fo. 232; BM, Harleian MS 360, fos. 32–33.

[6] CRO, EDV 1/3, fo. 33; PRO, SP 12/48, fo. 71; BIY, R VI, A 7, fo. 49, R VII, HCAB 9, fo. 172; BM, Harleian MS 360, fo. 32v.

conformed to the end.[1] Others were more steadfast. James Bell had
served the Anglican Church outside Lancashire for twenty years,
but in 1579 he returned to his native county and was reconciled to
Rome. He became an itinerant priest, and we know that he said mass
at Winwick in December 1583. But he was arrested in a drive against
recusants in January 1584, indicted at Manchester for denying the
royal supremacy, celebrating mass and being reconciled to Rome,
and was executed at Lancaster in April.[2] Thomas Williamson, who
had served as a recusant priest at Sefton since 1563, and Richard
Hatton, who had been working in Ormskirk and Prescot in 1578,
were taken at the same time as Bell, and were sentenced to life
imprisonment for denial of the supremacy.[3] By early in 1584
twelve priests were in custody in Salford gaol, all but one of them
recusant priests rather than seminarians. John Coppage, a former
fellow of Manchester College, had formed them into a 'college',
which presumably means that they followed a common devotional
life, and, as they exercised in a field behind the prison and spoke to
visitors through the gaol windows, Catholics were able, as Bishop
Chadderton complained, to 'receive both exhortations and absolu-
tions at their pleasure'.[4] James Stones, an old Durham priest, was
equally determined not to admit defeat. He was arrested at the house
of one of the earl of Derby's undertenants in 1585, complete with
Catholic books and massing equipment. Though he wished Elizabeth 'Nestor's years', he insisted that 'he thinketh her Majesty's
laws spiritual are not established according to God's laws'.[5]

One of the most dangerous revelations of the visitation of 1571 was
the support the recusant priests received from Anglican clergy.
Thomas Bland, rector of Whittington and rural dean of Lonsdale,
Kendal and Catterick, was 'supposed to have had mass lately said in
his house' and was 'a harbourer of runagate priests', while his curate
had similarly offended. Richard Dean, curate of Harwood, was
ordered that 'he shall not accompany, harbour nor relieve any
popish priests', and the vicar of Whalley 'harboureth papists'. None
denied the charges, and they were bound over to reform themselves.[6]
At this early stage it is unwise to draw too fine a line between
'recusant' and 'conservative' clergy, for there was a fifth-column
within the established Church willing to propagandise for Rome and

[1] *VCH*, VIII, 84; BIY, R VII, HCAB 4, fos. 113, 183; HCAB 5, fo. 19; HCAB 6,
fo. 93; HCAB 10, fo. 59v.
[2] *CRS*, V, 74–8; PRO, SP 12/167, fos. 123, 125, 12/168, fo. 34v.
[3] CRO, EDV 1/3, fo. 33; PRO, SP 12/48, fo. 71, 12/167, fo. 123; BIY, R VII,
HCAB 9, fos. 172, 174, R VI, A 7, fo. 49; *CRS*, V, 77–8.
[4] PRO, SP 12/120/21, 12/167, fo. 125; *Vaux's Catechism*, lxxvii; *CRS*, V, 46.
[5] PRO, SP 12/184, fos. 78–81.
[6] BIY, R VII, HCAB 6, fos. 64, 64v, 65v.

assist its priests. The Catholic clergy continued to receive recruits from within the Anglican fold. Christopher Thompson, presented to the rich rectory of Winwick in 1569, was evidently considered a promising young man, for in 1571 he was ordered by the High Commission to study so that 'he may be tried whether he be sufficient to be admitted to preach'. This encounter with officialdom may have worried him, for immediately after it he stopped performing services in his church. By 1574 he was said to have 'fled around disguised in apparel like a lay man', he 'divers and sundry times and at divers and sundry places taught unsound doctrine against the laws of God and this realm', and he was noted to 'frequent the company of notorious papists, uttering among them in secret with pernicious and papistical doctrine'. Thompson was removed from the rectory, and soon after he went to Douai to be ordained and returned immediately to be one of the first seminarians working in Lancashire.[1]

Throughout the 1570s the recusant priests provided a range of Catholic services for their followers. We know of masses at Whittington in 1571, Leyland in 1576, North Meols in 1577, and at Brindle, Croston, Wigan, Prescot, Preston and Bury in 1578; five priests were working in Prescot in 1578, and five laymen were said to have had masses in their homes.[2] There were Catholic weddings at Preston and Lytham in 1571, Manchester in 1578, and at Mitton in 1579, and Catholic baptisms at Blackburn in 1571, Preston in 1574, and Aughton, Whalley and Prescot in 1578; at Standish a midwife was presented at visitation because she 'goeth up and down the country with children to be baptised of popish priests'.[3] Catholic funerals were more difficult, for there was a conflict between the desire to have the traditional ceremonies and the desire to be buried in consecrated ground; in 1573 a recusant priest was buried in Whalley church in the middle of the night, apparently with no service at all.[4] The priests who provided these services served and were sheltered by a wide clientele, ranging from the prominent gentry families which became the backbone of local recusancy – such as, in 1571, Middleton of Leighton, Houghton of the Park, Ireland of Lydiate, Norris of Speke, Clifton of Westby and Rigmaiden of Weddicar[5] – to lesser figures. In 1571 Peter Carter, schoolmaster of

---

[1] *Ibid.* fo. 90; CRO, EDC 5, 1575; *Douai Diaries*, 117, 118, 260, 276; *APC*, x, 309.
[2] BIY, R VII, HCAB 6, fo. 64, HCAB 9, fos. 171–171v, 174, R VI, A 7, fo. 62, A 8, fo. 65; CRO, EDC 5, 1580; *VCH*, III, 294.
[3] BIY, R VII, HCAB 6, fos. 89, 92v, 110; HCAB 9, fo. 174, R VI, A 7, fos. 37, 47, 57, 58; LCL, RD/AC/1/4, No. 41; *Lancs. Chantries*, II, 206. It is difficult to agree with Dickens ('First stages of Romanist recusancy', 170) that clandestine marriages and baptisms were characteristic of seminarian-induced recusancy.
[4] *Chetham Miscellanies*, VI(1), 23–5.
[5] BIY, R VII, HCAB 6, fos. 69v, 86v, 87, 89, 91v.

Whalley, was 'privy with the roving priests', and a number of otherwise unknown men were receiving priests in 1571 and 1578. Roger Garnet's alehouse, somewhere in Blackburn deanery, was used as a base by recusant priests in 1571, and they were visited there by laymen. At Lawe in 1573 two former local curates who had become recusant priests stayed sometimes in the rooms they had used when serving there officially, and at Croston in 1578 William Wood was living at his own house; these men must have been concealed and assisted by local people.[1]

The 1571 visitation revealed a widespread and already well-established Catholic religious life; recusants certainly existed, and others, such as the five Blackburn men who had been reconciled to Rome but were as yet only non-communicants, were moving towards the same stand.[2] Of the 54 lay recusants presented, 40 were gentry and only 8 were women, which suggests that only the most obvious absentees from church were noted by wardens. The ineffectiveness of visitation makes it unlikely that these 54 represent anything like the sum total of recusants, and there was certainly a very much larger group than was reported. The strength of popular sympathy for the recusants, which protected them from presentment, is indicated by the inability of the authorities to track down any of the 38 priests whose arrest was ordered. In addition to the recusants, there was an indeterminate number of church-papists who had at least occasional access to the services of a priest; the total of 56 priests being sheltered and supported at this time suggests the extent of this group. Recusancy had existed for some time, and it is significant that the visitation which uncovered the scale of it was the first Elizabethan survey conducted with any intensity and by someone other than Bishop Downham. Thirteen of the gentlemen recusants had been proceeded against by the Chester Ecclesiastical Commission before the publication of the papal bull of 1570, and five of them had been charged in 1568. Of the recusant clergy, most of those whose earlier careers are known had left the Church by 1565, and nineteen of them were certainly active recusant priests by 1568. We can only conclude that recusancy began in Lancashire before the bull, before the northern revolt of 1569, and probably as a result of Laurence Vaux's mission of 1566.

The visitation of 1571 made clear the necessity of more intensive official activity in Lancashire, and in the following year the accession of Henry Stanley, called a 'passionate heretic' by the Spanish ambassador, to the earldom of Derby made such efforts possible.

[1] *Ibid.* fos. 67v, 77, 92, 114v, HCAB 9, fos. 169v, 174, R VI, A 7, fos. 58v, 62v; CRO, EDC 5, 1573.
[2] BIY, R VII, HCAB 6, fo. 114v.

After November 1570, when Bishop Downham was called up to London, the Chester Ecclesiastical Commission seems to have been passed over by the government, though in the next eighteen months it did proceed against 31 Lancashiremen and women for recusancy and non-communicating.[1] The centre of the anti-recusant campaign was now the York High Commission, which used the visitation return of 1571 as the basis for a concerted attack on the leading gentry recusants. Between the end of the visitation proceedings in November 1571 and October 1578, fourteen Lancashire gentlemen were called before the High Commission a total of more than 70 times, and poor John Rigmaiden had to appear on as many as 18 occasions.[2] Eight of the fourteen spent various periods in prison at York, but the Commission tried to vary its practice according to the character of the individuals concerned.

John Towneley was first called to York in July 1571, when he was dismissed until October, and when he appeared again he was bound over to receive communion and dismissed. Twelve months later he appeared according to his bond, but he had obviously not complied with instructions and he was sent to York Castle, where he remained until December. He was then sent to London in the hope that his half-brother, the dean of St Paul's, would be able to induce him to conform. Towneley reappeared at York in October 1573, but stated that despite Dean Nowell's efforts 'as yet he is not resolved in his conscience to communicate after the order in this realm established', and he was again imprisoned. In March 1574, after Nowell's intercession with the Privy Council, Towneley was released into the custody of a York citizen, but this leniency had no good effect and in December 1574 he found himself in prison once again. In July 1576 the Privy Council advised another dose of kindness, and he was released into the hands of a trustworthy Lancashire gentleman, but by October he was back in York and was transferred with other prisoners to the blockhouses at Hull. In April 1577 Dean Nowell again got Towneley freed on bonds, and by March 1578 he was in the dean's custody in London. As Towneley and Nowell both pointed out, his case was unusual, both in respect of the length and frequency of his imprisonments and in respect of the fact that he was not a recusant but a non-communicant. He was proceeded against not so much because of his own offences but because of his position. John Towneley was one of the wealthiest of the county gentry, and he was certainly by far the most prosperous

[1] CRO, EDA 12/3, fos. 2v–5v, 7, 13v–14v, 24v–26, 27, 28–28v.
[2] BIY, R VII, HCAB 6–9, *passim*. In this and the following paragraphs, references are, except where otherwise indicated, to these volumes, and can be found under the dates cited.

of the Catholics of the 1570s. The Council was much worried by 'his great power in the county', he had a household of 38, and his position as holder of several Duchy stewardships meant that 'he hath at his devotion great numbers of Her Majesty's tenants, which in a sort depend upon him'. It was clearly thought that if he could be broken it would be a great blow to Lancashire Catholicism.[1]

Cuthbert Clifton was first sent to York Castle in October 1571, as a recusant who was thought to have been reconciled to Rome, and as he refused to be examined on oath by the High Commission he was subjected to solitary confinement. In October 1572 he was allowed out of the castle for two months with a guard, for health reasons, but he was not freed from gaol until December 1573, after the death of his wife. His recognisances were regularly renewed until October 1574, when he was called back to confer with the dean of York, but Hutton's persuasions were fruitless and Clifton was again imprisoned. He was, however, released for a short time when he appealed to the Council that he needed to care for his children now that they had no mother. He was soon back in York, in the custody of one of the Commission's officers, until in November 1576 he was sent into Nottinghamshire to stay with a Lancashire gentleman who had lands there. His last appearance at York was in March 1577, when he was ordered to Chester to confer with one of the prebendaries, and thereafter he was allowed to return to his house at Westby.[2]

John Westby had also been put into solitary confinement in October 1571, though in July 1572 he was released from York Castle into the care of the recorder of Chester, where he was allowed to remain until April 1573 on a recognisance of £300. When he reappeared at York he asked 'to have a longer sparing for his coming to church', but the commissioners were not so easily outwitted, and when he refused to attend sermons in the Minster he was again committed to the castle. After three months in prison he was freed on heavy bonds into the custody of the archdeacons of Chester and Richmond at Chester, on condition that he did not visit his own house for more than two weeks in any half-year. Thereafter the High Commission troubled him no further.

The commissioners subjected this group of gentry to the maximum inconvenience and uncertainty. John Rigmaiden spent some time in prison and after he was released he was subjected to frequent journeys across the Pennines and increasingly heavy recognisances.

---

[1] *APC*, VIII, 170–1, IX, 157–8, X, 182, XII, 57; PRO, SP 12/118, fo. 104; *The Spending of the Money of Robert Nowell*, ed. A. B. Grosart, 360.
[2] *APC*, VIII, 299, where he is incorrectly given as 'Anthony Clifton'.

Thomas Catterall was sent to York Castle, and then to the household of the earl of Derby, while Edward Standish was not imprisoned but put into the custody of the sheriff of York. All those against whom this intense activity was directed had to find friends prepared to put up bonds for their release which eventually rose to £500; escape was therefore out of the question. In addition, attempts were made to break their local influence by keeping them out of the county. But despite its efforts the High Commission had very little success, and the men who were forced to conform did so only briefly. After a good deal of pressure Edward Standish finally agreed in November 1573 that despite his own conscience he would attend church if ordered to do so, and he was released into the charge of a Protestant J.P. Thereafter he was allowed to go free on recognisances but, on the expiry of one of his bonds in October 1574, he failed to make his usual appearance to certify his conformity. He lapsed into recusancy again, although he was able to avoid prosecution by moving between his estates in Lancashire and a house in Northamptonshire.[1] If the High Commission could not drive a small group of men under severe pressure into conformity, it would have little success with the county as a whole.

Official efforts in the 1570s seem to have been concentrated on these few gentlemen, but there were occasional attempts at wider harassment. In June and November 1574 Bishop Downham, the earl of Derby and the Lancashire members of the diocesan Ecclesiastical Commission were instructed to proceed against 'popish disorders' and those 'as are suspected to have reconciled themselves to the pope'. We do not know what action, if any, followed the June order but, when the second letter arrived, Downham finally bestirred himself. He compiled a list of 86 leading Lancashire recusants, whom he summoned to appear before the Ecclesiastical Commission; only 15 of them turned up and after persuasion agreed to conform, and the rest remained obstinate. In Lancashire the bishop confined himself to only four deaneries, of which the most dangerous were apparently Amounderness with 36 recusants and Blackburn with 29. The survey was not a complete census of recusants even in the four deaneries, for 66 of the 86 were gentry and their wives, while Warrington deanery, soon producing large numbers of recusants, had only 18 listed. Among those who failed to appear before the Commission when summoned were some of the leaders of county society: Sir John Southworth and his family, Lady Margaret Atherton, John Talbot, John Towneley and William Skillicorne. Downham concluded his report with a list of 10 Lancashiremen 'of

[1] BIY, R VII, HCAB 7, fos. 173, 178–178v, 202, HCAB 8, fo. 6; PRO, SP 12/118/48.

longest obstinacy against religion, who would be a good example if reclaimed'; 9 of them were gentry, 5 had been proceeded against in 1568, and 7 were among the 14 harried by the High Commission.[1] The authorities' campaign was producing few results.

Downham's next move against recusants was not until he was ordered by the Council in the autumn of 1577 to compile a return of recusants with an assessment of their wealth. Partly because of ill-health, the bishop's report was totally inadequate; only 54 recusants were listed, 3 of them were able to prove that they attended church, and the J.P.s who had to make up for the bishop's laxity by estimating the wealth of those listed were not impressed by his work. They found 'the matter so remissly handled' and noted that 'many others have been presented before us and other' for recusancy, while 'we hear an uncertain rumour of some lately revolted, who do not dutifully come to the divine service'.[2] Downham's list bears a close similarity to his return of February 1576, with many of the less important figures omitted; 45 of the 54 were of gentle rank, and most of those whose status was assessed by the justices were, in Lancashire terms, prosperous. Fourteen names had not been on the 1576 list, but five of these people lived in deaneries which had not been covered in the previous year; all those listed except three had already been proceeded against for recusancy. The bishop returned, in other words, only those names which could hardly be omitted, and his list represents nothing like a complete survey of recusants.

William Downham died in November 1577, and his departure might appear to have been followed by a rapid expansion of county recusancy. In fact, his death merely made possible the more intensive enquiries which revealed the widespread recusancy which had existed for some time. In July and August 1578 the diocese of Chester was visited, 'sede vacante', by Archbishop Sandys' commissaries. In Lancashire no fewer than 226 recusants and 29 noncommunicants and other church-papists were presented, and on the following 6 October 139 recusants and 15 non-communicants were called before the High Commission at York, of whom 78 recusants and 14 non-communicants had not been presented at the visitation.[3] A total of 304 recusants and 43 non-communicants had been detected, whereas in the visitation of Yorkshire, which Professor Dickens tells us was carefully conducted, only 32 recusants and 30 non-communicants were discovered.[4]

[1] *APC*, VIII, 258, 276–7, 302, 317; BM, Harleian MS 286, fo. 27, MS 360, fos. 67–68. [2] PRO, SP 12/118, fos. 103–104v, 111v–114v.
[3] BIY, R VI, A 7, fos. 34–103v, R VII, HCAB 9, fos. 168v–175.
[4] Dickens, 'First stages of Romanist recusancy', 182.

The emergence of recusancy

Though the number of recusants was dangerously large, there are good grounds for believing that many more went undetected. Seven parishes in the four deaneries which contained the largest recusant groups sent no representatives to the visitation, and four of them, Childwall, Kirkham, Leyland and Blackburn, were to return large numbers at later visitations. In 1580 Bishop Chadderton wrote that in the Fylde only fourteen or fifteen parishioners had attended each church in years past, but in 1578 only 45 recusants were reported in the parishes of St Michael's, Poulton, Garstang, Kirkham and Lytham.[1] The 12d absence fine had not been levied at twelve parish churches and probably an even larger number of chapels, while in the deanery of Warrington, later by far the most solidly Catholic in the county, the fine had been collected at only six of the ten parishes represented at the visitation. At Prescot it was said that 'the forfeiture is not levied, nor cannot be gotten of such as absent themselves from church', and further north at Lancaster in Amounderness it was admitted that the fine had never been imposed.[2] In these parishes there was no sanction to force the lower orders to attend church, and little attention was apparently given to the problem of recusancy.

Of the 304 recusants discovered in 1578, 42% lived in the deanery of Warrington, 24% in Amounderness, 16% in Blackburn, 8% in Manchester, and the rest were divided between the other deaneries. The distribution follows very closely the pattern of recusant priests working in the county in about 1570, when there had been 19 recusant priests in Warrington, 15 in Amounderness, 11 in Blackburn, 6 in Leyland, 4 in Manchester and one with an unknown area of operations. The visitation commissaries and the High Commission heard of 18 priests in five deaneries in 1578, 11 of them in the deanery of Warrington. Other sources give a total of 31 priests in the late 1570s, 14 of them in Warrington and the others fairly evenly distributed over the rest of the county. The clergy had been successful in instilling a true sense of recusancy into their followers; of 226 recusants cited to appear at the correction court only 41 did so, and only 6 of the 139 called before the High Commission turned up.[3]

It is usually suggested that widespread recusancy had been created by the seminary priests, but recusancy on a considerable scale existed in Lancashire by the middle of 1578 and this cannot have been the work of the seminarians. Only 44 priests had been sent into England by the end of 1577, and few of them had come to Lancashire. Evan Haydock had left Douai for England in February 1576,

---

[1] *CSPD*, Addenda (1580–1625), 11–12.
[2] BIY, R VI, A 7, fos. 37, 47, 48, 48v, 49, 49v, 55, 58v, 62, 62v, 63.
[3] *Ibid.* fos. 68–77, A 8, fos. 54–65v, R VII, HCAB 9, fos. 168v–175.

The emergence of recusancy

Christopher Thompson left in April 1577, and Richard Simpson set out in September 1577; these were the only seminarians to work in Lancashire who could have been in the county by the time the 1578 visitation took place.[1] The recusancy of mid 1578 was no newly created phenomenon. It is true that over half the recusants discovered in that year had not, as far as we know, been in trouble before,[2] but we are comparing the visitation of 1578 with one made seven years before, two lists by Downham which concentrated almost entirely on gentry, and the proceedings of the High Commission against a small group of particularly dangerous men. Almost all the gentry recusants presented in 1578 had been reported as dissidents earlier. We have already seen that by the late 1560s Lancashire was reputed to be the most conservative county in England, and its notoriety did not diminish later. In 1580 the state of the area was 'lamentable to behold', and in 1583 Lancashire was 'so unbridled and bad an handful of England'.[3] We are left, it seems, with an exceptional case: none of the counties most thoroughly studied, neither Hampshire nor Sussex in the south, nor Lancashire's neighbours Yorkshire and Cheshire further north, produced so much recusancy so soon; what made the palatinate so different?

The official answer stressed two points which were, as we shall see, to be reiterated with variations for the rest of the reign. First, the machinery of Church and state could not enforce religious change and detect offenders. It was noted, probably in 1583, that there was a shortage of J.P.s in the most dangerous areas, and there was a 'bad supply of the Church officers throughout all the country'; officials were lax and partial, and the activists lacked sufficient authority to carry out their task. Second, the Privy Council suggested in 1580 that 'this defection is principally begun by sundry principal gentlemen of that county, by whom the meaner sort of people are led and seduced'.[4] This, of course, begs at least part of the question, for why were the gentry so Catholic so rapidly? Historians might add what contemporaries were loth to say, that under the third earl of Derby and Bishop Downham negligence and conservative sympathy had given the recusant movement freedom to organise itself, but there was laxity in other areas too.[5] Part of the answer must lie in the weakness of early Elizabethan Protestantism,

---

[1] *Douai Dairies*, lxii, 24, 25.

[2] Although the records it produced are lost, there was a visitation, which detected recusants, in 1572 (CRO, EDA 1/3, loose leaf at fo. 24).

[3] PRO, SP 12/138/18; Peck, *Desiderata Curiosa*, 141.

[4] PRO, SP 12/120/21; Peck, *Desiderata Curiosa*, 85.

[5] R. B. Manning, *Religion and Society in Elizabethan Sussex*, xv, 23–5, 29–31, 47–50, 78–90.

for even in 1583 Lancashire was a county, as the Privy Council tactfully put it, 'where the Gospel as yet hath not been thoroughly planted'.[1] In a conservative area the reformed Church held few attractions, the clergy of the established Church were sympathetic to the recusant priests and, as the absence-fines were not collected, there was nothing to force conformity on any but the few troubled by the Ecclesiastical Commissions.

Another reason for the early recusancy of Lancashire can hardly be disputed; there was a large number of active recusant priests, who were able to work almost unhampered. But this too needs to be explained, and it is necessary to recall the position before, as well as after, 1559. The early Tudor Church in the county had exhibited some unusual signs of vigour, and the conduct of so many priests after the Elizabethan settlement becomes almost inexplicable unless one accepts this view at least in part. More immediately, it may be true that the considerable activity of Bishops Coates and Scott had revitalised the clerical body, so that a section of it found the new Church impossible to accept. It is significant that of all the clergy in the five southern deaneries of Lancashire *c.* 1570, 56 out of perhaps 160 were recusant Catholics, and at least 20 of the nominal Anglicans were practising conservatives. One of the priests most active in spreading Rome's views on church attendance, Laurence Vaux, had been a much respected warden of Manchester under Mary, worked as a recusant priest in the county and was, by 1566, in close contact with leading local Catholics.

However, the priests may have become recusants for less idealistic motives. A reformed Church needed a smaller clerical staff than traditional Catholicism, and there may have been a redundancy problem in the 1560s. Many of the clergy were unbeneficed men, dependent on the voluntary benefactions of the laity, but laymen may have been unwilling to pay the stipends of priests who could no longer provide mass, or the other Roman sacraments and prayers for the dead. Unemployed clergy may thus have been forced to provide as 'free-lancers' what they were not allowed to provide within the framework of the Elizabethan Church, while the laity gave them shelter and presumably money in return. Lay recusancy followed, perhaps, when laymen chose to follow the recusant priests who could supply the sacraments which led to salvation, rather than the unwilling conformists who peddled pale imitations. As Protestant opinion had made only a slight impact, the choice between the competing products was not a difficult one, and the benefits of the familiar Catholic brand outweighed even the disadvantages of abstention from the parish church.

[1] Peck, *Desiderata Curiosa*, 149.

The emergence of recusancy

A final, tentative suggestion might be made; despite current historical opinion, it is just possible that Lancashire was not an exception, merely an extreme case of what existed elsewhere, a sizeable, if largely undetected, recusant population. There were, after all, over 1,500 known recusants in England in 1577,[1] and the returns for other dioceses may have been as inadequate as that for Chester; Downham had listed 54 Lancashire recusants, but eight months later 304 were discovered. Even if the national figure represents something approaching the true number, one might wonder how many of them had been persuaded to recusancy by seminarians, when only 29 missioners had been sent to England by the end of 1576 and only 44 by the end of 1577. The argument that recusancy was created by seminary priests credits them with an instant impact that it is difficult to accept. If Catholics had conformed until the arrival of the missioners, if conservatism was almost dead by the mid 1570s, the successes of a handful of men in three or four years defy imagination. Either the conformist habits of half a generation were broken almost overnight, or the priests made new converts at an unbelievable rate. It might be doubted if the earlier visitation figures can be accepted, when the arrival of seminarians in Yorkshire seems to increase the number of recusants from 32 in 1578 to 329 (plus an unknown number in the Richmond deaneries which were not visited) in 1582. In addition, one might wonder why, when these so-effective new priests were trying hard to combat church-papistry, the number of non-communicants increased from 30 in 1578 to 151 plus in 1582 and 302 in 1590.[2]

The fundamental problem concerns the reliability of visitation returns as a guide to recusancy: it has already been suggested that the Lancashire reports were inadequate, and we shall return to this problem in the next chapter. For some areas it is difficult to accept Professor Dickens' contention that 'the character of contemporary parish life' made it difficult to conceal 'so public an offence as recusancy'.[3] This may have been true in small single-settlement parishes, but in large, especially northern, parishes with dispersed settlement and many chapels, recusants were extremely difficult to detect. The offence was not really 'public', since it involved a failure

---

[1] *CRS*, XXII, 9.

[2] Dickens, 'First stages of Romanist recusancy', 168–82. Dickens has rejected the 'negative evidence' that there was little Lollardy in Yorkshire, but accepted the 'negative evidence' that there was little recusancy. Though the Elizabethan sources are, certainly, much fuller than the Henrician, it is arguable that the acceptance and rejection should be reversed, on the grounds that popular hostility was greater towards heretics than recusants, so that the former were more likely to be presented and the latter were thus a larger number than the records suggest.

[3] *Ibid.* 159.

to perform an act rather than a public demonstration. Where the population of a parish was large, churchwardens could not know who was supposed to attend church, much less who did not. The efficient detection of recusancy required a regular parochial census combined with the weekly marking of a register, but in Lancashire at least this was not attempted until 1592, and then with only limited success.

Over time, and with determination, wardens might accumulate lists of those men to watch, and in time larger numbers of recusants might be presented, but this does not necessarily mean that recusancy had increased. The number of recusants detected reflects the intensity of the search: as James I told Parliament in 1621, 'I think there are more recusants discovered, but not that there are more indeed than heretofore.'[1] In the 1560s, and to a lesser extent in the 1570s, the Privy Council may have seen recusancy as a problem which would disappear with the death of the old priests, and if the recusants were left alone they really would go away. But the revolt of 1569, the bull of 1570 and the exiles' projects for invasion must have caused the authorities to think again. In the north, detection improved with the death of the third earl of Derby, the appointment of Huntington as Lord President and the nomination of Chadderton to the see of Chester. Finally, from 1575, the arrival of the seminarians and later the Jesuits who could sustain recusancy in the long term, completely altered official calculations. The early seminary priests may not have created recusancy, but they did frighten officials into tracking recusants down in the hope that the problem could be controlled. The executions of missioners, and official anxiety to catch them when the recusant priests had been little troubled, show the new sense of urgency; the higher presentments of recusants may reflect the same concern. It is not entirely coincidental, to continue with the Yorkshire example, that the number of recusants detected on visitation increased rapidly as soon as the High Commission abandoned its policy of dealing with selected gentry recusants and began in 1580–1 to seek out lesser offenders by means of local juries; over 400 were found.[2] Lancashire *may* have been an exception, but it is at least worth asking whether the peculiar influences stressed in this book were *really* so strong.

[1] Quoted in Magee, *English Recusants*, 101.
[2] Tyler, 'Ecclesiastical Commision', 251–60; BIY, R VII, HCAB 10, *passim*.

17

Recusants and church-papists

Though one may doubt whether the contrast between the 1560s and 1570s on the one hand and the 1580s and 1590s on the other was as marked as some have suggested, it is nevertheless true that there was a considerable expansion of recusancy after 1578. The most reliable of the visitations held after that date give the numbers of recusants detected in Lancashire, as shown in Table 1.[1] There are grounds for believing that the return for autumn 1590 was far too low: 600 recusants had been presented at quarter sessions in 1587, 800 had been indicted by February 1590, and in July 1590 the bishop of Chester was able to provide the Privy Council with a list of 700 Lancashire recusants.[2]

Table 1

Metropolitan	1578	304	recusants[3]
Metropolitan	1590	534	
Metropolitan	1595	481	
Diocesan	1596	724[4]	
Diocesan	1598	498[5]	
Diocesan	1601	754	
Diocesan	1604	3,516[6]	
Metropolitan	1630	3,433	

The visitations conducted by Bishop Chadderton in 1580–1, 1588, 1589 and 1592, that is, all the visitations held by him for which records survive, have been omitted from the table as inadequate, but a brief consideration of them will illustrate the weakness of visitations as a source for the enumeration of recusants. Though Chadderton was accused c. 1583 of over-friendliness with Catholic gentle-

[1] BIY, R VI, A 7, 8, 11, 12, 14, 15, 22; CRO, EDV 1/12a, 12b, 13; *CRS*, LIII, 70–86, 101–7.
[2] BM, Cotton MS, Titus B II, fo. 240, B III, fo. 65; *APC*, XIX, 337f.
[3] The recusants returned to the High Commission are included.
[4] This was not a visitation proper, but a survey conducted by visitation methods, i.e. churchwardens were asked for lists.
[5] The visitation return covers only five of Lancashire's eight deaneries, though the most Catholic are included.
[6] Only five deaneries.

men, and in 1590 he was rebuked by the Privy Council for inactivity,[1] he seems to have been a conscientious bishop and reasonably energetic in his pursuit of Catholics. But either his visitations were defective or he had a curious method of recording presentments of recusants. Despite the comprehensive set of articles compiled for his primary visitation of 1580–1, the surviving return lists mainly the inadequate provision of books in the churches and the poor repair of church fabric. It is true that various parishes had failed to list absentees, or had not collected the absence fines, or had lax churchwardens,[2] but it is curious that no recusants at all were listed. It is clear that Chadderton had recorded them separately, for in 1582 the government received from someone, presumably Chadderton himself, a certificate of 428 recusants in Lancashire, which was incorporated in a national survey also based on visitations.[3]

The visitation of 1588 raises similar problems; absentees had not been listed and fines were not collected at Ormskirk, the return for Leyland and Blackburn deaneries was very thin indeed, and only 4 recusants were listed in all.[4] The 1589 return lists only 17 recusants, again in a very thin set of presentments, and some ministers had failed to present recusants, but Chadderton reported to Walsingham that many recusants had been found and in mid 1590 he sent in a list of 700.[5] The visitation of 1592 is even more confusing for, in an extremely thorough visitation, the presentment of only 84 recusants, spread over four deaneries, is recorded; it is impossible to believe that after an underestimate of 534 in 1590 this represents the true position, but it is curious that so many were listed in the visitation 'detecta' if a separate survey of recusants was compiled. It is possible that in 1592 Chadderton encountered massive resistance from churchwardens, for no lists of recusants had been compiled at Prescot, the churchwardens of eleven churches and chapels failed to make presentments, and the wardens of sixteen churches and chapels had not collected the absence fines.[6] The historian who tried to write the history of Lancashire recusancy merely on the basis of Chadderton's visitations would reach some inaccurate conclusions.

The historian who assumed that even fuller visitation presentments provide a comprehensive coverage of recusants would also find himself in difficulties. It may be true that the visitation figures

[1] PRO, SP 15/27/94; *APC*, XIX, 340–1.   [2] CRO, EDV 1/6d, fos. 28, 28v, 29.
[3] PRO, SP 12/156, fo. 78. The Yorkshire figure was clearly taken from the visitation of 1582. Lancs. returned by far the highest number, 428 out of 1,939 in 23 counties.
[4] CRO, EDV 1/7, fos. 18v, 21, 24, 43.
[5] CRO, EDV 1/8a, fos. 60, 62, 1/8b, fos. 3, 5; *APC*, XVII, 309–10, XIX, 66, 337–8.
[6] CRO, EDV 1/10, *passim*. It is interesting that nine of the parishes which had not collected fines returned no recusants; if their wardens ought to have levied fines, this might imply there were recusants.

reflect the rate of increase of recusancy, but it cannot be assumed that they tell us how large the recusant community was. The effectiveness of visitation depended on the cooperation of local officers but, especially in the detection of Catholics, this was not always forthcoming. A group of Puritan ministers complained in 1590 that the gentry removed churchwardens who might present their offences, and we know that at Prescot the churchwardens were supervised by a group of local gentry dominated by Catholics.[1] In 1595 churchwardens were accused of 'colourable and cunning dealing', and were said to be 'infected with papistry, or placed by papists or their favourites of the baddest sort'.[2] Clergy, too, were not always diligent; in 1592 a renegade seminarian accused the incumbents of Sefton, Halsall, Croston and Preston of favouring papists and, though their parishes were in heavily recusant areas, few recusants were presented there in 1590 and later numbers were very much larger.[3] It was reported at the visitation of 1590 'that Mr Smith, vicar of Kirkham, doth bear with the recusants', and twelve months earlier the Privy Council had complained that 'the ministers do not in their several cures present them as they are by the statute prescribed'.[4] Other ministers may have been terrorised into inactivity; a paper was thrown into the rector of Wigan's pew which threatened to punish him for his persecution of Catholics, and especially for presenting fellow-townsmen on visitation.[5] Where there was a shortage of clergy, the corps of men available to detect offenders was small.

Even for the most conscientious, parochial conditions made the presentment of recusants difficult. Parishes were too large and populations too high for wardens to maintain any real check on attendance, so that families who were discreet about their absence might pass unnoticed. The conviction of a recusant required not simply that he be proved not to have attended his parish church, but that he had not attended *any* church,[6] and in the Lancashire situation this was extremely difficult. In 1570 Robert Morley admitted he had not attended Blackburn church, but claimed to have been to Langho chapel or Whalley church;[7] it was difficult to check a story such as this. Many who claimed to attend other churches were merely evading their duties; in 1578 the churchwardens of

[1] *State Civil and Ecclesiastical*, 9; Bailey, 'Churchwardens' accounts', II, 15–16.
[2] *Kenyon MSS*, 584.
[3] PRO, SP 12/243, fo. 223. The conservatism of two can be substantiated from other sources, and the others were negligent pluralists.
[4] BIY, R VI, A 11, fo. 77v; *APC*, XVII, 309–10.
[5] BM, Harleian MS 286, fo. 254; cf. *State Civil and Ecclesiastical*, 9–10.
[6] PRO, SP 12/136/16, fo. 4v.
[7] CRO, EDA 12/2, fos. 134v–135v, 12/3, fos. 4v–5v.

Middleton presented seven men from Oldham, Prestwich and Bury who 'being neigher their church than their own will rather lie abroad under some hedge or some such-like place after they have showed themselves once in the church than abide in the church the service time'.[1] These men were not, in fact, recusants, but any Catholic prepared to use a little ingenuity might well evade detection, or at least conviction. Large parishes also meant the additional complication of chapels, and it was always difficult to be sure whether men were absentees from the parish church or were attending chapels. In 1601 the churchwardens of Winwick reported that they 'have not levied 12d for absence by reason there are three chapels at least in the parish'.[2] When chapels were not served, recusancy was even easier, and the Puritan clergy complained in 1590 that 'most of the people refrain their parish church under pretence of their chapels, and having no service at their chapels come at [none] at all; but many of them grow into utter atheism and barbarism, many enjoy full security in popery and all popish practices'. It is not possible to show that the parishes with unserved chapels were those of the highest recusancy, as where there were no clergy there were no presentments at visitation. But there does seem to have been a general correspondence between recusancy and lack of clerical provision. Excluding Lonsdale, a poor area and one with, apparently, only a small recusant problem, the deaneries can be listed in order of the proportion of their chapels which had no ministers in 1610, that is, Warrington, Leyland, Blackburn, Amounderness and Manchester, an order which coincides almost exactly with the order of deaneries by the proportion of recusants in the population. The contrast between Warrington and Manchester, the deaneries with most and fewest recusants, is clear; in 1610 ten of Warrington's nineteen chapels had no minister, but only two of Manchester's nineteen were not provided for. When Baldeston chapel in Blackburn was not served in 1630, it was said to be 'the cause of the increase of popery'.[3]

The fundamental flaw in the visitation procedure was that it could cope only with minority problems. Where there were large numbers of recusants and no considerable anti-Catholic feeling, it was easy to avoid presentment. The outsiders who thought the whole county was Catholic[4] were exaggerating, but experienced local observers thought a substantial section was recusant or at least church-papist. A detailed report of *c.* 1590 pointed out that the churches were sparsely attended, in 1591 Chadderton's secretary wrote that as

---

[1] BIY, R VI, A 7, fo. 39.   [2] CRO, EDV 1/12b, fo. 142.
[3] *State Civil and Ecclesiastical*, 11; *Kenyon MSS*, 7–13; BIY, R VI, A 22, fo. 62v.
[4] e.g. *CSPS* (1568–79), 12, (1587–1603), 185.

many people went 'to places suspected in religion' as to parish churches, and in 1592 the Council remarked upon 'the great multitude of offenders in the said case generally in that shire, which was almost overflowen with a multitude of obstinate persons, offending publicly in the sight of the world'.[1] Paradoxically, in the 'least Catholic' areas recusants were likely to be presented at visitation, while in the 'most Catholic' districts detection was easier to avoid. The low presentments of recusants in the deanery of Manchester were much more accurate than the high presentments of Warrington and Amounderness, and the difference between them is therefore magnified. Though the Lancashire visitations, as a whole, did return remarkably higher numbers of recusants than those of any other part of the country, the county was also even more solidly recusant than, from the individual returns, it would appear to have been.

Visitation could only be made to work by vigorous effort at the local level. Prescot was a particularly difficult parish to supervise, covering 58 square miles, eight administrative divisions, fifteen townships, three chapelries and, in 1604, 2,000 communicants. The leading gentry were Catholic, and Bishop Vaughan described it as 'one of the most affected parishes in Lancashire, and most haunted by seditious priests'. The late-Elizabethan vicar was Thomas Meade, 'a bachelor of divinity, a diligent preacher', who was a noted anti-Catholic and moderator of the deanery exercise.[2] In 1592 only six recusants were presented at visitation, and the bishop warned the wardens to be more diligent in the listing of absentees. Chadderton apparently suggested specific improvements, and under Meade's leadership the wardens conducted a census of parishioners; at church services they crossed out the names of attenders, thus leaving the absentees.[3] Though the procedure was not adopted for the metropolitan visitation of 1595, it made a considerable difference thereafter. In 1590, when the parishes of Warrington deanery presented an average of 12 recusants each, Prescot had returned 18, but in 1598 Prescot presented 99 against an average of 21, in 1601 Prescot listed 184 to an average of 24, and in 1604 the average was 119 but Prescot's return was for 569 recusants.

The case of Prescot suggests that in the Catholic areas of Lancashire the number of recusants detected reflects not so much the incidence of recusancy but the effort put into finding them. The clergy's vigour in seeking out recusants depended partly on their theological standpoint: we have seen that conservatives reported few recusants, while Puritans were presumably the most anti-Catholic of

---

[1] PRO, SP 12/240, fo. 292, 12/235, fo. 146; *APC*, XXII, 369–70.
[2] *CRS*, LIII, 146; PRO, SP 12/175, fo. 41, 12/243, fo. 223.
[3] *Prescot Accounts*, 117–19, 127, 134–5; CRO, EDV 1/10, fo. 123v.

Table 2

	No. of parishes		No. of recusants		Average no. of recusants per parish		Recusants as a proportion of total population	
Visitation	I	II	I	II	I	II	I	II
1590	10	19	263	161	26	8	1:76	1:141
1601	11	18	393	267	36	15	1:57	1:77
1604	11	18	2,269	1,203	206	67	1:9	1:17

(Each column I gives figures for parishes with Puritan incumbents, a man being counted Puritan if he was proceeded against repeatedly for failure to wear the surplice and either was also in trouble for failure to comply with the rubrics of the Prayer Book or signed one of the Puritan manifestoes. Column II gives figures for the other parishes in the three deaneries. Population is calculated from the 1563 return of households. There is no evidence that Puritans were deliberately presented to the difficult cures; the Crown and ecclesiastical patrons were, for example, no more likely to present Puritans than others. Nor is there evidence that Puritans were more likely to secure wealthy parishes, in which population density might have been higher and Catholics may have hoped to find concealment easier.)

all. In 1590 a group of Puritan ministers claimed to have been used to detect recusants by the Ecclesiastical Commission, and their supporters asserted that the ministers had been active preachers against Catholics, a claim repeated in 1602.[1] To test if the Puritan clergy were more likely to detect recusants than their less-advanced colleagues, three 'high return' visitations of the 'Catholic' deaneries of Warrington, Leyland and Amounderness were studied, and the returns for parishes with Puritan incumbents compared with the presentments for other parishes. The results are indicated in Table 2. Puritans were very much more successful, on average twice as successful, in finding recusants than were other incumbents, but there seems to have been nothing to distinguish 'Puritan' parishes from the others except the views of their incumbents. Visitation returns of recusants may tell us more about the theology of the clergy than they do about the distribution of recusants. It is possible that if all parishes had had Puritan incumbents, or if all incumbents had been as eager to detect Catholics as were the Puritans, something closer to a full return of recusants might have been achieved. If non-Puritans had found recusants at the same rate as the Puritans, there would have been 754 recusants presented in the three deaneries instead of 424 in 1590, 1,044 instead of 660 in 1601, and 5,974

[1] *Kenyon MSS*, 597–9; *Salisbury MSS*, XII, 142.

instead of 3,472 in 1604. It can never be assumed that the number of recusants detected at visitation represents more than a part of the true number of recusants in the county.

Although there may be grounds for suggesting that Lancashire visitations were even more defective than those of other areas, they nevertheless show that the county was by far the most Catholic in England. In 1604 Yorkshire was reckoned to have 2,454 recusants and non-communicants, who represented about 0.8% of the total population and perhaps 1.2% of communicants.[1] The Lancashire visitation of 1604 revealed 4,037 recusants and noncommunicants, or 4% of the population, and 6.2% of communicants.[2] In Prescot, where the machinery for detecting recusants was operated efficiently, there were 682 recusants and non-communicants out of about 2,000 people of communicating age, perhaps 34% of the total.[3] An official return of 1603 estimated that well over a quarter of the known recusants in England and Wales lived in the diocese of Chester, and by 1641 9,000 of the 15,000 recusants on the subsidy rolls were Lancashiremen. James I wrote in 1617 that 'at our first entering to this Crown and Kingdom we were informed, and that too truly, that our county of Lancaster abounded more in popish recusants than any other country of England': his informants had been right.[4]

The core of Lancashire recusancy was surrounded by a fluctuating body of 'temporisers', church-papists, non-communicants and fair-weather Catholics, and the recusant household with an 'occasional-conformist' head seems to have been common among the gentry.[5] It is difficult to estimate the size of this crypto-Catholic group. Table 3 gives the numbers of non-communicants detected at various visitations compared with the number of detected recusants. In view of the comments which have been made on the efficiency of visitation, it is impossible to make any dogmatic statements, for the detection of those who missed one out of probably three services in a year was even more difficult than the detection of regular absentees. At each visitation one or two parishes returned a large proportion of the non-communicants presented; in 1595 70 of them were from Child-wall, in 1601 280 were from Prescot, and in 1604 166 were from Wigan and 113 from Prescot. This suggests that the recording of

---

[1] Dickens, 'First stages of Romanist recusancy', 179; A. G. Dickens, 'The extent and character of recusancy in Yorkshire in 1604', *YAJ*, XXXVII; H. Aveling, 'Some aspects of Yorkshire Catholic recusant history', *Studies in Church History*, ed. G. J. Cuming, IV, 111.
[2] The 1563 population was *c.* 90,000; for 1604 I have assumed a population of 100,000 with 65,000 communicants.
[3] CRO, EDV 1/13, fos. 132–142v; *CRS*, LIII, 146.
[4] Magee, *English Recusants*, 93; *Manchester Sessions*, ed. E. Axon, xxiv.
[5] PRO, SP 12/175, fos. 41–41v, 12/235, fo. 7v, 12/240, fos. 292–293v.

Table 3

Visitation	Recusants	Non-communicants
1578	304	29
1590	534	97
1595	481	233
1598	498	277
1601	754	349
1604	3,516	521
1630	3,433	65

non-communicants was generally neglected, except in the parishes with energetic incumbents, for the parishes which returned the highest numbers of non-communicants were normally those which returned most recusants. The nearest we are likely to get to a full census of church-papists is a return of 1613, which reported 2,075 recusants and 2,392 non-communicants, and it is probable that there were normally at least as many conforming Catholics as recusants.[1]

It may be, however, that the crypto-Catholic group was very much larger. Though a much more substantial proportion of the population was recusant in Lancashire than in any other area, the horror with which contemporaries regarded the county was hardly justified if, as the returns of 1604 and 1613 suggest, only 6% or 7% of the adult population was Catholic. In the three or four deaneries with the largest numbers of recusants, where there were normally at least half as many Catholic clergy as there were Anglicans, the prevailing opinion was probably Catholic. John Gerard, who did not think highly of his Lancashire co-religionists, wrote that in the 1590s very many of the people were Catholic, though they practised their religion only when it was safe to do so. Richard Cowling, a Jesuit who worked in the county, wrote in 1600 that 'Catholics are so numerous that priests can wander through the villages and country-side with the utmost freedom', and he thought that there was not a single 'heretic' in his area.[2] When the preaching of Protestantism, at least outside the deanery of Manchester, was so unsatisfactory, it might even be surprising if the majority of the people in the other deaneries were not at best mere conformists and at worst, from the official point of view, sympathetic to the Catholic cause. It is probably true that this 'non-recusant Catholicism' had been eroded by the Civil War, but it possibly existed on a considerable scale late in the reign of Elizabeth.

[1] Magee, *English Recusants*, 87–8. Cf. Dickens, 'Extent and character', 44–8.
[2] *Autobiography of John Gerard*, 32–3; P. Caraman, ed., *The Other Face*, 121.

276

Recusants and church-papists

How far it is justifiable to consider these conservatives as Catholics is, however, another question, and Dr Bossy has suggested that we ought to regard Catholics as 0% of the population of England in 1570 and thereafter count as Catholics only those claimed for recusancy by the seminarians. This view assumes a radical distinction between non-recusant 'old' Catholicism and a seminary-based Counter-Reformation brand,[1] and the Lancashire case provides little substantiating evidence. The available records tell us little of the interior religious life of the Catholic community, but there is no sign of conflict between the recusant clergy and the seminary priests, and the transition from pre-Tridentine to post-Tridentine religion seems to have taken place gradually and with little difficulty. The occasional conformists cannot be dismissed as mere conservatives when many of them received the ministrations of papist clergy and, as the visitation returns are normally inadequate, many of the apparent conformists may in fact have been recusants.

There was no sharp dividing line between recusants and church-papists. In 1595 there was a large body of Catholics in the Fylde who were recusants for most of the year but who conformed for a few weeks before each assize to escape prosecution.[2] John Gerard was probably right that many in the county were recusants when this was easy, and conformists when the position was more difficult, and most of them could never have been returned as recusants. In 1603–4 a proportion of those who had hitherto been non-communicants became recusants, or 'revolters since the beginning of His Majesty's reign', when it was widely expected that James I would grant toleration; the number of known recusants increased from 2,000 to 3,500 in a little over eighteen months. Late in 1604 there were roughly 3,500 recusants and 500 non-communicants, but by 1613 there were 2,000 recusants and 2,400 non-communicants, and it looks as if most of the 'new recusants' slipped back into limited conformity when persecution became a little more intense.[3] It seems from the large numbers who attended masses that many more than the detected recusants regarded themselves as Catholics,[4] and where we have lists of mass-attenders few of them had ever been presented as recusants. Thomas Burscough was arrested in 1604 while preparing to celebrate mass, and when 29 members of his congregation were brought to trial all but 3 of them agreed to attend Anglican services. Bishop Vaughan alleged in 1604 that he had 'reclaimed' more than 600 recusants in three years, and in 1605 at the spring

[1] Bossy, *English Catholic Community*, chs. 1, 6, 8.   [2] *Kenyon MSS*, 585.
[3] See below, pp. 330–1, and especially CRO, EDV 1/13, fos. 113v–114, where non-communicants and 'new recusants' are classed together.
[4] See below, pp. 292–3.

277   10-2

assizes 52 of the 56 recusants tried agreed to conform.[1] But when recusants conformed by attending church it was unusual for them to take communion,[2] and if conformity had been anything more than a temporary expedient, the Catholic body would have dwindled away instead of expanding.

Lancashire, then, was at the end of Elizabeth's reign by far the most Catholic county in England. This was partly because of the very slight impact Protestantism had made on the palatinate in the first two-thirds of the century. But the new religion had made no more promising strides further north, in Cumberland, Westmorland, Durham and Northumberland, which, nevertheless, with the exception of some parts of Northumberland, did not become recusant strongholds. Unsullied late-medieval Catholicism did not lead automatically to recusancy, and recusant and seminary priests never capitalised on the Anglican failure in the far north. In Lancashire, however, real efforts were made by Catholics to preserve their faith, and it is necessary to examine how the county was transformed from one of the least Protestant areas into one of the most positively Catholic and recusant.

The foundations of this thorough-going Catholicism had been laid early in the reign of Elizabeth. The Catholic tradition of the county had never been broken, but had been kept alive by the recusant clergy, so that the seminarians could build upon existing allegiances and did not have to create a whole new Catholic community. Though one would properly wish to ascribe the extent of county recusancy to the efforts of the missionary priests, it must be recalled that the first seminary was founded by a Lancashire-born exile in 1568, and that many of those who worked in Lancashire as seminarians had been recruited to Douai before the missioners themselves made any real impact on the shire; one-sixth of those who had entered Douai by 1584 came from Lancashire.[3] Early recusancy provided recruits for the seminaries, as is conveniently illustrated by the career of Laurence Yate, who was schoolmaster at Burnley between at least 1571 and 1578 and at Blackburn from *c.* 1584 until 1592 or 1595.[4] His house was described in 1592 as one of the worst in the county and, though he was officially recognised as schoolmaster at

---

[1] C. Dodd, *Church History of England*, ed. M. Tierney, IV, xcv; *Salisbury MSS*, XVI, 144–5; *CRS*, LIII, 147.

[2] e.g. PRO, SP 12/143, fo. 19.

[3] *VCH*, II, 54 and n.

[4] *Spending of the Money of Robert Nowell*, 356; BIY, R VI, A 7, fo. 52, A 14, fo. 33v; Stokes, *Records of Blackburn Grammar School*, I, 48, III, 393. It is curious that Stokes, and Beales in *Recusant History*, VII, 285, date Yate's 'Catholic' influence to his period at Blackburn in the 1580s, when several of his protégés had entered Douai earlier.

Burnley in 1578, he had already been a Catholic for some time. Yate, his wife, his daughter and a maid were recusants, and he and the maid were instrumental in sending at least nine young men who later became priests to Douai and Rheims; five of his ex-pupils had been received into the seminary by mid 1580.[1] The recusant clergy persuaded into recusancy several of the gentry families which were to provide sons, shelter and money for the seminarians. Christopher Southworth, Edward Osbaldeston, James Standish, Alexander and Gilbert Gerard, Thomas Hesketh, George Hathersall and John Worthington were all Elizabethan seminary priests whose gentry families were recusant by 1578. Christopher Southworth was recruited for Douai in 1579, when Thomas Worthington, one of the first of the Lancashire-born missioners, persuaded Sir John Southworth to allow his son to go abroad. By 1593 at least 32 sons of Lancashire gentlemen, most of them from early recusant families, had gone to the Continent without royal approval.[2]

In the last quarter-century of Elizabeth's reign, Lancashire attracted more than its quota of seminary priests, because the area was a fairly safe one in which to work and the prospects of success were so high. The *Douai Diaries* give the names of 452 missioners sent into England by the end of 1603, and perhaps as many as 66 of them worked at some time in Lancashire.[3] Some of these served in the county because they had been born there, and in the reign of Elizabeth probably 70 natives of the palatinate were ordained abroad, a larger total than for any other county except Yorkshire. About 25 Lancashire recruits returned to work in their native county, and in 1598 it was said that most of the priests serving in the north had been born in Lancashire or Yorkshire.[4] The county was normally well supplied with missioners, and in 1600 the Privy Council complained that 'there is more plenty in that county than in any other part of the realm'.[5] In 1580 there were probably 14 seminarians active in Lancashire, rising to 23 in 1585 and 29 in 1590; there may then have been a decline in the number of working priests, with a series of arrests, and we know of only 24 in 1595, 22 in 1600 and 16 in 1605. Thereafter there was a recovery, and there were 28 priests in the county in 1610; by 1639 there were 30 seculars, 23

[1] PRO, SP 12/240, fos. 228–231v; *Douai Diaries, passim.*
[2] PRO, SP 12/199, fo. 9; BM, Harleian MS 7042, fo. 164.
[3] I have been helped in this and other calculations by G. Anstruther, *The Seminary Priests*, but I have expanded and sometimes corrected his biographies. The true figure may be nearer 60, as some names are aliases and a few men may have been counted twice.
[4] *Salisbury MSS*, VIII, 152.
[5] *APC*, XXX, 321.

Benedictines and 25 Jesuits.[1] A more complete indication of the clerical staff is given by adding the recusant clergy, and this provides figures of 56 in 1570, 55 in 1580, 39 in 1590, 24 in 1600, 28 in 1610 and 78 in 1639. There was something of a shortage in about 1600, and in 1604 one local seminarian was contemplating forging letters of ordination for a young student he had converted, so that the student could 'go amongst Catholics in places unknown and there practise the priesthood, as and if he had been beyond the seas to take orders there'.[2] But with this exception there was usually a reasonable supply of priests, and they were fairly successful in evading detection; of 66 seminary priests only 26 had been arrested by 1605, and the remainder worked undisturbed.

Some priests reached Lancashire through Ireland or Tynemouth,[3] but others landed on the south coast, made their way to London and then were guided north by Lancashire laymen.[4] Within the county, too, strangers needed guides; in 1596 a priest was taken from place to place in the Fylde by a local recusant, and in 1604 James Bradley of Chipping was 'reported to be a leader of priests to men's houses'.[5] Though there were many official complaints that local officers were insufficiently diligent in their searches for missioners,[6] escape routes were also necessary and, when forced to flee, priests went north to Furness and then by boat to Scotland, Ireland or the Isle of Man, or through Cumberland into Scotland.[7] Within the county the priests were well organised and, from his arrival late in 1582 until his defection in 1592, the lead was taken by Thomas Bell, jocularly referred to as 'bishop of Chester'. He operated mainly in the Wigan area, but he knew of 93 households over the whole county where seminarians could find shelter and help.[8] The missioners had no difficulty in finding bases in Lancashire; in 1587 25 houses notorious for receiving priests were reported at quarter sessions, and in 1604 there were 13 households sheltering priests in the parish of Poulton alone.[9] During the reign of Elizabeth no fewer than 157 households are known to have received priests, 52 of them in Warrington deanery and 39 in Amounderness.

Missioners in Lancashire could be particularly effective, for they

---

[1] I have assumed continuous Lancashire service for those only known to have worked there, from their arrival in England to the last reference to them. See G. Anstruther, 'Lancashire clergy in 1639', *Recusant History*, IV.   [2] PRO, SP 14/8/33.
[3] *Salisbury MSS*, X, 30, 203; PRO, SP 12/266, fo. 40.
[4] *Salisbury MSS*, IV, 428; PRO, SP 12/243, fo. 223; *CRS*, V, 79–81.
[5] *Salisbury MSS*, XIII, 600; CRO, EDV 1/13, fo. 211.
[6] PRO, SP 12/240, fos. 292–292v, 295–295v; *APC*, XIX, 155–6.
[7] *CRS*, V, 180–1, 221; *CSPD* (1598–1601), 538, Addenda (1580–1625), 321–2; *APC*, XXIII, 365–6.
[8] PRO, SP 12/215, fo. 190; BM, Harleian MS 360, fo. 32; *CRS*, LIII, 123–5.
[9] BM, Cotton MS, Titus B. II, fo. 240; CRO, EDV 1/13, fos. 198v–199.

were not forced to depend on support from the gentry. Richard Cowling, as we have seen, reported that priests could work openly in some areas and, where secrecy was not essential, the clergy did not need to hide away in gentry households. Of the houses known to have sheltered priests, 65 certainly did not belong to gentlemen, and in 1604 three priests working in the Wigan area stayed at the homes of seven common people and provided regular masses for congregations which seem never to have included gentry.[1] Though itinerant clergy often lodged briefly in the houses of individual gentlemen, few seem to have become resident domestic chaplains, and even those who did, like Cowling, also provided the sacraments for local people. Later, the Benedictine Ambrose Barlow first used Thomas Tildesley's house in Leigh as his base but, though he continued to use its chapel for some of his masses, he soon found it more effective to work from the home of a poor family.[2] With widespread local support the missioners could afford a measure of confidence, and in 1591 they actually challenged the Anglican preachers to a disputation.[3] But the seminarians continued the work of the recusant priests rather than founding a new Catholic movement. The arrival of the missioners did not lead to a sudden expansion of recusancy, and though about 13 Douai priests were in the county by the latter date the 304 recusants presented in 1578 increased only to 428 by 1582. Campion's brief visit to Lancashire in 1581, which some have thought worked Catholic wonders, made little impact; he restricted his contacts to a group of gentry families, and he regarded the county as a safe retreat in which to finish *Decem Rationes* rather than an area still to be converted to recusancy.[4]

Many contemporaries identified the insidious influence of Catholic gentry as a central reason for the extent of local recusancy, and a group of Puritan clergy in 1590, the bishop's secretary in 1591, the earl of Derby in 1592 and an anonymous correspondent in 1595 all agreed on this score.[5] Officials were afraid of the influence of prominent Catholics, and efforts were made to keep recusant gentlemen out of the district. In 1573, 1578 and 1584, John Towneley was deliberately excluded from the county, as was Sir John Southworth in 1584, and in 1598 it was hoped that the Blundell family would at least be kept out of Sefton.[6] Attention was frequently

[1] PRO, SP 14/8/31, 33, 34.
[2] Caraman, *The Other Face*, 121; *Chetham Miscellanies*, II(2), 3–5, 10.
[3] PRO, SP 12/235, fo. 146, 12/240, fo. 292v.
[4] *Ibid.* 12/156, fo. 78; Strype, *Annals*, II(2), 359; *APC*, XIII, 184–5, 256–7.
[5] *State Civil and Ecclesiastical*, 3; PRO, SP 12/235, fo. 146; BM, Lansdowne MS 72, fos. 125–125v; *Kenyon MSS*, 584–5.
[6] *APC*, VIII, 170–1, X, 182, XII, 57; Peck, *Desiderata Curiosa*, 151–3; *Crosby Records*, xi–xii.

concentrated on gentry Catholics, and after the visitations of 1578 and 1590 it was the gentlemen recusants who were called before the High Commission as well as the correction court.[1] In 1580 Bishop Chadderton reported that the Ecclesiastical Commission intended to proceed against the gentry recusants because the commons depended upon them and, in February 1584, 50 of the 59 recusants prosecuted by the Commission were gentry.[2] The motive for attacking gentry was partly financial, for they could be fined more profitably, and imprisoning the poor merely increased the cost of the gaols.[3]

There was always a considerable group of gentry families which could be classed as 'Catholic'; in about 1590, 74 of the 129 families listed at the herald's visitation of 1567 and 65 of the families listed in 1613 were Catholic.[4] A survey of the deanery of Warrington *c.* 1591 gave 10 heads of gentry families as convicted recusants and another 43 as church-papists, while only 15 could be classed as 'soundly affected'.[5] Even if one applies the more rigid standard of recusancy, a difficult road for the gentry, 41 of the families of 1567 fell into this category in 1590, and in 1596 149 of the 724 known county recusants were from gentry families. A very much higher proportion of gentry families were Catholic in Lancashire than in, for example, Yorkshire.[6] The religious affiliation of some families was altered when Crown wards were educated as Protestants, and each drive against recusants produced a crop of those who agreed to conform, but the body of recusant gentry was whittled away only slowly, and there were still 114 gentry recusants in 1641.[7] Those who pledged conformity normally became church-papists and, though husbands might conform, recusant wives often brought up recusant children.[8]

Catholic gentlemen could make an important contribution to the number and the religious life of their co-religionists, especially as in the more difficult areas and periods their houses were the only ones large enough to conceal priests and masses. At Prescot in 1582 the

[1] BIY, R VII, HCAB 9, fos. 168v–175, HCAB 11, fos. 296–309.

[2] *CSPD*, Addenda (1580–1625), 11–12; PRO, SP 12/168, fos. 34–34v.

[3] Peck, *Desiderata Curiosa*, 118–19, 120–1, 136–7; *APC*, XIII, 279–80, XVIII, 278.

[4] Here 'Catholic' means that either the head of a family or a substantial number of its members occur in visitation or other official lists as recusants or church-papists.

[5] PRO, SP 12/235, fos. 6–8.

[6] *CRS*, LIII, 70–86, 101–7; Aveling, 'Aspects of Yorkshire Catholic recusant history', 117–18; Cliffe, *Yorkshire Gentry from the Reformation to the Civil War*, 188–9.

[7] J. D. Cosgrove, 'The position of the recusant gentry in the social setting of Lancashire', University of Manchester M.A. thesis, 1964, 190–2; K. J. Lindley, 'The part played by Catholics in the English Civil War', University of Manchester Ph.D. thesis, 1968, 26. Cf. Yorkshire, with only 116 gentry recusants at the same time, despite its much greater size.

[8] *Kenyon MSS*, 584–5; Bossy, *English Catholic Community*, ch. 7.

household of Richard Bold, Esq, was used by a recusant priest as a mass-centre, and a number of local people attended the services while the rest of the parish went to church. In the following year a series of priests took shelter in the house of John Rigmaiden of Garstang, where they said mass and were visited by other Catholics. Edward Norris' home in Childwall was used as a base by two priests in 1599, and strangers came to the house at night.[1] Dr Bossy has suggested that for security reasons such gentry households became religious 'closed shops', and in Lancashire entire households might be presented as recusants. In 1587 most of the Southworth household of half a dozen members of the family and more than thirty servants attended regular masses on the estate.[2]

The authorities were worried by the influence Catholic gentry might have on their tenants. Bishop Vaughan thought in 1600 that Catholic gentlemen in Warrington deanery were so powerful that their tenants dared not conform, and in 1604 he wrote that the 'persuasion' of 'backward landlords' was a reason for the heavy recusancy of Prescot.[3] On the Blundell estate at Crosby there were said to be only Catholic tenants in the seventeenth century, and the rate at which recusant burials took place at a Catholic cemetery there suggests that there was something in this.[4] But if the tenants of Catholics shared their landlord's religion it was less because they were coerced than, as Vaughan realised in a more thoughtful moment, because the landlords were able to protect them from the persecution which drove others to conformity. There is some evidence that recusants were thicker on the ground in parishes where there were more Catholic gentry; in the thirteen 'most Catholic' parishes there were, on average, three Catholic gentry families in each in 1590, but an average of two in each of the others.[5]

But in a county where, outside the deanery of Manchester, persecution was never severe, the role of the gentry was of less significance than in more dangerous areas. In 1596 gentlemen formed the highest proportion of the Catholic body in those areas where recusancy was least strong; 10 of the 16 recusants in Manchester deanery were gentry, but in Warrington deanery only 71 of the 443. The same was true in 1641, when the proportion of gentry to

---

[1] PRO, SP 12/153, fo. 121; Peck, *Desiderata Curiosa*, 143; *Salisbury MSS*, IX, 18.
[2] Bossy, *English Catholic Community*, ch. 7; CRO, EDV 1/12a, fos. 114, 114v, 1/12b, fo. 146v; H. Fishwick, *History of St Michael's-on-Wyre*, 152; *CRS*, LX, 38–9; BM, Harleian MS 360, fos. 32v–33.
[3] *Salisbury MSS*, X, 160; *CRS*, LIII, 146.
[4] *Cavalier's Notebook*, ed. T. E. Gibson, 52–4; *Crosby Records*, 41–2, 69ff.
[5] *Salisbury MSS*, X, 153–4. For the 'most Catholic' parishes, see below, pp. 318–19. Gentry families are those given in the 1567 herald's visitation.

other recusants was 1:5 in Manchester deanery, 1:38 in Amounderness and 1:64 in Warrington. Between 1596 and 1641 the numbers of recusant gentry in each deanery remained remarkably stable, but the total number of known recusants multiplied by more than six times. In Manchester deanery, where Protestantism was strongest and there was a substantial number of non-Catholic gentry, common Catholics were driven into conformity, leaving their Catholic landlords as lonely islands in a sea of Protestant opinion. Elsewhere, popular Catholicism was able to survive without the protection of Catholic landlords and, though the absence of gentlefolk from church was much more noticeable, they formed only 2½% of the recusants listed in 1641.[1] In the chapelry of Farnworth in 1604, only 15 of 208 recusants were of the gentry and all were minor figures, while the fourth earl of Derby, certainly no Catholic, had a good deal of trouble from recusants on his estates in Warrington deanery.[2] Poulton, Chipping, Ribchester, Eccleston and Huyton managed to become some of the 'most Catholic' parishes in Lancashire with only four Catholic gentry families between them. The incidence of recusancy owed much more to geography than to the protection of gentry families.

It would, of course, be absurd to suggest that the existence of prominent Catholic families did not assist Lancashire recusancy. The inactivity of the authorities in the 1560s must in part be ascribed to the conservative inclinations of the third earl of Derby, while Catholics had outnumbered reformers on the commission of the peace by 19 to 6. Though the situation improved later, many of the fourth earl's leading servants and advisers were at best church-papists, and many of the most frequent guests at his table were Catholics.[3] His successor was in close touch with recusants and exiles, who hoped for his conversion and put him forward as the Catholic candidate for the throne.[4] Many of the officers of the palatinate of Lancaster were Catholic in sympathy, and in *c.* 1592 complaints were made against the prothonotary, the clerk of the Crown, the clerk of the peace, the vice-chancellor's deputy and one of the receivers. The most dangerous case was that of Thomas Walmesley, one of the justices who held the assizes at which recusants were to be convicted; his father had been an obstinate recusant, he himself was 'not thought a Protestant', his wife was a recusant and in 1590 he

[1] Calculations based on *CRS*, LIII, 70–86, 101–7, and Lindley, 'Part played by Catholics in the English Civil War', 26. Cf. Dickens, 'Extent and character', 33–6, 40–2.
[2] *CRS*, LIII, 148–9; *APC*, XIX, 337, XXII, 369.
[3] PRO, SP 12/175, fo. 41v; BM, Cotton MS, Titus B. II, fos. 239–240, Harleian MS 286, fo. 133v; *Stanley Papers*, II, 22a, 41–83.
[4] *CSPD* (1591–4), 39–40, 519, 534, 546–7; *Salisbury MSS*, IV, 461–3, V, 58–9.

tried to switch the attention of the assizes from recusancy to Protestant nonconformity.[1]

There was always a substantial section of the commission of the peace which was less than trustworthy. In 1583 the working justices included three recusants, fourteen church-papists and eight men with Catholic families. An anonymous report of *c.* 1588 listed thirteen J.P.s who conformed themselves but had Catholic families and were 'intelligencers to the papists', and in about 1592 only five of the twelve justices in Warrington deanery were reliable and two of these were inactive.[2] In 1587 12 of the 50 justices on the commission of the peace were removed, but the earl of Derby's conservative advisers provoked him to resist, and some of the excluded were reinstated.[3] Although nineteen or twenty men who in normal circumstances would certainly have been justices did not have office in the 1590s, the chancellor of the Duchy was unable to form a commission which did not contain some Catholics, and as late as 1598 14 of the 43 working justices were church-papists, and another 10 had close relations who were recusants.[4]

The Privy Council, Bishops Chadderton and Vaughan, the registrar of the Ecclesiastical Commission, local clergy and anonymous correspondents, were unanimous in their opinion that the Lancashire J.P.s were not enforcing the laws against recusants.[5] In 1583 Chadderton remarked that 'the temporal magistrates will do nothing', in 1586 the vicar of Prescot noted that 'they that have the sword in their hands under Her Majesty to redress abuses among us suffer it to rust in the scabbard', and in 1590 it was reported that 'the number of justices of the peace within that county are but few that take any care in the reformation thereof'. In 1599 the Privy Council thought that recusancy was increasing, and argued that this was 'for want of due severity and by remissness of the government both civil and ecclesiastical in those parts'.[6]

This failure resulted from the number and distribution of justices as well as the composition of the commission of the peace. Despite a massive expansion in the reign of Elizabeth the commission remained far too small, and there was a severe shortage of justices in some hundreds; in Amounderness the combination of few justices

---

[1] PRO, SP 12/235, fo. 9; BM, Harleian MS 360, fo. 67, Lansdowne MS 31, fo. 12, Additional MS 48064, fos. 68–69.
[2] *THSLC*, XCV, 131–3; PRO, SP 12/240, fos. 293v–294, 12/235, fo. 6.
[3] BM, Cotton MS, Titus B. II, fos. 239–240; Lansdowne MS 53, fos. 178–179.
[4] Calculated from *Lancashire Quarter Sessions*, vi–vii.
[5] *APC*, XIII, 320, XXIX, 648–9, XXX, 321; PRO, SP 12/235, fo. 146, 12/240, fos. 292–293v, 295–295v; *Salisbury MSS*, X, 84, 153–4; *State Civil and Ecclesiastical*, 13.
[6] *CRS*, V, 46; F. A. Bailey, 'Prescot Grammar School in Elizabethan times', *THSLC*, LXXXVI, 4; BM, Cotton MS, Titus B. III, fo. 65; *APC*, XXIX, 606–7.

and many recusants was especially dangerous, and J.P.s had to be drafted in from more reliable areas to assist.[1] The Council was also worried by the number of inactive justices, whose laxity stretched resources and threw a heavy load onto the conscientious minority. In 1583–4 10 of the 40 active J.P.s attended only one or two of the twenty quarter sessions held in thirteen months, while three of the four most frequent attenders were church-papists.[2] Negligence was serious enough, for the inability of the established Church to gain converts made effective coercion essential, but there is also evidence of deliberate obstruction by justices. The Council protested in 1582 at the 'slackness and partiality' of J.P.s in their presentments, and in 1590 the rector of Wigan reported that justices omitted their friends among the recusants from returns.[3] Some J.P.s had fictitious grants of land from recusants, so that the property of those convicted could not be sequestered, and the justices then handed over the income from the estate to the recusant owners; others warned recusants when searches were to be made.[4]

The inevitable result of ineffective administration and widespread Catholic sympathy was that the sanctions which ought to have enforced conformity were only haphazardly applied. There was no consistent campaign against the recusants, and serious efforts were made only in 1580, 1584, 1590, 1592, and 1598, when the Privy Council insisted on action and the bishop of Chester or the earl of Derby exercised close supervision over lesser officers. To illustrate the ineffectiveness of persecution, the anti-recusant drives which seem to have been the most vigorous, those of 1580 and 1592, will be considered in as much detail as the evidence allows.

The 1580 campaign took place before the recusancy statute of 1581, so that prosecutions were undertaken by the Ecclesiastical Commission rather than the secular courts. A new Commission had been appointed in the early summer, with instructions to proceed against gentry recusants in particular, but there was an information leak, probably from conservative commissioners, and some of those sought were able to escape.[5] Between July 1580 and August 1581 the Commission held twenty sessions, and to assist in the detection of offenders local juries were empanelled. Though the jury system seems to have been a success in Yorkshire, it failed in Lancashire,

[1] Long, 'Wealth of the magisterial class', 2–3, 41–2; *Lancashire Quarter Sessions*, viii; PRO, SP 12/120/21, 12/282, fo. 170; BM, Cotton MS, Titus B. II, fo. 240.
[2] Peck, *Desiderata Curiosa*, 111–12, 114; *THSLC*, xcv, 131–3.
[3] Peck, *Desiderata Curiosa*, 114; BM, Additional MS 48064, fo. 68.
[4] PRO, SP 12/240, fo. 293v; Cosgrove, 'Position of the recusant gentry', 91.
[5] Peck, *Desiderata Curiosa*, 85, 87–8, 106–7; PRO, E 134/25 Elizabeth, Trinity No. 5, m. 1, SP 12/240, fos. 293–294. Information-leaks of this kind seem to have been common (*ibid.* 12/240, fo. 293, 12/282, fo. 170v, 12/266, fo. 40).

and nineteen gentry called to serve as jurors refused to do so and had to be fined for contempt. Bishop Chadderton reported that, of the recusant gentlemen who appeared, a minority agreed to attend Anglican services, but none was prepared to receive communion; a larger number refused to conform, and even more failed to appear before the Commission when summoned. During its year of intense activity, the Commission imposed 193 fines, but 178 of these were for contumacy in failing to appear before the court; more than four-fifths of those fined were later presented for recusancy. The Commission also imposed 41 conditional fines, in the hope that the accused would conform to avoid payment; there is no record of payment and all were said to have conformed, though almost all the 41 were in trouble again for recusancy. The first major effort against Lancashire recusancy had made a limited and temporary impact, and by 1582 the number of known recusants had risen to 428.[1]

The recusancy statute of 1581, which involved quarter sessions and assizes in the prosecution of offenders, ought to have led to considerable improvements in the campaign against Catholics. But there remained flaws in the procedure which was supposed to lead inexorably from the detection of an offender, through presentment, indictment, trial and conviction, to his punishment. We have seen that there were major faults in the main means of detection, the visitation, but not even all of those who were detected were ever presented to the secular courts. Chadderton thought that only half the recusants were presented at quarter sessions, and until 1590 there was no formal system of forwarding lists of recusants to the assize justices. Clergy and churchwardens were not always called to make presentments at quarter sessions, and the conservative ministers of heavily Catholic parishes made thin returns or none at all.[2] Attempts to supplement ecclesiastical presentments from secular sources proved abortive, as J.P.s failed to make adequate presentments: the constables of West Derby hundred made none until 1599, and in the most conservative areas few recusants were reported.[3] When a recusant had been presented at quarter sessions or assizes he could not always be indicted, for churchwardens often failed to supply the full details of absences which were needed; in 1590 over half the recusants presented at the autumn assizes could not be

[1] PRO, E 134/25 Elizabeth, Trinity No. 5, mm. 1–6, 10–11; Peck, *Desiderata Curiosa*, 89, 94; Tyler, 'Ecclesiastical Commission', 254–5; PRO, SP 12/143, fos. 19, 32v, 12/156, fo. 78.
[2] Peck, *Desiderata Curiosa*, 112–13; *APC*, XVII, 309–10, XIX, 335–7, 340–1; PRO, SP 12/240, fo. 292; BM, Harleian MS 360, fos. 32–33.
[3] *APC*, XIII, 320; *Prescot Accounts*, 130ff; *Lancashire Quarter Sessions*, 92–3; PRO, SP 12/167, fo. 123.

indicted for this reason.[1] In addition, the partiality and laxity of sheriffs, justices and juries, meant that only a minority of those presented were ever indicted; 600 recusants were presented in 1587, but in the time available only 87 could be indicted, and in 1590 only 126 of the 700 recusants presented were indicted.[2] There was even a gap between indictment and trial, and in 1590 it was estimated that only one in fifty of those indicted came to trial, 'for that the better sort of recusants are so linked into kindred and find so great favour at the hands of Her Majesty's officers', and 'the better sort of persons are passed over with silence and the poor sort only drawn to question'.[3] We are prevented by the loss of the Elizabethan assize records from checking statements such as these, but a number of commentators held similar views, and such figures as we have suggest that the majority of those indicted avoided trial; in 1605, for example, 600 recusants were said to have been indicted, but only 85 were actually tried. Those who were brought to trial could not always be convicted, for it was difficult to find juries which would convict Catholics, and in 1625 the chancellor of the Duchy complained that 'divers of very mean rank and quality', who might easily be intimidated, were used as jurors.[4] Finally, not all those recusants convicted were ever punished; penalties imposed were subject to 'remiss execution', and convicted recusants fled or went into hiding.[5]

The most intensive drive took place in 1592, but, despite the most promising opportunity the anti-Catholic campaign ever had, the expansion of recusancy was only temporarily halted. In February 1592 the earl of Derby instructed J.P.s to arrest all persistent recusants; the wives and daughters of knights and esquires were to be placed in the custody of reliable gentry, and all the rest were to be imprisoned. Some of those arrested were closely questioned on the activities of seminarians and Jesuits by the earl himself, but the enquiries did not lead to the detection of priests. Though he received congratulations from the Privy Council, the earl had achieved very little; soon, after disorders at a recusant funeral and during church services, the queen was complaining that the leniency of officials was allowing recusancy to increase.[6]

---

[1] F. X. Walker, 'The implementation of the Elizabethan statutes against recusants, 1580–1603', University of London Ph.D. thesis, 130–43; PRO, SP 12/167, fo. 123; BM, Additional MS 48064, fos. 68–69.

[2] BM, Cotton MS, Titus B. II, fo. 240; *APC*, XIX, 335–40; BM, Lansdowne MS 64, fo. 21.

[3] BM, Cotton MS, Titus B. III, fos. 65–65v.

[4] *Salisbury MSS*, IX, 398–9, XVI, 144–5; *Kenyon MSS*, 31.

[5] In the 1596 survey 37 recusants were 'fugitives' (*CRS*, LIII, 70–86, 101–7); see the case of William Blundell in 1598, *Crosby Records*, 23–4.

[6] *Kenyon MSS*, 603; *APC*, XXII, 325–6, 369–70, 529, XXIII, 64–5, 110–11.

The instructions for the arrest of recusants were therefore reiterated, and then, late in August, a potential disaster struck Lancashire
Catholics. Thomas Bell, the priest responsible for the organisation
of a network of 'safe houses' for the clergy in the county, surrendered himself to the authorities and offered to conform. Bell was
dispatched to London, where he provided the Council with information on seminarians, recusants, Anglican clergy sympathetic to
Rome and, most dangerous of all, temporising households which
had been able to shelter priests in comparative safety.[1] On the basis
of these revelations, a list was compiled of 16 men who were to be
sent up to London for examination, and 30 men and 16 women to be
detained in Lancashire, while Bell himself was sent north to act as
Derby's adviser on the execution of the new orders. The raids took
place in November. Sir John Southworth's house was ransacked but,
though an altarcloth, candlesticks, images and several Catholic
books were found, there were no priests there.[2] Many of those
arrested in the searches were examined by Derby, and the most
dangerous – such as William Blundell, Henry Lathom, Miles
Gerard and Edward Eccleston – were sent to London; others were
dispatched to Lancaster gaol, and recusant widows were imprisoned
in Radcliffe Tower.[3] The manouevre had, however, been of limited
success, for after Bell's defection the Catholics had been on their
guard, warning was given of the raids, and many of those on the lists
of wanted men escaped; several priests fled temporarily into
Cumbria.[4]

All this activity produced very little. Although 800 recusants were
presented at the assizes in 1592, only 200 of them were indicted and
only 11 ever paid recusancy fines.[5] Those taken to London gave
away no useful information, and one by one they were released from
custody.[6] Some remained in Lancaster gaol, but conditions there
were not onerous and Bishop Vaughan later complained that 'prisoners' were allowed to go hunting, hawking and racing, and they
even carried arms in the streets of the town.[7] In the middle of 1593
several of the women held at Radcliffe Tower were released for
conferences with ministers, but they immediately disappeared and

---

[1] *Ibid.* 163–4, 227; PRO, SP 12/243, fo. 223; BM, Lansdowne MS 72, fos.
125–125v; *CRS*, LIII, 123–5.
[2] *Salisbury MSS*, IV, 240–2; *CSPD* (1591–4), 283; *CRS*, LX, 37–41.
[3] *Crosby Records*, 22–3; Strype, *Annals*, IV, 261–2; *CRS*, LX, 42–3; *Salisbury MSS*,
IV, 265–6; *CSPD* (1591–4), 288; *APC*, XXIII, 354–5.
[4] PRO, SP 12/240, fos. 229f; *CSPD* (1591–4), 288; *APC*, XXIII, 365–6.
[5] PRO, SP 12/235, fo. 9; Walker, 'Implementation of the Elizabethan statutes
against recusants', 317, 366.
[6] *Crosby Records*, 23; *CRS*, LX, 42–3; *APC*, XXIV, 110–11.
[7] *CSPD* (1598–1601), 14–15; *Salisbury MSS*, XI, 123.

could not be traced.[1] Some of those brought before the assizes had agreed to conform, and during the winter of 1592–3 many seem to have done so, but by 1595 their 'conformity' amounted to a few appearances at church before each assize to avoid prosecution. If we can place any reliance on the visitation returns, this enforced conformity may explain the fall in presentments of recusants from 534 in 1590 to 481 in 1595, while non-communicants increased from 97 to 233. But there is probably nothing in this for, in the parishes which returned large numbers of non-communicants in 1595, recusancy had increased rather than fallen since 1590. If the regime made even minimal gains they were soon eroded, and the episcopal survey of 1596 provides a salutary comment on the effectiveness of the persecution: the number of detected recusants had risen to 724.[2]

The most serious failure, in 1592 and throughout the reign, was the inability of the authorities to track down Catholic clergy. We know of perhaps 145 recusant priests, Jesuits and seminarians who worked in Lancashire under Elizabeth, but only 42 of them were ever arrested. The attitude of Sir Richard Sherburne, a justice of the peace and member of the Ecclesiastical Commission, was probably typical; he was reported to have said 'that if he were so disposed he could easily apprehend massing priests at his neighbours' houses, but he would ransack no man for his conscience'.[3]

The most heavily Catholic deaneries in Lancashire, where persecution was lightest, provided a haven of comparative safety for recusants and priests. In 1577, Durham recusants fled into Lancashire to escape from Bishop Barnes' visitation, and in 1595 and 1600 fugitives from Yorkshire were concealed in Lancashire. At one stage it was complained, with some justification, that the Lord President of the North would never be able to control his area 'so long as Lancashire shall remain unreformed'.[4] In 1591 Roger Ashton, who had been taken on his way back from obtaining a marriage-dispensation in Rome, managed to escape from the Tower into Lancashire, and his brothers were able to conceal him and smuggle him out of the country despite an intensive search by the earl of Derby. In 1600 six seminarians escaped from Wisbech and fled into Lancashire; though Robert Nutter was taken the others remained free, and Christopher Southworth worked in the county until 1612.[5] By 1599, Vaughan thought, Lancashire Catholics were so well

[1] *APC*, XXIV, 281, 334–5, 361.
[2] PRO, SP 12/240, fos. 229f; *Kenyon MSS*, 585; *CRS*, LIII, 70–86, 101–7.
[3] PRO, SP 12/240, fos. 295–295v.
[4] Strype, *Annals*, II(2), 108; *Salisbury MSS*, V, 98, X, 154; PRO, SP 12/240, fo. 293v.
[5] *APC*, XX, 356–7, XXI, 127–8; Anstruther, *Seminary Priests*, 260, 328.

organised that they could not be taken by surprise, and we hear of surprisingly large gatherings which were not spotted by the authorities. John Gerard saw masses in the county attended by 200 people, Richard Cowling implied similar numbers, and in 1598 a group of priests held a series of revivalist meetings, at which they claimed to cast out evil spirits, and attracted large crowds. In the deaneries of Warrington, Amounderness and Leyland, where over half the gentry and several J.P.s were at least sympathetic towards Catholics, it was possible to pursue a separate religious life with only occasional harassment; John Gerard, who ministered in the harsher school of East Anglia, thought it was too easy to be a Catholic in Lancashire.[1]

Those who wished to do so could obtain the traditional rites of passage without difficulty and, except perhaps about 1600, the clerical staff was always sufficiently large for Catholics in central and south-west Lancashire to be within easy reach of a priest. At Kirkham in 1590, 16 couples were known to have had their children baptised illicitly, at Garstang in 1601 there had been at least 8 Catholic christenings and 6 marriages and in Prescot in the same year there were 25 secret baptisms and 11 weddings.[2] If, as was alleged, nothing was done to suppress these ceremonies, it was probably because some J.P.s preferred to have their own children baptised and married by priests. It was even possible for a poor man to have a full religious life outside the framework of the established Church; it was said in 1588 that Ralph Mercer of Walton had not attended his parish church or received communion, he and his wife had been married in secret, and their children had been baptised illicitly.[3]

In some deaneries a Catholic education could be obtained without undue difficulty. In Elizabethan Lancashire, 42 schoolmasters, of whom 34 worked in the deaneries of Warrington or Amounderness, were either presented as recusants or reported to be operating Catholic schools, and we know of another nine Catholic schools with unknown masters. No fewer than 27 schools are known to have been in existence between 1585 and 1595, and a group of ministers complained in 1590 that the youth of the county 'both of the gentry and of the common sort' were educated by Catholics; about the same time an anonymous report protested that the young were taught 'by such as profess papistry'. Where persecution was light, school-masters were not driven into the houses of the gentry, and only 18

[1] PRO, SP 12/266, fo. 40; *Autobiography of John Gerard*, 32–3; Caraman, *The Other Face*, 121; *Salisbury MSS*, VIII, 213–14, 293.
[2] BIY, R VI, A 11, fos. 73–73v; CRO, EDV 1/12b, fos. 151v–152v, 187, 187v.
[3] PRO, SP 12/240, fos. 292v, 293v; CRO, EDC 5, 1588.

of the masters were domestic tutors to the children of gentlemen.[1] At Prescot, where the Catholic gentry tried unsuccessfully to prise control of the grammar school from the reformist vicar, the people were, as the vicar complained, 'all unwilling to bring their children near to the church, lest happily they should be allured to love the Church and to have a liking of true religion, and therefore some of them have kept in their houses private schoolmasters corrupt in religion, who have taught their children the principles of papistry'. Prescot Catholics were served by a succession of four Catholic masters between 1578 and 1604, and none of them seem to have been mere family tutors.[2] Other heavily recusant parishes, such as Ormskirk and Warrington, provided work for a number of Catholic schoolmasters.[3] Papistical books were available to supplement a formal Catholic education. Edward Rishton seems to have established a network for sending books into Lancashire, and in 1583 300 copies of Vaux's *Catechism* were shipped in through a north-east port for sale in the palatinate. Gentry families such as the Blundells and the Southworths were able to accumulate libraries of recently-published recusant literature.[4]

Attendance at mass was crucial to the practice of the Catholic religion, and given the number of priests in Lancashire this must have been possible with fair frequency. In 1580, when a group of 60 people was arrested for attending mass, it was said locally that if the queen wished to proceed against all mass-goers 'she would have to imprison all the country'. In 1583 three or four masses each day were said in the Allen household at Rossall, a little later there were regular masses at the Worthingtons' in Standish, and in 1586–7 several priests were providing masses at Samlesbury, on the estate of Sir John Southworth. A Jesuit working in the county reported in 1600 that on Sundays and ordinary feast days 30 or 40 received communion at his masses, and on the important festivals only a selection of those who wished to attend his services could be admitted.[5] At the feast of the Purification in 1603, a mass was held in

---

[1] *State Civil and Ecclesiastical*, 3; PRO, SP 12/240, fo. 292. My figures are based mainly on A. C. F. Beales, 'Biographical catalogue of Catholic schoolmasters', *Recusant History*, VII, supplemented from visitation records.

[2] Bailey, 'Prescot Grammar School', *THSLC*, LXXXVI, 10; BIY, R VII, HCAB 9, fo. 174; *Lancashire Quarter Sessions*, 9; *CRS*, XVIII, 185; PRO, SP 12/243, fo. 180; CRO, EDV 1/12b, fo. 145, 1/13, fos. 132v–133.

[3] For Ormskirk, BIY, R VII, HCAB 9, fo. 172; Beales, 'Biographical catalogue', 269, 271; PRO, SP 12/175, fo. 41v; for Warrington, BIY, R VI, A 8, fo. 64v; PRO, SP 12/243, fos. 180–180v; *CRS*, LIII, 124; Beales, 'Biographical catalogue', 271.

[4] *APC*, XIII, 184–5, XIX, 310–11; *Vaux's Catechism*, lxxix; *CRS*, LX, 39f.

[5] Caraman, *The Other Face*, 93, 121; Allen, *Letters and Memorials*, 181; PRO, SP 12/175, fo. 41v; BM, Harleian MS 360, fos. 32v–33.

the house of John Linacre in Widnes, at which as many candles 'as a man would carry' were burned and 100 people 'reported to his house'. Early in 1604, three priests were working quite openly in Winwick, Wigan and Prescot, providing masses in private houses; about Shrove Tuesday a mass in Winwick was said to have been heard by 40 people, 4 of whom were named, in the middle of Lent a mass was said for 60 people, 8 of them named, and the Good Friday mass, which raised a collection of £4 for the celebrant, was attended by more than 100 people, 22 of them named.[1] Tudor Englishmen quoted numbers in cavalier fashion, but attendances at mass were clearly large on occasions and it is worth noting that these examples have been chosen from those which were not interrupted by pursuivants and which were, as far as we know, not followed by prosecutions.

Though in the relaxed atmosphere of Lancashire relations between Catholics and their non-Catholic neighbours were never bad, and though county recusants never became an exclusive and introspective group, there is evidence that the practice of an illegal religion was forging bonds of community between Catholics. The leading conservative families, the Sherburnes, Towneleys, Southworths, Ashtons, Standishes and Heskeths, were already inter-related, and efforts to marry within the faith created a network of relationships. Family ties played an important role in the creation and survival of recusancy; William Allen was related to many of the recusant families in the Fylde, and Sir John Southworth took Catholic friends and relations into his household.[2] Beyond family links, there was a web of recusant gentry households in close contact with each other. Thomas Clifton of Westby used one of his servants to carry letters to other Catholic families in 1583, and in the following year Bartholomew Hesketh's wife travelled round the principal recusant households of the county. Lesser men acted as guides to priests unfamiliar with Lancashire, and the speed with which news of drives against Catholics circulated suggests regular cooperation. In 1618 the justices of Salford hundred were worried by 'runners to and from recusant to recusant and from place to place, which are thought to be dangerous'.[3] For the the gentry at least, the formation of links such as these made the harbouring of Catholic priests and fugitives very much safer.

But safety existed only in those areas with a sizeable recusant population and considerable Catholic sympathy, and much of what

[1] *CRS*, LIII, 150; PRO, SP 14/8/31, 33, 34.
[2] Cosgrove, 'Position of the recusant gentry', 56–7; Allen, *Letters and Memorials*, cxix–cxxi, 371; *CRS*, XXII, 69; *CRS*, LX, 38.
[3] *CSPD* (1581–90), 139; Peck, *Desiderata Curiosa*, 149; *Manchester Sessions*, 49–50.

has been said on the practice of Catholicism is applicable only to a part of Lancashire, albeit the larger part. At each visitation the vast majority of detected recusants lived in the deaneries of Warrington, Amounderness, Leyland and Blackburn, which contained 84% of known recusants in 1578, 98% in 1590, 95% in 1595, 97% in 1601 and in 1604, when the three northern deaneries were not visited, 99%. Recusancy was always very thin in the deanery of Manchester, which contained 8% of known recusants in 1578, 1% in 1590 and 2% in 1601. In 1604 detected recusants formed perhaps 1 in 9 of the population in Amounderness, 1 in 13 in Warrington, 1 in 26 in Leyland, and 1 in 72 in Blackburn, but in the deanery of Manchester only 1 person in almost 2,500 was a recusant.[1] If Manchester was a deanery in which recusants were never numerous, Blackburn was one in which the advance of recusancy was at least contained. Though the number of recusants in the deanery increased, the percentage of the county's total who lived there fell from 18% in 1595 to 5% in 1604, followed by a rise to 9% in 1630. Among the five southern deaneries of the county, Manchester and Blackburn were exceptional, and it is to these two deaneries, in which Protestantism made significant advances, that we must now turn.

[1] These are slight exaggerations of the proportion of recusants in 1604, since the population figures used are those for 1563.

18

Protestantism and south-east Lancashire

It is in some ways easier to chart the rise of recusancy, a detectable offence which appears in official records, than it is to chronicle the growth of Protestantism, the established religion of the state. There is, therefore, a tendency for historians of the later stages of the Reformation to write not about Protestants, but about the sort of Protestants who got into the records, the Puritans who came into conflict with officialdom.

In the case of Lancashire there might be some justification for writing as if all Protestants were Puritans, for in the opinion of contemporaries they were. In 1590 some of the ministers of the county asked the archbishop of York to remember 'the general state of the people amongst whom we live, standing of two sorts, the obstinate papists and the zealous professors of religion', and they argued that the latter would 'leave us and our ministration if we should be brought under' the full liturgy of the Anglican Church.[1] The same point was made again in 1602, and two years later, at the Hampton Court Conference, it was requested 'that the ministers of Lancashire might be favourably dealt with in the matter of ceremonies, for that they had long been disused there, and the people would take great offence at the use of them'.[2] We might suspect special pleading to justify clerical nonconformity, but it was probably true that, in an area in which conservatism and outright recusancy were so strong, it was necessary for the ministers of the official Church to mark themselves out from the priests of Rome more vigorously than the Book of Common Prayer prescribed. It must have been a realisation of this which led to the vehemence of a Bolton minister when writing his will in 1582, for he said that he died 'hating with all my heart all popery and the filthy dregs thereof, wherewith our English Church is yet pestered to the great joy of the papists and the vexation of godly preachers'.[3] It was not only the ministers who contended that Lancashire was divided into two extreme religious factions. In 1608 Edmund Hopwood wrote to a friend: 'I beseech God deliver this kingdom and state from all my

[1] *Kenyon MSS*, 597–8.
[2] *Salisbury MSS*, XII, 142; Usher, *Reconstruction of the English Church*, II, 353.
[3] Raines, *Vicars of Rochdale*, 53.

sins, all atheism, popery and puritanism, which in this corner grows ripe for the sickle', and in 1617 James I complained 'that two sorts of people wherewith that country is much infected (we mean papists and puritans) have maliciously traduced and calumniated these our just and honourable proceedings'.[1]

The radical Protestantism which emerged in Lancashire became most firmly entrenched in the south-east of the county, in the area which had been canvassed by the reformist preachers under Edward VI. By 1581 the people of Manchester were described as 'generally well-affected in religion', and the earl of Huntingdon thought the town was 'the best place in those parts' for religion.[2] Dr Richardson found the signs of lay and clerical Puritanism revealed at visitation to be heavily concentrated in an area to the south and east of Ribchester in central Lancashire, and found the deanery of Manchester to be by far the most intensely Puritan in the diocese of Chester.[3] The religious radicalism of the area was not a temporary phenomenon either, and in the early nineteenth century Dissenters outnumbered Anglicans by two to one in Manchester.[4] Even at the census of 1851, before Irish immigration had thoroughly disrupted the pattern, it was possible to divide Lancashire into a Catholic north and west and a Protestant south and east along a line from Warrington to Burnley.[5] The brand of Protestantism which was first planted in the south-east of the county clearly found favourable soil in which to flourish, but it seems to have been less successful in other parts of the palatinate. The rest of this chapter will be devoted to evaluating the various reasons why the south-east was peculiarly receptive to radical Protestantism.

The Puritan ministers of the area were widely believed to have been responsible for the protestantisation of the Manchester region. In 1590 Edmund Bunny was told that 'some of them have been planters or founders of religion in these parts', and the vicar of Rochdale was described as 'the only first planter of sound religion in this corner of our country in Her Majesty's time'.[6] In 1604 a group of Protestant J.P.s told James I that although Lancashire had been 'overgrown with popery and prophaneness' when Elizabeth ascended the throne, 'it is now – and especially in the places in which these men have continued – so reformed that they are become unfeigned professors of the Gospel, and many recusants are yearly

[1] *Kenyon MSS*, 14; *Manchester Sessions*, xxiv.
[2] Peck, *Desiderata Curiosa*, 110–11.
[3] Richardson, *Puritanism in North-West England*, 8–9.
[4] D. Read, *The English Provinces, 1760–1960*, 21.
[5] J. D. Gay, *The Geography of Religion in England*, 93.
[6] *Kenyon MSS*, 599, 602.

conformed'.[1] Though one might be tempted to distrust *ex parte* statements in defence of Puritan ministers, the views of contemporaries have received some support from the most recent historian of Puritanism in the area, who has admitted the importance of the clergy at least in the first stages of the movement; the first example of detected lay nonconformity was apparently not until 1605 at Oldham.[2]

Local recruits to the clerical body were puritanised in the same way as the Edwardian preachers had been protestantised, by the experience of university education. The scholarships which had been endowed in the first part of the sixteenth century produced a crop of radical graduates in the second, and they help to explain the steady rise in the proportion of university men among the local clergy. Young scholars were helped on to Oxford or Cambridge by successful Lancashire churchmen like Alexander Nowell, the dean of St Paul's, or by local landowners such as Richard Ashton of Whalley – even by the church-papist William Farington and the recusant Sir John Southworth. Dean Nowell was particularly generous in his payments to students going up to his own college, Brasenose.[3] From a reformist point of view this was money well spent, for Brasenose had produced fourteen Puritan ministers who worked in the diocese by the Civil War. As well as locally-born graduates, the county was able to attract a considerable number of outsiders, and two-thirds of the graduate Puritan ministers of the diocese were not natives of the area. The university influence was probably fundamental in radicalising the clergy, and by 1642 60% of the known Puritan ministers of the diocese had attended Oxford or Cambridge; less than one-fifth of the total clerical body in 1578 had received a university education.[4]

The Puritan clergy who worked in Lancashire did not spread themselves evenly over the county, but tended to concentrate in the south-east. In 1595 21 of the 59 benefices in the county were held by ministers who might be classed as Puritans, but 10 of the 13 benefices in the deaneries of Manchester and Blackburn had Puritan incumbents.[5] Though there was a tendency for the curates of poor churches and chapels in outlying parts of the county to fail to wear the surplice for economic rather than religious reasons, cases of this

[1] Quoted Richardson, *Puritanism in North-West England*, 125.
[2] *Ibid.* 72, 76.
[3] *Spending of the Money of Robert Nowell*, 164, 168, 170, 216–17, 218, 222, 224, 228, 234, 236. See above, pp. 161–3.
[4] Richardson, *Puritanism in North-West England*, 58, 61, 64. My figure for 1578 is based on an analysis of BIY, R VI, A 8, Rolls A, B, F, I, K.
[5] From the lists of incumbents in *VCH*, III–VIII. For the classification of Puritan clergy, see above, p. 274.

Table 4

	1578	1590	1592	1595	1601	1604
Manchester deanery	5	15	7	8	5	6
Blackburn deanery	3	3	2	2	3	1
Other deaneries (6)	3	5	3	3	4	3

omission were detected at visitation much more frequently in the two eastern deaneries, as Table 4 shows. Early failures to observe the other rubrics of the Book of Common Prayer were also much more common in the south-east than elsewhere. The prescribed formula for baptism was not followed at Middleton in 1589, the rubrics were widely ignored at Manchester in 1590 and 1604, the liturgy was shortened at Rochdale in 1598 to allow more time for sermons, and in 1604 the curates of Didsbury and Oldham were not following the Prayer Book.[1] On the infrequent occasions when clergy outside the deanery of Manchester indulged in such experiments, they seem not to have endeared themselves to their people. In 1595 the rector and curate of Wigan were presented because 'they do not say service or minister the sacraments as by the Book of Common Prayer', and a similar charge was made in 1598, but as we shall see the rector's radicalism made him far from popular in his parish.[2] At Kirkham the Puritan vicar, Nicholas Helme, was said not to administer the communion with due reverence and to have preached against the use of the cross in baptism, and it was probably these faults which prompted his more conservative parishioners to accuse him of obtaining his vicarage by simony and keeping another man's wife in his house for a year.[3]

It is difficult to give any good reasons why Puritan ministers should, at least in the early stages of the expansion of Protestantism in the area, have been attracted to the deaneries of Manchester and Blackburn. It is possible that the composition of the clerical body was influenced by the distribution of patronage, for the Crown and ecclesiastical patrons presented to 7 of the 13 benefices in the two deaneries, but to only 10 out of 29 in the deaneries of Warrington, Amounderness and Leyland. But there is no evidence that, in the county as a whole, royal and clerical patrons were any more likely to present Puritans than were other patrons. There was certainly no

---

[1] BIY, R VI, A 11, fo. 80; CRO, EDC 5, 1604, EDV 1/8a, fo. 34, 1/12a, fo. 85v, 1/13, fos. 67v, 73v.
[2] BIY, R VI, A 15, fo. 5; CRO, EDV 1/12a, fo. 139v.
[3] *Ibid.* fo. 116.

strong financial motive for serving in Manchester and Blackburn and, excluding Manchester College, 43 of the 55 clerical posts in the area in 1610 were chapel curacies. The benefices of the two deaneries were no more attractive than those elsewhere in the county, and 8 of the 13 benefices had been impropriated and yielded only low stipends; in 1590 the Puritan vicar of Rochdale had to petition the archbishop of Canterbury for an increase in his total income of only £20.[1] It may be that Puritans went to the south-east of the county initially because it was that part of the county nearest to London and had the densest and most rapidly expanding population. There prospects for conversions may have been thought higher than in the more sparsely populated and isolated parishes. Once the earliest Puritan ministers had planted the Gospel, the process became self-perpetuating, for a responsive audience was clearly more attractive than possible hostility elsewhere. By 1609, as Edmund Hopwood remarked bitterly, 'all fanatical and schismatical preachers that are cashiered in other countries resort into this corner of Lancashire' in expectation of a welcome.[2]

Puritan ministers were, by doctrine and education, more likely to be preachers than were their less radical colleagues, and their concentration in the south-east was one of the main reasons for the better provision of preaching in that area than elsewhere. A survey of *c.* 1590 found ten preachers in 10 parishes of Manchester and Blackburn, but only eleven in 28 parishes of Amounderness, Leyland and Warrington, and six of those were non-resident. In 1610 there were sixteen preachers in the 15 parishes of Manchester and Blackburn, but only fifteen preachers for 28 parishes in the three other southern deaneries. The inclusion of Blackburn is perhaps a little misleading, since the two parishes of the deanery were particularly large and contained 23 chapels in 1610, but Manchester stands clear of all other deaneries with eight preachers in the 8 parishes of the 1590 survey, and thirteen preachers in the same number of parishes in 1610.[3] We have already seen that the fellows of Manchester College were not always diligent in the fulfilment of their preaching duties, but the impact of even intermittent sermons over a generation or more must have been considerable. As early as 1576, Alexander Nowell was reminding Burghley of the role of the college 'in respect of the good instruction of the whole people of that country in their duties'.[4] By 1600, preachers such as Oliver Carter had created a taste for sermons in Manchester which the fellows alone did not satisfy

[1] PRO, SP 12/31, fo. 86; *Kenyon MSS*, 9–10, 11–12; *Stanley Papers*, II, 182.
[2] *Kenyon MSS*, 15.
[3] PRO, SP 12/31, fo. 86; *Kenyon MSS*, 8–13.
[4] BM, Lansdowne MS 23, fo. 106.

and, after a petition to the Privy Council for a learned preacher, in 1603 the people of the town raised contributions to endow a lecture-ship for the Puritan William Burne.[1] At Bolton, too, parishioners wished to supplement the preaching provided by their vicar; the people were maintaining a preacher at their own expense by 1578, and from the mid 1580s the influential Puritan James Gosnell was serving as parish preacher.[2]

One of the most important reasons why ministers of the Puritan sort wished to serve in Lancashire was the leniency extended towards them by the ecclesiastical authorities. In June 1577 it had been suggested that the Puritan ministers who made a nuisance of themselves in the south of England should be sent into Lancashire and other difficult counties, where their energies could be directed to combatting the Catholics.[3] There is no evidence that this was ever followed up, but it does indicate that there was an awareness of the usefulness of the radicals, and perhaps a willingness to allow them a measure of toleration; certainly Whitgift's dreaded articles were not applied in the north.[4] The forbearance extended towards Lancashire Puritans is well illustrated by the career of Richard Midgeley, vicar of Rochdale, who seems never to have worn a surplice from at least 1571 until his resignation in 1595. Although he was summoned to correction for his failure at almost every visitation, there is no evidence that serious disciplinary action was ever taken, and he was appointed moderator of the official exercise in the deanery of Black-burn. After his resignation he was appointed one of the Queen's Preachers in Lancashire by Bishop Vaughan, who defended his choice with some vigour: 'As to Mr Midgeley, whatever exception may be taken to him, considering the good he has done in the last forty years, and the respect in which he is held, I am resolved for his continuance, unless by superior authority I am pressed to the contrary.' 'Superior authority' seems not to have pressed the point, and in 1604 Midgeley was King's Preacher, stationed in the Catholic stronghold of Leigh.[5]

William Langley, rector of Prestwich, was a more obstreperous character for, besides his persistent – but apparently acceptable – refusal to wear the surplice, he dared to criticise official religious policy and the relationship between Church and state. In 1591 he

[1] *APC*, XXXI, 44–5; *Salisbury MSS*, XII, 643.
[2] BIY, R VI, A 8, Roll I; R. Halley, *Lancashire: its Puritanism and Nonconformity*, 80; *Kenyon MSS*, 11.
[3] A. F. S. Pearson, *Thomas Cartwright and Elizabethan Puritanism*, 234.
[4] Halley, *Lancashire: its Puritanism and Nonconformity*, 80; Collinson, *Elizabethan Puritan Movement*, 253.
[5] BIY, R VII, HCAB 6, fo. 78, R VI, A 7, fo. 37, A 11, fo. 99v, A 14, fo. 22v; Raines, *Vicars of Rochdale*, 51; *Salisbury MSS*, IX, 91, X, 41.

preached a sermon 'concerning the queen's most excellent majesty and her royal prerogative in causes ecclesiastical, and against the lords and others of her majesty's most honourable Privy Council and against the justice of the land'. Langley seems to have suggested that the queen ought to have been subject to the discipline of the Church, and to have alleged that the authorities were conducting a 'prosecution of the sincere professors of religion'. His case was considered by Archbishop Whitgift, who was not usually tolerant in these matters, the earl of Derby and Bishop Chadderton, but his punishment was nothing more serious than a public confession of his faults in Prestwich church and an acknowledgement that 'all this realm and Church have and do daily receive at God's hands many singular blessings and benefits by the wisdom, care and great circumspection of her majesty's most honourable Privy Council, whom (as in duty I am also bound) I do hold to be persons of great virtue, honour and sincerity in true religion'. Though Langley may have found these words difficult to mouth, one cannot easily imagine such a light penalty being exacted in many other dioceses. His recantation, needless to say, did not curb his militance, and in 1595 he led the clergy of Manchester deanery in resisting a demand that they should wear the surplice.[1]

The official attitude towards clerical Puritans did not stop at mere tolerance of their offences, but extended to positive favour towards them and their methods. Though only one Puritan seems to have been given formal office in the diocesan administration – when Robert Osbaldeston was made rural dean of Blackburn – the ministers were given authority in other ways. In 1598 the episcopal visitation of Lancashire was conducted by three leading radical divines, who were a little more successful in uncovering conservative offences than they were in finding ministers who did not obey the Prayer Book.[2] But the most important involvement of Puritan clergy in ecclesiastical discipline was the use of 'exercises', which were placed under the control of the Puritan preachers. The exercises probably emerged from an order for quarterly synods for the improvement of clerical education given to his archdeacons by Archbishop Sandys in 1578. When William Chadderton was appointed to the see of Chester, he applied this plan to his own diocese, and he is said to have begun in 1579 with a monthly exercise for the clergy of Manchester deanery. We know nothing of what took place at the exercise, but it clearly developed into something more radical than Sandys had envisaged, for in 1581 he reminded the bishop of

---

[1] BIY, R VI, A 7, fo. 40, A 11, fo. 94v, A 14, fo. 20v, A 15, fo. 70; CRO, EDV 1/8a, fo. 41v, 1/12a, fo. 86v, 1/12b, fo. 104v, EDC 1/27, fos. 157–157v.
[2] CRO, EDA 3/1, fo. 170v, EDV 1/12a, fos. 81, 95, 106, 114.

Chester that he was 'noted to yield too much to general fastings, all day preaching and praying', and warned his suffragan that 'the devil is crafty, and the young ministers of these our times grow mad'.[1] By 1582 Chadderton had organised three annual meetings at Preston for the clergy of Lancashire, at which the ministers would study passages of Scripture which had been set for them, guided by four moderators, all noted Puritan preachers. Perhaps the most interesting departure was the disciplinary power given to the moderators, who were allowed to fine absentees from the exercise and issue public rebukes to those guilty of offences.[2]

These pilot schemes aroused the enthusiasm of men in high places and, in view of the benefits which were thought to have accrued, Chadderton was instructed by the Privy Council in April 1584 to hold more frequent exercises at additional centres. Accordingly, after first consulting the leading Puritan clergy, the bishop produced a scheme of exercises for the whole diocese, though only the Lancashire section need concern us. There was to be an exercise at each of five Lancashire towns each month between February and October, and all clergy and schoolmasters were to attend the synod for their own deanery. Absence was to be punished by a sliding scale of fines according to the status of the offender. Nineteen moderators were named, fourteen of whom were Puritans. Some of the clergy seem not to have appreciated this programme of disciplined study, and were not diligent in their attendance or in their preparation for the exercises, and in 1585 Bishop Chadderton found it necessary to increase the penalty for laxity from a fine to suspension from office; the Puritan moderators were allowed to suspend without reference to the bishop or his officers, although only the vicar-general could lift the suspensions.[3] The introduction of the exercises was hailed by the radical ministers as an important contribution towards clerical learning and prospects for reform in both theology and morals; the vicar of Prescot wrote that 'We hope that great reformation will follow the good and zealous use thereof.'[4] The exercises were also a contribution towards the puritanisation of the clerical body, especially as they were so firmly under the influence of the Puritan preachers.

Bishop Chadderton's alliance with the Puritans did not, however, remove the possibility of clashes between them and the establishment. In 1590, Archbishop Piers of York held a metropolitan visitation which Professor Collinson regards as an attempt to enforce

---

[1] Strype, *Annals*, II(2), 165; Halley, *Lancashire: its Puritanism and Nonconformity*, 72; Peck, *Desiderata Curiosa*, 102.
[2] Strype, *Annals*, II(2), 544–6; Richardson, *Puritanism in North-West England*, 65.
[3] *Ibid.* 65–6; Peck, *Desiderata Curiosa*, 149; Strype, *Annals*, II(2), 546–9.
[4] *THSLC*, LXXXVI, 4.

Whitgiftian policy on the northern province; if it was, it ended in ignominious failure. In Lancashire the visitation revealed the extent to which the rubrics of the Prayer Book had been disregarded under the benign eye of William Chadderton. The 'rag of popery', the surplice, was not worn or deliberately refused at 23 churches and chapels in the county, and the Prayer Book was flouted in other ways at Manchester College and probably elsewhere; in the deanery of Manchester the surplice was not worn by fourteen ministers and an unknown number of the clergy of the college.[1] The erring clergy were ordered by Piers' visitor to appear before Bishop Chadderton and promise future conformity, but this novel interference with their liberty prompted several of the ministers to a sharp response. Eleven of them, including seven from Manchester deanery, signed a protest to the archbishop, in which they argued both that they had obeyed the Prayer Book and that their disobedience was justified by the religious situation in Lancashire. Their justification pointed out that their own bishop and previous archbishops had been sympathetic towards their plight, and concluded with a broad hint that the archbishop should spend his time reforming more dangerous abuses than mere failure to wear a surplice: the ministers 'doubt not but your lordship shall find a far greater blessing to the good reformation of our country from the gross idolatry and heathenish profanations which yet continue with many amongst us, than if a more strict course were taken in these small matters of inconformity in the preachers'.[2] A local J.P. added his voice, and asked the archbishop to delay action against the clergy 'because some of them have been planters or founders of religion in these parts, continual well users of their liberty so many years enjoyed'. The Puritans seem also to have found more powerful influences to champion them, for some years later it was reported that members of the Privy Council had intervened to prevent the prosecution of Lancashire clergy. Although in January 1591 Bishop Chadderton, presumably under pressure from his metropolitan, instructed all churchwardens to supply surplices and certify that their ministers were wearing them; it was reported twice to Piers in the following month that the Puritans had not conformed. No disciplinary action was taken against them, which in itself suggests that the archbishop was called off by higher authority.[3]

If there was any improvement following the crisis of 1590 it was short-lived, and if – at least during the reign of Elizabeth – the number of men presented for ignoring the surplice never again reached the numbers of 1590, one suspects that this was because

---

[1] Collinson, *Elizabethan Puritan Movement*, 406; BIY, R VI, A 11–12, *passim*.
[2] *Kenyon MSS*, 597–8.
[3] *Ibid.* 599–600, 602; *Salisbury MSS*, XII, 142.

churchwardens were concealing offences of this sort.[1] By the visitation of 1595 the ministers of Manchester deanery were facing the metropolitan visitor with some truculence and, though he tried to persuade them to wear the surplice, they refused to do so.[2] There was another confrontation following Bishop Vaughan's visitation of 1601, when twelve cases of failure to wear the surplice were uncovered. Four were probably the result of laxity rather than principle, and Vaughan threatened to deprive the remaining eight. Again the clergy were able to obtain the support of government officials, and Robert Cecil was asked to prevent their removal; the bishop did not proceed against them.[3] The Lancashire Puritans had been able to forestall the attacks made on them, but they clearly felt vulnerable, and at the Hampton Court Conference of 1604 they attempted to secure from the king a grant of limited nonconformity in the county. Their intermediary was the Lancastrian Laurence Chadderton, 'the pope of Cambridge Puritanism', who asked that tolerance should be extended towards the Lancashire ministers who did not follow the rubrics of the Prayer Book as closely as they ought. James agreed to no more than that Vaugan should be instructed 'not to proceed over hastily or roughly against any of them', in the hope that they might in time conform themselves.[4]

What might have been a workable, if temporary, *modus vivendi* was, however, soon disrupted by the issue of the new ecclesiastical canons of 1604, which Bishop Vaughan tried to impose at his autumn visitation. He found that ten churches and chapels did not use the surplice, there were other non-conformist abuses at Didsbury and Oldham, and it is said that 21 ministers refused to subscribe to the canons. Vaughan did his best to proceed considerately and, after summoning the south-Lancashire Puritans before him, he gave them time to consider their position. It was probably at this point that twelve Puritan J.P.s, most of them from the Manchester area, petitioned the king in favour of the threatened ministers, and their intercession seems to have been effective, as no-one was deprived.[5] Except for the removal of Walsh of Blackburn and Joseph Midgeley of Rochdale by Bishop Lloyd in 1606, the ministers were not penalised for their offences, and there was no concerted attempt

[1] See, for example, Richardson, 'Puritanism in the Diocese of Chester', 68–70.
[2] BIY, R VI, A 14, fos. 19, 19v, 20, 20v, 22, 22v, 23v, A 15, fo. 70.
[3] CRO, EDV 1/12b, *passim*; *Salisbury MSS*, XII, 142.
[4] Usher, *Reconstruction of the English Church*, II, 353; S. B. Babbage, *Puritanism and Richard Bancroft*, 67–8.
[5] CRO, EDV 1/13, *passim*; D. Neal, *History of the Puritans*, 4 vols. II, 40; Raines, *Fellows of Manchester College*, 88; *CSPD* (1603–10), 175.

to bring them to heel until 1633.[1] The Puritan clergy of Lancashire were well treated throughout the reign of Elizabeth. Their usefulness against the papists secured them positions of great influence, immunity from all but intermittent harassment, and the protection of bishops and privy councillors. Dr Richardson has noted that conventicles emerged in Lancashire a generation after they became common further south;[2] this delay is probably to be explained by the dominance of Puritan ministers in south-east Lancashire and the indulgence allowed them, so that nonconformity outside the framework of the established Church was not necessary.

The influence of the Puritan clergy, especially with official support, was clearly of great significance, but it would be wrong to ascribe the protestantisation of south-east Lancashire to their work alone. There were hard-working pastors such as Richard Midgeley at Rochdale, but other Puritans were less conscientious. If one is tempted to assume that all radicals took their ministerial role as seriously as their theology implied, it is only necessary to recall the example of Manchester College, where in 1601 only one of seven clerics was fulfilling his duty to preach.[3] In the early 1590s the Puritan incumbents of Bolton, Winwick, Standish and Poulton were normally non-resident, Thomas Williamson held three posts in the deanery of Manchester, and even the curate of Oldham was sometimes absent at his benefice in Nottinghamshire.[4] Edward Fleetwood, rector of Wigan and an indefatigable anti-Catholic crusader, who sat as a J.P., preached at assizes and made personal and written reports to Lord Burghley, might more usefully have attended to his own parishioners. He was non-resident in 1578, he allowed his chancel to fall into serious decay, the children of the parish were not properly catechised, and he failed to provide curates for the chapels – at one of them in 1598 the people did not know their catechism and some could not say the Lord's Prayer and the Ten Commandments.[5] Manchester College, which might have been a powerful reforming agency, presents an equally dismal record. Financial problems drove the clergy to find additional employment, catechising was neglected in 1578, 1592, 1595 and 1601, the fabric was often in poor repair and sermons were not always provided.[6]

[1] Tupling, 'Causes of the Civil War in Lancashire', 4–5; Richardson, *Puritanism in North-West England*, 22.
[2] *Ibid.* 86.   [3] CRO, EDV 1/12b, fos. 109v–110; *Salisbury MSS*, XII, 643.
[4] PRO, SP 12/31, fo. 85, 12/235, fo. 8; BIY, R VI, A 11, fo. 65, A 14, fos. 20, 22, 26v; CRO, EDV 1/12a, fo. 89v.
[5] BIY, R VI, A 7, fos. 49–49v, A 12, fo. 73v, A 15, fo. 5; CRO, EDV 1/10, fo. 129v, 1/12a, fos. 136v, 137v, 139v, 1/12b, fo. 160.
[6] CRO, 1/10, fo. 168, 1/12a, fo. 89v, 1/12b, fo. 110, 1/13, fo. 64; BIY, R VI, A 11, fo. 79v, A 14, fo. 24v.

Though Bolton became the 'Geneva of the North', the parish was sadly neglected at the turn of the century; two successive vicars were absentees, the children were not catechised, books were not provided for the church, and the church fabric was in such poor repair that the chancel almost collapsed.[1] The people of Bolton, like those of Manchester, had to make up for the inadequacies of their parochial ministry by hiring a lecturer.

A second reason for casting doubt on the efficacy of Puritan preaching alone as a means of furthering reformation is the limited geographical impact of the ministers. We have seen that Puritan scruples over the use of wafers in the communion led to antagonism between ministers and their people in the 1580s, and it remained true that advanced clergy working outside the deaneries of Manchester and Blackburn aroused a good deal of hostility. Part of the unpopularity of the rector of Wigan arose from his position as lord of the manor, and it has been noted that Edward Fleetwood was threatened for his hostility towards Catholics. But it was alleged in 1598 that one of the reasons for the extent of recusancy in the parish was the nonconformity of the incumbent. Ralph Worsley, who had been cited before the Duchy court for assault on the rector, declared that he was

a dutiful hearer of divine service, and so hath always been, and hath also moved and persuaded others to do the like, which have been and yet are backward in religion, as he thinketh, much the rather by reason of the neglect and contempt of the complainant in not observing that form and order of prayer and administration of the Holy Sacraments which is, to this defendant's knowledge, appointed by the Book of Common Prayer.[2]

There was some trouble at Holland, one of the chapels of the parish, in the same year, when Fleetwood allowed an unlicensed Puritan minister to serve the cure. One of the congregation called out to the churchwardens during a service 'What, do you suffer yonder red-headed fellow to be in the pulpit or say service without a surplice', and walked out of the church, and another refused to attend the chapel unless the surplice was worn.[3] John White, the surplice-less vicar of Leyland, also drove people from his church; in 1598 and 1601 it was complained that he refused to use the sign of the cross in baptism, 'wherefore many of the parishioners do cause their children to be baptised at other churches'.[4] At Poulton in 1604 the vicar did not sign with a cross at baptism, with the same result, but if the minister would not provide the services demanded there

[1] *Ibid.* A 14, fo. 22; CRO, EDV 1/12a, fo. 91v, 1/12b, fo. 115v, 1/13, fo. 69.
[2] Bridgeman, *History of the Church and Manor of Wigan*, 160.
[3] CRO, EDV 1/12a, fos. 137v, 139.   [4] *Ibid.* fo. 96, 1/12b, fo. 122.

were priests available who would, and fourteen parishioners were presented for harbouring priests. At Ormskirk, Puritan sermons rather than Puritan services caused discontent, and there was a move to persuade the wardens to keep radical preachers out of the pulpit.[1] The bishops who claimed at the Hampton Court conference that Lancashire ministers, by their abuses in the administration of the sacraments, had driven 800 people into recusancy and 500 into non-communicating were presumably exaggerating, but they were right that Puritan departures could make Anglicanism less attractive in conservative districts.[2]

The Puritan ministers enjoyed success only when they worked in the south-east of Lancashire, so that other influences must also be considered to account for the peculiarity of the area. There are serious failings in any suggestion that the deanery of Manchester was a naturally radical region. The general theory that towns contain tradesmen who need to be literate and so can easily assimilate new ideas does not explain the Lancashire case. In the south-east of the county only Manchester provided anything approaching an 'urban environment', while the townships of Bolton, Rochdale and Bury were little more than focal points of dispersed settlement. Outside the deanery, Wigan, Preston and Lancaster were established boroughs and seats of government as well as trading towns, but Puritanism made no progress there in the sixteenth century and little in the seventeenth. It has also been suggested that radical Protestantism was characteristic of pastoral and weakly-manorialised areas such as south and east Lancashire, but it is surely more accurate to say that these were regions in which Anglicanism tended to fail, and either recusants or radicals might fill the gap. Establishment Anglicanism normally did well in the integrated village communities of arable and mixed-farming lowlands, so that the area which 'ought' to have been won for Anglicanism was the prosperous agrarian plain, the deaneries of Warrington, Leyland and Amounderness, the most Catholic part of all England. Pastoral uplands like eastern Lancashire were captured for Rome in other areas of the north.[3]

The most obvious characteristic of the Protestant part of Lancashire was that it was the 'inland' corner of the county, nearest to existing centres of radicalism in the West Riding, the Midlands and the capital. We have already seen that the villages to the north and east of Manchester were conveniently situated to draw raw materials

[1] *Ibid.* 1/13, fos. 198v–199; *Lancashire Quarter Sessions*, 224.
[2] Usher, *Reconstruction of the English Church*, II, 353.
[3] Thirsk, *Agrarian History*, IV, 112; Richardson, *Puritanism in North-West England*, 15, 94; Gay, *Geography of Religion in England*, 79, 111; Bossy, *English Catholic Community*, ch. 5.

Table 5

	1565–6	1582–3	1592–3
Packs of linen yarn	362	516	1,550
Stones of wool	561	1,561	6,479

from Ireland, north Lancashire and the West Riding, had fast-running streams for fulling mills, and could export across land to London or via Chester to Spain and Ireland, so that a flourishing textile industry developed there. The expansion in cloth production which had taken place in the middle of the century was followed by a more considerable growth under Elizabeth, as illustrated by Table 5, which shows raw material imports through Liverpool and Chester. New families were drawn into the industry as subdivision of landholdings through population growth made by-industries necessary, and textiles tended to creep further up the eastern fringe of the county into Rossendale. As the industry increased in size so its character began to change, and by the end of the century there were several rich clothiers in the Manchester area who might employ a dozen full-time workers in their houses.[1]

Woollen cloth was manufactured especially in Manchester, Bury, Bolton, Rochdale, Colne, Burnley and Blackburn, and expansion led to close links with the West Riding and London. The major wool market at Wakefield attracted broggers from east Lancashire, and the wool which Halifax clothiers found too coarse for their own use was sold to the men of Rochdale. Rochdale itself became a flourishing wool market, and Camden noted that it was 'well frequented'; merchants from Barnsley and Halifax used the market, and in 1608 it was said that a road from Rochdale into Yorkshire had been 'time out of mind a usual and common highway' for men 'to pass about their trades, being clothmakers, and other business'.[2] Late in the reign of Elizabeth, the Manchester region was more fully integrated into the radical and cloth-working West Riding of Yorkshire than it was into the much more conservative rest of Lancashire.

Woollens produced in the area were sold in the West Riding, the Midlands, south-west England and East Anglia, but their main destination was London, ready for export to the Continent. The

[1] Lowe, *Lancashire Textile Industry*, 14, 34; Wadsworth and Mann, *Cotton Trade and Industrial Lancashire*, 26–8.
[2] Bowden, *Wool Trade in Tudor and Stuart England*, 68–9; *Kenyon MSS*, 573, 620–1; J. F. Fox, 'Reformation and Tudor Rochdale', typescript deposited in Rochdale Public Library, 1972, 64–5.

cloth was carried south by professional carriers, and by 1580 there was a regular weekly service between Chester and the capital. In London the cloth was handled by members of the livery companies, who alone were allowed to export, but by the 1560s some Lancashire merchants were avoiding the use of Londoners, who took their own cut of the profits, by having more trustworthy family factors resident in the capital. Nicholas Moseley of Manchester settled in London in *c*. 1568, he became a member of the Cloth-workers' Company, and he was soon exporting cottons sent south by the Lancashire end of the family business. The Chetham family operated a similar system, with some of the sons apprenticed to the Tippings in Manchester and George Chetham, a member of the Grocers' Company, as London agent. The family ties with the capital which were created spread more widely, for it was common for a Lancashire emigrant to London to take friends and relations with him as servants.[1]

It is difficult to demonstrate precise connections between trade links and the flow of religious ideas, but over the four decades of Elizabeth's reign regular contacts with the capital must have had some effect. It is possible to show that emigré Lancashiremen, radicalised in London, remained aware of the religious needs of their native county, for the 55 Londoners (at least 44 of them originally from Lancashire) who made gifts to county charities between 1480 and 1660 gave no less than 28% of the known benefactions to the county. Two-thirds of their donations were for education, and part of the rest went to the building of chapels and the endowment of Puritan lectureships.[2] The frequent contacts with outside ideas which trading links brought were significant in the spread of religious radicalism, and Dr Richardson found evidence of Puritanism in 21 of the 31 market towns of Lancashire, and particularly in 12 of the 14 market towns of Blackburn and Manchester deaneries.[3]

Some market towns became radical, when others did not, because the trade with which they dealt came from radical areas. Towns outside the south-east of the county were involved in the cloth trade, mainly Preston, Wigan, Liverpool and Ormskirk, but there is an important distinction to be made. The textile industry in the west of the county was devoted to the weaving of linen rather than woollen

---

[1] Lowe, *Lancashire Textile Industry*, 3–4, 59, 64–5, 71; Wadsworth and Mann, *Cotton Trade and Industrial Lancashire*, 29–30; *Spending of the Money of Robert Nowell*, 88; Fox, 'Reformation and Tudor Rochdale', 67.

[2] Jordan, *Social Institutions of Lancashire*, 98–9.

[3] Richardson, *Puritanism in North-West England*, 13 and n. Richardson found Puritanism in 9 of the 17 market towns in the rest of the county, but my impression is that at least until near the Civil War the Puritanism of 8 of the 9 was clerical rather than lay; the exception was Liverpool.

cloth, while no area in the east specialised in linen alone.[1] The
Protestant towns of the east were those which drew their wool from
radical Halifax, Wakefield and the Midlands, as well as Ireland, but
the linen towns of the west used flax and hemp from Ireland and
from the Catholic parishes of the wet west coast of the county. In
addition, the textile industry of the western corporate boroughs,
Wigan and Preston, was in decay, with guild restrictions and inadequate water power, so that linen seems to have been sold over a
narrower area than Lancashire woollens and was not exported
through London. The trading connections created by the linen
industry were not extensive, and almost all of those who bought and
sold at Preston market lived within a radius of seven miles of the
town.[2] All this evidence points to the cloth trade as a protestantising
influence only in eastern Lancashire, where it reinforced the links
with radical areas outside.

The growth of the cloth trade influenced religious development by
the resources it made available for education as well as by its trading
contacts. The increase in the number of schools which took place
under Elizabeth far outstripped the increase in the first half of the
century. There were perhaps 25 schools in the county by 1560, but
this rose to 32 in 1570, 45 in 1580, 50 in 1590 and probably 56 by
1600; on the basis of the county population in 1563, the position
improved from one school for every 3,900 people near the beginning
of the reign to one for every 1,750 people at the end.[3] This expansion
was the result of heavy investment in education, and between 1561
and 1600 almost two-thirds of charitable benefactions went to education. Merchants were particularly aware of the poor educational
provision of the county, and almost three-quarters of their gifts went
to schools and scholarships; London merchants alone contributed a
third of the total given to education and, under Elizabeth, they
founded grammar schools at Blackrod, Heskin and Urswick.[4] A rise
of this magnitude in the number of school places available led in time
to an equally impressive increase in the number of local students
proceeding to higher education. It has been estimated that between
1500 and 1561 only 2 definite natives of the parish of Rochdale and 6
more possible natives proceeded to one of the universities or inns of
court, but that between 1561 and 1620 there were 42 definite natives

---

[1] For the details of the textile industry on which the following argument is based see
Lowe, *Lancashire Textile Industry*, 3–5, 6–10, 43, 58–9, 81–2.

[2] Rogers, 'Market area of Preston', 49–52.

[3] I have been helped in these calculations by Wallis, 'Preliminary register of old
schools in Lancashire and Cheshire', expanded where necessary from visitation
records and other sources.

[4] Jordan, *Social Institutions of Lancashire*, 7, 99, 113; *VCH*, II, 607–9.

and 28 more possibles.[1] This increase was clearly the result of the
foundation of Rochdale Grammar School in the 1560s, and the peak
period for admissions to higher education was the 1580s when the
first generations of scholars moved out of the school, probably under
the influence of the Puritan vicar, Richard Midgeley.

It is possible to demonstrate links between education and religious
reform, for example at Rivington School, founded by Bishop James
Pilkington in 1566. The master was to be 'a hater of popery and
superstition', boys were to be taught from Calvin's *Catechism* and
Institutes, and governors had to promise to ensure that the school
taught only 'that which is contained in the Holy Bible and agreeing
therewith'.[2] Grammar schools were founded by other Lancashire-
born ecclesiastics: Hawkshead by Archbishop Sandys, Warton by
Archbishop Hutton, and at Middleton, Dean Nowell was the power
behind the re-foundation of the school. Outsiders contributed, too,
and it was Archbishop Parker who prodded the farmer of the tithes
and the parishioners of Rochdale into establishing a school. The
creation of a literate laity made the task of reformist-minded clerics
easier, and in the 1580s Richard Midgeley, the Puritan vicar of
Rochdale, was able to hold Bible-study meetings for his people.
Educated laymen could themselves supplement the inadequate
propaganda effort of the established Church, and in 1574 Robert
Entwhistle left 'one little Bible to my son Richard and the said Jane
my wife, and they to see the same occupied every sabbath day
when there is no sermons nor sacraments in ministering, and in the
weekday my will and mind is that my poorest kinsfolks which are not
able to buy a Bible shall have the same lent unto them'.[3] It was
presumably with an eye to the failure of the clergy to catechise that
in 1578 the archbishop of York ordered after his visitation that each
parish should acquire copies of the official *Little Catechism* for sale to
the people, and in 1580 and 1585 Bishop Chadderton tried to force
parishioners to buy them.[4]

But to assume that educational improvements necessarily meant
the expansion of Protestantism, as some historians have come dangerously close to suggesting, is to beg some important questions.
Education assisted the process of reform only if it was the right sort
of education provided in the right place. Several official schools fell
into the hands of Catholics, and Burnley School under Laurence
Yate gained recruits for Rome and Douai rather than Canterbury or
Geneva. Even a Protestant-inspired education could be ineffective in
a Catholic area; the Puritan vicar of Prescot used his influence over

[1] Fox, 'Reformation and Tudor Rochdale', 61.   [2] *VCH*, II, 606, V, 289.
[3] *Chetham Miscellanies*, V(1), 46; *L & C Wills*, II, 222.
[4] *Great Harwood Reg.* 440; *Prescot Accounts*, 80, 85, 87–8, 97–8.

the local school, sited in the churchyard, to try to advance the new religion among the pupils, but conservative parents kept their children away, a group of local gentry tried to move the school beyond the vicar's control, and Catholic schoolmasters found plenty of employment in the parish. At Prescot, too, the attempt to force each household to buy a catechism was largely abortive, and the churchwardens were unable to sell 38 of the 60 copies they obtained in 1585.[1]

The more Catholic deaneries of Lancashire were, in fact, better provided even with officially approved schools than were the Protestant areas; at the visitation of 1578, 20 schoolmasters were recognised in the deaneries of Warrington, Amounderness and Leyland, but only 11 in the deaneries of Manchester and Blackburn.[2] Table 6 suggests that the distribution of schools changed little during the reign of Elizabeth, and that in relation to population the radical areas were, with the exception of the extreme north, the least well served:

Table 6

Deanery	1560	Ratio of schools to population, 1560	1570	1580	1590	1600	Ratio of schools to population, 1600
Manchester	4	1:6,199	9	11	12 [16]	12	1:2,066
Blackburn	3	1:4,428	4	5	5	6	1:2,214
Warrington	9	1:2,209	10	12	12	18	1:1,104
Amounderness	5	1:2,571	5	10	9	8	1:1,588
Leyland	4	1:2,572	4	4	4	7	1:1,470
Others	0		0	3	4	5	1:2,800
Total	25	1:3,900	32	45	50	56	1:1,741

The deanery of Warrington was always far better served than the deanery of Manchester, except perhaps in the 'freak' year of 1590, when four unlicensed additional schoolmasters were working in Manchester parish,[3] but Warrington had the highest density of recusants in the county and Manchester the lowest. It is probable that education, rather than necessarily causing Protestantism to spread, had the effect of deepening commitment to the prevailing religious views in each particular area. Education, like preaching, Puritan ministers and the cloth trade, was a protestantising influence only in the south-east of Lancashire.

[1] Bailey, 'Prescot Grammar School', *passim*; see above, p. 292; *Prescot Accounts*, 97–8.
[2] BIY, R VI, A 7, fos. 34v, 45, 52, 52v, 60v, A 8, Rolls A, B, F, I, K.
[3] *Ibid.* A 11, fos. 81, 95.

Our discussion of those influences which are normally considered to have led towards Protestantism must lead to the conclusion that an additional force helped them to operate more satisfactorily in one corner of the county than elsewhere. As we shall see, recusancy was never a strong force in some parishes of the more Catholic deaneries and, in the area to the north of Lancaster, though there was recusancy it was never a widespread popular movement. But Protestantism made no advances in these areas of Catholic failure, and irreligion, ignorance and passive conformity seem to have been the rule. It is significant that the most thoroughly Protestant and least Catholic parishes of Lancashire fell neatly within the political boundary of Salford hundred. It is true that there was some recusancy in Eccles, Dean and even radical Bolton, those parishes furthest from the Puritan influence of the West Riding and nearest to the Catholic parishes of west Lancashire. But Puritanism stopped, at least in the reigns of Elizabeth and James, at the western border of the hundred; ministers who ventured further aroused only resistance. Recusancy on a wide scale began immediately over the hundred border in Standish, Wigan and Leigh, though these parishes were hardly nearer the coast than they were to the solidly Protestant areas of Rochdale and Oldham. This suggests that a political and legal influence may have been important.

Salford hundred was probably better governed and more peaceable than the rest of Lancashire. The administration of justice may have been easier for, though the Pennine foothills began east of Rochdale and Ashton, the rest of the hundred was comparatively flat and, unlike West Derby hundred, there were few peat-bogs and overflowing rivers. Heavy investment in looms and fulling mills in the villages, and in shops in the towns, created a vested interest in order, while the needs of trade prescribed hostility to violence and theft. There was a class of politically-reliable lesser gentry, with no pretensions to feudal grandeur; of 31 families in the 1567 visitation, only 12 were in any way Catholic later in the century and the heads of 3 of the 12 were themselves anti-Catholic activists who happened to have recusant relations. From this group was drawn a high proportion of the working J.P.s of the county; 31 families in Salford hundred provided fourteen J.P.s in 1583, while 40 families in West Derby provided only eleven. Salford always had more than its share of resident justices; in 1583 there was roughly one justice for every 1,800 members of the population, as against one for every 3,000 elsewhere, and the distinction remained throughout the reign of Elizabeth. Salford justices, mainly lesser men anxious to improve their status by showing their worth, may even have been harder working than their fellows elsewhere. The prosperous town of

Manchester attracted justices to its quarter sessions, which in 1583–4 were each attended by an average of thirteen J.P.s as against only five at Preston and four at Lancaster.[1] It was said in 1587 that 'there be as many justices of peace in the hundred of Salford as are resident besides in all the whole county', and a dossier compiled in that year shows that Salford had 13 of the 32 resident J.P.s, 8 of the 16 members of the quorum and 6 of the 9 most reliable justices, some of whom also attended the quarter sessions of other hundreds to ensure that the anti-Catholic interest was properly represented there.[2] The hundred was well supervised by higher authority; the earl of Derby had a house in Manchester, and a succession of bishops of Chester made the town their headquarters for the drive against recusancy. The Ecclesiastical Commission held as many of its sessions at Manchester as it did in Chester, and there was a prison for recusants and priests in the town.[3]

A tradition of good government, Puritan J.P.s,[4] supervision from above, and a group of radical ministers ready to report any conservatism and recusancy, made the survival of popular Catholicism impossible. There had been many signs of conservatism in the area in the 1560s and 1570s, even in Manchester itself, and a not inconsiderable recusant body; at the visitations of 1571 and 1578 about 10 % of Lancashire recusants who were detected lived in Manchester deanery. There had been two hitherto powerful conservative families in Manchester, the Byrons of Clayton and the Radcliffes of Ordsall, but they declined in fortune, and their estates were finally broken up and divided between the small gentry and traders.[5] There remained a tradition of sabbath-breaking and reluctance to attend church,[6] but good government prevented the survival of recusancy except among a handful of gentry families. For the Catholic proselytiser the risk of detection was far too high in Salford hundred. Only 2 Catholic schoolmasters are known to have worked in the area, both as domestic tutors, during the reign of Elizabeth, while 24 worked in West Derby hundred, only 10 of them as private tutors. There were 4 recusant priests in Salford hundred in 1570 and 3 in 1580, but West Derby had 19 and 14 in these years, and though West Derby was served by about 14 seminary priests in 1590 there

---

[1] These remarks are based on an analysis of the commissions of the peace in 1564, 1583–4, 1595 and 1598 (*Camden Miscellany*, IX, 77–8; *THSLC*, XCV, 131–3; *Kenyon MSS*, 583; *Lancashire Quarter Sessions*, vi–vii).
[2] BM, Lansdowne MS 53, fos. 174, 178–178v, Cotton MS, Titus B. II, fo. 240.
[3] PRO, E 134/25 Elizabeth, Trinity No. 5, *passim*.
[4] 9 of the 12 signatories of the 1604 petition in support of nonconformist ministers were Salford J.P.s.
[5] *VCH*, IV, 176.
[6] e.g. *Kenyon MSS*, 572, 582–3, 601; CRO, EDV 1/10, fos. 168v–173v.

were none in Salford. His father's household in Manchester might have served as a base for Ambrose Barlow in the 1620s, but he preferred to work from Leigh, over the hundred border.[1] Without the support of priests and schoolmasters, the conservatism of the south-east died under a battering of Puritan sermons, and without clerical backing recusancy was impossible. Although it is not suggested that Protestantism was enforced by the justices of the peace and the Ecclesiastical Commission, these bodies made a crucial contribution by holding the Catholic clergy at bay. The Puritan clergy could therefore work without harassment, and radical ideas from the West Riding and elsewhere gained acceptance without contradiction from recusant priests or seminarians. Outside Salford, the Puritan ministers in Wigan, Standish, Prescot, Poulton and Kirkham were given a hostile reception by their parishioners because Catholic clergy were able to work comparatively freely. But in the south-east the authorities provided the machinery to implement the royal directives, and were able to create the conditions in which, by the 1590s, Protestant teaching could triumph.

[1]   *Chetham Miscellanies*, II(2), iii, 3–5, 12.

19

Catholics, Puritans and the establishment

By the end of the reign of Elizabeth there were marked geographical variations in the distribution of Protestants and Catholics, and these are illustrated by Table 7, which shows the number of recusants in each division relative to total population and area. The deaneries of Warrington and Amounderness were clearly much more Catholic than the others and, though large numbers of recusants were not reported there until 1604, Leyland ought to be included in this category. Until the late 1590s several Leyland parishes were staffed by lax and conservative clergy, who sometimes did not attend visitations and always made inadequate presentments, while Standish, with a Puritan incumbent, always returned very high numbers of recusants. The northern area, the deanery of Furness and the Lancashire parts of Lonsdale and Kendal, seems to have been non-Catholic, but there is little evidence of popular Protestantism. Manchester was certainly a non-Catholic deanery, and we have seen that it became heavily Puritan. Blackburn might be described as a 'mixed' deanery, for it contained both Puritans and recusants. In 1573 the deanery had been described as 'that part of the diocese which is the worst thought of',[1] but by 1604 only 5% of known recusants lived there, and thereafter there was extensive lay radicalism. Blackburn was too close to Manchester deanery and the West Riding to avoid Protestant influences, especially as the cloth industry grew in size, but the terrain was difficult and it was not well governed, so that Catholic clergy could work in reasonable safety.

The religious boundaries seem to have been finely drawn, as can be seen from a comparison of neighbouring parishes in different deaneries. Standish, in Leyland deanery, returned 12 recusants in 1592, 22 in 1596 and 265 in 1604, but at the same visitations the neighbouring parish of Dean, in the deanery of Manchester, presented 4, 4 and 0. Wigan, in Warrington deanery, presented 120 recusants in 1596 and 209 in 1604, but in the same years Bolton, in the deanery of Manchester, reported 6 and 4. A little further north, Ribchester in Amounderness, despite covering only one-seventh of

---

[1] *Chetham Miscellanies*, VI(1), 23–4.

Table 7[1]

Deanery	Recusants per head of population			Recusants per square mile	
	1590	1595	1604	1604	1641
Warrington	1:131	1:98	1:13	4.3	6.0
Amounderness	1:55	1:92	1:9	4.0	2.5
Leyland	1:234	1:302	1:26	4.0	5.0
Blackburn	1:156	1:150	1:72	0.7	2.6[2]
Manchester	1:3,542	1:3,100	1:2,479	0.03	0.15
Others	1:778	1:1,400	1:1,076[3]	0.03	0.6
All	1:178	1:131	1:27	2.0	2.5

the area and containing one-eighth of the population of nearby Blackburn parish, had 34 recusants to the latter's 25 in 1590, 5 to 21 in 1596, and 141 to 67 in 1604. It appears that Lancashire contained well-defined Catholic and Protestant deaneries, except perhaps for Blackburn, always at issue between the faiths, and the northern deaneries, where neither made much progress.

It would be dangerous, however, to draw these distinctions too sharply, indeed it would be amazing if religious allegiances followed ecclesiastical divisions exactly. Between Warrington and Leyland deaneries in the west and Manchester in the east there was something of a religious 'debateable land', and such recusancy as there was in Manchester deanery was heavily concentrated in the west. At the 1578 visitation 19 of the 24 recusants presented in the deanery lived in the border parishes of Eccles and Dean, and at the 1596 survey 14 of the 16 recusants lived in the western parishes of Bolton, Eccles and Dean. These parishes were sufficiently close to the 'safe' Catholic areas for recusants to receive the ministrations of papist clergy, and it is noticeable that while recusancy intruded into the 'Protestant' Manchester deanery, Puritanism did not overlap, except at the clerical level, into the 'Catholic' deaneries. The 'mixed' deanery of Blackburn almost defies geographical analysis; there were recusants from Samlesbury in the west to Colne in the

[1] Population figures are taken from the 1563 return of households. Recusants from visitations except for 1596 and 1641; my source for 1641 is Lindley, 'Part played by Catholics in the English Civil War', 26.
[2] The 1641 figures for Amounderness and Blackburn are distorted by the use of secular rather than ecclesiastical divisions, so that the heavily recusant parishes of Chipping and Ribchester are included in the hundred of Blackburn rather than the deanery of Amounderness.
[3] The northern deaneries were not visited in 1604; this figure is based on the 1596 return.

east, but apparently few at Rossendale in the south or Clitheroe in the north. The distribution of recusancy may have resulted from the distribution of leading Catholic gentry families; the central band running from Samlesbury through Blackburn itself to Harwood, Church, Padiham, Burnley and Colne – which produced 58 of the deanery's 88 recusants in 1595, 54 out of 69 in 1601 and 144 out of 183 in 1604 – contained the estates of the recusant Southworths, Talbots, Catteralls, Towneleys and Rishtons, and of the church-papist Sherburnes, who could shelter the priests who might keep recusancy alive.

Within the Catholic areas there were considerable variations between parishes. There were twenty-nine parishes in the 'Catholic' deaneries of Warrington, Leyland and Amounderness, and in 1604 2,661 of the 3,322 recusants presented were from only thirteen of them. The thirteen parishes were by far the most thoroughly recusant in Lancashire; in 1604 each had a density of over 5 recusants to the square mile, and in ten more than 1 person in 10 was a recusant. No other parish had anything approaching these concentrations.[1] There is no obvious geographical explanation for their peculiarity; Prescot, Childwall, Sefton, Kirkham, Poulton and Preston were parishes of the coastal fringe, but Chipping, Ribchester, Wigan and Standish were well inland and Huyton, Eccleston and Garstang were hardly coastal. The 'most Catholic' parishes were, on average, the same size as the other sixteen in the three deaneries, though the 'Catholic' parishes had a population density of 60 to the square mile and the rest only 49. The 'Catholic' parishes had more gentry families than the others, an average of 3.6 per parish as against 1.8, and had an average of 2.8 Catholic gentry families as against 1.1 in each of the other sixteen parishes. The 'Catholic' parishes were also the most fragmented, with an average of nine townships in each, as against an average of five in the remainder. Recusancy was most extensive where it was most difficult to control, in densely populated and fragmented parishes, protected by conservative gentry families.

In the three deaneries, five parishes showed very little sign of recusancy. These were North Meols, described in 1639 as having 'no Catholics or exceeding few and poor',[2] Lytham, Penwortham, Brindle and Croston; they were the only parishes in the three deaneries where, in 1604, detected recusants formed less than 1% of the population and there was less than one recusant to the square

---

[1] The 1604 distribution was checked against 1590 and 1596, and the three were found to be very similar. 6 of the 13 parishes had Puritan incumbents, so that detection may have been better, but this was only a little above average (see above, p. 274).

[2] Anstruther, 'Lancashire clergy in 1639', 44.

Table 8

	13 'most Catholic'	5 'least Catholic'	
Recusants to population, 1604	1:8	1:200	(1:700 without Croston)
Average parish size in square miles	27	15	(10 without Croston)
Average parish population	1,603	1,129	(736 without Croston)
Average number of townships	9.0	4.75	
Average number of Catholic gentry	2.8	0.6	

mile. Croston may be an exception in the group, for under Elizabeth it was served by a negligent conservative vicar who may not have presented the recusants in his parish, and in 1630 there were 150 recusants there. North Meols, Lytham and Penwortham were coastal parishes, near the 'most Catholic' Sefton, Preston and Kirkham, while Brindle and Croston were inland parishes near Eccleston and Standish. The five can, however, be distinguished from the other twenty-four in the deaneries; they covered, on average, an area of 15 square miles as against 30 square miles for the rest, their average population was 1,129 as against 1,551, and they embraced an average of 4.75 townships compared with 7 townships in each of the other parishes. There were thus significant differences between the five 'least Catholic' parishes and the thirteen 'most Catholic', as Table 8 shows. Recusancy was most likely in the large, well-populated parishes, which clergy and churchwardens found difficult to supervise, especially if there were gentry of Catholic sympathies to thwart the efforts of the ministers. But in smaller and consolidated parishes, where absence from church was more noticeable and there were few gentry to intimidate the incumbent, recusants were harried into submission and papist clergy found it more difficult to work.

The three northern deaneries, Lonsdale, Kendal and Furness, were neither obviously Catholic nor Protestant. There were isolated cases of recusancy, but its incidence was so erratic that one suspects the difficult terrain made proper detection impossible. The parish of Claughton, towards the southern end of Lonsdale and dominated by the Catholic Croft family, always returned a few recusants, 9 in 1590, 6 in 1595, 5 in 1596 and 13 in 1604. Nearby Tunstall rarely presented recusants at visitation, but in 1605 10 from the parish were indicted at quarter sessions; the Catholic Tunstalls, the wealthiest family in the deanery, held the impropriation of the rectory and the advowson of the vicarage, and they may have hampered the detection of recusants. Further north, in Furness, there were 14 recusants at Hawkshead in 1578 but only 1 in 1590, and Cartmel presented 1 recusant in 1578, 3 in 1590, 2 in 1595 and 3 in 1596. Recusants were never presented at Elizabethan visitations from the parish of Dalton, but in 1641 5 gentlemen and 42 commoners were given as convicted recusants.[1] It is probable that the detection machinery was inadequate in the extreme north of the county, far from both Chester and Richmond, rarely visited and with few J.P.s. Furness caused the government a good deal of worry, for it was thought Spanish invaders might land there, 'all that country being known to Dr Allen (who was born hard by the Pyle), and the inhabitants thereabouts all infected with his Romish poison'. There were masses held in Furness in the early 1590s, when William Battie, the deprived rector of Halton, James Dugdale, briefly vicar of Garstang under Mary, and Richard Bardsey were active in the area, and there was a boat used to carry escaping priests to safety.[2] Five recusant priests are known to have worked in the extreme north of the county, aided by Thomas Bland, the arch-conservative rector of Whittington, but except for fleeting visits to the Middletons of Leighton seminarians seem to have ventured so far north only in flight. Lonsdale and Furness were weakly-parochialised, pastoral areas in which Catholics ought to have done well, and it may be that the north of the county harboured recusants who were never detected.[3] But if the fragmentary evidence is to be taken seriously, it appears that seminary priests neglected the region for the more densely populated southern parts of the county. As in Manchester deanery, though for very different reasons, Catholicism may have declined for want of priestly support: 19 recusants were presented in the three northern deaneries in 1578, 14 in 1590, 8 in 1595, 7 in 1596 and 2 in 1601.

The losses of the Catholics were not paralleled by gains for the established Church. Poor northern benefices attracted few clergy of note, while those who held rich rectories such as Aldingham were normally non-resident. Late in the reign of Elizabeth the incumbents of Aldingham, Bolton-le-Sands, Halton and Kirkby Ireleth were absentees, and in 1610 there were 21 ministers, only 9 of them preachers, for seventeen parish churches and twelve chapels.[4] If the deanery of Manchester had more in common with the West Riding than with the rest of Lancashire, Furness, Kendal and Lonsdale

---

[1] *Lancashire Quarter Sessions*, 277; Lindley, 'Part played by Catholics in the English Civil War', 53.
[2] BM, Lansdowne MS 56, fo. 174; *CRS*, v, 180–1, 221.
[3] In 1593 it was said that during searches the hunted were 'conveyed into caves in the ground or secret places not possible to find them' (*ibid.* 221).
[4] BIY, R VI, A 7, fo. 65, A 11, fos. 38, 42, 55v; *Kenyon MSS*, 7–8.

might be seen as the southern extension of the diocese of Carlisle, where in 1599 the bishop found his people pitifully ignorant, the churches in decay and the clergy poorly-paid and insufficiently learned.[1] It is dangerous to try to sum up the religious history of almost a quarter of a county in one example, but it is worth re-telling John Shaw's story of the old man of Cartmel who, when told of the saving power of Jesus Christ, remarked 'I think I heard of that man you spake of once in a play at Kendal called Corpus Christi play, where there was a man on a tree and blood ran down.'[2]

It was not, however, in this northern area of both Catholic and Puritan failure that witchcraft and associated popular superstitions seem to have been most prevalent, unless they were so common that reports were not made. The loss of the assize records for the whole of the reign of Elizabeth and of the quarter sessions rolls for most of the period, makes any discussion of witchcraft accusations difficult, but in view of Lancashire's reputation as a witch-ridden region the problem can hardly be ignored. Between 1562 and 1604 28 individuals are known to have been accused of witchcraft or similar offences, 19 of them at visitations, 5 before the Ecclesiastical Commission, 2 are known from other sources to have been tried at assizes, 1 case went to Star Chamber and another led to proceedings in the Chester consistory. Unless accusations were normally made at assizes rather than at visitation, the number seems rather small; we have the returns for fourteen visitations between 1563 and 1604, but they produced only 19 accusations.

Only 7 of the 28 were actually accused of witchcraft, though 3 others were said to have gone to witches for help; there was 1 witchcraft charge in 1585, 1 in 1595, 2 in 1597, 2 in 1598 and 1 in 1601. The only well-documented case is that of Edmund Hartley, who was executed in 1597. Hartley acquired a reputation in the Leigh area for his skill with 'popish charms and herbs' and, when a seminary priest was unable to cure two children possessed by devils, Hartley was employed by their father, Nicholas Starkey, to treat the children for 40s a year. He then became a resident exorcist, but when Starkey refused to increase the salary and five children and two servants of the household fell ill, Hartley was tried for conjuring evil spirits.[3] The late 1590s saw a minor witch-craze in Lancashire; in 1594 Ferdinando, earl of Derby, was thought to have been murdered by witchcraft, in 1596–7 John Darrell, the Puritan exorcist, travelled through the county, in 1597 Hartley was executed and Alice Brereley of Castleton was pardoned for killing two men by witchcraft, and in

---

[1] *CSPD* (1598–1601), 362.
[2] Quoted Richardson, *Puritanism in North-West England*, 4.
[3] C. L. Ewen, *Witchcraft and Demonianism*, 186–7.

1598 two Rochdale women were accused of witchcraft and a group of seminary priests drew large crowds to public exorcisms.[1] There was certainly some fear at this time of the consequences of an accusation, and in 1595 Ellen Osbaldeston of Blackburn sued for slander those who had called her a witch.[2]

Seventeen of the accused were merely 'charmers' or 'blessers'; in 1595 Alice Staven of Stalmine was said to use 'charms upon the eyes of men', but those who used their skills to cure cattle were more common. A few, such as Thomas Batton in 1562, were more malevolent, and used charming to kill cattle.[3] The importance of exorcism, blessing and charming suggests that we are dealing with a debased form of Catholic piety, and there was a connection between assumed wizardry and assumed conservatism. The priest of Harwood and the schoolmaster of Whalley who were accused of sorcery in 1571 had been aiding recusant clergy, Catholics were thought to have bewitched the fifth earl of Derby to death, Edmund Hartley's charms were 'popish' and he was only called in when seminarians had failed, and the outbreak of accusations in the late 1590s coincided with increased official activity against Catholics.[4] Some support for this view comes from the geographical incidence of accusations. We know the home parishes of 26 of those charged: 13 lived in the deanery of Warrington, 4 in the deanery of Blackburn, 3 in Leyland, 3 in Lancashire north of the Ribble and 3 in Manchester deanery. We might expect that the virtual exclusion of Catholic clergy from the south-east of the county forced men to turn to lay charmers and exorcists for protection, while accusations might be more likely in an anti-superstitious Protestant area.[5] But, on the contrary, the use of charms and Catholicism tended to go together for, though the records for the heavily recusant deanery of Warrington are no better than those for other areas, it produced half the known cases of witchcraft and related practices. Seven of the eighteen accusations made between 1590 and 1601 came from the 'Catholic' parishes of Prescot and Wigan, and were presumably made by the Puritan incumbents.

There is some evidence, however, that concern over witchcraft proper was more common in the radical south-east. Three of the seven accusations of actual wichcraft were made in Manchester deanery, all three at Rochdale in 1597-8, and all the known charges in the area were of witchcraft rather than mere charming. But later

[1] *Ibid.* 174-5; K. Thomas, *Religion and the Decline of Magic*, 483; *CSPD* (1595-7), 406; CRO, EDV 1/12a, fo. 85v; *Salisbury MSS*, VIII, 213-14, 293.
[2] CRO, EDC 5, 1595.   [3] BIY, R VI, A 14, fo. 74v; CRO, EDA 12/2, fo. 82.
[4] BIY, R VII, HCAB 6, fos. 64v, 67v.
[5] Thomas, *Religion and the Decline of Magic*, 477-501.

accusations of witchcraft came almost entirely from conservative areas; the four major Lancashire trials of the early seventeenth century all originated in the deanery of Blackburn, and there were several lesser trials at the quarter sessions of West Derby hundred.[1] Accusations of witchcraft, charming and sorcery were most common in the Catholic sections of the county, rather than in the Puritan south-east or the neutral north. There was, no doubt, a widespread 'magical' element in religion at the popular level in addition to the denominational loyalties discussed here but, even allowing for our almost total reliance on ecclesiastical sources, witchcraft does not appear to have been a major problem in the Elizabethan period. The Puritan ministers who complained about the state of Lancashire religion in 1590 found much to say about popery, but they failed to mention witchcraft.[2]

The religious characteristics of Lancashire, excluding Lonsdale, have been defined in terms of a relatively strong Catholicism in the deaneries of Warrington, Leyland and Amounderness, a relatively strong Protestantism in Manchester deanery, and a mixed situation in Blackburn. There were several general forces which may have shaped this distribution, and they will be considered in turn. First of all, there is no straightforward link between the pattern of religious allegiance and the pattern of agriculture. Although it is true, as Dr Bossy has pointed out, that the 'agrarian plain' of central and south-west Lancashire tended towards Catholicism while the pastoral uplands of the east tended to be Protestant, the structure of land-usage was rather more complex.[3] The demarcation line between the 'Protestant' Manchester deanery and the 'Catholic' deaneries of Leyland and Warrington was not the edge of the upland pastoral area to the west of the Pennines; rather it ran down the middle of the broad arable band which stretched from Preston to Manchester. Leyland and Warrington included not only the western portion of this strip, but also the wet lands of south-west Lancashire, which made arable farming difficult and enforced specialisation in stock-rearing. The 'Catholic' deanery of Amounderness included another badly drained pastoral area on the Fylde coast and the pastoral uplands to the north, but the two were separated by an arable belt set back from the Fylde and no perceptible religious variations followed these lines. Pastoral farming went with Catholicism in south-west Lancashire and the Fylde, but with Protestant-

---

[1] *Ibid.* 220, 234, 525, 557; Ewen, *Witchcraft and Demonianism*, 213–23, 226–8, 244–51, 408–13.
[2] *State Civil and Ecclesiastical, passim.*
[3] Bossy, *English Catholic Community*, ch. 5; Rogers, 'Land use in Tudor Lancashire', *passim.*

ism in the east and south-east, while arable areas included the 'Protestant' eastern section of the central arable band and the 'Catholic' inner Fylde. Within these areas no more than 60 % of the land was devoted to specialisation in either stock or crops, so that there were no wide agrarian distinctions which might have provided the foundations for religious differences.

It seems, however, that there were fewer social disruptions in the 'Catholic' region than in the 'Protestant', though much work remains to be done on this point. The agrarian life of western Lancashire changed very little during the Tudor period, and the drastic increases in entry fines which caused so much rancour elsewhere appear to have come to the county only under the Stuarts. In the sixteenth century the Farington family built up a whole new complex of estates in the west of the palatinate, but did not attempt to increase rents on their newly acquired lands and cultivated only a small proportion of the estate themselves, while on the demesne the emphasis was on production for household consumption rather than exploitation for the market.[1] In Warrington, Leyland and Amounderness, landlord–tenant relations were good, and the area's tradition of country sports may suggest a harmonious and well-ordered society; in Manchester deanery, on the other hand, the Puritan gentry fought for more than a generation to suppress Sunday and May games.[2] If there was disruption in the 'Protestant' sector of the county it probably resulted from population pressure on land. In 1563 the population density was 57 to the square mile in Warrington deanery and 38 in Amounderness, but 76 in the deanery of Manchester, while the tendency for more families to turn to weaving in the east of Lancashire as land became scarce indicates that thereafter the disparity increased. There was certainly a marked difference between south-west and east Lancashire by the time of the Civil War; the absence of conflict in the former made it possible for royalist landlords to raise forces from among their tenants, but in Rossendale, with population pressure and agrarian grievances, the people were anti-royalist.[3] Under Elizabeth, tenants in the more peaceful areas were willing to follow many of their landlords and remain Catholic, accepting the ministrations of the priests who often came

[1] Long, 'Wealth of the magisterial class', 111–12; Atherton, 'Estates of William Farington', 37–40, 104–15, 122–4.

[2] Walker, *Historical Geography of South-West Lancashire*, 62; Blackwood, 'Lancashire cavaliers and their tenants', 21; Bossy, *English Catholic Community*, ch. 5; *Farington Papers*, 128–9; Baines, *History of the County Palatine and Duchy of Lancaster*, I, 549–50; J. Tait, 'The declaration of sports for Lancashire', *EHR*, XXXII.

[3] BM, Harleian MS 594, fos. 101, 102, 108; Lindley, 'Part played by Catholics in the English Civil War', 193–5; Tupling, *Economic History of Rossendale*, 76–96, 167, 235.

from the local gentry, rather than throw in their lot with a strident and aggressive Puritanism. In the deanery of Manchester, however, Catholic gentry were unable to hold the allegiance of their tenants, who declared their independence by opting for Protestantism.

There does seem to have been a correlation between the pattern of industrial and commercial development and the distribution of sectarian loyalties. The parishes which specialised in linen weaving – Wigan, Ormskirk and Preston – tended towards Catholicism, while the areas of woollen manufacture and of both linen and woollen weaving were largely Protestant. The linen weavers drew their raw materials from Catholic Ireland and the Fylde and sold their wares locally, but woollen weavers bought from broggers who dealt mainly with radical districts, and their cloth was sold in the West Riding, East Anglia and especially London. The Protestant parts of the county were those most open to outside influences; 14 of the county's 31 markets were in the deaneries of Manchester and Blackburn, giving a market for every 42 square miles, but only 12 were in Warrington, Leyland and Amounderness, where there was a market for every 70 square miles. The number of markets probably reflects the frequency of contact with the outside world, a world from which traders might bring Protestantism as well as merchandise. Lack of regular contact with the rest of England could, however, be an advantage; there were several outbreaks of plague and similar diseases in Manchester in the sixteenth century, but the first serious plague to hit Preston since the Black Death was not until 1630–1.[1] West Lancashire was insulated from dangerously contagious radical ideas as it was insulated from dangerously contagious diseases.

The distribution of religious opinion both resulted from, and determined, the nature of clerical activity. In 1590 10 of the 13 incumbents in the deaneries of Manchester and Blackburn were Puritan, but only 10 of the 29 incumbents in Warrington, Amounderness and Leyland shared their views. The inactivity of the established Church in some districts contributed to the survival of Catholicism; in 1596 only 1 of the 9 incumbents in Amounderness was making serious efforts to convert his Catholic parishioners. The network of exercises established by Bishop Chadderton lapsed during the 1590s in the conservative areas, but continued in the Puritan deaneries.[2] Protestantism could be created and sustained only by the vigorous preaching provided by the Puritan ministers, while recusancy was impossible without the support of the seminary priests. There were about 29 seminarians and ageing recusant clergy in the three 'Catholic' deaneries in 1590, but there were only 2 in

[1] J. F. D. Shrewsbury, *A History of Bubonic Plague in the British Isles*, 362–3.
[2] *CRS*, LIII, 101–5; Richardson, *Puritanism in North-West England*, 66–7.

Blackburn and none in Manchester. In the western deaneries conservative sympathy made it fairly safe for seminary priests to operate, but the Protestantism of the south-east made that area too dangerous for them; conversely, Puritan clergy might reap a harvest of souls in Manchester deanery, but they were given a hostile reception elsewhere. Whereas Salford hundred provided Protestant J.P.s to staff quarter sessions in other districts, the few Catholics in Salford were cared for by priests from the rest of the county.[1]

Behind agrarian, industrial and even clerical influences on the religious development of Lancashire lay a fundamental geographical distinction. The most Protestant deanery was Manchester, that area nearest London, the Midlands and the West Riding, while the second most radical district was the deanery immediately to the north. The trading and intellectual links which were established were naturally between Manchester and London rather than Preston and London, and between Rochdale and Halifax rather than Wigan and Halifax. The more Catholic deaneries were the fringe coastal ones, where priests could land from Ireland and fugitives could escape,[2] and where recusants were fairly safe behind the peat-mosses which separated them from Manchester. As in Yorkshire, the Catholic parts of Lancashire were those well away from the most important town, the centre of operations for anti-recusant activity.[3] Unlike Yorkshire, however, the most thoroughly Catholic parishes were not those furthest from Manchester, for Warrington, Winwick, Leigh and Wigan, to the east of the deanery of Warrington, had recusant groups as large as those in Sefton, Ormskirk and Halsall in the west. The same was true in Leyland – with a significant amount of recusancy in eastward Standish as well as Eccleston in the west – and in Amounderness, with Catholics in Ribchester and Preston in the south-east of the deanery as well as further north and west in Poulton and Lancaster.

Although there were 'border' areas of potential conflict where 'Catholic' and 'Puritan' deaneries met, and though there might be trouble when Puritan clergy intruded into 'Catholic' parishes, the two religious extremes were segregated in separate compartments of the county and there was little sectarian friction. Where there was conflict it was not normally between Puritans and Catholics, but between Puritans and Catholics alike and the established Church. From about 1590, first under pressure from Archbishop Whitgift, bishops of Chester and archbishops of York tried to drive Lancashire Puritans into conformity. Increasingly, the radicals were pre-

---

[1] BM, Cotton MS, Titus B. II, fo. 240; *Recusant History*, IV, 39.
[2] PRO, SP 12/266, fo. 40; *Salisbury MSS*, IX, 19.
[3] Aveling, 'Aspects of Yorkshire Catholic recusant history', 113–14.

sented as dangerous subversives rather than, as they had been under Bishop Chadderton, the mainstay of local Protestantism, and the Puritans reacted by turning to conventicles and eventually to Presbyterianism.[1] Anglican assertiveness against Puritans was paralleled by more vigorous attempts to bring Catholics under control. There were drives against recusants and even church-papists in 1590, 1592 and 1598, and in 1599–1600 at least seven priests were arrested; in 1600 the first executions of seminary priests in Lancashire took place, and officials saw this as the end of an era of undue tolerance.[2]

In the 1560s and 1570s, when a substantial section of clerical conservative opinion remained within the established Church, when many of the recusant priests were recent colleagues of the conformists, and when recusancy was not considered a dangerous force, Catholics were rarely reported, and were proceeded against even less often. But as the Puritan element among the clergy of the official Church grew and as the authorities became worried by what seemed to be a Spanish 'fifth-column', the detection and punishment of Catholics increased. Yet the confidence of the recusants grew with the size of the seminarian element among their clergy, and from about 1590 they began to defend themselves against attack. A group of Puritan ministers complained in 1590 that the Catholics were trying to switch official attention from the failings of recusants to those of Protestant nonconformists, and at the autumn assizes Justice Walmesley, whose wife was a local recusant, stressed the danger of Puritan rather than Catholic offences.[3] In the following year, when the bishop's secretary complained of the arrogance of the papists towards the secular magistrates, events took a more serious turn. Two officers of the Ecclesiastical Commission were sent to Wigan to seize the property of a convicted recusant, but they were driven off by a group of Catholics. When a search for those guilty of the attack was conducted, they could not be found, and they were presumably concealed by conservative sympathisers. In the middle of 1592 some papists were backing physical resistance by open criticism of royal policy towards them, and complaint was made of 'unreverent and audacious speeches' at a recusant funeral.[4]

After the great anti-recusancy drive of 1592 had passed, Catholics became quiescent once more, although official pressure might still encounter opposition and in 1595 a captured priest was rescued by his co-religionists.[5] But in 1598, when action against recusants was

[1] Tupling, 'Causes of the Civil War in Lancashire', 3–5.
[2] *Salisbury MSS*, X, 283–5.
[3] *State Civil and Ecclesiastical*, 11; BM, Additional MS 48064, fos. 68–69.
[4] PRO, SP 12/235, fo. 146; *APC*, XXII, 92–3, 468–9, 529, XXIII, 64–5.
[5] *Kenyon MSS*, 585–6.

again stepped up, there began six years of intermittent resistance by local Catholics. Bishop Vaughan had trouble in collecting the 1598 assessments on some recusants towards the cost of the queen's forces in Ireland, and early in the following year he sent pursuivants to arrest a group of defaulters in the notoriously recusant parish of Prescot. As had happened at Wigan in 1591, the messengers were assaulted by local Catholics and magistrates found it difficult to apprehend the malefactors. Sir Richard Mollineux found the names of fourteen of those responsible, though he was unable to arrest them, and Vaughan thought they were hidden by recusant gentry. By the November assizes some of the rioters had been taken, but the justices thought the case might not be proved and doubted if a jury which would convict could be found in such a corrupt county. In January 1600, a year after the event, eight of those indicted were still free, and there were others who had been involved but whose identity had not yet been traced.[1]

The Prescot affair was still unsolved when trouble began further south in equally Catholic Childwall. In May 1600 there were riots led by the tenants of the church-papist Edward Norris, and in August Norris' men were involved in an assault on a justice of the peace and the constable of the hundred; some weeks after the August incident cattle belonging to the constable were maimed. A mob of about fifty people was involved in the attack on the justice, and the Privy Council regarded Norris, 'on whom the whole rabble of these malefactors seem to depend', as responsible; it later emerged that a seminary priest had been involved in the planning. Despite intensive enquiries, only eleven of the participants were taken, and there was much official concern at 'such audacious insolencies'.[2] On the evening of 20 August 1600, an equally serious incident took place in Garstang, another centre of recusancy. After some local Catholics had been arrested, the pursuivant, the vicar and a Puritan Queen's Preacher based in the parish were besieged in the vicarage by a score of armed men, some of whom fired muskets at the house. All 73 of the people later interviewed by the sheriff and three justices denied any knowledge of the rioters and marksmen, and no-one seems to have been punished.[3] There was further violence late in September, when a captured seminarian named Middleton was being moved from Preston to Lancaster gaol. A band of mounted men attacked the escort and tried to free the priest, though they were beaten back and one of the assailants was taken.[4]

[1] *APC*, XXIX, 300–1, 604–5, 606–7; *CSPD* (1598–1601), 389–90; *Salisbury MSS*, IX, 398–9.
[2] *Ibid.* X, 160, 311, 373; *CSPD* (1598–1601), 482; *APC*, XXX, 662–3, 746, 757–8.
[3] PRO, SP 12/275, fos. 124–128; *Salisbury MSS*, X, 311, 315.
[4] *Ibid.* 335–6; *CSPD* (1598–1601), 485–6; *APC*, XXX, 720–1.

The new prisoner turned out to be Thurstan Hunt, a seminary priest who had organised the Childwall disorders and the attempt to rescue Middleton, and who was said to have been responsible for all the recent troubles. His explanation of the violence was simple: if the government treated Catholics as traitors, they had the right to defend themselves, and it is true that the recorded attacks were designed to forestall arrests or free captured Catholics. Hunt had another plan to prevent persecution by discrediting those responsible. He wrote to the queen and had broadsheets ready to be printed, alleging that those leading the drive against Catholics in Lancashire saw the defeat of the papists, whom Hunt represented as the bastions of the throne, as the preliminary to the overthrow of Elizabeth and the crowning of the earl of Essex. Among those he accused were Bishop Vaughan, who had ordered the attempted arrests early in 1599, Sir Richard Mollineux, who had led the enquiry into the Garstang shooting and arrested Robert Middleton, and the dean of Chester, who in 1598 had harassed the recusants of Sefton.[1] Hunt was clearly a determined and imaginative fellow, and no mean propagandist.

The apprehension of Thurstan Hunt and his execution at Lancaster in April 1601 did not bring an end to Catholic resistance. In August 1601 the Ecclesiastical Commission sent two pursuivants to arrest a group of recusants in Chipping, but the officers were driven back by the offenders and their supporters. A few months later a goldsmith from Claughton, who had been one of the ring-leaders in the 'Garstang seige', was taken, but he too was rescued and twelve months later the authorities were still unable to find those who had freed him.[2] In 1604 James Gardiner, a seminary priest, was arrested at Poulton, but while being carried to Lancaster he was rescued, though one of his deliverers was himself taken and later executed. By this stage, priests seem to have been taking care for their own protection, and three seminarians in the Winwick area had a bodyguard 'who usually doth carry pistols for defence of the said seminaries'.[3] The years 1603–4 saw, in fact, a flurry of plots and half-hearted military activity in Lancashire. Soon after Elizabeth's death some local recusants, apparently in concert, began buying up arms but nothing came of this; two years later Bishop Lloyd was still worried by the number of recusants who had weapons purchased in 1603.[4] James I's proclamation of February 1604 that all priests were

[1] *Salisbury MSS*, X, 335–6, XI, 109, 160, 165–8; *CSPD* (1598–1601), 486–7, Addenda (1580–1625), 399–400.

[2] *Lancashire Quarter Sessions*, 116–17, 127–8.

[3] Anstruther, *Seminary Priests*, 126; PRO, SP 14/8/34, fo. 1v.

[4] *Salisbury MSS*, XV, 88, 92–3, XVI, 320–1. The purchases may have been linked to talk elsewhere of seizing James and forcing him to grant Catholics toleration.

to leave England provoked a few Lancashire missioners to draw up one of the most hare-brained schemes that even English Catholics produced. The priests intended to raise support in Lancashire and seize the port of Chester, and then either hold it against the king or plunder it and escape by sea, presumably taking the city's wealth to help finance the seminaries abroad.[1] The severely practical Thurstan Hunt would have had none of this nonsense, and lay Catholics had more wit than to force a confrontation with the new king.

The years 1598–1604, which saw successful efforts by Catholics at self-protection, also saw a massive expansion of Lancashire recusancy, and there was a mood of confidence among local Catholics. The probably inadequate visitation of 1598 had detected 498 recusants, but in 1601 the bishop found 754, and by January 1603 there were almost 2,000 recusants in five deaneries; by Vaughan's visitation in the winter of 1604 there were 3,516 known recusants in the same five deaneries.[2] Unless we assume that the 1601 visitation was particularly careless and that of 1604 especially diligent, we must concede impressive gains by the seminary priests. It is surprising that recusancy should have gained ground in the years immediately before Elizabeth's death, when the Appellant controversy raged and the local Catholic clerical staff was weakened by the arrest of at least seven priests and the death of one more in 1599–1600. Perhaps the age of the queen, and the tentative negotiations between some Appellant clergy and the government, held out hopes of toleration and gave church-papists confidence to take the step into recusancy. Perhaps the anti-Catholic effort slackened as a result of disputes over the division of the Stanley inheritance, or the capture of the priests may have made the authorities complaisant, or the rescues of 1599 and after may have persuaded officials to leave Catholics in peace. These explanations seem inadequate, and the 1604 count of 'old recusants' probably included many who had not attended church in 1601 but had not been returned at that visitation. Certainly three normally heavily recusant parishes, Sefton, Winwick and Lancaster, had presented no recusants at all in 1601, and the lists for Halsall and Standish were totally unsatisfactory; a supplement for these parishes alone would add another 200 recusants to the 754 detected.

There can be no doubt that an increase in recusancy followed the death of Elizabeth. Archbishop Hutton noted it, and remarked sourly that it was because the government was wasting its time

[1] PRO, SP 14/8/31, 34.
[2] CRO, EDV 1/13, *passim*. The January 1603 figure is calculated from the 1604 visitation, which distinguished between 'old recusants' before the queen's death and those who had 'revolted' from the established Church since.

chasing Puritans: 'I wish with all my heart that the like order were given not only to all bishops but to all magistrates and justices of the peace, etc., to proceed against papists and recusants; who of late, partly by this round dealing against the Puritans and partly by some extraordinary favour, have grown mightily in number, courage and insolency.'[1] In the eighteen months following the queen's death, the churchwardens of Sefton thought the number of recusants in the parish had risen from 42 to 101, the Prescot wardens thought their increase was from 157 to 569, and at Wigan the increase was from 113 to 209.[2] The 1604 visitation was careful, but it seems unlikely that a visitation at which eleven churches and chapels did not make proper presentments could have been so much better than that of 1601 that detections could multiply by five times while recusancy remained stable. Vaughan observed cryptically 'many fallen away by reason of the cessation of the commission ecclesiastical', and thought that at Prescot 'the persons named in this presentment are of mean reputation and of no force or ability of themselves, and many may for the most part easily by authority be reclaimed when their hopes are at an end and the laws executed'. He was, to a point, correct that the increase of recusancy was due to temporary phenomena, especially the laxity of persecution in James' first year and the 'great hope' of toleration reported by Garnet.[3] But even after the proclamation of February 1604 the confidence of Lancashire Catholics remained high. Prescot recusants flaunted their absence from services, walking up and down outside the church, while Edward Millington, a seminary priest, 'went openly from house to house in the town of Wigan in the day time, and namely was at the house of Grace Mason, widow, there drinking'.[4] Congregations of over a hundred attended masses in Farnworth and Winwick, and five years later a worried local Protestant bewailed

the ruins of the Church of God [in] many places of this county, by reason of the increase of papists' profaning of the sabbath and other enormities, which the most are not ashamed to commit without remorse of conscience or fear or law. The Lord redress it in his good time; for the which let us all strive with the Highest in prayer most fervently to obtain.[5]

The Catholic gains of 1603–4 were, in substance, retained and, although there is evidence of a drift from recusancy into noncommunicating about 1613, the number of recusants detected remained remarkably stable; the 3,516 presented in 1604 were almost

[1] Babbage, *Puritanism and Richard Bancroft*, 113–14.
[2] CRO, EDV 1/13, fos. 88v–92v, 95v–111, 132v–142v.
[3] *CRS*, LIII, 146–7; Caraman, *Henry Garnet*, 305.
[4] CRO, EDV 1/13, fos. 143v–144v; PRO, SP 14/8/33.
[5] *CRS*, LIII, 150; PRO, SP 14/8/34, fos. 1v–2; *Kenyon MSS*, 16.

exactly matched by the 3,433 presented in 1630. Lancashire recusancy had not been crushed, and the county palatine had become what it was to remain, by far the most Catholic shire in England.

The established Church was no more effective in its efforts to combat clerical Puritanism, and from about 1604 there was increasing evidence that radical Protestantism was firmly established among the laity of the south-east of the county. Official pressures late in the reign of Elizabeth and early in that of James had done nothing to weaken either of the religious extremes, and there were few hints of a substantial Anglican presence, except in the sense of mere passive conformity, until after the Civil War. Whatever may have been true elsewhere, the Reformation in Lancashire did not see the replacement of one uniform orthodoxy by another, but the division of the community into two competing religious factions. During the course of the sixteenth century, Lancashire changed from one of the counties least divided by religious allegiances to probably the most deeply divided area of England; monopoly gave way to competition, and the palatinate became, in Fuller's words, 'the cockpit of conscience'. Reformation by official decree failed to destroy widespread popular Catholicism, while the unofficial Reformation of preachers and traders failed to capture more than one corner of the county. The uneven infiltration of reformist beliefs followed most nearly the uneven control exercised by ecclesiastical and secular authorities, since the machinery for change was fundamental to the implementation of the Reformation. Thomas Fuller's description of the results of the Reformation in Lancashire was that:

The people, generally devout, are (as I am informed) northward and by the west popishly affected, which in the other parts (intended by antiperistasis) are zealous Protestants. Hence it is that many subtle papists and Jesuits have been born and bred in this county which have met their matches, to say no more, in the natives of the same county.[1]

---

[1] T. Fuller, *History of the Worthies of England*, ed. P. A. Nuttall, II, 189.

Appendix 1

Deprivations of Lancashire clergy, 1559–1575

A. THOSE DEFINITELY DEPRIVED

1559 Laurence Vaux, warden of Manchester College
(He did not appear at the 1559 visitation, and by 1560 he had been replaced as warden; he was ordered to remain at Worcester, but by 1561 was working secretly in Lancashire; PRO, SP 12/10, fo. 51; *VCH*, IV, 195; *CSPD*, Addenda (1547–65), 522.)

Richard Hart, fellow of Manchester College
(He appeared at the visitation but refused to subscribe, and was ordered to appear at Lambeth; he did so and was apparently deprived and restricted to Kent or Sussex, but by 1561 he was 'lurking' in Lancashire; PRO, SP 12/10, fos. 51, 184; *CSPD*, Addenda (1547–65), 522.)

John Coppage, fellow of Manchester College
(He failed to appear at the visitation and must have been removed with the others; he was a recusant priest in Lancashire by 1568, and was in prison at Chester by 1577; PRO, SP 12/10, fo. 51; 12/152/48; CRO, EDA 12/2, fo. 118.)

John Hampson, archdeacon of Richmond and vicar of Rochdale
(He was removed from the archdeaconry in October 1559, though he sat as official at Chester until February 1561; his successor at Rochdale was presented, 'per deprivationem', in March 1561, and in that year he fled overseas; PRO, SP 12/10, fos. 74–74v; CRO, EDC 1/16, fo. 80; *Reg. Parker*, II, 778–9; *CSPD*, Addenda (1547–65), 524.)

Thomas Dobson, vicar of Urswick
(He was replaced as vicar by a previous married and deprived incumbent; PRO, SP 12/10, fos. 72v–73.)

1562 James Hargreaves, vicar of Blackburn
(He was replaced, 'per deprivationem', in 1562, and by 1568 was active as a recusant priest; *Reg. Parker*, II, 787; CRO, EDA 12/2, fo. 118.)

1569 William Langley, rector of Prestwich
(He refused to perform the Prayer Book services and was replaced 'per deprivationem'; CRO, EDA 12/2, fos. 119v–120, 121; EDA 1/1, Part 3, fo. 1.)

1571 William Battie, rector of Halton
(He was replaced 'per deprivationem' and by 1590 was living secretly and saying masses in Furness; *Reg. Parker*, II, 600; *CRS*, V, 181.)

1572 Elizeus Ambrose, vicar of Ormskirk
(He was replaced 'per deprivationem' in 1572, and died later in the same year; *VCH*, III, 244; *Ormskirk Reg.* 152.)

1575 Christopher Thompson, rector of Winwick
(He stopped performing Prayer Book services in 1571 and began consorting with papists; after trial before the consistory he was replaced 'per deprivationem'; CRO, EDC 5, 1575; *VCH*, IV, 128.)

Ten men were deprived; six became recusant priests and one went into exile.

B. THOSE POSSIBLY DEPRIVED

There is a gap in the institution act book series, covering the years 1561–9, and the entries are scrappy thereafter; unexplained disappearances by known conservatives may suggest deprivations.

? James Dugdale, ? fellow of Manchester and ? vicar of Garstang
(If the Crown's presentations of Dugdale to either or both of these posts were effective, he must have been deprived; he was assisting at masses in Cartmel *c*. 1590; *CPR*, Philip and Mary, IV, 247, 447; *CRS*, V, 181–2.)

1564–5 Edward Lowe, vicar of Huyton
(He was disciplined in 1564 for using holy water and encouraging his people to pray in the old ways; he was no longer vicar by July 1565; CRO, EDA 12/2, fo. 80; EDV 1/3, fo. 71.)

1572 James Lingard, vicar of Ribchester
(He was called before the York Ecclesiastical Commission in November 1569 with a group of known conservative clergy to answer articles alleged against him, and was placed in the custody of the sheriff of York; he was released when he agreed to read a declaration in his parish church, which he duly did; replaced in 1572; BIY, R VII, HCAB 4, fos. 184, 198, 199, 210v; HCAB 5, fo. 2; *VCH*, VII, 42.)

Appendix 2

Resignations by possible conservatives

1559 Robert Ashton, rector of Middleton and Radcliffe
(He resigned both rectories, and died in 1563; *VCH*, V, 65, 158.)

1562 James Anderton, vicar of Garstang
(*VCH*, VII, 298.)

1563   Robert Brooke, rector of Aldingham
(He failed to appear at the royal visitation in 1559, and resigned in 1563; PRO, SP 12/10, fo. 158; *VCH*, VIII, 326.)

Anthony Mollineux, rector of Walton
(He failed to appear at the visitation of 1559, and by the visitation of 1563 he was 'ultra mare'; successor instituted in 1565; PRO, SP 12/10, fo. 157v; CRO, EDV 1/3, fo. 33v; *VCH*, III, 7.)

1570   William Crosse, vicar of Childwall
(He was excused the oath at the 1563 visitation, and resigned in 1570; a William Crosse, curate of Hale in Childwall, was a 'naughty papist' in 1571; CRO, EDV 1/3, fo. 33; *VCH*, III, 106; BIY, R VII, HCAB 6, fo. 87.)

1571   William Blackleach, rector of Wigan
(*VCH*, IV, 63; *Reg. Parker*, II, 598.)

Gowther Kenyon, rector of Bury
(He was called before the York Ecclesiastical Commission in 1571 for an unknown offence, but was dismissed when he agreed to resign his benefice; BIY, R VII, HCAB 6, fo. 72; *VCH*, V, 125.)

1581   George Dobson, vicar of Whalley
(He was frequently in trouble for conservative words and practices, and finally resigned; he was said to have been induced to do so by Bishop Chadderton; he died in 1583; see above, pp. 217–18; *VCH*, VI, 358–9; *Whalley Reg.* 153.)

1583   Edward Croft, rector of Heysham
(He resigned his benefice and seems later to have been a recusant; *VCH*, VIII, 117; *Lancashire and Cheshire Exchequer Depositions*, 13.)

Bibliography

I MANUSCRIPTS

Bodleian Library, Oxford
Brasenose College Manuscripts
Tanner Manuscripts

Borthwick Institute of Historical Research, York (BIY)
PN   Precedent Papers
R/I   Archbishops' Registers
R VI, A   Visitation Act Books
R VII, G   Consistory Cause Papers
R VII, HCAB   High Commission Act Books

British Museum (BM)
Additional Manuscripts
Cotton Manuscripts: Cleopatra, Titus, Vespasian
Harleian Manuscripts
Lansdowne Manuscripts

Cheshire County Record Office, Chester (CRO)
EDA 1   Institution Act Books and Ordination Registers
EDA 2   Bishops' Registers
EDA 3/1   Bishop Bridgeman's Register
EDA 12   Proceedings of Royal Commissioners
EDC 1   Consistory Act Books
EDC 2   Consistory Depositions Books
EDC 5   Consistory Cause Papers (these are unsorted; references in the
    footnotes and appendixes are to years)
EDR 1   Registrar's Memoranda Book, 1575–7
EDR 6   Registrar's Precedent Book
EDV 1   Visitation Correction Books
EDV 2   Visitation Call Books

Lancashire County Record Office, Preston (LRO)
DDBl   Blundell of Crosby Papers
DDCl   Clifton Papers
DDF   Farington Papers
DDHu   Hulton Papers
DDIb   Ireland Blackburne Papers
DDIn   Blundell of Ince Blundell Papers
DDK   Stanley of Knowsley Papers
DDM   Mollineux Papers
DDN   Hesketh Papers
DDPt   Petre Papers
DDTo   Towneley Papers

Bibliography

Leeds City Library, Department of Manuscripts (LCL)
RD/A   Richmond Consistory Act Books
RD/AC   Richmond Consistory Cause Papers
RD/RP   Richmond Probate Registers

Lichfield Joint Record Office (Lich. RO)
B/A/1   Bishops' Registers
B/C/2   Consistory Act Books
B/C/13 Episcopal Court Book, 1511–12
B/V/1   Visitation Books

Public Record Office (PRO)
Chancery Records:
C 1   Early Chancery Proceedings
Duchy of Lancaster Records:
DL 1   Bills and Answers
DL 3   Depositions and Examinations
DL 5   Entry Books of Decrees and Orders
DL 14   Colleges and Chantries
DL 28   Various Accounts
DL 29   Ministers' Accounts
DL 41   Miscellaneous Documents
DL 42   Miscellaneous Books
DL 43   Rentals and Surveys
DL 44   Special Commissions
Exchequer Records:
E 36   Exchequer of Receipt, Miscellaneous Books
E 134 Exchequer Depositions
E 334 First Fruits and Tenths Office, Composition Books
Palatinate of Lancaster Records:
PL 15   Plea Rolls
PL 20   Writs Prothonotary
PL 25   Assize Rolls
PL 26   Indictments
Records of the Court of Requests:
Req. 2   Proceedings
Special Collections:
SC 6   Ministers' Accounts
SC 11   Rentals and Surveys, Rolls
SC 12   Rentals and Surveys, Portfolios
Records of the Court of Star Chamber:
Sta.Cha.2   Proceedings
State Papers:
SP 1   Henry VIII
SP 2R   Henry VIII, large folios
SP 10   Edward VI
SP 11   Mary
SP 12   Elizabeth I, Domestic
SP 14   James I, Domestic
SP 15   Addenda, Edward VI–James I

Bibliography

II PRINTED WORKS AND THESES

Act Book of the Ecclesiastical Court of Whalley, ed. A. M. Cooke, CS, NS, XLIV, 1901.

Acts of the Privy Council of England, ed. J. R. Dasent, 32 vols. 1890–1907.

Allen, W., *Letters and Memorials*, ed. T. F. Knox, 1882.

Anstruther, G., 'Lancashire clergy in 1639', *Recusant History*, IV. *The Seminary Priests*, nd.

Ascham, R., *Works*, ed. J. A. Giles, 3 vols. 1864–5.

Ashmore, O., 'The Whalley Abbey bursar's account for 1520', *THSLC*, CXIV.

'Aske's Examination', ed. M. Bateson, *EHR*, V.

'Aske's Narrative', ed. M. Bateson, *EHR*, V.

Aston, M., 'Lollardy and the Reformation: survival or revival?' *History*, XLIX.

Atherton, A. J., 'The estates of William Farington, 1537–1610', University of Manchester M.A. thesis, 1953.

Aveling, H., *Northern Catholics*, 1966.

'Some aspects of Yorkshire Catholic recusant history', *Studies in Church History*, ed. G. J. Cuming, IV, 1967.

Autobiography of an Elizabethan, The, (John Gerard), ed. P. Caraman, 1951.

Axon, E., 'The King's Preachers in Lancashire, 1599–1845', *TLCAS*, LVI.

Babbage, S. B., *Puritanism and Richard Bancroft*, 1962.

Bagley, J. J., 'Matthew Markland, a Wigan mercer', *TLCAS*, LXVIII.

Bailey, F. A., 'Churchwardens' accounts of Prescot, 1523–1607', *THSLC*, XCII, XCV.

'Prescot grammar school in Elizabethan times', *THSLC*, LXXXVI.

Baines, E., *History of the County Palatine and Duchy of Lancaster*, ed. J. Croston, 5 vols. 1888–93.

Baskerville, G., 'Married clergy and pensioned religious in Norwich diocese', *EHR*, XLVIII.

Bayne, C. G., *Anglo-Roman Relations, 1558–1565*, 1913.

Beales, A. C. F., 'Biographical catalogue of Catholic schoolmasters', *Recusant History*, VII.

Beck, T. A., *Annales Furnesienses*, 1844.

Bennett, W., History of Burnley, II, 1944.

Bill, P. A., *Warwickshire Parish Clergy in the Later Middle Ages*, Dugdale Society, Occasional Papers, XVII.

Bindoff, S. T., *Tudor England*, Pelican History of England, 1963.

Blackwood, B. G., 'Lancashire cavaliers and their tenants', *THSLC*, CXVII.

Booker, J., *Memorials of the Church in Prestwich*, 1852.

Bossy, J., *The English Catholic Community, 1570–1850*.

'The character of Elizabethan Catholicism', *Past and Present*, XXI.

Bouch, C. M. L. and Jones, G. P., *Economic and Social History of the Lake Counties, 1500–1830*, 1961.

Bibliography

Bowden, P. J., *The Wool Trade in Tudor and Stuart England*, 1962.

Bowker, M. *The Secular Clergy in the Diocese of Lincoln, 1495–1520*, 1968. 'Non-residence in Lincoln diocese in the early sixteenth century', *J. Eccl. Hist.* XV.

Brasenose College Register, 1509–1909, Oxford Historical Society, LV, 1909.

Bridgeman, G. T. O., *History of the Church and Manor of Wigan*, CS, NS, XV–XVIII, 1888–90.

Brigg, M., 'The Forest of Pendle in the seventeenth century', *THSLC*, CXIII.

Buckatzsch, E. J., 'The geographical distribution of wealth in England, 1086–1843', *Economic History Review*, 2nd series, III.

Burnet, G., *History of the Reformation*, 6 vols. 1820.

Calendar of Moore Manuscripts, ed. J. Brownbill, Record Society of Lancashire and Cheshire, LXVII, 1913.

Calendar of Papal Registers, XII, ed. J. Twemlow, 1933.

Calendar of Patent Rolls, Edward VI, 6 vols. 1924–9, Philip and Mary, 4 vols. 1936–9.

Calendar of Standish Deeds, 1230–1575, ed. T. C. Porteus, 1933.

Calendar of State Papers, Domestic Series, of the Reigns of Edward VI, Mary, Elizabeth I and James I, ed. R. Lemon and M. A. E. Green, 12 vols. 1856–72.

Calendar of State Papers, Foreign Series, of the Reign of Edward VI, ed. W. B. Turnbull, 1861.

Calendar of State Papers, Foreign Series, of the Reign of Mary, ed. W. B. Turnbull, 1861.

Calendar of State Papers, Spanish, 1485–1558, ed. G. A. Bergenroth, P. de Gayangos, M. A. S. Hume and G. Mattingley, 15 vols. in 20, 1862–1954.

Calendar of State Papers, Spanish, 1558–1603, ed. M. A. S. Hume, 4 vols. 1892–9.

Calendar of Wills in the Consistory of Lichfield, Index Library, VII, 1892.

Cambridge University Grace Books, 1454–1659, ed. S. M. Leathes *et al.*, 5 vols. 1898–1913.

Camden Miscellany, IX, 'A collection of original letters from the bishops to the Privy Council, 1564', ed. M. Bateson, 1895.

Caraman, P., *Henry Garnet, 1555–1606, and the Gunpowder Plot*, 1964.

Caraman, P., ed., *The Other Face: Catholic Life under Elizabeth I*, 1960.

Catholic Record Society Publications:

I	*Miscellanea*	'Official lists of prisoners', ed. J. H. Pollen.
II	*Miscellanea*	'Official lists of prisoners', ed. J. H. Pollen.
IV	*Miscellanea*	'Lord Burghley's map of Lancashire', ed. J. Gillow.
V	*English Martyrs, 1584–1603*, ed. J. H. Pollen.	
XVIII	*Recusant Roll, 1592–3*, ed. M. M. C. Calthrop.	
XXII	*Miscellanea*	'Diocesan returns of recusants, 1577'.
LIII	*Miscellanea, Recusant Records*, ed. C. Talbot.	
LVII	*Recusant Roll, 1593–4*, ed. H. Bowler.	
LX	*Recusant Documents from the Ellesmere Manuscripts*.	

Bibliography

Cavalier's Notebook, A, ed. T. E. Gibson, 1880.

Chambers, D. S., *Cardinal Bainbridge in the Court of Rome, 1509–1514*, 1965.

Chandler, G., and Saxton, E. B., *Liverpool under James I*, 1960.

Chantry Certificates for Cornwall, ed. L. Snell, 1953.

Chantry Certificates for Devon and the City of Exeter, ed. L. Snell, 1961.

Cheshire Sheaf, 3rd series, I, 'Signatories to three articles, 1563', ed. W. F. Irvine, 1896.

Chester Customs Accounts, 1301–1566, ed. K. P. Wilson, Record Society of Lancashire and Cheshire, CXI, 1969.

Chetham Miscellanies, OS, V, 'State civil and ecclesiastical of the county of Lancaster', ed. F. R. Raines, CS, OS, XCVI, 1875.

Chetham Miscellanies, OS, VI, 'The Rent Roll of Sir John Towneley, 1535–6', ed. F. R. Raines, CS, OS, CIII, 1878.

Chetham Miscellanies, NS, II, 'The apostolical life of Ambrose Barlow', ed. W. E. Rhodes, CS, NS, LXIII, 1909.

Child Marriages and Divorces, ed. F. J. Furnival, Early English Text Society, 1897.

Chronicles and Political Papers of Edward VI, ed. W. K. Jordan, 1966.

Churchwardens' Accounts of Prescot, Lancashire, 1523–1607, ed. F. A. Bailey, Record Society of Lancashire and Cheshire, CIV, 1953.

Churton, R., *Lives of Smith and Sutton*, 1800.

Life of Alexander Nowell, 1809.

Clemensha, H. W., *History of Preston in Amounderness*, 1912.

Cliffe, J. T., *The Yorkshire Gentry from the Reformation to the Civil War*, 1969.

Cobban, A. B., *King's Hall, Cambridge*, 1969.

Cockersand Chartulary, ed. W. Farrer, CS, NS, XXXVIII–XL, XLIII, 1898–1900.

Collectanea Anglo-Premonstratensia, ed. F. A. Gasquet, Camden Society, 3rd series, X, 1906.

Collinson, P., *The Elizabethan Puritan Movement*, 1967.

Commonwealth Church Survey, ed. H. Fishwick, Record Society of Lancashire and Cheshire, I, 1878.

Cook, G. H., *Medieval Chantries and Chantry Chapels*, 1963.

Cooke, W. H., *Students Admitted to the Inner Temple*, 1878.

Correspondence of Edward, third Earl of Derby, ed. T. N. Toller, CS, NS, XIX, 1890.

Correspondence of Matthew Parker, ed. J. Bruce and T. T. Perowne, Parker Society, 1853.

Cosgrove, J. D., 'The position of the recusant gentry in the social setting of Lancashire, 1570–1642', University of Manchester M.A. thesis, 1964.

Court Rolls of the Honour of Clitheroe, ed. W. Farrer, 3 vols. 1897–1913.

Coward, B., 'The lieutenancy of Lancashire and Cheshire in the sixteenth and early seventeenth centuries', *THSLC*, CXIX.

Crofton, H. T., *History of the Ancient Chapel of Stretford*, I, CS, NS, XLII, 1899.

Crosby Records, ed. T. E. Gibson, CS, NS, XII, 1887.

Dansey, W., *Horae Decanicae Rurales*, 2 vols. 1835.

Bibliography

Darby, H. C., ed., *Historical Geography of England before AD 1800*, 1936.

Davis, J. F., 'Lollard survival and the textile industry in the south-east of England', *Studies in Church History*, ed. G. J. Cuming, III, 1966.

De Houghton Deeds and Papers, ed. J. H. Lumby, Record Society of Lancashire and Cheshire, LXXXVIII, 1936.

Diary of Henry Machyn, ed. J. G. Nichols, Camden Society, OS, XLII, 1848.

Dickens, A. G., *Lollards and Protestants in the Diocese of York*, 1959.

  Robert Holgate, Borthwick Papers, VIII.

  The Marian Reaction in the Diocese of York, I & II, Borthwick Papers, XI–XII.

  The English Reformation, 1966.

  'The first stages of Romanist recusancy in Yorkshire, 1560–90', *YAJ*, XXXV.

  'The extent and character of recusancy in Yorkshire in 1604', *YAJ*, XXXVII.

  'Heresy and the origins of English Protestantism', *Britain and the Netherlands*, ed. J. S. Bromley and E. H. Kossman, II, 1964.

  'Secular and religious motivation in the Pilgrimage of Grace', *Studies in Church History*, ed. G. J. Cuming, IV, 1967.

Dillingham, W., *Life of Laurence Chadderton*, trans. E. S. Shuckburgh, 1884.

Dixon, R. W., *History of the Church of England*, 6 vols. 1878–1902.

Dodds, M. H. and R., *The Pilgrimage of Grace and the Exeter Conspiracy*, 2 vols. 1915.

Dodd, C., *Church History of England*, ed. M. A. Tierney, 5 vols. 1839–41.

Ducatus Lancastriae, ed. R. J. Harper, J. Caley and W. Minchin, 3 vols. 1823–34.

Dugdale, W., *Monasticon Anglicanum*, ed. J. Caley, H. Ellis and B. Bandinel, 6 vols. in 8, 1817–30.

Dunham, W. H., *Lord Hastings' Indentured Retainers*, 1955.

Durham Obituary Roll, ed. J. Raine, Surtees Society, XXXI, 1856.

Edwardian Inventories for Bedfordshire, ed. F. C. Eeles, Alcuin Club, VI, 1905.

Eeles, F. C., 'On a fifteenth-century York missal formerly used at Broughton', *Chetham Miscellanies*, NS, VI, CS, NS, XCIV, 1935.

Ellis, H., *Original Letters*, 1st series, 3 vols. 1824.

Elton, G. R., *The Tudor Revolution in Government*, 1953.

  Policy and Police, 1972.

Emden, A. B., *Biographical Register of the University of Cambridge*, 1963.

Episcopal Court Book for the Diocese of Lincoln, An, ed. M. Bowker, Lincoln Record Society, LXI, 1967.

Everitt, A., *Change in the Provinces*, Leicester University Department of English Local History, Occasional Papers, 2nd series, I, 1969.

Ewen, C. L., *Witchcraft and Demonianism*, 1933.

Farington Papers, ed. S. M. ffarington, CS, OS, XXXIX, 1856.

Fines, J., 'Heresy trials in the diocese of Coventry and Lichfield, 1511–12', *J Eccl. Hist.* XIV.

First and Second Douai Diaries, ed. T. F. Knox, 1878.

Bibliography

Fishwick, F., *History of the Parish of Kirkham*, CS, OS, XCII, 1874.
    History of the Parish of St Michael's-on-Wyre, CS, NS, XXV, 1891.
    History of the Parish of Preston, 1900.

Foley, H., ed., *Records of the English Province of the Society of Jesus*, 8 vols. 1877–83.

Fox, J. F., 'Reformation and Tudor Rochdale', typescript deposited in Rochdale Public Library, 1972.

Foxe, J., *Acts and Monuments*, ed. J. Pratt, 8 vols. 1870.

France, R. S., 'Lancashire Justices of the Peace in 1583', *THSLC*, XCV.

Frere, W. H., *The Marian Reaction*, 1896.

Froude, J. A., *History of England, from the Fall of Wolsey to the Defeat of the Spanish Armada*, 12 vols. Longmans, Green and Co., London, nd.

Fuller, T., *History of the Worthies of England*, ed. P. A. Nuttall, 3 vols. 1840.

Furness Coucher Book, ed. J. Brownbill, CS, NS, LXXIV, LXXVI, LXXVIII, 1915–19.

Garrett, C. H., *The Marian Exiles*, 1938.

Gastrell, F., *Notitia Cestriensis*, ed. F. R. Raines, CS, OS, VIII, XIX, XXI, XXII, 1845–50.

Gay, J. D., *The Geography of Religion in England*, 1971.

Gee, H. and Hardy, W. J., *Documents Illustrative of English Church History*, 1896.

Gillow, J., *Biographical Dictionary of English Catholics*, 5 vols. 1885–1903.

Glynne, S. R., *Notes on the Churches of Lancashire*, CS, NS, XXVII, 1893.

Grieve, H. E. P., 'Married clergy in Essex', *TRHS*, 4th series, XXII.

Haigh, C., *The Last Days of the Lancashire Monasteries and the Pilgrimage of Grace*, CS, 3rd series, XVII, 1969.
    'A mid-Tudor ecclesiastical official: the curious career of George Wilmesley', *THSLC*, CXXII.
    'Slander and the Church courts in the sixteenth century', *TLCAS*, LXXVIII.
    'The Reformation in Lancashire to 1558', University of Manchester Ph.D. thesis, 2 vols. 1969.

Hall, E., *The Triumphant Reign of King Henry VIII*, ed. C. Whibley, 2 vols. 1904.

Halley, R., *Lancashire, its Puritanism and Nonconformity*, one-volume edition, 1872.

Hay, D., 'The Dissolution of the Monasteries in the diocese of Durham', *Archaeologia Aeliana*, 4th series, XV.

Heath, P., *The English Parish Clergy on the Eve of the Reformation*, 1969.
    'The medieval archdeaconry and the Tudor bishopric of Chester', *J. Eccl. Hist.*, XX.

Heaton, H., *The Yorkshire Woollen and Worsted Industries*, 2nd edition, 1965.

Hewart, B., 'The cloth trade in the north of England in the sixteenth and seventeenth centuries', *Economic Journal*, X.

Hibbert-Ware, S., *History of the Foundations in Manchester*, 3 vols. 1834.

Hill, C., *Society and Puritanism in Pre-Revolutionary England*, Panther edition, 1969.

Bibliography

Economic Problems of the Church, Panther edition, 1971.

'Puritans and the "dark corners of the land"', *TRHS*, 5th series, XIII.

Hill, R. M. T., *The Labourer in the Vineyard*, Borthwick Papers, XXXV.

History of the Chantries within the County Palatine of Lancaster, Reports of the Chantry Commissioners, ed. F. R. Raines, CS, OS, LIX, LX, 1862.

Hollingworth, R., *Mancuniensis*, ed. W. Willis, 1839.

'Homage Roll of the manor of Warrington', ed. W. Beaumont, *Miscellanies relating to Lancashire and Cheshire*, Record Society of Lancashire and Cheshire, XII, 1885.

Hughes, P., *The Reformation in England*, 3 vols. in 1, 1963.

Hurstfield, J., *The Queen's Wards*, 1958.

Inventories of Church Goods for the Counties of York, Durham and Northumberland, ed. W. Page, Surtees Society, XCVII, 1897.

Inventories of Church Goods in the Churches and Chapels of Lancashire, 1552, ed. J. E. Bailey and H. Fishwick, CS, OS, CVII, CXIII, NS, XLVII, 1879, 1888, 1902.

Jacob, E. F., *The Fifteenth Century*, 1961.

James, M. E., 'The first earl of Cumberland and the decline of northern feudalism', *Northern History*, I.

Johnston, P. F., 'The life of John Bradford, the Manchester martyr', University of Oxford B.Litt. thesis, 1963.

Jones, B. C., 'Westmorland packhorsemen in Southampton', *Transactions of the Cumberland and Westmorland Antiquarian and Archaeological Society*, NS, LXIX.

Jones, H. L., 'The development of leasehold tenure in south Lancashire', University of Manchester M.A. thesis, 1924.

Jordan, W. K., *The Charities of Rural England*, 1961.

Philanthropy in England, 1961.

The Social Institutions of Lancashire, CS, 3rd series, XI, 1962.

Journals of the House of Lords, I, 1509–77, 1846.

Kenyon Manuscripts, Historical Manuscripts Commission, 14th Report, App. 4, 1894.

Kerridge, E., *Agrarian Problems in the Sixteenth Century and After*, 1969.

Knowles, D., *The Religious Orders in England*, III, 1959.

Knowles, D. and Hadcock, R. N., *Medieval Religious Houses: England and Wales*, 1971.

Lambert, D., 'The lower clergy of the Anglican Church in Lancashire', 1558–1642, University of Liverpool M.A. thesis, 1964.

Lancashire and Cheshire Antiquarian Notes, ed. W. D. Pink, 2 vols. 1885–6.

Lancashire and Cheshire Cases in the Court of Star Chamber, ed. R. Stewart-Brown, Record Society of Lancashire and Cheshire, LXXI, 1916.

Lancashire and Cheshire Exchequer Depositions, ed. C. Fishwick, Record Society of Lancashire and Cheshire, XI, 1885.

Lancashire and Cheshire Wills and Inventories, ed. G. J. Piccope, I–III, CS, OS, XXXIII, LI, LIV, 1857–61.

Lancashire and Cheshire Wills and Inventories, ed. J. P. Earwaker, CS, NS, III, XXVIII, 1884, 1893.

Lancashire and Cheshire Wills, ed. W. F. Irvine, Record Society of Lancashire and Cheshire, XXX, 1896.

Lancashire Lieutenancy, ed. J. Harland, CS, OS, XLIX, L, 1859.

Lancashire Quarter Sessions Records, ed. J. Tait, CS, NS, LXXVII, 1917.

Laslett, P., *The World We Have Lost*, 1965.

Leach, A. F., *English Schools at the Reformation*, 1896.

Leland, J., *Itinerary in England*, ed. L. Toulmin Smith, 5 vols. 1907–10.

Le Neve, J., *Fasti Ecclesiae Anglicanae*, ed. T. D. Hardy, 3 vols. 1854.

Letters and Papers, Foreign and Domestic, of the Reign of Henry VIII, ed. J. S. Brewer, J. Gairdner and R. H. Brodie, 23 vols. in 38, 1862–1932.

Letters of Stephen Gardiner, ed. J. A. Muller, 1933.

Lindley, K. J., 'The part played by Catholics in the English Civil War', University of Manchester Ph.D. thesis, 1968.

'List of the clergy in eleven deaneries of the diocese of Chester, 1541–2', ed. W. F. Irvine, *Miscellanies relating to Lancashire and Cheshire*, Record Society of Lancashire and Cheshire, XXXIII, 1896.

Liverpool Town Books, ed. J. A. Twemlow, I, *1550–70*, 1918.

Loades, D. M., *The Oxford Martyrs*, 1970.

'The enforcement of reaction, 1553–1558', *J. Eccl. Hist.*, XVI.

Logan, F D., *Excommunication and the Secular Arm in Medieval England*, 1968.

Long, P. R., 'The wealth of the magisterial class in Lancashire, *c.* 1590–1640', University of Manchester M.A. thesis, 1968.

Longfield, A. K., *Anglo-Irish Trade in the Sixteenth Century*, 1929.

Lowe, N., *The Lancashire Textile Industry in the Sixteenth Century*, CS, 3rd series, XX, 1972.

McConica, J. K., *English Humanists and Reformation Politics*, 1965.

McGrath, P., *Papists and Puritans under Elizabeth I*, 1967.

Magee, B., *The English Recusants*, 1938.

Mamecestre, ed. J. Harland, CS, OS, LIII, LVI, LVIII, 1861–2.

Manchester Court Leet Records, ed. J. Harland, CS, OS, LXIII, 1864.

Manchester Sessions, 1616–1623, ed. E. Axon, Record Society of Lancashire and Cheshire, XLII, 1901.

Manning, R. B., *Religion and Society in Elizabethan Sussex*, 1969.

Marchant, R. A., *The Church under the Law*, 1969.

Mason, R. J., 'The income, administration and disposal of monastic lands in Lancashire', University of London M.A. thesis, 1962.

Mather, W., 'Some aspects of parochial administration in the archdeaconry of Chester in the latter half of the fourteenth century', University of Manchester M.A. thesis, 1932.

Mayor, J. E. B., *The College of St John the Evangelist*, 2 vols. 1869.

Milne, J. G., *The Early History of Corpus Christi College*, 1946.

Montagu of Beaulieu Manuscripts, Historical Manuscripts Commission, LIII, 1900.

Bibliography

Morris, R. H., *Chester in the Plantagenet and Tudor Reigns*, 1893.
  Diocesan Histories: Chester, 1895.
Moyes, J., 'The collegiation of Manchester church', *TLCAS*, XXIV.
Mozley, J. F., *John Foxe and his Book*, 1940.
Muir, R., *History of Liverpool*, 1907.
Mullinger, J. B., *The University of Cambridge*, II, 1884.
  St John's College, 1901.
Mumford, A. A., *Hugh Oldham, 1452–1519*, 1936.
Neal, D., *The History of the Puritans*, 4 vols. 1732–8.
Norris Deeds, ed. J. H. Lumby, Record Society of Lancashire and Cheshire,
  XCIII, 1939.
'Ordination register of the diocese of Chester, 1542–1558', ed. W. F.
  Irvine, *Miscellanies relating to Lancashire and Cheshire*, Record Society
  of Lancashire and Cheshire, XLIII, 1902.
Ormerod, G., *History of the County Palatine and City of Chester*, 3 vols.
  1882.
Oxley, J. E., *The Reformation in Essex*, 1965.
Palatine Note Book, 4 vols. 1881–4.
Parkes, J., *Travel in England in the Seventeenth Century*, 1925.
Pearson, A. F. S., *Thomas Cartwright and Elizabethan Puritanism*, 1925.
Peck, F., *Desiderata Curiosa*, one-volume edition, 1779.
Pilkington, J., *Works*, ed. J. Scholefield, Parker Society, 1842.
Pill, D. H., 'The administration of the diocese of Exeter under Bishop
  Veysey', *Transactions of the Devonshire Association*, XCVIII.
Pleadings and Depositions in the Duchy Court of Lancaster, ed. H. Fishwick,
  Record Society of Lancashire and Cheshire, XXXII, XXXV, XL, 1896–9.
Plumpton Correspondence, ed. T. Stapleton, Camden Society, OS, IV, 1839.
Pollard, A. F., *The Reign of Henry VII from Contemporary Sources*, 3 vols.
  1913–14.
Porter, H. C., *Reformation and Reaction in Tudor Cambridge*, 1958.
Porteus, T. C., *History of the Parish of Standish*, 1927.
Prescot Records, 1447–1600, ed. F. A. Bailey, Record Society of Lancashire
  and Cheshire, LXXXIX, 1937.
Prest, W. R., *The Inns of Court under Elizabeth I and the Early Stuarts*, 1972.
Price, F. D., 'The abuses of excommunication and the decline of ecclesias-
  tical discipline under Queen Elizabeth', *EHR*, LVII.
Proceedings and Ordinances of the Privy Council, ed. H. Nicholas, 7 vols.
  1834–7.
Rae, T. I., *The Administration of the Scottish Frontier, 1513–1603*, 1966.
Raine, J., *Historians of the Church of York*, Rolls series, 3 vols. 1879–94.
Raines, F. R., *Vicars of Rochdale*, I, CS, NS, I, 1883.
  Wardens of the Collegiate Church of Manchester, I, CS, NS, V, 1885.
  Fellows of the Collegiate Church of Manchester, I, CS, NS, XXI, 1891.
Ramsay, G. D., 'The distribution of the cloth industry in 1561–2', *EHR*,
  LVII.
Read, D., *The English Provinces, 1760–1960*, 1964.
Register of the Archbishop of Canterbury's Faculty Office, ed. D. S. Chambers,
  1966.

Bibliography

Register of the University of Oxford, ed. C. W. Boase, I, Oxford Historical Society, I, 1885.

Registers of Cuthbert Tunstall and James Pilkington, ed. G. Hinde, Surtees Society, CLXI, 1952.

'Registers of the archdeacons of Richmond, 1361–1477', ed. A. H. Thompson, *YAJ*, XXV, XXX, XXXII.

Registers of Farnworth, Great Harwood, Middleton, Ormskirk, Standish and *Whalley*, Lancashire Parish Register Society.

Registrum Matthei Parker, ed. W. H. Frere and E. M. Thompson, Canterbury and York Society, XXXV, XXXVI, XXXIX, 1928, 1933.

Reid, R., *The King's Council in the North*, 1921.

'The political influence of the "North Parts" under the later Tudors', *Tudor Studies*, ed. R. W. Seton Watson, 1924.

Remains of Archbishop Grindal, ed. W. Nicholson, Parker Society, 1843.

'Rent Roll of Sir John Towneley, 1535–6', ed. F. R. Raines, *Chetham Miscellanies*, OS, VI, CS, OS, CIII, 1878.

Report of the Deputy Keeper of the Public Records, XL.

Richardson, R. C., *Puritanism in North-West England*, 1972.

'Puritanism in the diocese of Chester to 1642', University of Manchester Ph.D. thesis, 1969.

Richmond Wills, ed. J. Raine, Surtees Society, XXVI, 1853.

Ridley, N., *Works*, ed. H. Christmas, Parker Society, 1841.

Rogers, H. B., 'Land use in Tudor Lancashire: the evidence of final concords, 1450–1558', *Publications of the Institute of British Geographers*, XXI.

'The market area of Preston in the sixteenth and seventeenth centuries', *Geographical Studies*, III, Part 1.

Roper, W. O., *Materials for the History of the Church of Lancaster*, CS, NS, XXVI, XXXI, LVIII, LIX, 1892, 1894, 1906.

Rupp, E. G., *Studies in the Making of the English Protestant Tradition*, 1947.

Russell, J. C., *British Medieval Population*, 1948.

'The clerical population of medieval England', *Traditio*, II.

Rutland Manuscripts, Historical Manuscripts Commission, 4 vols. 1888–1905.

Rymer, T. *Foedera*, Record Commission, 20 vols. 1727–35.

Salisbury Manuscripts, Historical Manuscripts Commission, in progress, 1883–.

Savine, A., *English Monasteries on the Eve of Dissolution*, 1909.

Scarisbrick, J. J., *Henry VIII*, Pelican edition, 1971.

Schofield, R. S., 'The geographical distribution of wealth in England, 1334–1649', *Economic History Review*, 2nd series, XVIII.

Sermons of Thomas Lever, 1550, ed. E. Arber, English Reprints, 1871.

Shrewsbury, J. F. D., *History of Bubonic Plague in the British Isles*, 1970.

Short Title Catalogue, 1475–1660, ed. A. W. Pollard and G. R. Redgrave, 1946.

Simpson, R., *Edmund Campion*, 1896.

Smith, R. B., 'A study of landed income and social structure in the West Riding of Yorkshire, 1535–46', University of Leeds Ph.D. thesis, 1962.

Somerville, R., *History of the Duchy of Lancaster, 1265–1603*, 1953.

Bibliography

Spence, R. T., 'The Cliffords, earls of Cumberland, 1579–1646', University of London Ph.D. thesis, 1959.

Spending of the Money of Robert Nowell, The, ed. A. B. Grosart, 1877.

Spenser, E., *A View of the Present State of Ireland*, ed. W. L. Renwick, 1970.

Stanley Papers, ed. F. R. Raines, II, CS, OS, XXXI, 1853.

'State civil and ecclesiastical of the county of Lancaster', ed. F. R. Raines, *Chetham Miscellanies*, OS, V, CS, OS, XCVI, 1875.

State Papers, Henry VIII, 11 vols. 1830–52.

Statutes of the Realm, 11 vols. 1810–28.

Steel, R., *Tudor and Stuart Proclamations*, 2 vols. 1910.

Stocks, G. A., *Records of Blackburn Grammar School*, CS, NS, LXVI–VIII, 1909.

Stokes, C. W., *Queen Mary's Grammar School, Clitheroe*, CS, NS, XCII, 1934.

Stone, L., *The Crisis of the Aristocracy, 1558–1641*, 1965.

Storey, R. L., *Thomas Langley and the Bishopric of Durham*, 1961.

Strickland, H. H., *Lancashire Members of Parliament, 1290–1550*, CS, NS, XCIII, 1935.

Strype, J., *Ecclesiastical Memorials*, 3 vols. in 6, 1822.
  Annals of the Reformation, 4 vols. in 7, 1824.
  Memorials of Archbishop Cranmer, 2 vols. 1840.

Sturgess, H. A. C., *Register of Admissions to the Middle Temple*, 3 vols. 1949.

Survey and Account of the Estates of Hornby Castle, ed. W. H. Chippindall, CS, NS, CII, 1939.

Tait, J., 'The declaration of sports for Lancashire', *EHR*, XXXII.

Tempest, A. C., 'Nicholas Tempest, a sufferer in the Pilgrimage of Grace', *YAJ*, XI.

Thirsk, J., ed., *Agrarian History of England and Wales*, IV, *1500–1640*, 1967.

Thomas, K., *Religion and the Decline of Magic*, 1971.

Thompson, A. H., *Parish History and Records*, 1919.
  'Diocesan organisation in the Middle Ages: archdeacons and rural deans', *Proceedings of the British Academy*, XXIX.

Thomson, G. S., *Lords Lieutenant in the Sixteenth Century*, 1923.

Thomson, J. A. F., *The Later Lollards, 1414–1520*, 1965.

Tudor Royal Proclamations, ed. P. L. Hughes and J. F. Larkin, 3 vols. 1964, 1969.

Tupling, G. H., *Economic History of Rossendale*, CS, NS, LXXXVI, 1927.
  'Parish Books', *TLCAS*, LXII.
  'The causes of the Civil War in Lancashire', *TLCAS*, LXV.
  'Pre-Reformation parishes and chapelries of Lancashire', *TLCAS*, LXVII.

Tyler, P., 'The Church courts at York and witchcraft prosecutions, 1567–1640', *Northern History*, IV.
  'The Ecclesiastical Commission for the province of York, 1561–1640', University of Oxford D.Phil. thesis, 1965.

Usher, R. G., *The Reconstruction of the English Church*, 2 vols. 1910.

Bibliography

Valor Ecclesiasticus, ed. J. Caley and J. Hunter, 6 vols. 1810–34.

Vaux's Catechism, ed. T. G. Law, CS, NS, IV, 1885.

Venn, J. and J. A., *Alumni Cantabrigiensis*, Part 1, 4 vols. 1922–7.

Victoria History of the County of Lancashire, ed. J. Tait, 8 vols. 1906–14.

Visitation of Lancashire, 1533, ed. W. Langton, CS, OS, XCVIII, CX, 1876, 1882.

Visitation of the County Palatine of Lancaster, 1567, ed. F. R. Raines, CS, OS, LXXXI, 1870.

Wadsworth, A. P. and Mann, J. de L., *The Cotton Trade and Industrial Lancashire, 1600–1780*, 1931.

Walker, F., *The Historical Geography of South-West Lancashire*, CS, NS, CIII, 1939.

Walker, F. X., 'The implementation of the Elizabethan statutes against recusants, 1580–1603', University of London Ph.D. thesis, 1961.

Wallis, J. E. W., *History of the Church in Blackburnshire*, 1932.

Wallis, P. J., 'A preliminary register of old schools in Lancashire and Cheshire', *THSLC*, CXX.

Wark, K. R., *Elizabethan Recusancy in Cheshire*, CS, 3rd series, XIX, 1971.

Watson, J. B., 'The Lancashire gentry and the public service, 1529–1558', *TLCAS*, LXXIII.

'The Lancashire gentry, 1529–1558, with special reference to their public services', University of London M.A. thesis, 1959.

West, T., *Antiquities of Furness*, 1732.

Westerfield, R. B., *Middlemen in English Business*, 1915.

Whalley Coucher Book, ed. W. A. Hulton, CS, OS, X, XI, XVI, XX, 1847–9.

Whitaker, T. D., *History of the Parish of Whalley*, ed. J. G. Nichols and P. Lyons, 2 vols. 1872–6.

Whittle, P. A., *Bolton-le-Moors*, 1855.

Willan, T. S., *The English Coasting Trade, 1600–1750*, 1938.

Williams, G., *The Welsh Church from Conquest to Reformation*, 1962.

Williams, N., *Thomas Howard, Fourth Duke of Norfolk*, 1964.

Williams, P., *The Council in the Marches of Wales under Elizabeth*, 1958.

Wood, A., *History of the Colleges of Oxford*, ed. J. Gutch, 1786.

Wood-Legh, K., *Perpetual Chantries in Great Britain*, 1965.

Woodward, D. M., 'The foreign trade of Chester in the reign of Elizabeth I', University of Manchester M.A. thesis, 1965.

Writings of John Bradford, ed. A. Townsend, Parker Society, 2 vols. 1848, 1853.

Yorkshire Chantry Surveys, ed. W. Page, Surtees Society, XCI, XCII, 1894–5.

Youd, G., 'The Common Fields of Lancashire', *THSLC*, CXIII.

Index

349

Index

Blakey, Roger, 32, 238–9

Bland, John, 165

Bland, Thomas, dean of Furness, etc., 11, 14, 212, 257, 320

Bleasdale (Lancs.), 256

Blundell, family, 251, 281, 283, 292

Blundell, Richard, 250, 251, 256

Blundell, Robert, 95, 250, 251

Blundell, William, 94, 288n, 299

Blyth, Geoffrey, bp of Lichfield, 77

Bold, Richard, 90, 283

Boleyn, Queen Anne, 26, 84, 109, 111

Boleyn, William, archdeacon of Winchester, 26

Bolton, Robert, 171, 177

Bolton-le-Moors (Lancs.), xii–xiii, 63, 64, 66, 78, 151, 159, 164, 168, 169, 193, 235, 306, 307, 308; conservatism in, 220–1, 313, 316, 317; radicalism in, 168, 169, 173, 175, 176, 177, 188, 295, 300, 306; vicars of, 172, 193, 305, 306

Bolton-le-Sands (Lancs.), xii–xiii, 242, 320

Bonner, Edmund, bp of London, 12, 24, 50, 179, 189, 190, 193, 248, 255

Books: Catholic, 116, 253, 289, 292; in churches, 115, 143, 202, 237, 244, 270, 306; clergy and, 69, 82, 124; laity and, 101; reformist, 82, 101, 171, 187, 188, 194; trade in, 81, 101, 171, 172, 292; see also Bibles; Prayer books

Booth, Elizabeth, 68

Booth, Thurstan, 54

Bordeaux (France), 89

Bossy, Dr John, vii, 97, 247 & n, 277, 283, 323

Bostock, Maria, 228

Bourne, Sir John, 189

Bowdon (Cheshire), 9

Bowker, Margaret, 27, 28, 30 & n, 138n

Bowland (Lancs.), 91

Braboner, Robert, r Ashton, 240

Braddyll, John, 69, 101

Bradford, family, 167, 171, 173

Bradford, John: conversion of, 161, 165–6, 167; examinations and trial, 189–90, 192, 193, 203, 204; letters of, 170, 175, 185–6, 188–9, 191; work in Lancs., 168–9, 170–2, 174 & n, 175, 176, 189

Bradford, Margaret, 167, 171

Bradley, James, 280

Bradley (Staffordshire), 10

Bradshaw, family, 173, 176, 177

Bradshaw, –, 75

Bradshaw, James, 171, 174

Bradshaw, John, 176

Bradshaw, Laurence, 171

Bradshaw, Roger, 154

Bradshaw, William, 64

Brasenose College, Oxford, 39, 162, 163–4, 255, 297

Brassey, Dr Robert, v Prescot, 184

Brerely, Alice, 321

Brereton, Sir Richard, 55

Brereton, Thomas, 248

Brettan, Richard, 39

Briddock, Robert, 53

Bridgeman, John, bp of Chester, 102, 226, 233

Brindle (Lancs.), xii–xiii, 220, 258, 318–19

Bristol (Gloucestershire), 89

Brockhurst (Lancs.), 152

Brooke, Robert, r Aldingham, 199, 335

Brooks, James, bp of Gloucester, 203–4

Broughton, John, 112

Broughton (Lancs.), 66, 67, 68

Brown, Hugh, 38–9

Bruche, family, 52

Bucer, Martin, 145, 164, 166, 170, 171, 197

Buckingham, duke of, see Stafford, Henry

Buckinghamshire, 50, 65

Buckley, Francis, 15

Buckley, James, 157

351

Index

Index

Justices of the peace (*cont.*)
284–5, 286, 291; failure to act
against Catholics, 213, 280,
285, 286, 287, 288, 290;
inadequacy of, 106, 213, 286;
local interests of, 89, 106;
Puritans among, 304, 305,
314 & n; in Salford hundred,
313–14, 325; shortage of, 106,
265, 285–6, 320

Kay, John, 33
Keble, Edward, r Warrington, 24, 181
Keighley, Sir Henry, 52
Kelver, Richard, 41
Kendal, deanery of, xii–xiii, 11, 243,
316, 319–21; dean of, *see* Bland,
Thomas
Kendal (Westmorland), 77, 113,
119, 122n, 123, 133, 134, 321
Kent, 79, 80, 84, 107, 202, 204, 333;
Nun of (Elizabeth Barton), 111
Kenyon, Gowther, r Bury, 214–15,
335
King's College, Cambridge, 205
King's Hall, Cambridge, 164
King's Lynn (Norfolk), 80
Kirkby, family, 89
Kirkby, Thomas, 14, 35–6, 68
Kirkby (Lancs.), 241, 255
Kirkby Ireleth (Lancs.), xii–xiii, 15,
110, 180, 244, 320; church, 55,
66; disputes in, 54, 63
Kirkham (Lancs.), xii–xiii, 38, 41,
68, 264, 315; anti-Puritanism
in, 298; recusants in, 264, 291,
318, 319; vicars of, *see* Helme;
Smith, James
Knight, William, archdeacon of
Chester and Richmond, 2, 5,
6–7, 110, 199
Knox, John, 169

Lambert, John, 124
Lambeth (Surrey), 333
Lancashire: communications
within, 1, 91, 326;
communications with other
areas, 80–2, 88–9, 159, 160,
163, 253, 280, 307–10, 325,
326; ecclesiastical
government, problems of, 3–4,
5, 8, 10, 12, 14, 16, 17, 18–19,
30, 31–2, 44–5, 78, 102, 140,
212–13, 223–4, 225–36, 264,
269–73; most Catholic
county, 222–3, 265, 273, 275,
278; religious antagonism in,
193–4, 209, 218, 221, 222, 232,
326–32; secular government,
problems of, 19, 96–7, 100–8,
136–8, 145, 213, 222, 284–6,
286–90, 328; strength of
religious extremes, 295–6,
306–7, 332; wealth of, 20, 74–5
Lancaster, duchy of, 21, 23, 106,
202, 205, 261; administrative
weakness of, 52, 103, 104, 105;
council of, 31, 46, 52, 60, 96,
103, 104; court of, 17, 18, 19,
59, 60, 96, 103, 177, 201, 306;
and Edwardian confiscations,
147–50; officers of, 52, 59,
85, 87, 92, 140, 213, 222, 240,
285, 288; and suppression of
monasteries, 126–9
Lancaster, palatinate of, 87, 96,
103–4, 140, 236, 284, 288
Lancaster (Lancs.), xii–xiii, 96, 114,
131, 134, 135, 176, 179, 231,
244, 246, 257, 307, 313, 329;
chantries, 34n, 148; courts at,
35, 104, 132, 133, 176, 191,
314; disputes in, 53, 57; gaol,
52, 173, 183, 184–5, 186, 187,
192, 289, 328; mayor of, 131,
137n, 176, 206; recusancy in,
256, 264, 326, 330; school, 42,
176, 206; trade and industry,
82, 92, 175
Landholdings: services linked to,
94–5; sub-division of, 92,
159, 308, 324
Langho (Lancs.), 271
Langley, family, 173
Langley, Robert (d. 1528), 64, 70

362